Daughters
of the
Conquistadores

Daughters of the Conquistadores

Women of the Viceroyalty of Peru

Luis Martín

UNIVERSITY OF NEW MEXICO PRESS
Albuquerque

Library of Congress Cataloging in Publication Data

Martín, Luis.
  Daughters of the conquistadores.

  Bibliography: p.
  Includes index.
  1. Women—Peru—History.   2. Spaniards—Peru—History.
3. Peru—History—1548–1820.   I. Title.
HQ1572.M37   1983   305.4′0985   83-6625
ISBN 0-8263-0707-8
ISBN 0-8263-0708-6 (pbk.)

First Edition.

For
Glenda and J. W. Davis
and their children
Christy and Jake

Contents

Illustrations

Preface

THE PRESENT BOOK, WHICH TODAY comes to light thanks to the interest and professional skills of the staff of the University of New Mexico Press, has been in the making for more than a decade. A continuous commitment to undergraduate teaching in the humanities, an ever expanding involvement with the community, administrative and bureaucratic duties, and serious financial constraints have unduly delayed the completion of this present book. The rather large and complex subject of women's history in the viceroyalty of Peru has presented many theoretical and research problems, which may also explain this delay and the limitations of the completed work. A word about the title of the book is perhaps needed to understand clearly the intended scope of the present monograph.

"Daughters of conquistadores" is an expression found in many colonial documents of the sixteenth and seventeenth centuries, and frequently used by viceroys, royal administrators, ecclesiastical authorities, and women themselves. They used the expression, as it is clear by the context of those documents, in a rather loose fashion and without any pretense to being historically objective or literally accurate. The term, as used in the documents of the period and in the title of this book, does not exclusively mean the young women born in the first generation of Spanish Peru, whose fathers had participated directly in the conquest of the Incan empire. It means, rather, women of Spanish Peru born

of Spanish ancestry, either pure criollas or mestizas, regardless of
any provable filial or genealogical links with the early conquistadores and settlers. "Daughters of conquistadores" meant, to those
who first used the expression, women who were, at least in part,
racially Spanish, spoke only the Castilian language, were mostly
urban dwellers, and had been deeply affected by the value system
of Spanish culture and Spanish Catholicism. The present book
deals only with those women of Spanish Peru, and makes no
attempt to study black or Indian women. Black and Indian women
need, of course, to be studied for a fuller understanding of the
female world of the viceroyalty of Peru, but neither time nor
financial means have allowed me to explore that fascinating world.
The few black and Indian women that appear in the following
pages are mentioned only because their paths crossed those of
the daughters of conquistadores.

Although this book has been written not with the professional
historian but with the student of history in mind, I hope my
colleagues in the history profession will also appreciate my efforts
in breaking this uncharted ground of women's history in the viceroyalty of Peru. Although a great number of prominent historians
today borrow heavily from the methodology of the social sciences
and are true masters at historical quantification, I must openly
confess, with a bit of embarrassment but without apology, that I
cannot quantify, even if my life depended on it. As a member of
an older generation of intellectual historians, I have been guided
in arranging my findings by the insights of theology, art, literature,
popular legends, and folklore. All I have intended to do is to tell
another story, to explore a little bit further the open-ended mystery of our common humanity. If my reader gains some new
insights into the variety, the splendor and, at times, the sorrow of
being human, my efforts will not have been in vain.

It would be practically impossible to thank and acknowledge all
those who have helped me during a decade of research and writing. The staffs of the National Archives of Peru, the Cathedral
Archives of Lima, and the Archives of the Indies in my home
town of Seville have been extremely generous with their time and
professional expertise, and time and time again have steered me
in the right direction. My colleagues in the history department of
Southern Methodist University in Dallas have given me constant
moral support, and have created around me an intellectual climate

in which research and writing flourish almost naturally. Our former chairman and now dean of the college, R. Hal Williams, the
present chairman and great historian of the Southwest, Don David
J. Weber, and my great friend, historian, and novelist, Ronald L.
Davis, have generously given me their advice, criticism, friendship,
and moral support. To all of them and to all my Dallas friends
who have encouraged and supported me with their friendship
and love, I offer in return this book with my thanks and heartfelt
gratitude.

Dallas, Texas
April 1, 1983

I

Introduction

IN 1532 FRANCISCO PIZARRO'S SEARCH for a kingdom of gold led a band of Spanish adventurers to the shores of Peru. After founding the city of San Miguel de Piura, the Spaniards crossed the Sechura Desert and climbed the Andes in what was one of the great epic marches of history. Pizarro dealt a fatal blow to the Incas of Peru in the treacherous massacre of Cajamarca and made emperor Atahualpa a captive of the Spaniards. The victory of Cajamarca opened the era of the conquistadores in Peru, and for several decades, the empty spaces of the South American continent were filled with men in armor restlessly searching for the gold of the Incas. They fought not only against the Indians, but also against each other in bloody civil wars that for years rocked the fragile foundations of Spanish Peru. Another army of men of the cloth soon joined the soldiers to begin the spiritual conquest of Peru. Friars and priests imposed on the Incas the heavy, juridical structures of the Roman Church and engaged with zest in converting the "children of the Sun" to the Christian, European God of the Spaniards.

It is obvious that the military and spiritual conquest of Peru was the exclusive work of males, who would continue to dominate Peruvian life throughout the colonial period. Men monopolized the political, governmental positions, manned the tribunals, managed the economy, and enjoyed the exclusive right of governing the powerful Catholic church. Colonial Peru appears to the mod-

1

ern student of history as a world of men, where women fade into
the historical backdrop of the period. Although Spanish women
were in Peru from the early days of the conquest, it was not easy
to detect their presence in the historical spectrum of colonial Peru.

Were women just a silent, passive element in Peruvian colonial
society? Were they so rigidly controlled and conditioned in a world
of men that they were impotent to chart their own lives? Was there
any effort to educate them? What was their position and role in
marriage? How did women live in colonial days? How did they
fit in the two dominant institutions of church and state? Did women
have any collective and institutional impact in their society? Were
there any outstanding women who left a visible mark in Peruvian
history? In trying to answer some of these questions, one must
consider three powerful cultural forces which through the centuries have shaped women's life in Iberian societies—Don Juanism, marianism, and the strong Iberian tradition of courtly, romantic
love.

Don Juanism implies an obsessive exaltation, an almost religious
cult of virility, and at the same time a Faustian, satanic conviction
of the boundless nature of the male ego. Don Juan is not merely
a selfish lover who uses and abuses women without regard to their
human, personal worth, he is a pathological egotist who dreams
of reshaping the universe with himself at the center, and who
constantly hears resounding at the core of his being the satanic
rebellion of the biblical *non serviat:* I shall not serve! Don Juan
defies secular and religious conventions with exaggerated ag-
gressiveness and derives a diabolical pleasure in acting against the
established norms. Naturally, Don Juanism converts women into
charming, decorative objects, whose sole function is to fulfill the
passions and the daydreams of the male ego. And yet, as Gregorio
Marañón has rightly noted, Don Juan tends to be a weak personality, easily shaped by the female objects of his passion. He may
appear to the superficial observer as a strong *macho*, who despot-
ically rules and dominates women, but in many instances he is, in
fact, ruled and dominated by the women in his life. Turned into
a worshipper and slave of female beauty, the conqueror is manipulated and ultimately conquered by women of strong personality and talent.

One should not overemphasize the obvious sexual overtones
present in the character of Don Juan, since Don Juanism is not

limited in Iberian history and literature to the great Latin lover immortalized by Tirso de Molina and by Zorrilla. A sort of cultural and psychological Don Juanism also gripped many stern, puritanical Castilians, who ruled their households with the iron hand of an unchallenged patriarch. Wife, daughters, unmarried sisters, poor female relatives, and servant girls formed within the home a cultural harem guarded by the head of the household. The pride and honor of the family name was tightly bound to female behavior, which was zealously dictated and controlled by the family patriarch. Any serious stain on that honor caused by female misconduct could, and at times did, demand the blood of the culprit, as much of the Spanish literature of the Golden Century readily attests. But, again, many of those family harems could dominate a man and drain his economic, social, and political power as much as an Arab harem could sap the vitality of its master.

A final characteristic of Don Juanism, not stressed sufficiently by historians and literary critics, is that within Iberian societies the cultural attitudes of the selfish, domineering personality do not occur exclusively among the males. Spanish history and literature offer too many examples of women who share the rebellious and diabolical independence of Don Juan for us to ignore the pervasive nature of Don Juanism, which, at times, does not seem to recognize any sexual boundaries.

The strong women who have sat on the Spanish throne could be profitably studied under this light. Many historical examples of domineering females come readily to mind: the fierce independence of Queen Isabella, the Catholic, who repeatedly checked and controlled the boundless ambition of her consort, Ferdinand; the Princess of Eboli, daughter of a viceroy of Peru, who rocked the austere, puritanical court of Philip II with scandals and intrigues; the rebellious reformer Theresa of Avila, who against insurmountable odds accomplished the reform of the Carmelites; the hispanicized Princess de los Ursinos, who manipulated many affairs in the court of the first Spanish Bourbon and became a notorious political intriguer; Queen Isabel de Farnesio, second wife of Philip V, who dominated her husband, and who reshaped for selfish motives the foreign policy of the Spanish Empire with unshakeable stubbornness; Queen María Luísa, immortalized by Goya, whose blind passion for the commoner Godoy made her husband Charles IV the laughingstock of Spanish society and helped bring a decadent Spain to its knees before the victorious armies of Napoleon; the Duchess of Alva, lover of Goya, who allowed herself to be painted with a defiant look at the world, pointing her finger to the ground of her garden where she had just written "sólo Goya"; and Queen Isabel II, Don Juan in petticoats, whose notorious love affairs scandalized Spanish society for several decades.

One also encounters hundreds of domineering, independent women in the pages of Spanish literature; women who built a world of their own and ruthlessly dominated it. The Doña Barbara of Rómulo Gallego comes to mind as a modern example. The passionate women of García Lorca, who defy conventions and challenge traditional values, are distant cousins of the *mujeres viriles* so dear to the heart of Saint Theresa of Avila and the playwrights of the Golden Century. The female adventurer and man-hunter, who burned with jealousy and concealed a jackknife in her stocking, is undoubtedly an exaggerated and colorful symbol created by Spanish folklore, but her basic profile is readily recognizable in many women of Spanish literature and history.

At the other extreme of the cultural spectrum of Spanish history, one detects the ideological current of marianism. The cult of Mary, the Virgin Mother, permeated Iberian society from an early date, and by the time of the conquest of Peru, the figure of Mary had become the most popular and the most beloved religious symbol of the Spanish people. The Mother of Christ was exalted as the ideal woman, not only by missionaries and theologians, but also by writers, playwrights, sculptors, painters, and musicians. Often in the Spanish literature of the Golden Century, Mary appears as the fulfillment and blossom of womanhood. The voices of Tirso de Molina, Lope de Vega, Cervantes, and Calderón, to name a few, sang the praises of the Mother of God, and anonymous bards composed thousands of popular marian songs and poems, which became a very important part of the Spanish folklore. Painters like El Greco, Velázquez, Murillo, and Zurbarán brought Mary to the common people by painting in a simple fashion the complex marian thought developed by the writers and theologians of the Counter-Reformation.

The cult of Mary came to America with the early Spanish conquistadores who, although often oblivious to the tenets of orthodox Christianity, always maintained a strong emotional attachment to popular mariology. Soon hundreds of marian shrines dotted the landscape of South America. In almost every colonial city there were cofradías and sodalities under the patronage of Mary, which attracted to their membership not only the Spanish settlers, but also Indians, mestizos, and even black slaves. Following the marian fervor of Spain, the American colonial cities, the cabildos, the guilds, the professions, the schools, and the universities took a vow to defend, even at the risk of one's own life, the mystery of the Immaculate Conception. By the middle of the seventeenth century, it had become almost impossible for any individual to enter the corporate life of the colonies without first taking the marian vow. The Holy Tribunal of the Inquisition kept a sharp eye from its See of Lima for any doctrine that could cast the slightest shadow on the exalted privileges of the Virgin Mother.

This intense religious, cultural current produced in Iberian societies the conviction that to fulfill their potential, women had to approach, as much as possible, the exalted model of Mary, the ideal woman. Those who did were accorded authority and respect and could exercise in society a moral influence, which at times surpassed that of many males. It was common in the period to accept that women were spiritually superior to men. Women could become, as Mary, quasi-angelic creatures, examples of human and supernatural virtues, while men were weak, sinful beings ruled by lust, pride, and the love of money and power. Although dominated and manipulated by men, women could become spiritual beings inspiring awe and veneration, and intercessors between the supernatural world of God and the sinful world of men. Women, thus perceived, could escape through marianism to strike at the very roots of Don Juanism.

This curious metamorphosis of women from sexual objects to spiritual intercessors was but a reflection of the popular social awareness of the dogmatic mariology developed by the theologians of the Counter-Reformation. Although Jesus was the son of God and the sole redeemer of the human race, Mary was chosen to be the sole mediator between men and God. According to Catholic theology, Mary was conceived without the stain of original sin, was free from all moral imperfections, became mother without the instrumentality of a male, and was the sole distributor of God's grace. In the institutional and social unfolding of these Christian marian mysteries, many women were seen as the silent, invisible

soul of the church. Bishops and priests (all of them male) were
the official leaders of the church, but hundreds of women were
considered by the Christian communities as reservoirs of spirit-
uality and holiness.

It is doubtful that the church would have become as all-powerful
and dominant an institution in the Spanish colonies without the
role played within it by devout women. More receptive perhaps
to religious symbols and ideas than men, and less occupied with
the material aspects of the earthly city, women of the period crowded
the colonial churches daily, flocked by the hundreds to the confessionals of renowned priests, donated their time and money to
further the work of the church, and established dozens of colonial
nunneries. These nunneries can be rightly counted, as we hope
to show, among the most powerful and influential institutions of
Peruvian society of the period. When we consider the great popularity of female monasticism in Spanish Peru, and the extraordinary numbers of young women who chose the conventual life
of consecrated virgins, we cannot help entertaining the suspicion
that their motivations were not solely religious. By entering the
convent where the ideals of marianism were institutionalized, women
cut themselves off from the constant influence of men and could
move toward a degree of personal freedom and autonomy that
was not easily attainable in the male-dominated secular society.
The colonial nunnery became a fortress of feminism, a true island
of women, where, under the cloak of marianism, women could
protect themselves from the corrosive and dehumanizing forces
of Don Juanism.

Blending with marianism and enlarging and enriching it was a
third cultural current first introduced in Iberian society by the
lyric Arab poets of Al-Andalus—the tradition of courtly love with
its romantic, lyric view of women. This lyric tradition, like marianism, also elevated women to a level of perfection not attainable
by men. Women appear in this literary tradition more as angelic
creatures than as mere mortals. Their physical and moral beauty
is described with elaborate literary metaphors which, like the stucco
ornamentation of the Alhambra, hide the coarse surface of reality.
Those women created by the poets of Al-Andalus did not have
just eyes, but "stars reflecting at midnight in the dark pools of the
Alhambra." Their teeth were compared to rare, oriental pearls,
and their limbs to the marble columns of the great mosques. If

Don Juan debased women as objects of lust, the Arab lyric poets elevated them to objects of admiration and worship.

Don Quijote, the most outstanding symbol of the Golden Century of Spain, was a worthy heir of the literary tradition of Al-Andalus. The Knight of the Sorrowful Countenance transformed an ordinary, unattractive peasant woman into Lady Dulcinea, whom he served selflessly and without conditions and loved "chaste and pure from afar." Her name was invoked in times of personal crisis as a magic, religious incantation. Don Quijote would have been horrified by the gross selfishness of Don Juan in dealing with women.

In spite of the pervasive Don Juanism of Spanish culture, not all Spanish males behaved toward women in the style of Don Juan. The Don Quijote type was also as abundant in Spanish society as the Don Juan character, and many women found themselves placed on a pedestal—venerated by husbands, sons, lovers, and male relatives. The thread of courtly, romantic love in Spanish culture unites the medieval bards to the songs and poems of modern Spanish literature and folklore. This strong tradition provided many women with another escape from the constraining and debasing forces of Don Juanism.

The philosopher Ortega y Gasset once wrote, in an effort to clarify the nature of the personal self, *"Yo soy yo y mis circunstancias"* ("I am I plus my cultural environment"). Ortega meant that, in spite of our dreams of personal freedom and autonomy, the core of our selves is partly shaped and conditioned by cultural, historical forces, which are not of our own making.

The women of colonial Peru were caught in a historical environment in which the three cultural forces of Don Juanism, marianism, and courtly love played a dominant role in shaping their self-awareness and in conditioning their behavior. Those forces had been unleashed in Spanish history at an early period and had created a widely accepted image of women which would be reflected in Peruvian history. Modern feminists could rightly point out that marianism and the tradition of courtly love had the same truncating effects on women as Don Juanism. Although in different ways, the three cultural attitudes robbed women of their true humanity and denied their essential equality with men. The women exalted by marianism and courtly love to a level of sexless beings of angelic properties are incapable, as much as those de-

based by Don Juanism, to participate as equal in the earthly affairs
of the city of men. Yet, most women of colonial Peru seem to have
accepted the basic assumptions of their culture and to have found
meaning and fulfillment within the religious and cultural framework of their own society. Many of them, far from being mere
passive elements of Peruvian life, made significant contributions
to their society. Contemporary Peru owes much to the women of
its colonial past.

In the following pages, we will examine the role played by women
at the dawn of the Spanish colonization of Peru, the system of
female education, the colonial marriages, the daily life of women
in the colonial cities, and their impact on the colonial church.
Although the subject is vast and complex, we hope that our efforts
will be a modest and preliminary contribution to the study of
women in Spanish Peru.

2

❦

The First
Spanish Women
of Peru

THE DISCOVERY AND EARLY SETTLEMENT of the New World by the Spaniards, one of the great landmarks in the history of civilization, were accomplished under the firm guidance of Queen Isabella. The queen was a highly educated person, who understood better than most the shattering implications of Columbus's dreams. After the early success of 1492, Isabella accepted the dream with great empathy, and supported the dreamer with all the power of her royal authority, even when Columbus's demands seemed to most royal councillors to be overly ambitious and unreasonable. By the time the queen died in 1504, the mark of a Spanish colonial society was already clearly discernible in the scattered islands of the Caribbean. Isabella had toiled for more than a decade to shape that emerging profile and had planted the legal and institutional seeds, which would blossom years later into the strong Spanish-American society of the mainland. To call the Catholic queen "mother of the Spanish American Empire" is not hollow rhetoric but an undeniable historical fact.

Other Spanish women also played important roles in the colonization of America, though never matching the impact of Queen Isabella. Shortly after the discovery and the foundation of the first Spanish town in Hispaniola, the early settlers, and the crown itself, became aware of the importance of having Spanish women in the new colonies to create and maintain a healthy and stable society. On the third voyage of Columbus in 1498, the crown issued a license allowing thirty Spanish women to join the expedition, provided that they were willing to become permanent residents of the colony.[1] Those thirty women represented only 10 percent of the total expedition. However, their presence can be seen as an early attempt to avoid making the "enterprise of the Indies" exclusively the domain of men. Historians of the period, including the knowledgeable Bartolomé de las Casas, did not mention their names, and there are some grounds to doubt that all thirty of them crossed the Atlantic in 1498. Nevertheless, the royal license and the efforts to recruit those thirty women stand as a proof that the gates of America were open to Spanish women at an early date and that their presence was considered vital in the New World. Queen Isabella was not thinking of a military expedition of conquest when she issued the license to bring Spanish women to the Caribbean islands. She was undoubtedly thinking of the unfolding of Spanish society in America in the best tradition of Greek and Roman colonization.

The license of 1498 signaled the beginning of women's immigration to America, and in the opening decade of the sixteenth century, the tempo of that immigration increased. In 1508, when Diego Columbus, the oldest son of the discoverer, was readying himself to sail for Hispaniola to take over as viceroy of the islands, he was joined in Seville by his wife Doña María de Toledo. Doña María, who was a daughter of Don Hernando de Toledo and a niece of the Duke of Alba and of King Ferdinand, arrived in Seville with a large household, ready to sail for the Indies with her husband. In Doña María's household, there were several married women whose husbands were members of Diego Columbus's administration, some dueñas or ladies-in-waiting, servant girls, and a group of young unmarried girls, all of them hijasdalgo, daughters of the lesser nobility of Castile. In the late spring of 1509, these young ladies waited impatiently at Seville to start a new life, and hoped to find suitable husbands from among the early settlers of Hispaniola. One of them was Doña María de Cuellar, daughter of a royal treasurer. In the colonies she would marry Diego Velázquez, the governor of Cuba. Among the married women in the household of Doña María de Toledo was Doña Francisca de Peralta. Her daughter Doña Inés Bravo, who would be born in Hispaniola, would play an important role in colonial Peru in later years.[2]

Doña María de Toledo arrived with her female companions in Santo Domingo on July 10, 1509. Never before had so many distinguished Spanish women arrived in the colony at one time, and the island, rocked years before by riots and rebellions, acquired an easy, holiday mood. There were parties, concerts, dances, and plays. A great number of Spanish settlers crowded into the town from all over the island to see and welcome the newcomers, and in some cases to find a Castilian wife. The marriages that followed the arrival of Doña María de Toledo became a strong, stabilizing social force in the island, and the raucous atmosphere of a frontier camp began giving way to the orderly life of a civilized town. Married settlers, whose wives had been left in Castile, brought them now to Santo Domingo and changed from restless seekers of adventure and easy wealth to husbands and fathers working to support a family. A shrewd observer of the period noted that before the arrival of Doña María de Toledo and her companions, "there was a great need of such Castilian women, . . . and with these Castilian women who arrived (with Doña María) the town was ennobled a great deal. . . ." He goes on to explain that the families established and ruled by these women became the true foundations of the colony, and that thanks to them, the "city has already increased its population and forms a healthy republic."[3]

As the years went by, a ship seldom arrived in the islands from Seville without some Castilian women on board. By 1514, of the fourteen towns founded on Hispaniola by the Spaniards, thirteen had Spanish women living on them, and two out of three married settlers were married to women from Castile. Married men whose wives had been left in Spain, were under social and legal pressure to bring their spouses to the island and to lead the orderly life of family men. The official catalog of those licensed to immigrate to the colonies, an incomplete and not altogether reliable source, shows that in those early years 10 percent of the immigrants were women. Given the higher rate of male mortality in the Spanish settlements of the New World, the actual proportion of Spanish women in the colonies must have been substantially higher.[4]

The pattern established in the Caribbean islands was to be repeated on the mainland. In April 1514, Doña Isabel de Bobadilla, following the example of Doña María de Toledo, sailed for the New World accompanying her husband, Pedro Arias, who had been appointed governor of Panamá. As a governor's wife, Doña

Isabel must have brought with her a household of relatives and servants, and in Panamá, one of her four daughters was promised in marriage to Balboa, the discoverer of the Pacific. By 1532, when Francisco Pizarro conquered the Incan empire, most of the Spanish settlements in Hispaniola, Cuba, New Spain, and Central America had Spanish women living in them, and not all of those women were immigrants from Spain. By the time Pizarro conquered Peru and founded the city of Lima, a new generation of Spanish girls, born in the colonies of Spanish parents, was maturing in the Caribbean islands and in Panamá.

As the news of recent conquests arrived in Spain, the demand for immigration licenses increased in Seville, the port of exit for the Indies. This increased demand, coupled with the traditional slowness of the Spanish bureaucracy, produced a black market, where licenses were sold to anyone with ready cash. At least one woman, Francisca Brava, was active as a "broker" in this black market around the middle of the century. The following advertising leaflet offering the services of Francisca Brava was distributed in the narrow backstreets of Seville:

> Whoever would like to buy a license to go the the Indies, may go to the Gate of San Juan and Santisteban, in the road to Tudela, near the stone bridge, and in that street he should ask for Francisca Brava, and she will sell it to him there.[5]

Early Spanish Women in Peru

The years from 1532 to 1550 were not easy in Spanish Peru. The conquest had begun with the brutal massacre of Cajamarca and the legalized murder of the Inca emperor, Atahualpa. After the first shock of the conquest, the Indians had revolted and trapped Francisco Pizarro in the newly founded city of Lima. While he fought for his life in the coastal lowlands, his brothers were surrounded by thousands of Inca warriors in the ancient city of Cuzco, the imperial capital of the Incas. These Inca rebellions were followed by the bloody civil wars of the conquerors, who fought first among themselves for control of the Incan empire, and later against the crown to resist encroachment in Peru of the royal bureaucracy of Castile. By the time the civil wars came to an end in 1548, Francisco Pizarro and his brother, Martín de Alcántara, had been assassinated in Lima by the followers of the Almagros. Almagro and his son had been brutally executed in the central plaza of Cuzco by the Pizarro faction. The first Spanish viceroy of Peru, Blasco Núñez de Vela, had been deposed by a *coup d'état* organized by the early settlers, and finally killed in the battle of Añaquito. Gonzalo Pizarro, leader of a popular revolt against royal authority, had been captured and executed in the plaza of Cuzco. Hundreds of Spanish men had been wounded, killed, or exiled from Peru.[6]

The early stage of Spanish Peru, with its battlefields and violent clashes of male egos, would not appear to be a suitable place for gentle women. The secluded and pious wives, the dueñas, the illiterate servant girls, and the overprotected young maidens could not play any role in the bloody games of the civil wars. And yet in those early years, Peru saw the arrival of several hundred Spanish women, who concealed under feminine veils the restless selfish personality of a Don Juan or the hidden powers of a religious madonna. They stole silently, almost undetected, onto the Peruvian stage, and the whirlwind of the civil wars was affected by their presence. They became secret plotters and vocal protestors, peacemakers and intercessors, as the occasion warranted. Some of them could not resist the lure of the expanding frontier and became itinerant campfollowers. Others, ignoring the rigid demands of their own society, openly became mistresses and "women of love." Many were undisputed rulers of large households. While men fought for power and wealth, the early Spanish women of Peru introduced European plants, crops and home industries; taught the Spanish way of life to the first generation of Spanish children born in Peru; played a dominant role in the acculturation of Indian servant girls and black slaves; raised many mestizo children; opened domestic businesses; and even became heads and rulers of powerful encomiendas.[7]

Among the first Spanish women to arrive in Peru were two adventuresses who joined the conquistadores shortly after the occupation of Cajamarca in 1532. They followed the men of Pizarro from Cajamarca to the heart of the Inca empire in Cuzco as the first soldaderas or campfollowers in the conquest of Peru. One was Isabel Rodríguez, who soon was known as La Conquistadora. This nickname, given to her by the soldiers of Pizarro, clearly indicates that Isabel was a woman of courage and well known around the campfires of Pizarro's army in the early Spanish marches toward Jauja and Cuzco. The other woman was Beatriz, whose surname now is forgotten. She was simply known among the soldiers as La Morisca. Beatriz was the first of the Peruvian *moriscas*, Spanish-born women of low social status and Muslim descent, who came to Peru either as servant girls or, as Beatriz, to live on the fringes of social respectability.

While La Conquistadora and La Morisca followed the soldiers of the conquest, another small group of Spanish women arrived with Almagro from Panamá and began to settle in the first Spanish town in Peru, San Miguel de Piura. Among them was Doña Inés Muñoz, wife of Martín de Alcántara and sister-in-law of Francisco Pizarro, of whom a colonial historian wrote that "she was the first Spanish woman to enter this kingdom (of Peru), accompanying her brother-in-law Don Francisco Pizarro, when he began the conquest. . . ."[8] Doña Inés herself corrected this statement when she wrote years later to the crown that she was the first *married* Spanish woman to enter Peru to begin populating the land.

The year 1534 was a landmark in the early immigration of Spanish women to Peru. Pedro de Alvarado, the companion of Cortés and veteran of the conquest of Mexico, arrived in Peru to join the Pizarro brothers. He had been back to Spain in 1527, and when he returned to Mexico the following year, he brought to the colonies several marriageable girls. The amusing and embarrassing encounter of those girls with their prospective husbands has been preserved in the work of the Inca Garcilaso, the great Peruvian mestizo. A welcome party was organized by the old conquistadores and veteran settlers. The young ladies huddled together in a corner of the room to gossip and share first impressions. In the spirited conversation that followed, they amused themselves by making fun of the old, worn-out conquistadores, and some went as far as to declare that they had no intention of marrying "those rotten old men." One of the girls retorted that she did not share those misgivings and that in fact the men would make ideal husbands. She hastened to explain, amidst the laughter of her companions, that the men would soon be dead, leaving them the wealth and social prestige accumulated during a lifetime of hardship and toil. Then, she went on, "we will be able to choose a young man of our liking to take the place of the old one, as one changes an old, broken pot for a new one in good condition." Such selfishness and cynicism in the proverbial shy maiden, educated in a convent to be subservient to a man, was, needless to say, unexpected. Unfortunately for the strong-minded and cunning young ladies, their conversation was overheard by one of the old conquistadores, who stormed out of the room shouting that he would rather marry his Indian mistress than one of those proud and crafty girls of Castile.[9]

Some of these women followed Alvarado to Peru in 1534. Like the household of Doña María de Toledo two decades before, Alvarado's entourage included married women, servant girls, and young daughters of good families to be married in Peru. They arrived in Quito and followed the Inca highway into Peru as members of an expedition composed of several hundred persons. Slowed down by the women and children in the march, they inched their way south over the crest of the Andes. When they arrived at the Sierra Nevada, not far from the snow-covered Huascarán, a woman and her two small daughters refused to go on and collapsed exhausted by the roadside. The husband tried desperately to help them to their feet as he begged them, in vain, to continue marching. The four of them froze to death in the snow. Their trail could perhaps serve as a silent symbol of the many courageous women who found their way to Peru in the footsteps of the early conquistadores.[10]

The women brought by Alvarado were not the first, but they constituted the largest group of Spanish women to arrive in Peru since 1532. By the 1540s, there was one Spanish woman in Peru for every seven or eight Spanish men. New Spanish towns had been founded, where the slow, painful task of transforming the conquistador into merchant, artisan, and farmer had begun. The presence of women in those urban centers served as a powerful catalyst to hasten that metamorphosis vital to a viable and orderly society. There were Spanish women in Piura in 1533. Spanish women had settled in Jauja and Cuzco by 1534, and some of them followed Pizarro in 1533 to found Lima. Two years later, Lima had at least fourteen well-known Spanish ladies. Spanish women were also living in Trujillo during the great Indian rebellion of 1536–37, and Pizarro ordered the city fathers to evacuate them

and their children to the safety of Panamá. By 1541, the year
Pizarro was assassinated in his palace at Lima, the whole of Peru
probably had about three hundred Spanish women. This figure
reached one thousand by mid-century. Almost half of them are
mentioned in the written records of the period. Some of them
became legendary and are still known in Peru after four centuries.[11]

In 1544, the first Spanish viceroy, Blasco Núñez de Vela, arrived
in Peru, and the old settlers led by Gonzalo Pizarro revolted against
him. The main grievance of the rebels was that the viceroy brought
with him a royal order to apply to Peru the drastic New Laws of
1542 abolishing encomiendas, which meant undoubtedly the destruction of the economic basis on which the most powerful settlers
had built their own large households. The New Laws had raised
a storm of protest in Mexico and Guatemala. The settlers of those
northern regions wrote to the Emperor Charles that they had
brought their wives and fiancées from Spain and raised new families in the colonies because they felt financially secure with the
possession of encomiendas. They were sure that without the encomienda system, they and their newly formed families would die
in misery and despair.[12]

In Peru, Viceroy Núñez de Vela, the enforcer of the New Laws,
was met with urban protests, in which the women of the cities of
Piura and Trujillo played a vociferous part. Obviously, those women
were fully aware of the economic and political implications of the
New Laws and did not hesitate to take to the streets to voice their
protest in the face of the viceroy. In the city of Piura, the women
gathered on the balconies and in the windows, rhythmically shouting insults at the passing Núñez de Vela, *maldiciéndole a boca llena
y ofreciéndole al demonio,* cursing him and offering him to the devil.
In Trujillo, the viceroy was received by a large group of angry
women who mockingly sounded cowbells and cursed the royal
representative. They accused him of destroying the emerging
Spanish society of Peru and demanded his immediate return to
Castile. These rioting women of Piura and Trujillo were far from
the stereotype of the secluded and male-dominated matrons. They
understood the consequences of the New Laws and did not hesitate to confront the viceroy with their protests and insults. The
voices of those angry women were, in fact, the first rumblings of

a society that was about to explode into open rebellion and civil war.[13]

When the war finally came and the rebels of Gonzalo Pizarro clashed with the royal officials, the women of Spanish Peru followed the conflict closely and played the diversified roles of plotters, messengers, collaborators, intercessors, and peacemakers. This female participation was not restricted to discussions in the safety of the drawing rooms, but took the form of personal, active involvement in which some of those women risked their freedom and lives to support their cause. A group of strong women, who chose to remain loyal to the crown, clustered around Doña María Calderón in the city of Arequipa, ready to do their best to keep Peru moored to Castile. Although the viceroy had been defeated and the rebel Gonzalo Pizarro ruled Peru, Doña María Calderón and her female companions spoke freely against the rebellion and urged peace and compromise with the crown. Doña María, who obviously possessed some historical knowledge, explained to the people of Arequipa that "the Romans had obtained more victories (than Gonzalo Pizarro), and yet at the end they had perished." Doña María's implications was quite clear to her listeners: the time had arrived to make peace with royal officials. This was not simply harmless female gossip. The impact of this loyalist propaganda was so great among the people of Arequipa that the rebels began worrying about the outspoken friends of Doña María. Finally, one of Pizarro's captains, Francisco de Carbajal, felt obliged to imprison Doña María Calderón and the other twenty women of her group. They were brought as prisoners to Cuzco, the headquarters of the rebellion.[14]

The female loyalists of Arequipa were placed under preventive custody in several private houses of Cuzco. Not even that could silence the stubborn Doña María. She went on openly speaking against the rebels to all who would listen, calling Gonzalo Pizarro a bloody tyrant. She was admonished several times by Francisco de Carbajal, Pizarro's lieutenant, a man whose brutal deeds had merited him the nickname of the "demon of the Andes." Other prominent citizens of Cuzco, fearing for her life, sent messages to Doña María begging her to restrain herself, accept the situation, and keep silent. But Doña María Calderón had the rebellious nature of Don Juan and the idealism of Don Quijote, and "instead of restraining and correcting herself, spoke from then on with more freedom and disrespect (for the rebels). . . ." The men of Pizarro could no longer tolerate her verbal dissent since she was undermining their support in Arequipa and Cuzco. Francisco de Carbajal had Doña María strangled to death by his black body-guards. Her body was hung from an upstairs window as a macabre warning to all dissenters of Cuzco. Mindful of the incredible stubbornness of Doña María, Carbajal spoke to the corpse amidst the laughter of the soldiers: "Comadre, if this remedy does not silence you, I do not know what I shall do!" Carbajal tried to make a sarcastic joke about a woman whom he saw as a vain, chatting gossip. In fact, Doña María Calderón should be seen as one of the first Peruvian martyrs for freedom of speech and as a sterling example of female Don Juanism. She would not bend to the demands of desperadoes, and she readily gave her life for the conviction that Peru should remain loyal to the crown of Spain.[15]

The group formed in Arequipa was not an isolated example of female activism during the civil war. The chronicles of the period have preserved the names of two other women, who made themselves heard by the leaders of the rebellion. They were the noble lady, Doña Inés Bravo de la Laguna, and the humble maid, Juana de Leytón. Doña Inés was born in Santo Domingo, the daughter of one of the ladies-in-waiting of Doña María de Toledo. After the death of her mother, the young Doña Inés played the same role in Lima during the rebellion of Gonzalo Pizarro that Doña María Calderón played in Arequipa. According to the notarized testimony of eyewitnesses, Doña Inés was the only person in the early days of the rebellion who spoke publicly in Lima against the rebels and formed among relatives and friends a group loyal to the viceroy and the crown. She helped her husband and several of his friends to escape from Lima when it was occupied by the rebels and urged them to join the royalist army in the north. She alone stood up to the wrathful Gonzalo Pizarro, who had given orders to have her palace looted and destroyed.

Doña Inés did not flee, but waited for Pizarro and his men under the lintel of her mansion. She confronted the man who had become a legend and recriminated Pizarro for his disloyalty to the crown, accused him of treason, and praised the actions of her husband. Gonzalo Pizarro must have been impressed by the courage of Doña Inés because her house was spared. Several weeks later, he yielded again to this energetic woman, who begged for the life of an imprisoned loyalist. The ill-fated viceroy, Núñez de Vela, was also impressed and was moved to inform the crown that nobody in Lima had followed the royal banner with the loyalty and steadfastness of Doña Inés Bravo de la Laguna.[16]

Juana de Leytón, a woman of humble origin and little education, came to Peru as a maid in the household of Catalina de Leytón, the mistress-wife of Francisco de Carbajal. By the time of Pizarro's rebellion, Juana was already married and living in her own house. In spite of the fact that her former master was Pizarro's lieutenant, Juana declared herself for the crown and made her house a haven for hunted loyalists. She provided them with food and shelter and risked her own life trying to hide them. Once Francisco de Carbajal came into Juana's house looking for three fugitives, whom his spies had reported were hidden there. Juana did not falter before the most feared man of Peru. Realizing that her secret was known to Carbajal, she calmly offered to bring a knife so that he could satiate his thirst for human blood by slaying the fugitives with his own hand. Carbajal was paralyzed at the sight of that woman holding the knife and left the house abruptly shouting, "Leave me alone, woman, and go with the devil!"[17]

María Calderón and her twenty female friends, Inés Bravo, Juana de Leytón, and the protesting women of Piura and Trujillo were not passive spectators of the early civil wars of Peru. They were aware of the issues involved and did not hesitate to take sides in the conflict. Echoing the voices of the Spanish settlers of Guatemala and Mexico, the women of Piura and Trujillo protested the abolition of encomiendas as a threat to the stability of their families, and therefore to the stability of an orderly Spanish society in Peru. The crown would eventually vindicate them by withdrawing the New Laws so vehemently opposed by those women. The women of Arequipa and Lima helped moor that emerging society to the Spanish throne by remaining loyal to the crown, and played a modest but important role in bringing about the defeat of the rebels. Two decades later, the women of Arequipa were still involved with political issues affecting the Spanish monarchy. In 1580, King Philip II wrote a letter to the city of Arequipa praising and thanking the ladies who had sent to Spain money, jewelry, and gold ornaments to support the Spanish struggle against the Turks and the infidels.[18]

Campfollowers, Mistresses, and "Women of Love"

Although early in the colonization of America the sexual needs of the male settlers were easily fulfilled by Indian women, many Spanish women of loose morals arrived in the colonies to trade their bodies for a share in the wealth of the Indies. As early as 1527, the crown had issued a royal license to Bartolomé Cornejo in Puerto Rico and Juan Sánchez Sarmiento in Santo Domingo to open "a house for public women . . . in a suitable place, because there is need for it in order to avoid (worse) harm."[19] In 1537, the Bishop of Panamá found to his chagrin that Spanish women of loose morals were not an uncommon sight on the isthmus. When the news of the conquest of Peru and of the untold wealth of the Incas began circulating in Panamá, naturally some of those women drifted south toward Peru.

Most of them were not common prostitutes and were not going to Peru to inhabit full-fledged prostitution houses. They were, to use an expression of the period, "women of love" who, for the most part, attached themselves to one man at a time to be his mistress and lover. When their men were conquerors and explorers, the women became campfollowers who abandoned the relative comforts of cities and towns to follow them into the unknown. Sometimes they ended by marrying their lovers, but they did not always abandon the campfires for the hearths of a traditional household. There was undoubtedly a touch of Don Juanism in those mistresses and campfollowers. They shamelessly challenged the strong religious and social conventions of the period and chose to live their lives as they saw fit. They were condemned by the stern moralists of the Catholic church and ostracized by the "decent people," but they won the respect and love of those unencumbered by religious dogmatism and social conventions.

As mentioned, Isabel Rodríguez, La Conquistadora, and Beatriz, La Morisca, were the pioneers of the campfollowers and "women of love" of colonial Peru. They were not alone for long around the campfires of the conquerors. During the civil wars, María de Toledo and the spirited Mari López became the lovers and constant companions of the soldiers Alonso Camargo and Bernardino de Balboa.

Mari López was a "veteran" who, in the true tradition of the soldadera or campfollower, had participated in the Indian uprisings. On one occasion, she guarded a group of Indian prisoners while the town was surrounded by Indian attackers and did not let a single prisoner escape. On another occasion, Mari López went even further in her role as soldadera and took an active part in the battle itself. Together with her friend, Leonor de Guzmán, wife of Hernando Carmona, and armed with sword and shield, Mari López fought to defend one of the gates of the town. Eyewitnesses said that the two women fought *varonilmente,* in a virile fashion, and the gate was not overrun by the Indians. The fighter Mari López ended by marrying her lover and fading into a "respectable" family life after the civil wars.

María de Toledo had a career similar to that of Mari López. She had followed Alonso Camargo through the turmoil of the civil wars, but their relationship ended in tragedy. Camargo was taken a prisoner and condemned to death by Francisco de Carbajal. A pious Dominican friar brought María to Carbajal to plead for the life of Camargo. The friar explained to Carbajal that, if spared, Camargo would marry María to atone for the sin in which they had lived. The "demon of the Andes" was not moved by theological arguments. He mocked the friar and the unhappy María and rejected their pleas. Camargo was executed, and María probably drifted to another lover.[20]

The mistresses and campfollowers were not always attached to men of lower ranks, nor were they a unique product of the conquest and civil wars. Well into the second half of the sixteenth century, one finds them as lovers of captains and expeditionary leaders, and on the fringes and frontiers of the expanding empire. Some of those campfollowers were, as suggested before, devoted wives who rejected the traditional roles of mothers and housekeepers to follow their spouses into the unknown danger of the frontier. Catalina de Leytón, Inés Suárez, Inés de Atienza, Isabel de Vergara, and Isabel de Barreto stand out as unforgettable names among the mistresses and campfollowers of the period.

Catalina de Leytón was, as already mentioned, the lover of Francisco de Carbajal, Pizarro's lieutenant during the great rebellion. It seems that later they had legalized their union by marriage. Catalina followed Carbajal from Spain to Mexico and then to Peru, where she remained loyally by the side of the most cruel and most feared of the conquistadores. Catalina and her maid Juana de Leytón were the only two persons who ever dared to confront

Carbajal, and who, at times, succeeded in taming the beast. Catalina could even tease and mock the man in front of whom other men trembled. On one occasion during a respite from the civil war, Carbajal prepared a banquet in Cuzco for his most important captains, who proceeded to get royally drunk. When Catalina de Leytón entered the banquet room, bodies were lying on the floor and slumbering in chairs and on benches. Catalina began deriding Carbajal and his men, and with a sarcastic smile exclaimed: "Oh poor Peru! See how its rulers look!" Carbajal would have not tolerated the insult from anybody else, but to Catalina he only said: "Keep quiet, old woman, and let them sleep a couple of hours that anyone of them could rule by himself half the world!" Carbajal saw his men as boundless Don Juans who could readily rule the world. Catalina saw them with the naked eye of reality as helpless, pitiful drunkards, who were ruining themselves and everything they touched.[21]

The restless, free spirit of the female conquistador was best personified by two women named Inés, who operated on the southern and northern fringes of the Peruvian viceroyalty in the sixteenth century. Inés Suárez, lover of captain Pedro de Valdivia, took part with him in the conquest of Chile. Inés de Atienza left behind the comforts of the town of Trujillo and descended with her lover, Pedro de Ursúa, into the "green hell" of the Amazon. Inés Suárez had sailed for the New World in 1537, accompanied only by a young niece, and had settled in the imperial city of Cuzco. In Peru, she met Don Pedro de Valdivia whose lawful wife was still living in Spain. In defiance of the laws of the church and of the state and in open challenge to the social conventions of respectable people, Inés and Valdivia became lovers and constant companions.

When Pedro de Valdivia left Peru in 1540 to conquer Chile and to subdue the Araucanian Indians of the southern frontier, Inés Suárez was the only Spanish woman of the expedition. During the long marches toward Chile, across the crest of the Andes, and later in the war-torn Araucanian frontier, Inés became the guardian angel of the rough Castilian adventurers. Many eyewitnesses spoke of her great love for the men of Valdivia, and of the countless hours spent nursing the sick, healing the wounded, and encouraging the disheartened. Inés saved the life of Valdivia several times by exposing the plot of mutinous soldiers. She became the eyes and ears of Valdivia, and little transpired in the Spanish camp that was not soon reported to Inés by friendly and grateful soldiers.

On September 11, 1541, the famous battle of Santiago took place. It was one of the most violent clashes between Indians and Spaniards in the entire history of the conquest. On that occasion, when the Spanish settlement was almost destroyed by the Araucanians, Inés Suárez proved to friends and enemies alike that, besides the tenderness of a lover and the concern of a mother, she also possessed the steel and ruthlessness of the conquistadores. The Indians, enraged like wounded animals, attacked Santiago to free seven of their most important caciques, who had been imprisoned by the Spaniards. Inés did not remain secluded away from the fighting, but rushed to the defense of the town wearing armor, exhorting the soldiers to the battle, and helping to evacuate the wounded. When, in spite of the Spanish efforts, the settlement was overrun by the Indians, and the Spanish soldiers were already tasting the bitterness of defeat, Inés conceived a brutal, desperate idea, which turned the tide of the battle. She proposed to slay the imprisoned caciques, and to throw their severed heads into the midst of the onrushing waves of Indian attackers. Inés herself was one of the slayers, and her brutal deed so horrified the Indians that they fled in fear at the sight of the mutilated bodies of their leaders.[22]

When the battle was over and the men of Valdivia had collapsed among the burning ruins of the small town, Inés alone seems to have realized that the struggle for survival was not yet over. She busied herself by searching among the ruins for the few domestic animals brought from Peru by Valdivia, and she "managed to save a young hen and a rooster, a hog and a sow." One does not know whom to admire more, the woman-warrior who fought in the battle of Santiago, or the woman of domesticity who thought of saving a few animals to secure the development of the colony.

Inés obviously knew that the true conquest of Chile could not be fully accomplished by a few military victories. On that day, while chasing pigs and chickens among the dead and wounded, Inés Suárez was thinking ahead into the future. She was also thinking of the future when she persuaded the friendly cleric Rodrigo González to teach her to read and write. After months of painful drills, Inés, a woman almost fifty, mastered the art of reading and writing. She went on with her studies, ignoring the criticism of some of the men who thought that literacy was unbecoming to a woman. They gossiped among themselves, fearing that *de leer verna a otras cosas* (from reading she will graduate to other things). Whatever those other things were in their minds, the men obviously did not like the prospect.

The life of Inés Suárez as mistress and lover of Valdivia came to an abrupt end because of the pressures of the bureaucracy of Lima. The royal governor of Peru, Pedro de la Gasca, who was a man of religion and law, opened an inquiry into the affairs of Chile. He ordered Valdivia to bring his lawful wife from Spain and to terminate his relationship with Inés. Valdivia had to obey and arranged the marriage of Inés to an important man in the colony, Don Rodrigo Quiroga. Inés accepted the painful decision with awesome restraint and dignity. Years later, when her husband became governor of the southern colony, Inés spent the twilight years of her life as the revered first lady of the kingdom of Chile.[23]

The most tragic figure among the campfollowers of early Peru was Inés de Atienza, a young widow and a mestiza of disturbing, sensuous beauty. Together with twelve other Spanish women, she was caught in the greatest orgy of greed, brutality, and lust unleashed in the sixteenth century by the seekers of El Dorado.

In 1555, when the marquis of Cañete arrived in Peru, he found a viceroyalty still threatened by the presence of ruthless adventurers and displaced veterans of the civil wars. To get rid of them, the viceroy organized a new expedition to the lands of El Dorado and appointed Pedro de Ursúa to lead the expedition out of the Andes into the heart of the Amazon forest.[24] By 1559, Ursúa was building a fleet of brigantines near Moyobamba, on a branch of the Huallaga River. He was ready to seek El Dorado through the tangled maze of rivers in the Amazon valley. Ursúa had recruited three hundred adventurers, and among them the notorious López de Aguirre, known in Peru as "Aguirre the madman." He had a long history of crimes and rebellions and would transform "Ursúa's expedition into a wild orgy of bloodshed and mad cruelty."[25] Twelve women were also in Ursúa's camp on the eastern slopes of the Andes. Seven of them were married to members of the expedition and had chosen to follow their spouses in the elusive search for El Dorado. Five of the women were still single and had joined the expedition in the hopes of finding suitable husbands, who would one day become wealthy and famous in the lands to be conquered. Doña Inés de Atienza, who had the reputation of being the most beautiful woman of Peru, had become the lover and mistress of Captain Pedro de Ursúa. She also joined the tragic expedition with several of her black and Indian maids. In the opening months of 1560, all of them waited impatiently for the launching of the ships and for the expedition to get under way.

In distant Lima, some friends of Ursúa, anxious about the future of the expedition, wrote letters warning Ursúa against the madman Aguirre and strongly advised him to leave Doña Inés and the other women behind. Ursúa ignored his friends' advice, and the expedition began moving down the Huallaga River in early July 1560. The excitement of building the ships, and the feverish activity of gathering men and supplies was soon replaced by the monotony and drudgery of following the meandering rivers, hoping against hope that El Dorado would materialize behind the next bend of the river. The enervating heat and humidity of the jungle, the lack of comforts and of a proper diet, and the constant aimlessness soon had the men of Ursúa wrapped in stupor and numbness.

Weeks went by, and Captain Pedro de Ursúa began to lose his courage and the will to find El Dorado. He refused to meet with his officers, neglected his role as a leader, and spent his days alone in the company of Doña Inés. There is no doubt that Ursúa had become seriously ill in the insalubrious climate of the Amazon forest, but his men, who were overwhelmed by the haunting beauty of Doña Inés, spoke of witchcraft and spells cast by the sensuous mestiza. Rumors circulated in whispers among the expeditionaries that Ursúa was *embebecido,* stupefied and absorbed by Doña Inés. Whatever the reasons, Ursúa became more and more reclusive and communicated his orders and heard complaints only through his companion and lover. With Ursúa thus secluded in his cabin or his tent, Doña Inés de Atienza appeared to some as the only remaining visible symbol of authority in an expedition that had begun to disintegrate.[26]

López de Aguirre, a rebel against all authority and a misogynist at heart, could not tolerate Doña Inés's new role in the expedition. He soon began plotting the assassination of Ursúa and found willing conspirators in Juan Alonso and Lorenzo de Salduendo, whose motivation in joining the plot sprang from their blind passion for Doña Inés.

January 1, 1561 was the day set for the assassination. A black slave, who had gotten wind of the plot, tried to warn Ursúa, but as usual the captain refused to be disturbed. Ursúa was taken by surprise, and the assassination was consummated.

The crime did not restore discipline to the expedition, but opened instead a brutal struggle among the leading officers for the possession of Doña Inés de Atienza. Hernando de Guzmán, a vain, lesser noble, was named the new leader of the expedition, but he could not control the storm raised among the men by the magnetic beauty of the Peruvian mestiza. Juan Alonso, Baltasar de Miranda, Pedro Hernández, and Lorenzo de Salduendo fought among themselves for the woman. Juan Alonso took the prize after killing Miranda and Hernández, while Salduendo had to settle for Doña María de Sotomayor, a friend and companion of Doña Inés. But Lorenzo de Salduendo could not free himself from the torturing longings for Doña Inés and eventually, through a new assassination, supplanted Alonso as the lover of the beautiful mestiza.

The haunting beauty of Inés de Atienza brought to Salduendo the same fate it had brought to Pedro de Ursúa. The young mestiza dominated her new lover to the point that Salduendo "would never leave her sight either during the day or at night." He neglected his duties, and the seeking of El Dorado was almost forgotten by his total absorption in pleasing Doña Inés and enjoying her company. The other women in the expedition had, perhaps to a lesser degree, a similar effect on their lovers. Doña María de Sotomayor, who was a married woman, changed lovers several times as the expedition sailed down the Amazon toward the sea, and also saw men fighting and killing for her love and company.

The cruel and misogynist López de Aguirre understood better than most the devastating effect the passion for women was having on the expedition and conceived a deep hate for the women in the expedition. The most beautiful and the most desired woman in the group, Doña Inés de Atienza, became the main target of Aguirre's hate. After a few days camping rest, a fight broke out between Salduendo and Aguirre over some extra mattresses for Doña Inés and her companions, which ended with the assassination of Salduendo. Aguirre was not satisfied with Salduendo's death; he decided to kill Doña Inés and put an end to what he conceived to be the cause of so much evil.

> *The cruel beast Aguirre, now bathed in the blood of Salduendo, longed to shed that of Doña Inés, and calling to mind his distaste for her . . . he determined that she should suffer a similar punishment; so he ordered one of his sergeants, called Antón Llamoso, and one Francisco Carrión, a mestizo, to go and kill her wherever they might find her. . . . The murderers went to where Doña Inés lodged, and rushing upon her with drawn swords took her life in such barbarous manner that after her death, even the most hardened men in the camp, at the sight of the mangled victim, were heartbroken for this was the most cruel act that had been perpetrated.*[27]

After the assassination of Doña Inés, the expedition exploded into an orgy of crimes, and Aguirre led an open rebellion against the authority of the distant crown. Lost in the middle of the Amazon jungle, he planned a new conquest of Peru to make it into a kingdom independent of Castile. He even wrote the king an abusive letter informing him that he and his men had severed their allegiance to the Spanish crown and were about to liberate Peru from the tyrannical rule of Castile. Aguirre also wrote that he would "kill all the women [in the expedition] because they were the cause of all the great evils and scandals in the world." He went on to say that "he had already killed Governor Ursúa and many others because of one woman brought by the governor."[28] True to his word, Aguirre assassinated his own daughter, Elvira, to prevent her from becoming "the mattress of villains." In the sick mind of López de Aguirre, women were only sexual objects, who weakened and destroyed men.

López de Aguirre could never have accepted that the camp-followers were, at times, a source of support and strength for their men. He saw no difference between lust and love and would never have understood a woman like Inés Suárez and her heroic role in the conquest of Chile. Aguirre also would have been confused by the unselfish behavior of the female campfollowers, who arrived at the Rio de la Plata in 1536 with Don Pedro de Mendoza in his ill-fated attempt to found the colony of Buenos Aires. There

were at least eight women among almost fifteen hundred persons
brought by Mendoza to Rio de la Plata in 1536: María Dávila, the
companion of Mendoza himself; Elvira Pineda, the "maid" of captain Juan Osorio; María de Angulo, the wife of Francisco de Mendoza; her two daughters, Juana and María; Francisca Josefa de
Bocanegra, who was destined to play a vital role in the development of the new colony; Catalina de Vadillo, wife of a soldier;
and Isabel de Guevara, wife of Pedro de Esquivel, a gentleman
from Seville. Twenty years later and from the city of Asunción in
Paraguay, Isabel de Guevara wrote a letter to Queen Doña Juana
to remind her of the services performed in 1536 by those women,
and to request for them royal recognition.

Isabel still remembered vividly in 1556 the horrors of her first
months on the mouth of the Rio de la Plata. Hunger, pestilence,
and Indian attacks ravaged the men of Mendoza, and in three
months, about a thousand of them had died. The remainder of
the expedition, ill and broken-hearted, clung in despair to the
eastern edge of the South American continent. The women, Isabel
de Guevara wrote to the queen, nursed the sick, gathered food
and cooked it to feed the starving men, were the lookouts for
surprise Indian attacks, kept watch over the campfires, and had
the weapons always clean and ready for the fight. When the Indians did attack, the women fought by the side of their men in
the true tradition of the campfollowers.

When the survivers of Mendoza's expedition abandoned Buenos Aires and sailed north on the Paraná toward the city of Asunción, the women went along. If we are to believe Isabel's letter to
the queen, the women saved the men from starvation and death.
Some of the men were so weak that the women had to carry them
aboard the brigantines like children. Most of the time the women
manned the rudders and sails, and frequently went ashore searching for food and fuel. They performed other services for the men,
not mentioned in Isabel's letter in order "not to hurt the men's
pride and honor." Isabel explained her almost unbelievable story
by saying that the women would, by their nature, survive with less
food and comforts than the men, and could remain stronger and
less despondent. Besides, "God wanted the women to survive mi-
raculously to show that women are the source of men's life." Whatever one may think of the objective value of those reasons, they
say a great deal about Isabel's self-awareness and about the way

she saw herself in relation to men. For Isabel de Guevara, women were physically and psychologically stronger than men because God had made them the source and the sustenance of men's life.[29]

The Queen of Sheba

Before the sixteenth century came to an end, another remarkable woman won the admiration and elicited the fear of men sailing the Pacific Ocean. Her name was Doña Isabel de Barreto, but sailors and soldiers called her in respectful fear "la reina de Saba," the Queen of Sheba. She became admiral of the South Pacific fleet, and governor and captain-general of the Solomon Islands. Her name became well known in the ports of Callao, Manila, Acapulco, and in the scattered islands of the South Pacific. The saga of her life gives clear testimony that the boundless, selfish ego of a Don Juan could, at times, belong to a woman. Isabel de Barreto's ambition, strength of character, and brutal selfishness compare to the qualities found in men like the Pizarro brothers, Carbajal, and López de Aguirre.[30]

Isabel de Barreto was born in Spain and came to Peru with her three brothers, Lorenzo, Diego, and Luís, when she was still a young girl. Little is known of her early years in Peru, but by 1557, she was a lady-in-waiting of Doña Teresa de Castro, wife of Viceroy García Hurtado de Mendoza, marquis of Cañete. Isabel's charm and beauty made her the favorite of the viceroy's wife, and like many young ladies of her station, she hoped to contract a marriage of economic and social prestige. Isabel was more ambitious and more adventurous than most of her female companions in the viceregal court, and she set her eyes upon Don Alvaro de Mendaña de Neira.

In the 1580s, Mendaña was in his early forties and was the most eligible bachelor of Peru. His past accomplishments had given him the aura of a romantic conquistador. Mendaña had come to Peru in the entourage of his uncle, the royal governor of Peru, Lope García de Castro. In 1567, he was given command of the fleet of the South Pacific, and in February of the following year, he discovered one of the archipelagoes of the South Pacific. They landed on an island with a river of auriferous currents and named the island Guadalcanal after the town in Spain where the chief pilot of the fleet had been born. The sight of gold in Guadalcanal made Mendaña think of the Queen of Sheba and of her lover, the biblical king; he named the entire archipelago the Solomon Islands.[31]

By 1580, Mendaña had spent two decades fighting the viceregal and royal bureaucracy and trying to establish his claims to the Solomon Islands. Tired of the slowness and pettiness of the Lima bureaucrats, he went to Spain to see King Philip II, who granted Mendaña the right "to conquer and pacify the islands of the South Sea."

When Isabel de Barreto met Alvaro de Mendaña in Lima, he had the royal titles of admiral of the fleet, *adelantado,* governor, and captain-general of the Solomon Islands. He also had the authority of passing his titles and rights to his lawful heir. The ambitious young lady saw a marriage with the mature explorer and navigator as the fastest possible way to a life of wealth, social prestige, and political power. The wedding took place in Lima in May 1586, and Isabel plunged with zest into all the preparations for the long trip to this new kingdom of King Solomon.

Forty married women were allowed by royal charter to accompany their husbands to the South Pacific, but some single girls were also persuaded to join the expedition, which promised famous and wealthy husbands. After years of delay, Mendaña tried to prod the bureaucracy into action by explaining to the royal authorities that those single girls, recruited for the expedition, ran the serious danger of falling into prostitution in the raucous atmosphere of the port towns, if the ships were delayed any longer.

Finally, the expeditionaries sailed in four ships on July 16, 1595. There were 350 persons on board and "among them women and some children." Doña Isabel de Barreto settled with a queenly wardrobe and several maids in the best cabin of the flag ship and expected in her floating court the same gracious and luxurious living that she had enjoyed at the viceregal court of the marquis of Cañete. Her sensitive pride and her arrogance soon became apparent to all.

Toward the end of July, after failing to find the elusive Guadalcanal and its auriferous river, the ships landed on a new archipelago not seen by Mendaña in his first expedition. Mindful of the friendship between his wife and Doña Teresa de Castro, the marchioness of Cañete, Mendaña named this new archipelago "Islas Marquesas" in honor of Doña Teresa.[32]

For more than four months, the small fleet threaded its way through the scattered islands in vain search of Guadalcanal. By the second week of August, food and water were running short, and the first rumblings of protests were heard aboard the ships. The women complained to Mendaña bitterly and sarcastically, saying they had been brought to the expedition "to collect the promised pearls from the deep bottom of the sea." The soldiers and sailors also protested that, on top of all the hardship and futility of the trip, their salaries were weeks in arrears. They resented that "only with the value of Doña Isabel's wardrobe their salaries could have been paid for two years." Doña Isabel de Barreto haughtily ignored the criticism and kept flaunting her wealth and luxurious style of life. It must have been about this time when the sailors began calling her in bitter resentment "the Queen of Sheba."

By the time Mendaña had given up hope of finding Guadalcanal and had begun building a Spanish settlement on the island of Santa Cruz, sailors and soldiers had almost reached the state of open mutiny. Doña Isabel, always arrogant and domineering, pressed for a hard line in dealing with the men and advised her husband and brothers to execute the *maese de campo* or commander of the troops. Her anger toward the *maese* was such that one day she attacked him with a dagger, and only the intervention of the bystanders saved his life. Doña Isabel finally had her way and, with the excuse of maintaining discipline and giving an example to the soldiers, she had the *maese* executed by her brother, Don Lorenzo de Barreto. Her hard line toward the mutinous crew and her rationing of water and food were not only signs of selfishness and cruelty, but also symbols of a stubborn determination to reach, at all cost, the elusive archipelago of the Solomons.[33]

A turning point in the life of Doña Isabel came toward the middle of October 1595, four months almost to the day since the expedition had sailed from Peru. Alvaro de Mendaña had fallen gravely ill and by the fifteenth of October, all hopes to save his life had been relinquished. On a lost island of the South Pacific, hundreds of miles from any Spanish settlements, surrounded by a mutinous crew and besieged by thirst and hunger, the Queen of Sheba got ready for an orderly and legal transfer of power. On October 17, Mendaña dictated his last will and testament and, by virtue of the royal cedula of 1574, he transferred to Doña

Isabel all his titles and all the rights and privileges granted by the crown for the government of the islands of the South Sea. The following day, Alvardo de Mendaña died and was buried in a grave facing the blue Pacific. Isabel de Barreto was now the undisputed "queen" of the South Pacific.

A few days after the death of Mendaña, Isabel de Barreto was confronted with a petition signed by many members of the expedition, in which they demanded that the ships return immediately to Peru. Doña Isabel tore up the petition and announced that the first to sign a new petition would be hanged from the mast of the flag ship. The men knew that she meant what she said, and grudgingly busied themselves loading the ships to sail once again into the unknown in search of Guadalcanal.

By the end of December, after nearly two months of search and desperate conditions on the ship, even this woman of steel had to yield to the unavoidable. She called off the search for Guadalcanal, and allowed Fernández de Quirós, the chief pilot, to set course for Manila. On January 20, 1596, they sighted a small island, where one of the natives understood the Castilian language. Manila was near at last, but Doña Isabel did not relax her iron discipline and continued to ration food and water. By the time the ships entered the Bay of Cavite on the eleventh of February, fifty persons had died of dehydration and hunger. And yet, Doña Isabel still had in the storeroom of the ship two large sacks of flour and twenty casks of fresh water. Although many of her men would have liked to see her thrown into jail, she was received with honor and acclaim by the people of Manila. Acknowledging her titles and authority, the governor of the Philippines lodged her in his palace.

The ambitious Doña Isabel was well aware that a woman alone would encounter almost insurmountable odds in organizing a new expedition to the Solomon Islands, and she knew the advantages in the society of her day of being married to a powerful husband. In November 1596, ten months after her arrival in Manila and twelve months after the death of Alvaro de Mendaña, she married Don Fernando de Castro, a member of the ruling class of the Philippines, a nephew of a former governor of the islands, and since 1593 *general de La Carrera de Filipinas,* commander of the Acapulco-Manila sea route. He had prestige, money, political power, and experience as a navigator in the Pacific and was well qualified to fulfill the ambitions of Isabel de Barreto.

The newlyweds publicly declared their intentions to sail to the Solomons to settle there as rulers of the islands of the South Sea, and they produced the royal cedula of 1574 and the last will and testament of Mendaña to support their claims. They needed new ships, a large supply of tools, seeds, livestock, a new, experienced crew to man the ships, and volunteer settlers to join the expedition. Manila, still a small, developing town at the edge of the empire, was hardly a suitable place to outfit an expedition of such magnitude. The eyes of Doña Isabel and Don Fernando turned toward Mexico and Peru.[34]

On August 10, 1597, Doña Isabel and Don Fernando sailed from the Philippines on the Manila-Acapulco galleon on their way to Peru. The Manila-Acapulco route was the longest and most dangerous sea route of the Spanish empire, and it took them four months to reach the Bay of Acapulco. From Acapulco, Doña Isabel traveled to Peru, where the cumbersome and slow Spanish bureaucracy began grinding her dreams into dust. For twelve years, she fought the petty bureaucrats of Lima to have her rights to the Solomons recognized and to obtain a license to outfit a new expedition. In 1609, almost a quarter of a century after her marriage to Alvaro de Mendaña, Doña Isabel de Barreto decided to pass over the viceroy of Peru and present her case directly to the king of Spain. Isabel de Barreto probably died in her ancestral lands of Galícia, convinced to the end that she alone was the lawful governor of the Solomons and a new, legendary Queen of Sheba.

Isabel de Barreto, Isabel de Guevara, Inés de Atienza, and Inés Suárez were a few of the women who shared with their men the excitement of the conquest and of the expanding frontier in sixteenth-century Peru. They were strong persons with a touch of Don Juanism in their character; they challenged the laws and conventions of their society to live their lives as they saw fit. They influenced and, at times, dominated their husbands and lovers, and they played a vital role in the shaping of events. Some of their lesser-known sisters, La Conquistadora, La Morisca, Mari López, and María de Toledo, also crossed Peru in the wake of the conquest, and during the civil wars moved with complete ease from being tender lovers to being soldaderas and fighters. They did not hesitate to take an active part in the battles of the period. Even some ladies who did not become campfollowers and chose to remain within the traditional structures of family and home were politically aware and openly voiced their feelings and opinions on the vital issues of the day. The protesting ladies of Piura and Trujillo, Doña María Calderón in Arequipa, and Doña Inés Bravo de la Laguna in Lima are fine examples of female involvement in the political life of early Spanish Peru. They all played visible and important roles in the development of colonial Peru, and yet they should not share the spotlight of history alone. There was a large, silent majority of Spanish women in early Peru who, as homemakers, wives, mothers, and rulers of large households, also helped plant the solid foundations of a Spanish society.

3

(❀❀)

Homemakers
and Encomenderas

THE CAMPFOLLOWERS AND SOLDADERAS of early Spanish Peru were undoubtedly a small minority among the Spanish women who settled in Peru during the sixteenth century. The majority of their Spanish sisters settled in the newly founded Spanish cities of Peru and assumed the female roles traditionally found in the Iberian peninsula. They became wives, mothers, homemakers, and took upon themselves the early education of the first criollo and mestizo children. These women were the most important channel of Iberian acculturation for the generation born in Peru after the conquest. By 1550, only fifteen years after the foundation of Lima by Pizarro, these Spanish women numbered one thousand. They lived in Piura, Trujillo, Jauja, Cuzco, Lima, and Arequipa. Their numbers increased dramatically during the second half of the sixteenth century, while their proportion to Spanish males also increased noticeably, owing to the large numbers of males killed during the civil wars. In the opening decade of the seventeenth century when the viceroy marquis of Montesclaros ordered the census of Lima, the findings were striking. In a population of 26,441 inhabitants, the Spanish women numbered 5,359—a figure which surpassed by 101 the number of Spanish males in the city, and this figure does not take into consideration the 820 Spanish women who lived as consecrated virgins in the nunneries of Lima.[1]

Knowing that, in the Iberian tradition, these women became the heart and center of their families, it is impossible to dismiss their historical importance. Within the strong institution of the family, they had an almost absolute power. They taught their children and their black and Indian maids the Castilian language, the Christian religion, and the Spanish way of life, from preparing food and sewing clothes to taking care of all the other daily details in running a large household. It was not uncommon for some of these women, moved by Christian piety and spurred by the traditions of their culture, to accept into their houses mestizo and mulatto children to be raised and educated in the Spanish fashion.

Almost 95 percent of the first generation of mestizo children were born out of wedlock and therefore without the benefit of established families. By 1610, Lima alone had almost a thousand of these children. Some of them were placed by their Spanish fathers under the care of Spanish women of lower rank, who received some economic incentives to act as foster mothers. Francisca Suárez, La Valenciana, was one of those women. In 1544, she accepted into her house a mestizo girl, born of a Spanish father and an Indian mother, and received from the girl's father a black female slave to compensate her for the expenses of raising the child. Women of means did the same thing out of Christian charity. Isabel de Ovalle was the prototype of this kind. She had been married twice but had not had any children of her own, so she took under her care three mestizo girls and two Spanish orphan girls, whom she raised as her daughters. The maternal love of these women helped form the solid foundation of a new nation, part Indian and part Spanish.[2]

The lives of these Spanish women was by no means confined to the realm of the family and the household. Before the end of the sixteenth century, one finds many of them exercising their influence well beyond the boundaries of their homes and families and making contributions of a general nature to the development of Peruvian society. The detailed records of the colonial notaries have preserved the names of hundreds of women, who, even in the first half of the sixteenth century, engaged in a variety of socioeconomic activities outside the home. Either to supplement the family income or to make up for the absence of a husband, many of them developed some home skills into personal businesses. The *panaderas* or female bakers were ubiquitous in almost all the Spanish cities of Peru, and they sold bread, biscuits, and pastry to the general public for a profit. The *curandera* or practical healer was also a familiar figure in early Spanish Peru. The lack of doctors and of medical facilities in the first years of the colonization facilitated the development of this female profession. *Curanderas* were usually older women of rather low social class, whose knowledge of folk medicine, tinted with religious superstitions, became for them a means of livelihood. It also brought them social recognition and prestige. A more specialized "medical" profession, which was totally monopolized by women because of tradition and religious-ethical beliefs, was the profession of *partera* or midwife. In a society of prolific mothers, the midwife was always in demand and could earn a substantial living.[3]

Spanish women in Peru engaged in other professions as well. Needlework was an essential part in the training and education of all young girls in Iberian society. Once in Peru, some Spanish women of lesser means used that skill not only to supply the needs of their own families, but also to sew for the public to supplement their incomes. Some of those women were undoubtedly professional seamstresses. With the aid of Indian maids and orphan girls, they often converted a home occupation into a modest business. One also finds potters, candlemakers, innkeepers, landladies, buyers and sellers of black slaves, and speculators in urban real estate among these women.

The already mentioned Francisca Suárez typifies the many avenues open to enterprising women outside the home. In the 1540s, she was a well-known *curandera,* who obviously prospered in her profession. Francisca was able to open a handsomely furnished boardinghouse staffed by several of her own slaves, where she also sold bread and biscuits to the public. In addition to the boardinghouse, Francisca also owned several other houses in Lima that she rented for a profit.

Luísa de Rosa was a skilled potter, who had been officially recognized with membership in the potters' guild of Lima. She was the only female among the fourteen members of the guild, and in 1596, she paid her dues and was active in the affairs of the profession. In the same year, Elvira Rodríguez was a member of the hatters' guild and was recognized as a master hatter in the official rolls. Their guild memberships meant that they both had trained for several years under a master, had produced a "masterpiece" to the specifications of the guild, had received the official title of master, and were from then on allowed to keep and train their own apprentices.[4]

María Escobar and Inés Muñoz

The early socioeconomic activities of Spanish women in Peru were not always restricted to the modest enterprises of healing, sewing, baking bread, or manufacturing pottery. Women played a vital role in one of the most important aspects of colonization, the transfer and adaptation to Peru of European domestic animals, European plants, vegetables, fruits, and trees. One can easily imagine the consternation of the early wives and homemakers when they realized that they could not obtain eggs, milk, wheat flour, olive oil, Castilian fruits, beef, or pork in Peru. They could not conceive of running a normal home without these items, and they took a greater interest than the men in introducing and popularizing them in Peru.

Inés Suárez, the first lady of the frontier of Chile, clearly dramatized this concern and interest after the battle of Santiago. As mentioned, she was the only one who tried to save the few domestic animals brought from Peru after the Indians had scattered them. Running among the burning ruins, she managed to save a hen, a rooster, a hog, and a sow. She was clearly more aware than the men just how important these animals were for the survival of the colony. What Inés Suárez did in a dramatic fashion after the battle of Santiago had been done before in hundreds of courtyards in Piura, Trujillo, Lima, and Arequipa. While the men were outside doing the "important" things, the women took care of the few domestic animals available in those early days to make sure that the animals would multiply.

For centuries, wheat flour and olive oil had been among the main staples of the Iberian diet. The Spanish colonization of Peru was made easier and more thorough by the early introduction of wheat and olive oil, for which two Spanish women, María Escobar and Inés Muñoz, can claim the honor.

María Escobar had been married to Captain Martín de Arrete and had lived in Trujillo as one of the wealthiest women in the city. In the late 1530s, she lost her husband and married again, to Captain Francisco de Chávez, friend and companion of Pizarro. She moved from Trujillo to Lima and was living in the city, when her second husband was killed on June 26, 1541. A year or so before the assassination of her second husband, María Escobar received a sack of wheat from Spain, and aware of her treasure, she distributed from twenty to forty grams of wheat among several farmers of Lima and Cañete. The first crop from María's wheat was produced at Cañete, and for about three years the entire crop was resown before the authorities allowed the wheat to be ground into flour to begin the production of bread. From the reward offered to María Escobar, one may gather the importance attached to this event by the colonial authorities and the crown.

Although she was very well off and had inherited the estates of two wealthy husbands, María was given an encomienda-repartimiento of Indians in the province of Lima. This was the same reward given to the early conquistadores and to the most distinguished servants of the crown. Obviously, the introduction of wheat was thought to be worthy of the same reward as the heroic deeds of the conquest.[5]

According to the colonial historian Bernabé Cobo, María Escobar was not the first to introduce wheat into Peru; it was Inés Muñoz, the wife of Martín de Alcántara and sister-in-law of Pizarro. Although the distribution of wheat by María Escobar in 1540 cannot be questioned, Inés Muñoz had experimented with the cultivation of wheat in Lima almost five years before. Cobo, who had arrived in Lima just a few years after the death of Inés Muñoz, and whose knowledge of plants, grains, and trees was unsurpassed, wrote in his monumental *Historia del Nuevo Mundo* that Inés Muñoz "through her ingenuity and diligence, took the steps to bring from Spain the majority of trees and plants, which we enjoy in this land today; and she was finally the person, who gave wheat to this kingdom of Peru, from where wheat spread later to all other provinces of this southern America."[6] Cobo goes on to describe with a great wealth of details the arrival of the first wheat grains to Peru.

In 1535, Pizarro had descended with a few companions from the Andean valley of Jauja to found near the Pacific coast the new Spanish capital of Peru, the City of the Kings, later known as Lima. About a dozen women were among the founders of the city, and one of them was Inés Muñoz. A few months after the foundation of Lima, Inés received from Spain a barrel filled with rice, another Spanish staple. One day Inés sat to pick and clean some of the rice with the intention of preparing a rice pottage for her brother-in-law, Pizarro. (Cobo adds that in those days a rice dish was considered in Peru *regalo extraordinario,* an extraordinary treat.) While cleaning the rice, Inés noticed a few grains of wheat mixed in with the rice which she picked out carefully with the intention of planting them to see if wheat would grow in Peru. She planted the few grains of wheat in a flowerpot "with the same care and attention she would give carnations or sweet basil." Inés took unusual care of her flowerpot, and was delighted when a bundle of large, healthy spikes of wheat grew from the few grains she had planted.

Those were years filled with momentous events: the Indian rebellions had occurred in 1536–37; Almagro had led his ill-fated expedition to Chile; and finally the men of Pizarro had clashed with the men of Almagro in the first civil war of the conquerors. Nevertheless, the humble agricultural experiment conducted by Inés Muñoz in her house of Lima did not go unnoticed. When the first spikes of wheat were threshed by hand and Inés replanted her first tiny crop, "all the inhabitants of this city (Lima) were filled with the greatest of joy, because they conceived the hope that from such humble beginnings would result the sustenance and fullness of this kingdom. . . ." Cobo goes on to say that with the intense care and interest of Inés Muñoz, the wheat multiplied so much that within three or four years the production of bread began in Lima. The first mills were built in 1539, and the following year the city council set the price of bread at one *real* per pound. The efforts of Inés were so successful that by 1543 one *real* could buy three and a half pounds of bread in Lima.[7]

Five years after the foundation of Lima, Inés Muñoz was one of the most revered matrons in the city and was considered by many of her fellow citizens a sort of secular madonna, benefactress, and protectress of the emerging Spanish society of Peru. This feeling of respect increased in 1541 when tragedy struck and disrupted her personal life and the life of her beloved city. On June 26, 1541 in the governor's palace, just a stone's throw from the house of Inés, her husband Martín de Alcántara and her brother-in-law, Francisco Pizarro, the conqueror of Peru, were assassinated by the Almagro faction. Francisco de Chávez, husband of María Escobar, neighbor and friend of Inés, also fell to the sword of the assassins.

Panic spread through the city, and the friends and supporters of Pizarro went into hiding, fearing for their lives. The plaza in front of the palace and the adjacent streets were filled with the cries of revenge of the rebels, who began to vent their hate of the Pizarros by desecrating their bodies. A group of courageous women, led by Inés Muñoz and María de Lezcano, prevented this last ignominy. They crossed the plaza, defying the insults of the rebels, and recovered the bodies of Pizarro and his companions. Following an ancient tradition, the women washed the bodies stained by blood, dressed them, and made the arrangements for an honorable, although hasty, burial. Controlling her own grief with the fortitude of a stoic Roman matron, Inés Muñoz protected the mestizo children of Pizarro from the threat of the rebels and took them under her guardianship. On the day of the assassination, she was the only person who dared to confront the assassins. She called them tyrants and traitors to their faces.

In the days following the assassination, Inés saw her house looted and almost destroyed by the new masters of Lima, but nothing would make her relent on her open protests and vocal opposition. Two weeks after the assassination, she appeared in front of the city council of Lima. She was dressed in mourning, her face and body covered by the black veil of a wealthy widow; she held the hands of six-year-old Gonzalo Pizarro, the mestizo son of Pizarro, and of an Inca princess. She did not humbly beg the city fathers, but with courage and dignity demanded justice for the crime and protection for young Gonzalo, whom she considered the sole rightful heir of his assassinated father.[8]

The citizens of Lima equated Inés Muñoz with the Pietá and the Virgin Mother. The great artists of the Counter-Reformation had already popularized in paintings and statues the sorrowful figure of Mary. Holding the lifeless body of her husband and protecting the young children of Pizarro, Inés Muñoz was a living replica of the madonnas venerated in the churches and homes of Lima.

The assassination of Pizarro and the civil wars of the conquerors disrupted the life of Inés Muñoz, but did not diminish her commitment to bring to Peru the plants, grains, trees, and domestic animals of Spain. Like most wealthy widows of early Peru, Inés

married again. Her new husband was Antonio de Rivera, a well-
known gentleman of Lima, who enjoyed a good economic position
and who would share with Inés her interest in the transfer of
plants and animals from Spain to Peru. In 1560, returning from
a trip to Spain and well aware of what would please Inés most,
Antonio brought to Lima the first olive trees to arrive in Peru.

Antonio had gathered many young olive trees from the *aljarafe*
(hill country) near Seville, but only two or three survived the long
journey to Peru. The surviving trees were protected like a rare
treasure and were planted with the utmost care in the vegetable
garden that Inés kept on the outskirts of Lima. Day and night a
group of slaves accompanied by Castilian watchdogs kept a vigil
in the garden, while many citizens of Lima glanced with envy at
Inés's growing young trees. In spite of that protection and perhaps
with the connivance of a bribed slave, one of the olive trees was
stolen one night from the garden to reappear months later on
the frontier of Chile. In Chile, the stolen tree multiplied with ease,
and in a few years groves of olive trees overlooked the Pacific
Ocean.

The spread of the olive tree from the garden of the Rivera-
Muñoz family did not take place only by an act of thievery. On
the feast of Corpus Christi, the pious Antonio and Inés donated
an olive branch, the traditional symbol of peace, to adorn the float
of the Blessed Sacrament. As the float wound its way through the
streets of Lima surrounded by clerics and friars, a canon of the
cathedral, Bartolomé Leones, kept his eyes on the precious olive
branch while daydreaming of future wealth. After the procession
returned to the cathedral, the canon took the olive branch from
the float and gave it to Gonzalo Guillén, one of the best-known
farmers in early Lima. The two of them formed a partnership to
cultivate the olive and share the profit. Guillén took the olive
sprout and planted it in his vegetable garden, where he was already experimenting with other trees and plants from Castile.
The sprout blossomed into a healthy tree, and soon Guillén was
selling its shoots to other farmers of Lima, making a profit of
almost five thousand pesos. In his garden the original tree multiplied, and Guillén became the proud and wealthy owner of one
of the first olive groves in Peru.

In the 1620s, Bernabé Cobo, the best agricultural historian of colonial Peru, saw the original tree of Inés Muñoz, still alive but old and twisted. He also saw the olive tree of Gonzalo Guillén and believed that those two trees were the parents of all the olives of America. Cobo was convinced that "to this household of Inés Muñoz owes this republic the bread and olive oil. . . ," and he also knew that wheat and oil were as important in the true conquest of Peru as the swords of the Pizarro brothers. While the olive trees grew and multiplied, Inés and her husband kept experimenting with "many other fruits and vegetables which they brought from Spain with great diligence and planted in their gardens. . . ."[9]

While Doña Inés Muñoz worked in Lima to introduce Spanish plants into Peru, Doña Usenda Loazzo y Bozán worked for the same purpose in Cuzco, the imperial capital of the Incas. By the beginning of the seventeenth century, Doña Usenda had brought the Spanish grapevine to Cuzco. She had 60,000 grapevines planted in her lands of Cupino, and from there the grapevine spread through the entire province of Moquegua. Although the Spanish grapevine had been brought to the valley of Lima around 1550 by Hernando de Montenegro and had spread through the coastal valleys, Doña Usenda Loazzo played an important role in introducing the vine into the Andean regions of Peru.

If the feeding of their families with a proper Castilian diet was a great concern to the early housewives of Spanish Peru, clothing them with the materials and in the fashion of Spain was not a lesser concern. As already indicated, many Spanish women supplemented the family income by sewing, and some of them introduced their Indian and black maids to the European art of needlework. One of their greatest problems was the scarcity of Castilian cloth in Peru. In 1548, the cortes of Valladolid, aware of the decline of the cloth industry in Spain, forbade the settlers in the overseas colonies to import the Castilian cloth industry to the colonies. The alternative was obviously to create a cloth industry in the colonies. The resourceful Inés Muñoz was one of the first persons to understand the nature of the problem, and to do something about it, even before the drastic order of the cortes of Valladolid. Inés was fully aware of the abundance of raw materials—cotton and wool—and of the availability of cheap Indian labor. Under those conditions, it would only take determination, capital, and technical know-how to launch the industry of Castilian cloth in Peru. Inés Muñoz again, with her husband, would provide all three.

The first merino sheep were brought to Peru by Captain Salamanca around 1537. By mid-century, the Andean valleys were teeming with herds of seven hundred or a thousand merino sheep "with their good meat and fine wool," to use the words of a colonial observer. The meat was readily consumed in the growing urban centers, while most of the wool was simply wasted. Many herd owners gave the wool to anybody who would care to shear the sheep. Inés Muñoz put an end to this waste when around 1545 she established the first Peruvian *obraje* or factory of Castilian cloth.

The *obraje* was founded in the small village of Sapallanga nested in the Andean valley of Jauja, where the Rivera-Muñoz family owned an Indian encomienda. The Indians of their encomienda supplied the labor, while the hundreds of sheep herds around the valley of Jauja provided an abundance of the finest merino wool. Fifteen years later, the *obraje* of Inés Muñoz, which began producing cloth in 1545 by aboriginal techniques and in simple, domestic Indian looms, was a full-fledged European industry. In 1559, the Rivera-Muñoz family brought from Spain sixteen officials to work full time. The master weaver of Segovia, Felipe Briceño de Valderrabano and his son Felipe, who was also a master weaver, headed the group of officials. There were also two carders, two shearers of cloth, and one master dyer to supervise the dyeing of fabrics in the Castilian fashion. The Briceños brought with them some of the most "modern" equipment available in the textile factories of Spain at that time: spinning wheels, European looms, cards to disentangle the fibers of wool, weaver's reeds, and the parts needed to install a fulling-mill to clean, shrink, and thicken the cloth.[10]

By 1560, Inés Muñoz had converted a very common concern, the proper clothing of the family, into one of the most important industries of colonial Peru. Her *obraje* of Sapallanga was not only the first, but also the most modern and the most successful of the Peruvian *obrajes* of the sixteenth century. One could say that Inés Muñoz, with the sound of her looms and the deafening noise of her fulling mill, awakened the Spanish settlers of Peru to the untold potential of the textile industry. Her example was followed by many, and soon hundreds of *obrajes* of Castilian cloth were founded from Quito in the north to Chile and the Jesuit missions of Paraguay in the south. In the seventeenth century the viceroyalty of Peru had about three hundred large *obrajes* with several hundred Indian workers each, plus countless small ones or *chorrillos* run by single families. A colonial friar could write with understandable hyperbole that the whole of Peru had become an uninterrupted loom.

Pizarro's conquest of the Incan empire, Almagro's expedition to Chile, and Ursúa's descent into the Amazon valley were undoubtedly fateful events in the history of European expansion. And yet the introduction of wheat, the planting of olive trees, the development of a textile industry, and the education of the first generation of mestizo children were more important in forming the lasting foundation of a stable and orderly Spanish society in Peru. Bernabé Cobo was right when he wrote that Spanish Peru owed as much to Inés Muñoz as it owed to Francisco Pizarro himself.

Encomenderas

In the new society, which emerged in the lands of the Incas after the conquest of Peru by Pizarro, the encomenderos or holders of encomiendas occupied the highest level of the social pyramid. Their social prestige and the incomes derived from their encomiendas made them the new nobility of Hispanic America. The encomienda was a legal institution by which the crown bestowed on individual Spaniards the right to collect and enjoy the tributes of a certain number of Indians living within the boundaries of a specified region. It imposed on the encomendero the duty to protect the entrusted Indians, teach them the Christian religion, and promote their Spanish acculturation. Although the encomienda did not carry by itself any grant of land, it was easy for the encomenderos to go beyond the narrow boundaries of the law and eventually to control the land in which the encomienda was located. It was easier still to use the Indians as laborers in the field or hire them to landlords and miners for a handsome profit.

In early Spanish Peru, the encomienda was the safest way to acquire economic power and social prestige. Many encomenderos built palatial homes in Lima, Cuzco, Arequipa, and Trujillo and kept large households of administrators, retainers, and servants; they were frequently elected to the city councils. They were undoubtedly the social, economic, and political elite of Spanish Peru.

Encomenderos were by no means all male. In colonial Peru, some powerful women held encomiendas in their own right. Like their male counterparts, they reached the pinnacle of colonial society, controlled thousands of Indians, and governed large households of relatives, servants, and retainers. The custom of granting encomiendas to women was well established even before the conquest of Peru. One of the first Spanish women to obtain an encomienda in America was Doña María de Toledo, the daughter-in-law of the discoverer, who with her husband, Diego Colón, arrived in Hispaniola in 1509. This precedent was followed later in Panamá and Mexico, where women encomenderas date back to the early days of the conquest.

In Spanish Peru, one of the first encomenderas was Doña María Escobar, who was granted an encomienda in the province of Lima as a reward for the introduction of wheat. Besides this encomienda, Doña María inherited two more which had been granted in 1536 and 1538 to her husband, Francisco Chávez, by Francisco Pizarro. With her three encomiendas, Doña María Escobar was undoubtedly one of the most powerful and wealthy women in the colony. Years later, in the aftermath of the civil wars of the conquerors, when Governor Vaca de Castro revised the legal titles of the encomiendas and took away the two encomiendas inherited by Doña María, she fought back with all the legal means at her disposal until her voice was heard in the distant Spanish court. On March 23, 1543, Doña María appeared before Alcalde Ordinario Juan de Barbarán and presented the original documents by which Pizarro had granted the encomiendas to her husband. She demanded that the notary public witness the fact that she was in possesion of the valid legal documents. She was quick to point out that her husband was given the encomiendas not only because of his great services to the crown, but also because he had married with the intention to remain in Peru and help populate the land. In October of the same year, disgusted with the slowness of the colonial bureaucracy, Doña María gave the power of attorney to Juan de Cáceres so that he could represent her before the Council of the Indies in Spain, the supreme governing body of the overseas

Spanish empire. She wanted the decision of Vaca de Castro over-turned so that all her Indians could be restored to her.[11]

Two other encomenderas of the first Spanish generation in Peru were Doña Inés Muñoz and Doña María Sánchez, La Millana, who had suffered the same fate as María Escobar by the high-handed policies of governor Vaca de Castro. Both of them were widows in 1543 and were in peaceful possession of the encomiendas in-herited from their husbands when Vaca de Castro took them away. Aware that without the encomiendas they could not maintain their privileged economic and social status, the two women, like María Escobar, fought in court to recover their Indians. Both of them gave powers of attorney to representatives in Spain to appeal over the head of the governor to the Council of the Indies. Like Viceroy Toledo years later, Vaca de Castro strongly opposed the idea of widows and single women holding encomiendas. Perhaps he be-lieved that unattached women could not manage and administer by themselves the all-important institution of the encomienda, or perhaps he feared that these women could become the victims of unworthy and unscrupulous suitors.[12]

Although the crown would never fully accept the policies of Vaca de Castro, the governor's fears were not totally without foun-dation. There were too many widows or elder daughters of de-ceased encomenderos, who wittingly or unwittingly helped through their marriages to transfer important encomiendas from worthy conquerors or settlers to men who had not distinguished them-selves in the establishment of Spanish Peru. The new husbands acquired, if not the full legal title, at least the control and admin-istration of the encomiendas. The case of the young wife of Juan Pérez in 1547 may serve to illustrate the point.

Juan Pérez held an important encomienda inherited from a close relative, who had distinguished himself fighting for the crown against the rebel Gonzalo Pizarro. When Juan Pérez was overtaken by a serious illness and was on his deathbed, he had recourse to a legal trick to be able to transfer the legal title of his encomienda to a friend and relative named Juan de Vergara. Juan Pérez pro-posed marriage to a young girl recently arrived in Peru from Avila, Spain, under the condition that upon his death she would marry his relative Juan de Vergara. The governor approved this legal fiction and was ready to grant the encomienda to Vergara as soon as he would marry the young Spanish widow. The young lady,

who must have had a mind of her own, surprised everybody by
repudiating her promise to Juan Pérez and hastily marrying an
unknown gentleman from her hometown of Avila. Vergara was
left without any legal grounds to claim the encomienda, and the
new husband became the encomendero.[13]

In 1563, the viceroy count of Nieva wrote a letter to the king
trying to explain that the ownership of encomiendas by women
could result in the encomienda eventually being transferred to
the hands of an unworthy man. To make his point, the count gave
the king the specific example of the encomienda granted to Antonio Picado, a worthy settler. When Picado died, his widow, Ana
Suárez, inherited the encomienda. According to law, she became
the sole legal holder of the encomienda and collected the tributes
from the Indians, who had been granted to her deceased husband.
Ana Suárez eventually remarried Sebastian Sánchez de Merlo,
who became the administrator of the encomienda. When Ana
Suárez died a few years later, Sebastian inherited the legal title to
an encomienda that the crown had initially intended for Antonio
Picado and his heirs.

But the story did not end there; Sebastian Sánchez de Merlo,
the widower of Ana Suárez, married Beatriz Marroquí, who became the legal holder of the encomienda when Sebastian died and
one of the most eligible young widows of Spanish Peru. Among
the many potential suitors attracted by her wealth, Beatriz chose
as a husband Don Diego Carvajal. By July 1563, when the count
of Nieva wrote to the king, Diego Carvajal was enjoying the fruits
of an encomienda that the crown had never intended to be his.
He had come into possession of that encomienda through two
women, Ana Suárez and Beatriz Marroquí, because the law recognized the right of women to hold encomiendas and to transfer
them to their husbands and heirs. The count of Nieva had reason
to feel uneasy about this situation.[14]

The Spanish crown had recognized the problem even before
the warnings of the county of Nieva, but to its credit, the crown
refused to abolish the rights of women to hold encomiendas. Instead, royal approval was required before a single encomendera
could marry, and viceroys and governors had the *de facto* power
to choose the future husbands of encomenderas from among all
potential suitors. In this way the encomenderas themselves could
be "protected" from the unscrupulous manipulations of relatives

and suitors, and the crown would always maintain strict control of who had access to the elite class of colonial Peru, the encomendero class.

One wonders if the proposed solution was not worse than the problem it intended to solve. Many wealthy encomenderas were deprived of the freedom to choose their own husbands, and at the hands of royal officials, they became reluctant pawns in the economic and political power play of colonial society. The danger of the new policy was not purely theoretical, as can be seen by events that took place in Lima under the viceroy marquis de Cañete.

Soon after the viceroy marquis de Cañete took office in 1556, he shocked colonial society with his ruthless policies toward the marriages of wealthy girls, encomenderas, and rich widows. A secret, anonymous report was hastily compiled and sent to the king, protesting the policies of Cañete. The viceroy was accused of defiling the sanctity of matrimony by forcing wealthy women to marry for pure economic reasons and to reward his friends and servants with encomiendas and princely dowries. The viceroy had forced a wealthy encomendera to marry his relative, Don Pedro de Mercado, who was a man "recently arrived from Castile and who has not served in this land (of Peru)." The encomienda of the reluctant wife was transferred to Mercado to enjoy for two generations. Doña Beatriz de Santillana, widow of Captain Rodrigo de Piñeda and holder of a good encomienda, was forced to marry Pedro de Villagra to whom the viceroy transferred all the Indians of the encomienda. The same indignity was suffered by Doña Bernardina de Heredia, who saw all the Indians of her encomienda go to Hernando de Pantoja, the new husband the viceroy chose for her. But the most blatant case of abuse was a daughter of Doña María de Sandoval. Although the girl was only ten years old, she was already the owner of an encomienda in the province of Guayaquil. The viceroy chose a young boy, also ten years old and the son of his doctor, and had the two children married. Then the viceroy transferred the encomienda of Guayaquil to the child-husband to enjoy for two generations.[15]

Although all these facts cannot be doubted, the motivation that prompted this report is less certain. One suspects that the anonymous authors of the report were more concerned with being left out in the manipulation of the marriages of their daughters and female relatives than they were with the sanctity of matrimony and the freedom of choice. They seem to resent that the viceroy alone was ruthlessly controlling one of the most efficient tools for economic and social mobility in colonial Peru. This suspicion is reinforced when one reads that years later fathers, brothers, and male relatives were still manipulating the marriages of young encomenderas for their own selfish economic and social reasons.

In 1573, the situation was such that the new viceroy, Don Francisco de Toledo, felt compelled to inform King Philip II of the dangers to colonial society if women were allowed to hold encomiendas. Toledo, who was the great lawgiver and organizer of colonial Peru, was honestly convinced of that danger. In a letter to the king, dated in La Plata on November 30, 1573, the viceroy explained his reasons. There were too many young widows and girls in Peru who had inherited encomiendas. Their male relatives were using them to further their own family interest without regard for the intentions and the benefit of the crown. Some of those encomenderas were forced to marry or the encomiendas were sold to persons whom the crown would have never distinguished with the award of an encomienda. Toledo believed that the only way to stop this abuse was to make women legally incapable of holding encomiendas.[16]

King Philip II must have ignored the recommendation of his Peruvian viceroy because in 1583, when the official census of all the encomiendas of Peru was taken, the rolls show that sixty encomiendas were still held by women. These sixty women held the encomiendas in their own right, either by direct grant of the crown or by inheritance from deceased husbands. Among all of them, the Peruvian encomenderas of 1583 controlled an Indian population of 239,856 Indians, of whom 46,876 were tributary Indians. Considering the amount of income derived from so many tributaries and the amount of labor and personal services the encomenderas could obtain from the total population of the encomienda, it is no wonder that the viceroys worried about the final disposition of those encomiendas. They worried that male relatives of these encomenderas would pressure their women to use them in ways that were detrimental to the welfare of the realm, and contrary to the wishes of the crown.

Undoubtedly, the sixty women listed in the census of 1583 formed the female elite of colonial society. They were wealthy, respected, and heads of large households filled with poor relatives, administrators, male servants, maids, and black slaves. All of them, with the exception of three, seem to have been women of pure Spanish ancestry, closely related to other prominent members of the colonial society. The three non-Spanish women in the census were Indians of the royal blood of the Incas: Doña Beatriz Ysasaga, Doña Beatriz Sayrecoya, and Doña Beatriz Coya.

Doña Beatriz Ysasaga was a daughter of Atahualpa, the Inca emperor executed by Pizarro in Cajamarca. Her encomienda was among the best held by women, with a total population of 9,434 Indians and 1,742 tributaries. The encomienda of Doña Beatriz Coya, also a daughter of the Inca and wife of the Spanish captain Martín García de Loyola, had a population of 1,289 Indians, of whom 264 were tributaries. Finally, Doña Beatriz Sayrecoya held an encomienda of 3,433 Indians, and 708 of them were obliged by law to pay their tributes to her.

The elite of these encomenderas was formed by four Spanish women, who among themselves controlled a population of 62,802 Indians living in their encomiendas. Doña Jordana Mexía had an encomienda of 15,240 Indians, and every year she collected tributes from 2,678 of them. Doña Lucía de Montenegro's encomienda had a population of 13,955 Indians, of whom 2,466 were tributaries. In the encomienda of Doña Florencia de Sandoval lived 14,431 Indians, and 2,476 of them payed the yearly tribute to Doña Florencia. Doña Mayor de Berdugo enjoyed an encomienda with 19,176 Indians and 3,770 tributaries. Below this encomendera class were thirteen women whose tributary Indians fluctuated between one and two thousand Indians.[17]

The concentration of wealth in the hands of a few powerful women, so feared by men like Viceroy Toledo, was, in many instances, a blessing and an asset for the developing Spanish society of Peru. The wealthy encomenderas were more ready than their male counterparts to support schools, hospitals, orphanages, and other works of social welfare. Many colonial institutions, which for more than three hundred years played important social roles, were established by the generosity of wealthy encomenderas. The case of Doña Florencia de Mora y Sandoval is one example of a common pattern in the use of female wealth.

Doña Florencia was the rich widow of a former governor of Piura. She held a large encomienda in the provinces of Huamachuco and Puno. Moved by the plight of the Indians, Doña Florencia freed seven towns of her encomienda from the duty to pay her the yearly tributes. With the income derived from her haciendas and her *obrajes* of Tulpo and Sinsicapa, she established a foundation to feed and clothe the poor Indians of the region, and gave administration of the foundation to the bishops of Trujillo. Doña Florencia also made large contributions to build the church and convent of St. Augustín, and endowed there several perpetual chaplaincies.[18] The generosity of Doña Inés Muñoz became legendary in colonial Peru. She spent thousands of pesos to support the welfare works of the church and to educate and care for orphan and mestizo girls; late in her life, she pledged her large fortune to the foundation and support of the school and convent of La Encarnación.

Even on the frontier of Chile, far from the most developed civic centers of the viceroyalty, one finds examples of female generosity that show that the wealth of the encomenderas did play a very important social role. In 1595, Doña Agueda de Flores signed her last will in the presence of Ginés de Toro Mazote, a notary public of Santiago. Her testament, similar to hundreds of others preserved in the colonial archives, clearly shows the distribution of wealth after the death of rich encomenderas. After distributing part of her fortune among her children and relatives, Doña Agueda made generous grants to her favorite charities. She left a sizable amount of money to all the monasteries and convents of Santiago and to the city hospital, named as beneficiaries some of her servants and slaves, and donated a herd of fifteen hundred sheep to the Indians of her encomiendas. She also left two hundred pesos to clothe the poor Indians of her hacienda of Talagante.[19]

Doña Florencia, Doña Inés, and Doña Agueda were not the exceptions, but the rule among the wealthy encomenderas of colonial Peru. Perhaps their generosity was one of the reasons why the crown never abolished the female encomiendas. In the seventeenth century, women encomenderas were still a part of the Peruvian elite, and the crown was still granting new encomiendas to worthy women. In 1619, King Philip IV wrote to his Peruvian viceroy, the count of Chinchón, ordering him to grant to Doña Guiomar Manrique de Lara, marchioness of Santa Cruz, an encomienda "of 3,000 pesos of income to enjoy during her life time and the life of one heir." Three years later, in 1631, when the king was informed that his order had not yet been executed, he insisted that the marchioness should not be kept on the waiting list, but should be given the encomienda ahead of any other person as soon as any became vacant. The preference shown Doña Guiomar was not unique, and the king also granted encomiendas of Peruvian Indians to the duchess of Huesca, the countesses of Navas, Galves, and La Palma, and to Doña Margarita de Aragón, countess of Cabra.[20]

La Quintrala

Although the wealth of the encomiendas enabled many women of colonial Peru to play the role of secular madonnas by educating orphans, supporting hospitals and schools, and protecting their Indians, that same wealth could also corrupt the encomenderas and give them the tools of exploitation. The female Don Juan with a boundless ego, who manipulated the world around her for her own selfish motives, was by no means absent from the ranks of the encomenderas.

In the sixteenth and seventeenth centuries the Lisperguer-Flores family of Chile produced a group of women, who exhibited all the characteristics of Don Juanism to its most satanic extremes. In an effort to reshape their colonial world with themselves at the center, they manipulated parents, husbands, children, servants, royal officials, and even powerful members of the clergy. Some of the Lisperguer-Flores women did not hesitate to break the law and the most basic, moral tenets of the Christian religion, and committed some of the most hideous crimes recorded in the history of colonial Peru. The most notorious of those women was the encomendera Doña Catalina de los Rios y Lisperguer, feared and hated by her contemporaries, and known as La Quintrala. A modern Chilean historian has rightly called her the Lucrecia Borgia of the frontier of Chile.

La Quintrala was born around 1604, a third-generation child of one of the most socially prominent and wealthy families of Chile. She came from a line of ruthless women, who by 1600 had already left behind them a wake of abuses, unpunished crimes, and blood. Her paternal grandmother was María de Encio, who assassinated her husband by poisoning him with mercury, according to the testimony of Don Francisco de Salcedo, Bishop of Chile, in a letter to the crown.[21]

On her maternal side, Doña Catalina belonged to a family founded by Captain Pedro Lisperguer, whose surname was synonymous with wealth and social prestige. The Lisperguers enjoyed such high social status that one could hear in the streets of Santiago the saying that "in Chile, if you are not a Lisperguer, you are a mestizo!" Don Pedro Lisperguer married Doña Agueda Flores, the maternal grandmother of La Quintrala, whom popular gossip accused of being a notorious *encantadora* or witch. Her three daughters, Doña María, Doña Catalina, and Doña Magdalena, were also accused of practicing witchcraft and of being powerful *encantadoras*. These rumors and accusations may have had some basis because in 1604 the sisters were indicted for attempting to assassinate the governor of Chile, Don Alonso de Rivera. The indictment claimed that in their frustrated attempt, Doña María and Doña Catalina had used the help and knowledge of an Indian, who was an expert in magic herbs.[22] The two women fled and found refuge with friars, who were presumably paid off by the Lisperguer family. The legal action was finally dropped when the governor was replaced and the star witness of the prosecution, the Indian expert in magic herbs, was found dead. A letter from the bishop of Chile informed the crown that the Indian was killed by orders of Doña Catalina, mother of La Quintrala, who was also accused in the same letter of assassinating her step-daughter, a half sister of La Quintrala.[23]

None of these crimes were ever punished, and Doña Catalina Lisperguer y Flores married the wealthy Don Gonzalo de los Rios, son of María de Encio, and led the life of a wealthy encomendera in Santiago. Their daughter, Doña Catalina de los Rios y Lisperguer, La Quintrala, would add a new tragic, bloody chapter to the history of Chile, and in the process became the most hated and the most feared encomendera of colonial Peru.

Pampered by an overindulgent grandmother, the child grew up in one of the wealthiest households of Chile like an untamed animal, led by instincts and blind passions. By the early 1620s, La Quintrala was a totally selfish, unscrupulous young woman, who terrorized servants and slaves with her cruelty and outbursts of sadism. Around 1623, she was officially accused by one of her aunts of patricide. The judicial inquiry affirmed that La Quintrala poisoned her father, Don Gonzalo de los Rios, while feeding him a chicken meal. It was never known whether the crime was committed to obtain the expected inheritance or whether it was simply the result of a deranged mind.

Three or four years later, La Quintrala was again accused of murder. She had written an amorous note to Don Enrique Enríquez de Guzmán, knight of Malta, inviting him with seductive language to visit her in the seclusion of her home. The gentleman kept the date only to be found murdered in the house of La Quintrala, who accused one of her slaves of the crime. The authorities opened a judicial inquiry and as a result of it, they placed under arrest not only La Quintrala, but also her grandmother, Doña Agueda Flores, and her aunt, Doña Magdalena Lisperguer. The three women obtained their freedom under bond, and the slow process of colonial justice was stopped at every turn by the unscrupulous manipulations of the Lisperguers. The final sentence was another travesty of justice. Doña Agueda and Doña Magdalena were fined five hundred pesos each, while La Quintrala had to pay a fine of six thousand pesos.

Doña Agueda Flores must have known by 1616 that the destructive personality of her granddaughter could one day ruin the family, and decided to ease her out of the home by finding her a husband. La Quintrala's history of sadism and crimes should have deterred all potential suitors, but her wealth was such that there were men ready to take the risk of marrying her. The man finally chosen by Doña Agueda as a husband for her granddaughter was Don Alonso Campofrio de Carvajal, an impoverished gentleman and a captain in the royal militia, with an illustrious and noble surname. The marriage took place in September 1626, and soon after the couple abandoned the capital of Santiago and retired to her haciendas and encomiendas in the secluded valley of La Ligua. For the next forty years, La Quintrala, hidden away in her rural empire, and unchecked by any human or divine authority ruled her possessions like an absolute mad queen.[24] In 1660, an official inquiry discovered that La Quintrala had worked her Indians, servants, and slaves to exhaustion, and through the hacienda stores had kept many of them under a brutal system of debt-peonage. Those who incurred her displeasure were punished with a refined sadism. Among the incredible tortures inflicted by La Quintrala were daily whippings, covering the bleeding wounds with salt and chili, beatings with clubs, stonings, burning the body with candles, and forcing the "culprits" to drink boiling milk. Thirty-nine persons had lost their lives, either under torture or murdered by orders of La Quintrala. La Quintrala was placed under house arrest, but again the powerful Lisperguer family interfered with justice.

In January 1665, Doña Catalina de los Rios y Lisperguer, La Quintrala, died without ever having been brought to trial. Her funeral, dictated to the last detail in her will, was a final mockery of the most elemental human decency. She was buried in the Augustinian church, wearing the holy robe of the Augustinian order, and her body was accompanied to its final resting place by forty-eight friars, twenty secular priests, the entire ecclesiastical cabildo, and the banners of eight religious confraternities. This final testimony of "respect" cost the executors of the testament 1,129 pesos and six *reales*, without counting the price of 25,000 masses said for the repose of La Quintrala's soul. The overwhelming presence of the clergy at the funeral, and the thousands of services held in memory of La Quintrala seem to indicate that the leaders of the church in Chile could be bought and manipulated as easily as judges of the audiencia of Santiago.[25]

The machiavellian shrewdness of La Quintrala, her legendary fortune, and the tribal loyalty and social prestige of the Lisperguers formed the steel armor that kept her untouched for more than forty years. She was ruthless in her use of Indians and servants; she bought judges and prosecutors as she bought supplies for her rural empire; and she made her many relatives in the priesthood and in the orders into shields to protect her from the reach of justice.

Before we turn our attention to the education of women in colonial Peru, we should reflect once more on the wide spectrum of female activities in the Peruvian viceroyalty. Women were present in all the social strata: they accompanied the conquerors and explorers; they labored as maids, bakers, potters, seamstresses, and innkeepers; they owned real estate and were proprietors and managers of small businesses; and finally they belonged to the exclusive and powerful elite of the encomendero class. Women made lasting and essential contributions to the future development of Spanish Peru. They educated in Spanish ways the first generation of mestizo and criollo children born in Peru after the conquest. They played a vital role in the transfer of European plants and domestic animals to Peru, and they helped to develop the first *obrajes,* where the Peruvian textile industry was born. Many of them were prolific mothers who helped "to populate the land," a goal considered by the Spanish crown vital and paramount in the colonization of Peru. In short, this remarkable group of colonial women spanned the wide spectrum of human possibilities.

The Immaculate Conception, by Juan Sevilla (1643–95). (Meadows Museum, Southern Methodist University)

A mestizo family, painter unknown. (Museo Nacional de Ethnologia, Madrid)

Portrait of a Girl, by Mariano Fortuny (1838–74). (Meadows Museum, Southern Methodist University)

A. Sᵗⁿ Prinsipal con su negra, esclava
B. Arbol de Granadillas, y su Fruta.
C. Arbol del Níspero, y su Fruta.
D. Fruta con nombre de Narangillas.
E. Palma de Cocos grandes.
F. Arbol de Coquitos de chile.

Vicen Alban pincxor en
Quito á 1783.

A society lady attended by her black slave, by Vicente Albán, 1783. (Museo de America, Madrid)

Concubine or mistress of a wealthy man in colonial Quito, painter
unknown. (Museo de America, Madrid)

Women flower and pastry sellers, watercolor by Léonce Angrand, 1837. (Bibliothèque National de Paris)

Three *tapadas* buying tickets for the cockfights, watercolor by Léonce Angrand, 1837. (Bibliothèque National de Paris)

Women returning from a fiesta on the outskirts of Lima, water-color by Léonce Angrand, 1837. (Bibliothèque National de Paris)

A high-society lady in her calesa, watercolor by Léonce Angrand,
1837. (Bibliothèque National de Paris)

A street in the nunnery St. Catherine of Arequipa.

Cloister of the confessionals in the nunnery St. Catherine of Arequipa.

Elegant entrance to the cell of the nun Doña Rosa Cardenas in St. Catherine of Arequipa.

Back patio of the same cell.

St. Rosa of Lima, by Claudio Coello (1642–93). (Museo del Prado, Madrid)

4

❦

Women's Education

BY THE MID-SIXTEENTH CENTURY, an educational system, manned by professional teachers, had begun to emerge in colonial Peru, and by the opening decades of the following century that system was easily comparable to the one existing in the Iberian peninsula. Wealthy families began by hiring clerics or well-educated laymen to come to the home and serve as private tutors of their children. Parents and tutors signed formidable legal documents in the presence of a notary public specifying the subjects to be taught, the number of hours, the methods of teaching, the salary of the tutor, and, at times, even disciplinary matters. Some of those contracts clearly stated that the payment of the salary depended upon the intellectual progress made by the pupils—a condition that would horrify today's professional, unionized teacher. A perusal of those contracts reveals that the children were taught reading, writing, arithmetic, some Latin, and music. As the population of children in the viceroyalty increased, so did the demand for instructors and tutors to the point that private, personal instruction was no longer possible for all those who wanted to learn. By the second half of the sixteenth century, the first grammar schools were formed, and education in Peru became institutionalized. Both the civil and ecclesiastical authorities kept a close eye on this process of institutionalization and required that the teachers obtain an official license to teach, after having proven that they possessed the knowledge and were worthy Christians.[1]

In those early stages of Peruvian education, both girls and boys had access to private tutors and private instruction; but when the first formal schools were opened, girls were not allowed to attend classes with boys. Peruvian colonial society, like its European counterpart of the period, abhorred the idea of coeducation. Above all, the church was strongly opposed, on moral grounds, to allowing males and females to attend the same schools. In 1594, an official instruction was issued in Lima, "which those who teach how to read, write, and count in this City of the Kings should observe for the good education and training of the children." The very first directive contained in that instruction was that the licensed teachers "should not accept girls into their schools to teach them to read and pray, because it is not proper and certain inconveniences could follow."[2] Although this guideline was issued under the authority of the viceroy, its author was a Jesuit educator whose objections were not against the education of girls, but against coeducation. Coeducation was opposed because it was "not proper." In other words, it was against the accepted and established norms of society. The "inconveniences" feared by the author of the instruction were probably of a moral, ethical character. The constant proximity of the two sexes in the same classroom could lead to risky sexual confrontations.

Once this opposition to coeducation was firmly established, Peruvian colonial society saw no other course of action than to establish separate schools for girls. A testimony to the importance attached to female education is the fact that by the mid-seventeenth century Lima alone had four or five convent schools for girls, and half a dozen institutions established by individual benefactors for the education of orphans, mestizas, and Spanish girls. Among these institutions were the School of Our Lady of Mount Carmel, the School of San Juan de la Penitencia, the Colegio de Santa Cruz, a girls' school attached to the hospital of charity, and another to the Jesuit mission church of El Cercado. The nunneries of Lima that accepted female students were the Convent of La Concepción founded in 1561 by Doña Leonor de Portocarrero, the Convent of La Encarnación founded in 1573 by the already mentioned Doña Inés Muñoz de Rivera, the Convent of La Santísima Trinidad established in 1584 by Doña Lucrecia de Sansoles, and the nunnery of Santa Catalina founded in 1624 by the two noble sisters, Doña Lucía and Doña Clara de la Daga.[3] These convent schools, charging a sizable tuition, seem to have been reserved for the daughters of prominent, wealthy families, while orphans, mestizas, and poor Spanish girls were educated in the private institutions mentioned above.

Convent Schools

The first female students received in the colonial convents were usually young nieces or other relatives of the professed nuns, who, in a rather informal fashion and as a favor to their married brothers and sisters, took the responsibility of raising and educating the young girls. By the end of the sixteenth century, the process of admission had been formalized, and true convent schools had taken shape. In 1591, Don Francisco de Quiñones, brother-in-law of the then archbishop of Lima, applied formally to the Holy See for an official license to place his two young daughters as students in the convent of Santa Clara. Pope Paul Clement VIII, informed of the great need to educate daughters of prominent families in the viceroyalty of Peru, granted the request, and the two girls began their education in Santa Clara. The fact that the young ladies were the nieces of the archbishop explains, in part, the prompt and positive response of the pope. The example of the Quiñones family moved other prominent families to request the same privilege from the ecclesiastical authorities. The petitions must have been numerous because four years later, in 1595, the pope, in a personal letter to the archbishop, granted a general license to the Convent of La Trinidad to accept female students. La Concepción also obtained the ecclesiastical license to operate a school within the cloister, and Abbess Doña Isabel de Uceda proudly kept in the conventual archives the official papal bull allowing the convent to run its own school.[4]

By the opening decades of the seventeenth century, the custom of accepting girls in colonial convents had become so widespread and common that a papal license was no longer required. The process of admission was simplified and became strictly a local matter. After obtaining approval of the bishop of the city, the conventual chapter was convened and took a secret vote to accept or to reject the candidate. The cases of Doña Mayor de Arbildo and Doña María Ruíz Naharro may serve to illustrate that process

of admission into the conventual schools. In 1630, the father of
Doña Mayor, Don Ambrosio de Arbildo y Berriz, wrote to the
archbishop of Lima requesting approval to place his daughter as
a "lay student" in the Convent of La Encarnación. Don Ambrosio
had been appointed corregidor of Chachapoyas and, being a widower, he felt that he could not take his daughter to such a distant
province. Since there were no other female relatives to take care
of the girl in Lima, the school of La Encarnación was the best
possible alternative. Don Ambrosio agreed to pay the customary
fees and promised to provide his daughter with the services of a
trusted maid, who would take care of Doña Mayor while in the
convent.

The archbishop of Lima informed the abbess of La Encarnación, Doña Casilda de Illescas, of Don Ambrosio's request, and
Doña Casilda called a preliminary meeting of the conventual chapter to discuss and vote on the matter. Two hundred and four nuns
cast their secret ballots. Doña Mayor de Arbildo was accepted as
a student in La Encarnación without a single dissenting vote. This
unanimity, Abbess Doña Casilda explained to the archbishop, reflected the nuns' conviction that Doña Mayor was "noble and virtuous," and that her tuition would help support the nunnery.[5]

A few months later, the same procedure was repeated in the
case of Doña María Ruíz Naharro, a noble young lady ten or eleven
years old. Her uncle was one of the best-known and most prominent clergymen in the viceroyalty of Peru. His name was Fray
Pedro Ruíz, and he held the office of provincial superior for all
the Mercedarian friars of Peru. His brother and sister-in-law had
died and left him with the legal custody of his young niece, María.
Fray Pedro, like Don Ambrosio de Arbildo before him, wrote to
the archbishop requesting permission to place his niece as a student in the school run by the nuns of La Encarnación. Doña
Casilda wrote to the archbishop in October 1630 to inform him
of the acceptance of Doña María, and to give him a short report
on the status of the school. The convent had built separate facilities
for the school within the cloister, where the girls could live by
themselves without mixing with the nuns and servants. A headmistress had been chosen from among the best-qualified nuns—
Doña María Desturisaga, who in October 1630 was teaching seventeen girls of the most prominent families of Lima.[6]

This pattern of admission was observed in the many convent

schools scattered throughout the viceroyalty. The consent of the local bishop was always required, but the actual admission of a candidate rested with the secret vote of the community. The girls accepted to be educated into the colonial nunneries were, almost without exception, daughters of prominent merchants, encomenderos, royal officials, or relatives of powerful clergymen. The fees and tuition required by the convents were not within reach of families of modest means. It was a universal custom, approved by the ecclesiastical authorities, to collect a yearly payment of fifty pesos per student *"por solo pisar el suelo de dicho monasterio"* (just to stand on the ground of said nunnery). Furthermore, families had to pay between one hundred to two hundred pesos a year for room and board, and to take care of expenses for clothing, medicines, and doctor's visits. These payments represented, as Abbess Doña Catalina de Illescas explained to the bishop in 1630, a handsome income to help support the nunnery, and were, therefore, collected regularly and faithfully. In the case of default, the nuns did not hesitate to take recourse to legal action, as the example of Doña María de Cardenas well illustrates.

Doña María was the daughter of a prominent lady of Huancayo, Doña Gerónima de Cardenas, and her parents had sent her to Lima to be educated in the convent school of La Encarnación. The Cardenas family had appointed Juan de Villar their agent in Lima, charging him to pay the room and board of Doña María while in the convent. On June 16, 1632, Juan de Villar notified the abbess of La Encarnación of his inability to pay, stating that the Cardenas family was not remitting sufficient funds from Huancayo. After a reasonable waiting period, the nuns brought the case to the attention of the ecclesiastical authorities. The ecclesiastical judge, Don Francisco de la Vega, examined the case and heard both parties. The final decision was that if sufficient funds did not arrive from Huancayo soon, the nuns had the right to expel Doña María de Cardenas from the school and send her to her parents in Huancayo.[7] This principle was maintained well into the eighteenth century since the bishops were deeply concerned that the girls should not become an unbearable economic burden on the nunneries.

The entrance into a convent school was a fateful and sometimes traumatic event in the lives of colonial girls. Once they crossed the threshold of the nunnery, they were bound by the rules of the cloister, where they would spend the next six or seven years. During that period, they could never return to their homes, wander outside the boundaries of the cloister, or receive any visitors without the approval of the headmistress, who also censored their correspondence. Their dress and life-style frequently imitated that of the professed nuns. They got up before sunrise to attend mass and devotions, followed a strict schedule of work and study during the day, ate their meals in silence, and went back to the chapel for evening prayers before retiring. The prospect of that kind of life would certainly horrify a modern seven-year-old girl, yet it seemed to have been fairly well accepted in colonial times.

There were several good reasons for this acceptance on the part of the colonial young ladies. Their lives "in the world" were not greatly different from what they encountered in the cloister. In some instances, the girls were allowed to bring their favorite maids into the convent. In wealthy families, these maids sometimes had closer contact with the children than the parents themselves. Most of the time the convent chosen by the family was one where close female relatives were either novices or professed nuns. Consecrated great-aunts, aunts, and elder cousins poured affection on the young girls, who found within the cloister a new, conventual family as affectionate and protective as the one they had left. The convent itself, with its ample courtyards and well-tended gardens, its frequent fiestas and excellent music, did appear to many women not only as an acceptable, but even an attractive place to live.

As we shall see later, the conventual life was popular in colonial Peru. The case of the convent school of La Concepción is one example of that popularity. In 1629, the school had only eleven students: Isabel Barreto, Mariana de Herrera, María de Ribera, María de Alcor, Ana Solano, Isabel de Francia, Catalina de Vargas, Catalina de Meneses, Luisa de Gevara, Ana Jiménez, and Catalina de Burgos. By 1700, the number of lay students in the convent of La Concepción had climbed to one hundred forty-seven—an increase also reflected in other convent schools.[8]

What kind of education did the girls receive in the convent schools? In our era overly concerned with accreditation, pragmatic skills, "meaningful" courses, freedom of choice, and direct preparation for future occupations, the education provided by the convent schools may appear meaningless and restrictive. Yet, the conventual education of colonial Peru should not be compared with the complexities of the modern industry of education, but must be judged within the ideals held by the society of colonial days. Those ideals stressed human and religious development, the basic skills of reading and writing, and in the case of wealthy girls, the many skills needed to run a large household successfully. Within these ideals, the convent schools performed a rather creditable job. The students of the convents did learn how to read and write; they were also trained in simple elementary arithmetic, enough to handle the household finances. Three to four hours a day were spent learning how to sew and embroider, and how to prepare the culinary delicacies for which many colonial convents were rightly famous. In some convents, elementary Latin was taught so that the girls could participate in the Latin liturgy of the Catholic church.

In an effort to develop the character and potential of the young students, the convents used both music and drama to a degree unknown today. The girls had voice lessons and joined the nuns in the choirs, which attracted hundreds of persons to the conventual churches and made the convents important musical centers in colonial America. They also learned how to play musical instruments either from the nuns or from lay musicians like the master organist Gonzalo Mateos, who was frequently hired to teach organ to the girls around 1650.

Drama had been refined by the Jesuits into a precise instrument of humanistic education, and was widely used in their excellent schools for boys. The nuns of the convent schools followed the Jesuits' example, and the presentation of plays also became a common feature in the colonial convents. In fact, some ecclesiastical authorities felt that the nuns had gone too far and were afraid that the convents might, in the popular mind, become another center of dramatic entertainment. One bishop was shocked to hear that the girls and nuns appeared on the stage wearing men's clothing and that they were helped in their rehearsals by lay professional actors. The synod of 1688 issued an order prohibiting presentation of plays in convents, but it was obviously ignored since convents still produced plays during the eighteenth century.[9]

Since the foundation of the convent schools at the end of the sixteenth century, it had been common practice to accept pupils who were at least six or seven years old. But in the seventeenth century an "abuse" crept into the convents which deeply worried the ecclesiastical authorities of the period—the widespread custom of accepting babies and infants into the convents. This practice turned the nunneries into noisy nurseries. Some of these babies were brought to the convents when they were only a few months old and remained there until they were ready to join the convent schools at age six or seven. These girls spent their entire young lives in an isolated island of women, and the convent was the only world they ever knew. It was not unusual, therefore, that upon reaching their teens, most of those girls requested the veil and exchanged their school uniforms for the robes of a professed nun. They formed the only group in the history of the Americas who lived from cradle to grave in a cloistered world of women.

One can hardly blame the bishops for being disturbed by this unusual development. The presence of baby girls within the cloister was not conducive to a life of silence, prayer, and monastic discipline. The ecclesiastical authorities questioned the objectives that had brought these infants to the convents, and they felt uneasy when they discovered that those motives were not "pure" or "religious" enough. Many of the babies came to the convent through the pressures of families and relatives. It must have been an easy way out for a young mother of seven or eight children to place one or two of her babies under the care of a consecrated aunt or sister. The nuns, obviously, thought that it was their duty in Christian charity to help out those relatives by raising some of their children. According to social standards, orphan baby girls of wealthy families could not be placed in public orphanages with mestizo and poor Spanish girls, so they also found their way into the convent nurseries. Most disturbing to the bishops was the fact that some nuns, perhaps motivated by a frustrated maternal instinct, went out of their way to obtain baby girls they could raise in their cells. Perhaps the inmates of the nunneries also justified these unusual nurseries as an easy way to secure the natural growth and future membership of the orders.

The conventual records have preserved the names and histories of some of those babies, whose cases may serve to illustrate the generalizations made above. Felisa Márquez de Mansilla was only four years old when the nuns of La Concepción took her into the convent in 1669. Fourteen years later, in 1683, she petitioned the ecclesiastical authorities to take the veil and became a novice and eventually a professed nun. Melchora de Estrada was only four months old when she lost her parents and was taken by her aunt, Doña Beatriz de Estrada, into the convent of La Concepción. Doña Beatriz was the abbess of the nunnery and for seventeen years took care of her young niece, educating her like a true daughter. Around 1610, the abbess wrote to the bishop of Lima to inform him that her niece, Melchora, had reached the age of seventeen and had no desire to return to the world. The girl wanted to become a nun but, unfortunately, did not have the dowry required by canon law. The bishop readily granted a dispensation, and the candidacy of Melchora was submitted to the secret vote of the community. Being the niece of the abbess and having lived in the convent for seventeen years, the result of the vote was never in question. She obtained the unanimous vote of the two hundred and ninety-two nuns who formed the community of La Concepción.

These nuns of La Concepción had a rather liberal policy toward the kind of baby girls accepted into the convent. Besides relatives of the nuns and daughters of good families, they also took mestizo, mulatto, and black babies, who were born to the maids and slaves of the nunnery. In the second half of the seventeenth century, the mulatto babies Sancha de Cordoba, Luísa Bravo, Catalina de la Madre de Dios, María Ustaque de Zárate, and the blacks Feliciana Betanzos and Beatriz de Arco were among the babies raised by the nuns of La Concepción.[10]

La Concepción was by no means the only nunnery that accepted baby girls in the seventeenth century. La Trinidad also had its population of baby girls raised and educated by the nuns. Isidora de la Cruz was taken into the convent around 1653 when she was a baby. She grew up in the cell of Doña Gerónima Meléndez, an important nun, who by 1668 had been elected abbess of La Trinidad. In that year, Isidora de la Cruz, already a young lady of fifteen, petitioned the bishop to take the veil. Being recognized by all as the spiritual daughter of the mother abbess, Isidora easily obtained the episcopal license and the unanimous vote of the community, and in 1668 formally became a nun of La Trinidad. Inés Carbajal, an orphan of reputable Spanish parents, was placed in La Trinidad under the care of the nun Doña Catalina Delgadillo, who raised the girl in her cell for seven years. In 1665, Doña Catalina wrote to the bishop to inform him that Inés was ready to take the veil. The bishop granted permission, and Inés was accepted by the community on November 12 of that year. María Manuela de Quirós and Tomasa de Igarsa also grew up in the convent of La Trinidad from a young age, and both eventually became nuns. In fact, this seems to have been a consistent characteristic of the Convent of La Trinidad: all the girls raised or educated in the convent ended up by taking the veil. A careful check of the documents of acceptance shows that, in the case of candidates applying to the school, their desire to become a nun was a condition for admission. Obviously, the nuns of La Trinidad saw their nursery and school as a great tool to secure the future membership of the order.[11]

At times, the acceptance of a new baby into the convent exhibited all the characteristics of a *sainete*, the short, comic-dramatic plays so popular in the sixteenth century. Such a case occurred in the convent of La Concepción one evening in 1668. As was customary, the mother abbess, Doña Juana de Amaya, secured the three different padlocks of the door with three large keys. She kept one of the keys, handed another to the door keeper, and entrusted the third to one of the oldest members of the community. From that moment on, the only way to communicate with the outside world was through the famous monastic *torno*. The torno resembled a large, cylindrical lazy susan built into the wall of the nunnery. Through it voices could be easily heard and letters and packages passed via a simple revolving movement. As Doña Juana de Amaya and her nuns were about to return to their cells on that particular night, somebody knocked on the outside wall of the *torno;* when opened on the inside of the convent, the torno revealed a newborn baby girl. Hearing her cries, nuns and servants ignored the rules of canonical silence and retreat and rushed from their cells to the entrance hall of the convent. Everybody wanted to see, touch, and hold the little girl, who was described by an eyewitness as *"acabada de nacer y tan linda"* (just born and so pretty). The abbess tried to restore order, but the confusion did not subside until everybody's curiosity was satisfied. Confusion arose once more when the nuns began discussing what to do with the baby.

The abbess, Doña Juana, aware that the bishop frowned upon the presence of babies in the convent, suggested that they send the girl to the public orphanage or place her with a good family outside the cloister. Most of the nuns objected. If God had sent the baby to La Concepción, it was obviously His will that the nuns take care of her. One of the black servants of the convent came forward and volunteered to work extra hours to pay for the milk needed to feed the infant. The nun Doña Manuela de Luna offered herself as a substitute mother, and promised to keep the girl in her cell and raise her at no cost to the community. Doña Juana de Amaya hesitated, and finally decided to consult with the canon of the cathedral, Don Cristóbal Bernardo de Quirós. The canon was summoned to the convent the following day to discuss the matter with the abbess and her advisors. Don Cristóbal not only went along with the desire of the majority, but volunteered to be the godfather of the little girl. The baptism was a solemn occasion, and the baby was baptized Ursula María de La Concepción.

Ursula grew up in the cell of Doña Manuela de Luna, who was a nun of means. When the baby became a young child, Doña Manuela, through her mother, Doña Bentura de Luna, hired private tutors to educate the girl. Ursula María learned to read and write well, mastered the organ and the harp, and developed a pleasant singing voice. By 1683, Ursula María was an attractive and well-educated young lady, fifteen or sixteen years old. On July 3 of that year, she requested permission to take the veil. For fifteen years she had been the darling of the convent, and two hundred and fifty professed nuns gave their votes to accept her formally as a nun. Ursula María never saw the outside world. With the exception of those moments after birth, when she was rushed through the darkened streets of Lima toward La Concepción, her entire life was spent hidden in an island of women.[12]

The example of Ursula María was the typical and frequent case of the unwanted or abandoned child. In 1664, there was another case in La Trinidad, which seems to have no parallel in the long history of the colonial nunneries. It involved the young girl, Juliana María de Zuñiga, legitimate daughter of Doña Ana María de Zuñiga y Sotomayor. At the beginning of March 1664, the young Juliana María was kidnapped and brought by force and deception to the convent of La Trinidad. The nun, Doña María de Orozco, who seems to have been involved in the plot to kidnap Juliana María, took the girl into her cell and was planning to raise her in the convent. The heartbroken mother appealed to the nuns to return her young daughter and, when this failed, presented a legal complaint before the vicar of the archbishopric, Don Pedro de Villagómez.

A formal inquest was held by the ecclesiastical tribunal on March 24, 1664, and witnesses were called to testify. The witnesses were the Spaniard Diego Flores de Paredes, the free black Ana María de Mora, one of the city midwives, and the mulatto woman Tomasa de Sanabria, a washerwoman. The three of them confirmed under oath that the child Juliana María was in the Convent of La Trinidad, but denied any knowledge of how the girl was brought there. Since no formal suit was filed after this inquest, one may safely assume that the girl was finally returned to her mother. The case nevertheless proves the incredible extent to which some nuns would go in order to raise and educate young children in their cells.[13]

There is no question that in the seventeenth century the number of babies and young girls in the convents created all kinds of unpleasant problems for the ecclesiastical authorities. Since their frequent remonstrances had been mostly ignored by the nuns, the archbishop of Lima, Don Fernando Arias de Ugarte, decided in 1630 to take stronger action. He sat down and wrote an official letter to all the nunneries of the archbishopric. The letter was addressed to the abbess of each of the convents, and it read in part:

> *I understand that in that holy house there are many girls not yet eight years old, and that they disturb the nuns in their prayers and divine exercises, and take a great deal of their time. Your Ladyship should not consent to this, and the girls living in your convent should be returned to their mothers or persons who brought them, to be raised by them.*[14]

The efforts of Don Fernando Arias de Ugarte did not have any appreciable results, and the nuns continued happily to play the roles of substitute mothers. In 1687, a new archbishop, Don Melchor de Liñán y Cisneros, had to face the same problem once again. He repeated the order of 1630, but the nuns ignored it as they had for four decades. This time the archbishop, Don Melchor, refused to accept defeat. After a few weeks of waiting, he issued an official canonical decree depriving all the nuns who would dare disobey of any voice and vote in the conventual elections. To avoid delays and misunderstandings, he commissioned the ecclesiastical notary, Don José Bravo, to deliver the decree personally to the abbess of each convent. Bravo fulfilled his commission by handing the decree directly to Doña Gregoria Becerra, abbess of La Encarnación, Doña Juana de Acevedo, abbess of La Trinidad, Doña Manuela Blazquez de Arriaga, abbess of La Concepción, and Doña Micaela de Juan, abbess of Las Descalzas. After almost a year had gone by, the effect of that decree was still minimal.

The nuns had recourse to a clever legal fiction to be able to keep their adopted daughters, disobeying the archbishop, and at the same time avoiding the canonical penalties formulated by Don Melchor. The nuns shifted the legal guardianship of those young children to trusted lay servants or slaves who lived within the convent serving the nuns. Then they claimed that the lay maids and slaves of the convent were not bound by strict canonical rules and were not directly affected by the canonical directives of the archbishop. An ecclesiastical court would have probably upheld the nuns' claims, but Don Melchor de Liñán was incensed with his stubborn and rebellious subordinates. In 1688, a year after his initial order, he chose four loyal matrons of the city to go inside the cloister of each nunnery, take a census of all the girls in the convent, and physically remove those who were not old enough to attend the convent school. This drastic measure must have been only partially successful, because at the end of the century one still finds babies and young girls living with the nuns in the colonial nunneries.[15]

Lay Schools

Aside from convent schools, there were many other schools for girls scattered throughout the viceroyalty of Peru. Both civil authorities and private citizens showed a remarkable concern for the proper education of young girls. This concern gave rise to a widespread net of institutions specializing in female education. Already in 1540, Emperor Charles V gave instructions to his governor in Peru, Vaca de Castro, to look for some "honest women" who could teach the daughters of the principal Indians in the way of life and culture of Spain. By 1550, the number of mestizo girls had greatly increased in the viceroyalty of Peru, and on January 23, the city council of Lima wrote to the king requesting royal patronage for the foundation of a school to educate the mestizas. That letter was followed in July 1550 by another written by Fray Domingo de Santo Tomás, the leading intellectual of the vice-royalty, author of the first Quechua grammar, and first rector of the University of San Marcos. Fray Domingo urged the king to support the foundation of a school system which would educate mestizo girls. He suggested that all the principal cities of the kingdom should have such a school, but especially Lima, Cuzco, La Plata, and Quito.

This idea caught the imagination of the early settlers of Peru, many of whom had mestizo children. Private donations began pouring in. In 1553, the wealthy Doña Catalina de Castañeda and her husband, Don Antonio de Ramos, moved the idea from the realm of dreams to that of reality with a generous and splendid gift. They donated some valuable real estate within the city of Lima, several vegetable gardens, farms, livestock, and slaves. Other powerful families followed suit, and the first school for mestizo girls named San Juan de la Penitencia was opened in Lima.

In September 1556, the new viceroy, the marquis de Cañete, could write to the king that the school of San Juan de la Penitencia was well endowed with a yearly income of one thousand pesos, had one of the most imposing buildings in the city, and was educating "the great amount of mestizas . . . daughters of conquistadores. . . ." In fact, by that year the building and income were large enough that the school also admitted "poor Spanish maidens." The viceroy appointed the widow Doña Catalina de Arguelles the first headmistress of San Juan de la Penitencia, which became the most popular girls' school for the lower classes of Lima. About ten years later, in 1577, when Viceroy Francisco de Toledo decided to move the University of San Marcos away from the Dominican convent, no better place could be found for the fledgling university than the buildings of San Juan de la Penitencia. The girls were moved, and the university took over the old school for mestizo girls.[16]

San Juan was by no means the only lay school for girls in Lima. There was another one called the School of La Caridad, attached to the Hospital of San Cosme and San Damián. This hospital dates back to 1559, when Don Pedro Alonso de Paredes began gathering poor patients and providing them with medical care. A few years later, the wealthy widow Doña Ana Rodríguez de Solor used her fortune to establish a hospital for women, and at the same time began to accept poor girls to be educated and to serve as nurses' aides. By the early seventeenth century, the school of La Caridad had its own exclusive part of the building and sufficient income to accept mestizo and Spanish girls. The first headmistress of the school was Doña Isabel de Porras Marmolejo, who, under a board of laymen, was responsible for the administration of the school and the education of the girls. To be accepted in La Caridad, a girl had to be of legitimate birth, poor, and between eight and twelve years old. One third of them had to be mestizas. They learned reading and writing, domestic skills, and, as a unique feature of La Caridad, they received instructions to become nurses' aides. The girls devoted time to working in the hospital, making beds, and reading to the patients. To compensate them for this work, they not only received free room and board, but upon graduation, they were given a dowry either to marry or to take the veil in one of the nunneries. A dowry of three hundred pesos was given to mestizas, while Spanish girls received four hundred pesos.[17]

Another girls' school with a very humble beginning, the School of Our Lady of Mount Carmel, became well known in the viceroyalty. The founder of the school was Catalina María Pérez de Silva, who had received an excellent education in her native Italy. As an orphan, Catalina María attended a school for girls in Milan founded by Cardinal Borromeo, a true Renaissance man and one of the leaders of the Counter-Reformation. Her education was so refined that upon graduation she was chosen as one of the young ladies-in-waiting of Doña Brianda de Guzmán, the wife of the Spanish governor of Milan. After the governor's term of office expired, Catalina María moved to Spain with her mistress, and eventually traveled to Peru as the wife of Domingo Pérez de Silva.

Once in Lima, Catalina María showed a remarkable interest in and talent for the education of young women. She began her teaching career by accepting private pupils in her own house, and she was constantly sought out by the best families of Lima. She educated the two daughters of Don Francisco de la Cueva, knight of Alcántara, and the daughters of other royal officials. By 1619, the petitions were so numerous that private tutoring became an impossibility. Therefore, the Pérez de Silvas used all their economic resources to buy a new property and build a chapel and the School of Our Lady of Mount Carmel. Soon the school was filled with "a large number of girls. . . . Some of those girls are brought there by their parents, and others are poor orphans maintained and supported by the material means of the Pérez de Silva."

The students lived a rather secluded and cloistered life. Their uniform was the habit of the Carmelite nuns, and only their parents could visit them while they were at the school. Perhaps reflecting the intellectual climate of late Renaissance Italy, Catalina María devised one of the best curricula available to women in the viceroyalty of Peru. The girls were taught Castilian and Latin so that they could read and understand the liturgy of the day. Music was also stressed. The girls took voice lessons and were taught to play musical instruments. The female Latinists who existed in seventeenth century Peru were most probably disciples of Catalina María.

By 1626, the work of Catalina María had been brought to the attention of the viceroy, the marquis of Guadalcazar, who took steps to perpetuate and consolidate the efforts of this excellent female educator. On August 30, 1627, he appointed a board of twenty-four directors "who will care for the welfare and development of the . . . school." This board of directors, among other things, raised enough capital to give a dowry of one thousand pesos to all the orphan girls who completed the course of studies under Catalina María.[18] The excellent education, plus the hope of a sizable dowry, attracted many girls to the School of Mount Carmel. One observer tells us that those girls came not only from Lima, but also from the provinces and some even from outside the kingdom of Peru—a clear proof of the reputation enjoyed by the school of Catalina María.

This Italian woman was not the only private educator in the viceroyalty. Almost every important city had some women, called amigas or beatas, who took an interest in the education of poor girls. Most of them operated in their own houses, and their efforts never blossomed into the institutional results we have witnessed in the School of Mount Carmel. Yet there are examples of female educators who, in the provinces, matched the accomplishments of Catalina María in Lima.

One of the most outstanding of those educators was Doña Francisca Josefa de Bocanegra in the city of Asunción. In 1536, as a young girl, she had arrived in the regions of the Rio de la Plata with the expedition of Pedro de Mendoza, and was one of the few survivors of the terrible hardships encountered by the early Spanish settlers of the Atlantic seaboard. Francisca Josefa found her way to the inland city of Asunción, where for almost forty years she would dedicate all her energies to the education of young girls. By 1575, her school for girls was already known in the La Plata region, and a few years later Francisca Josefa and her school came under the influence of the Jesuits, the best educators of the viceroyalty. For almost thirty years, her counselor and confessor was the Jesuit Marcial de Lorenzana, and all the girls, led by Francisca Josefa, attended services in the Jesuit church of Asunción.

Early in the seventeenth century, the school had seventy or eighty students for whom Francisca Josefa provided not only education, but also room and board. Since the school had no endowment, the girls had to dedicate a great deal of time "weaving, sewing, and other skills proper to their sex, so that they could support themselves with the fruits of their hands. . . ." The economic hardships of the school troubled the citizens of Asunción, and efforts were made to establish an endowment. On April 5, 1604, the governor himself, Hernandarias de Saavedra, wrote to the crown that Francisca Josefa was supporting sixty "poor orphan girls, daughters of noble parents" in her own house. He went on to request a license to import one hundred African slaves at the expense of the government. With the profit from their sale he proposed to establish the endowment of the school.

Three years elapsed without an answer, and in 1607 Hernandarias insisted once more. He explained to the king in a new letter the great economic needs of the school, and in an effort to win the sympathy of the crown, he stressed the social quality of the girls educated by Francisca Josefa. According to Hernandarias, the girls were "all daughters of conquistadores, some of them relatives of mine, daughters of my sister and of General Don

Antonio de Añasco." The slow and entangled bureaucracy of Spain ignored a second time the urgent plea of the governor, while Doña Francisca and her students worked long hours trying to stay alive. In a third and last letter of 1609, the governor sounded downcast and despairing: if Doña Francisca "dies before a decision has been made on this matter of the endowment, the whole work will be lost."

We do not know what happened to the school after the death of Doña Francisca, who lived until 1617 and died an octagenarian. But while she was alive, the school remained open and merited the respect and praise of some outstanding intellectuals and educators, including the Jesuit Pedro de Oñate, who, in 1614, put into writing his feelings about the school directed by Doña Francisca. In Spain, Oñate had been the assistant to the chair held at the University of Alcalá by Francisco Suárez, the philosophical genius of sixteenth-century Spain. Years later Oñate held a chair in the College of San Pablo in Lima and became one of the most prolific authors in the viceroyalty. In 1614, three years before the death of Doña Francisca, Oñate lived in Asunción and as Jesuit provincial was directing the remarkable anthropological and cultural experiment of the Jesuit missions of Paraguay. Writing to Europe in that year, Pedro de Oñate praised Doña Francisca who, in her eighties, was still supporting and educating about eighty girls in her house. The quality of the school truly impressed Oñate, who compared it favorably to similar institutions in the most developed civic centers of Europe. From a professional educator, who was thoroughly familiar with academic institutions in Rome, Madrid, Salamanca, and Alcalá, those were impressive words indeed.[19]

Although the many lay schools for girls founded in the old viceroyalty of Peru were very similar to each other in origin, structure, and goals, some exhibited certain unique characteristics. Efforts were made in 1615 to convert a girls school in Santa Fe into a combination vocational school and factory to solve the perennial economic problem of supporting the institution. The local authorities thought that the school was an ideal place to start *un grande obraje*, a big cloth factory, where the girls could work and earn the money to support themselves and pay for their education. A thirty-year-old master weaver, Lorenzo Gutiérrez, was hired to teach the girls weaving and to run the *obraje* for a profit. An investment was made in looms, cotton as well as wool, and the *obraje* was ready for production.

Unfortunately, the originators of the idea forgot to take into consideration the aristocratic feelings of the society of Santa Fe and the aversion of most seventeenth-century Spaniards to manual labor. Many in the city objected to forcing Spanish girls "of good families" to do the kind of work that was done in commercial *obrajes* by drafted Indian laborers. Obviously that type of work was considered by the best society of Santa Fe as servile and dishonorable. Some of the girls shared the opinion of their elders, refused to work at the looms, and even tried to escape from the school. The leader of the "rebels" was eighteen-year-old Francisca Ortiz, who twice in one week jumped over the fence and ran away from the school. She was caught both times, brought back, and kept in the school shackled with irons. A harsh discipline was imposed to contain the spirit of the rebellion. The girls were forced to work at the looms, and everyday were given a certain amount of wool to be woven. Those who failed to finish their assigned amount had to complete it by candlelight after all other girls had retired for the night. After almost one year of this rigid discipline and unable to survive against the ever-increasing opposition of public opinion, the experiment had to be abandoned.

Toward the middle of the seventeenth century, owing to the efforts and contributions of Don Juan de Saavedra, another curious development took place in the orphanage-school founded in Buenos Aires. For the first one hundred years nothing distinguished the school of Buenos Aires from any other school in the viceroyalty. Then, by the second half of the eighteenth century, the school began to develop a unit of adult education. The headmistress at the time was Doña Josefa Bacco, and the faculty was made up of Doña Ignacia Paniagua, Doña María Isabel, and Doña Antonia Bacco. Some leading ladies of Buenos Aires and benefactors of the school begged the headmistress to provide some hours of weekly instruction for their illiterate maids and other female servants. The idea was accepted, and a class was begun with the maids of Doña Josefa Rodríguez, Don Pedro Mazón, Doña Josefa González, Doña Ana Bracho, Don Felix de la Rosa, and Doña Rosa Bracho. The experiment must have been very suc-

cessful because a few years later we find that a group of society
ladies was emulating the maids and occasionally taking instruction
at the school.[20]

School of Santa Cruz

Among the many lay schools for girls in the viceroyalty of Peru,
the School of Santa Cruz in the House of Our Lady of Atocha
merits special consideration for the importance it acquired in the
colonial society of Peru. In 1596, the city of Lima, filled with
expectation and new hope, was getting ready for the arrival of a
new viceroy. Nothing broke the monotony and increased the tempo
of colonial life like the arrival of a new representative of the king.
Weeks of parades, fireworks, bullfights, and solemn religious services filled the city with noise, color, and excitement. In 1596, Don
Luís de Velasco arrived, surrounded as usual by relatives, courtiers, friends, and new royal officials. The parades and receptions
were a splendid opportunity for the newcomers to show the latest
fashions of Europe—robes, military uniforms, and academic
gowns—to the multitude lining the streets. However, in that year,
all this European finery did not attract the attention of the crowd
as much as did the ascetic figure of a man who, dressed in sack-
cloth, eyes downcast, was walking among the courtiers of Viceroy
Don Luís de Velasco. He called himself Luís "the sinner," and soon
he was revered by the superstitious masses as a "holy man and
servant of God." From the day he arrived in Lima, Luís collected
alms for the poor and tended to the needs of the indigent. As his
reputation as a holy man of God increased, so did the amount of
alms given by the pious citizens of Lima. Soon Luís had enough
money to buy a city lot, and began dreaming of buildng a hospital
for indigent blacks.

While he was making plans to start the building, a tragic accident
occurred one night in the streets of Lima which changed Luís's
plans. Fray Juan de Roca, a Franciscan friar and confessor of Luís,
on his way one night to administer the last rites to a dying person
came upon a pack of hungry stray dogs fighting noisily over the
half-eaten body of a newborn and abandoned baby. Some time
later when the horrified friar encountered an almost identical
scene, he persuaded Luís to abandon his idea of a hospital for

blacks and build instead an orphanage for foundlings. When the house was finished, it was called the House of Our Lady of Atocha and, in time, it became one of the principal orphanages of Peru.[21]

Early in the seventeenth century, the scholar Bernabé Cobo visited the house and wrote a chapter of his famous *Fundación de Lima* describing the institution. It is clear from Cobo's description that the orphanage had already begun to evolve into a full-fledged school. When Cobo visited the institution, the House of Our Lady of Atocha was taking care of 120 foundlings. Eighty of them were under the care of hired wet nurses, who kept the babies in their homes until they were weaned and then returned to the orphanage. Between forty and fifty children lived in the orphanage itself, and by the 1630s, they were under the care of a professional schoolteacher, who conducted regular classes and taught all the orphans how to read and write. Two decades later the School of Santa Cruz for orphan Spanish girls evolved from this humble beginning.

A well-to-do lady of Lima, Doña Francisca Vélez Michel, persuaded her husband, the pharmacist Mateo Pastor de Velasco, to will all their possessions to found the School of Santa Cruz in the House of Our Lady of Atocha. Their last will and testament was signed in Lima on June 16, 1654, before the notary public, Martín Ochandiano. Article five of that testament created the School of Santa Cruz for Spanish foundling girls, and placed the new institution under the government and patronage of the Holy Tribunal of the Inquisition. In 1655, when both Mateo Pastor and Francisca Velez died, the inquisitors of Lima, acting as a board of trustees, opened the new school for girls in the old building of the orphanage of Our Lady of Atocha. The assets of the philanthropic couple amounted to 341,626 pesos and six and one-half *reales*, and produced a yearly income of almost 15,000 pesos. The inquisitors used this amount to pay the salaries of a headmistress, a female teacher, an administrator, a lawyer, a doctor, and several maids. About 8,000 pesos were spent every year to pay these salaries, and the rest of the money was kept in a trust fund to furnish the dowries of the girls upon their graduation from the school.[22]

The constitution and by-laws of the school, written in 1659 by the inquisitor Don Cristobal de Castilla y Zamora, which according to observers of the period were strictly observed, provide the modern reader with a unique insight into the life of a colonial institution dedicated to the education of young women. The School of Santa Cruz, following the last will of the founders, was an autonomous institution, free from the ordinary jurisdiction of both civil and ecclesiastical authorities. A board of trustees, formed by the judges of the Holy Tribunal of the Inquisition, had full and independent government of the school. The inquisitors could appoint and remove at will the headmistress, the teacher, and all other officials of the institution. At least once a year the board had the duty of visiting the school to audit the accounts and to assure that the educational goals of the institution were properly fulfilled. The constitution also required that the headmistress and the teacher be well-educated matrons of a mature age and, if possible, without children, grandchildren, or any other close relatives. In this way it was hoped both of them would be free of all earthly attachments and exclusively dedicated to the welfare of the school.

The students were examined and accepted at Santa Cruz by the inquisitors of Lima, who had to ascertain before admission that the candidates were female, foundlings from the orphanage of Our Lady of Atocha, and of Spanish parents. This last condition was obviously hard to establish since the girls had been abandoned at birth, and their parents were unknown. To make up for the lack of documentation on the racial origins of the girls, the inquisitors relied on common sense and public opinion. The documents of admission stated time and again that the candidate in question "is a little Spanish girl, generally judged and considered as such by her skin color and the fine features of her face." In other words, a girl was Spanish if the people thought she was, and the inquisitors accepted that common opinion.

Race in seventeenth-century Peru was much more a question of social acceptance than of strict biological ancestry. Once these conditions had been fulfilled, the candidate had to prove that she was a baptized Catholic, raised in the orphanage, and between the ages of eight and sixteen. The girls who were finally accepted into the school were entered in the official rolls under their given Christian names, with the common and shared surname of "de Atocha." This surname would mark them for life as foundlings, raised in the orphanage founded by Luís "the sinner."

Life behind the thick walls of the School of Santa Cruz evolved in an atmosphere of monastic discipline. Students and teachers were bound by the rules of the cloister. Outside visitors were rarely allowed, and on those few occasions, always in the presence of the headmistress or another mature woman. Save in cases of emergency, the girls could not go beyond the front door, which was always locked by two different keys, kept by two different persons. Every evening the headmistress, accompanied by the schoolteacher and two of the oldest girls, inspected all the doors and windows to make sure that the cloister had not been, and could not easily be, violated.

The daily schedule followed by the students added to the climate of discipline and austerity. The girls were awakened at a quarter to six every morning, and by six o'clock all of them were gathered in the school chapel for two hours of vocal prayers, meditations, and the celebration of the mass. Breakfast was served at eight o'clock, and classes began at half past eight to last until half past eleven. Right after these morning classes the main meal of the day was served in the community dining room. The meal was abundant, consisting of three courses, followed by a dessert of either fresh fruit or pastry. After the meal, the girls were allowed a period of recreation and rest until two o'clock. They could talk among themselves, exercise, play games, or indulge in that most sensible of pleasures, the traditional Latin siesta. By two o'clock, all students were once again gathered in the chapel for a few minutes of reflection and prayers. Classes occupied most of the afternoon, from half past two until six o'clock. The following couple of hours were divided into evening prayers and free time, when the girls could read, study, or engage in other activities of their own choice. A supper of either meat or fish was served at eight o'clock, followed by a period of community recreation. By half past nine the day ended, when all girls went to bed and the lights were extinguished.

What kind of education did the young foundlings receive at the school of Santa Cruz? Obviously, in a school governed and controlled by the Holy Tribunal of the Inquisition, the curriculum emphasized religion. Many hours were devoted to memorization of the catechism and to the practicing of a large variety of religious exercises. Yet a more humanistic and secular learning was not neglected. Reading and writing were constantly stressed, and we can safely affirm that all students of the school mastered these two basic intellectual skills. The girls were encouraged to read, and at certain periods during the day they took turns reading aloud to the rest of the class to facilitate comprehension and delivery. Skills such as sewing, embroidering, cooking, and housekeeping, considered essential in the education of young women by colonial society, were also systematically taught at the School of Santa Cruz. Music and singing formed a very important part of the curriculum, and many girls spent the entire afternoon taking voice lessons, learning how to read music, and how to play several musical instruments. No expenses were spared in hiring lay musicians, master organists, and professional singers, who came daily to the school to conduct small classes. As has been stated before, this type of education did not prepare the girls for any specific profession—a goal Peruvian colonial society would not have understood anyway—but was an excellent preparation for future wives and future nuns. In accordance with the constitution of the school, the inquisitors provided all graduating girls with a dowry to marry or to take the veil according to the inclination of each one. Considering then that the future of the girls was either an arranged marriage or a nunnery, the education received at Santa Cruz must be judged good and proper.[23]

A few specific cases, preserved in the colonial archives, may serve to illustrate the background common to the majority of the girls educated at Santa Cruz. Agustina de la Rosa y Atocha, for instance, was placed in the *torno* of the orphanage on the evening of August 17, 1694. A newborn baby, she came wrapped in a torn blanket so old that it had to be discarded. A note was pinned to the blanket saying that the name of the girl was Agustina de la Rosa, that she was Spanish, and that she had already been baptized. Following the regular procedure, Agustina was kept in the House of Our Lady of Atocha only a few days until a foster mother could be found. In her case, the foster mother was an unmarried Spanish woman, Doña Micaela Ortega.

She kept the girl under her care for fourteen years, an indication perhaps that Agustina may have been the illegitimate child of a close relative or of Doña Micaela herself. In 1608, Agustina was brought to the School of Santa Cruz, and a formal petition was presented to the inquisitors to request the admission of the girl into the school. After a long investigation into the background of Agustina, the inquisitors accepted her with a full scholarship and the promise of a dowry upon her graduation from the school.

On January 6, 1720, Melchora María de Atocha was also placed in the *torno* of the orphanage. Another unmarried Spanish woman, Doña Melchora Clara de Avendaño, was chosen as a foster mother but was unable to keep the baby. When young Melchora María was returned to the orphanage, a well-known gentleman of Lima, Don Juan Manuel del Molino, senior notary of the ecclesiastical tribunal, came forward and volunteered to take the responsibility of raising the baby. One of his black slaves breast-fed the young child, who remained for several years in the house of Don Juan Manuel. Again one wonders if Melchora María was not the child of an illicit love affair between Don Juan Manuel and Doña Melchora Clara de Avendaño. One thing seems certain: the unusual procedure of looking for foster parents gave an opportunity to "respectable people," who may have had an affair, to keep the child, save face, and even project the image of concerned, charitable citizens. In any case, Melchora María de Atocha was accepted at the School of Santa Cruz when she was about ten years old, and in 1729 moved as a novice to the Convent of La Encarnación with a dowry of 2,000 pesos granted by the inquisitors.

One final example of alumnae of Santa Cruz was María Antonia de Atocha. She was abandoned at the door of the orphanage in the 1730s, and shortly thereafter placed under the care of Doña Gregoria de Leyva, a professed nun in the convent of Santa Catalina. The nun had one of her black slaves raise the child until 1745. On June 23 of that year, María Antonia was accepted as a student at Santa Cruz, where she remained for three years. In 1748, the young foundling, homesick for her foster mother and for the peace and quiet of the cloister of Santa Catalina, wrote to the inquisitors of Lima requesting permission to return to the convent as a novice. Her request was granted, and with a dowry of 2,000 pesos, she entered the nunnery of Santa Catalina under the name María Antonia de Leyva y Atocha. Like many other young ladies before her, María Antonia lived her entire life in a hidden, cloistered world.

The founders and patrons of Santa Cruz must have realized as early as 1659 that the rigid discipline and almost monastic austerity envisioned for the school would create serious disciplinary problems in the future. When they wrote the first constitution and by-laws of the school, they took into account the possibility that some of the girls might one day revolt against the stern regimen of Santa Cruz. Mindful of this possibiity, they approved as article twenty-six of the constitution a provision shocking to the more permissive mentality of our times:

> The school should have a well established jail, where could be imprisoned the students who show themselves incorrigible, arrogant, or inclined to commit crimes worthy of punishment. For cases of excessive outrage, the jail should be furnished with stocks to confine offenders by the ankles, wrists, or head. The girls who have merited to be confined in the stocks must fast at least one whole day having only bread and water once they have been freed from the stocks. . . . If these punishments are not sufficient to reform the offenders, the Patrons [Inquisitors] should be notified so that they can devise a greater punishment or expel the offenders from the school. . . .[25]

The concern and fear shown in this article was not unfounded, and the few extant papers of the school archive clearly show that serious disciplinary problems did occur at Santa Cruz. Two cases, one of the seventeenth century and the other of the eighteenth, may serve to establish the fact that some of the colonial young ladies did not peacefully accept the disciplinary yoke imposed by the inquisitors.

In 1667, fourteen-year-old María Rafaela de Atocha and sixteen-year-old María Josefa de Atocha had to be expelled from the school. For months they had exhibited a constant pattern of disruptive behavior by ignoring the rules of the school, neglecting their studies, disobeying direct orders from the teachers, and showing unmistakable signs of a precocious lewdness. When another student, María Santos, climbed the fence of the cloister and fled from Santa Cruz, María Josefa was her accomplice.

None of the punishments established by the constitution of the school seem to have worked in the case of the two young girls. In fact, their behavior became more rebellious and independent, and it was finally discovered that several times they had scaled the fence of the cloister and had spent the night roaming the streets of Lima. The scandal created by these nightly adventures was such that the inquisitors had little choice: the two teenagers were declared "incorrigible" and were expelled from Santa Cruz.

The case involving Mariana de Atocha y Zurvarán in 1771 was even more serious, and the Holy Tribunal of the Inquisition opened an official inquiry, summoning witnesses and taking sworn depositions. Mariana had been accepted at the school in 1765, and very early had begun showing a rebellious character and a notorious lack of obedience and submission. In 1771, in an outburst of rage and violence, Mariana attacked the associate headmistress, pulling her hair, kicking her, and with long fingernails scratched her face and arms until she drew blood. The inquisitors were shocked by this criminal act of physical violence and opened an inquiry. Sworn depositions of the associate headmistress, the teacher Doña Petronila Boller, the maid Catalina Cifuentes, and the student Rosa Eugenia de Atocha revealed some discrepancies in the testimony, but the substance of the event was well established.

It seems that Mariana had formed a strong attachment for a younger girl, Manuelita de Atocha. One day the associate headmistress ordered Manuelita to go to the kitchen and help do the dishes. Mariana resented the order and protested, using abusive language against the headmistress, provoking her to slap Mariana's face. Mariana exploded in a rage and attacked the associate headmistress.

The prosecutor in the case asked for a harsh punishment, explaining that "if one tolerates such horrible crime, it will be the cause of the total ruin and loss of the said school of Santa Cruz." Then he added a comment which speaks louder than many volumes about the racial prejudices in the colony. The prosecutor noted that such shocking behavior seemed to indicate that Mariana was a *chola* or mestiza, not a true Spanish girl. Mariana was finally confined to the school jail, placed in the stocks, and obliged to fast for several days.

That jail sentence was not the end of Mariana's troubles. Five years later, in 1776, she was a senior, and like others, she was promised a dowry either to take the veil in a convent or to be married to a suitor acceptable to the inquisitors. Mariana had chosen to marry, and was awaiting someone to come along and request her hand from the school authorities. Finally, a young man approached the headmistress asking for Mariana as his bride.

One can imagine the excitement of the young woman, who was about to abandon the cloister of Santa Cruz and start her own family. Yet, following the established custom of the school, there were still several months to wait. The request of the young man was forwarded to the inquisitors, who would conduct a thorough investigation into the suitor's background before giving their final and official approval to the proposed marriage.

During those months of waiting, Mariana could see her suitor only for brief, formal visits in the school parlor and, of course, always in the presence of an elderly matron. Yet, in view of later developments, it was almost certain that the rebellious Mariana managed to avoid the constant vigilance of her teachers and to meet the young man alone and in compromising situations. As other girls had demonstrated before, the fence of the garden was not difficult to scale, and there were windows on the lower floor that could easily be pried open. When Mariana was informed that the inquisitors had rejected her suitor as unacceptable, she was ready to take drastic action. Mariana paid no attention to the reasons behind the rejection. The man in question was a "foreigner" whose legal status in Peru was doubtful. He had no occupation nor any known skills to support the burden of a family. The investigation also suggested that he was not committed to a permanent union with Mariana but was simply trying to get her dowry.

Mariana ignored all these reasons and made secret plans to elope with her lover. They took advantage of the approaching feast of the Nativity, when the school was caught in a multitude of activities to prepare for Christmas. The regular schedule was suspended, and the girls worked in small groups around the house, decorating the halls and chapels, rehearsing carols and plays, and baking the traditional desserts and pastries of the season. On December 22 at about eight o'clock in the evening, when the doorkeeper was about to lock the front door for the night, perhaps with the complicity of other girls, Mariana managed to distract her and run into the shadows of the street. Her boyfriend, armed with pistols, was waiting in an adjacent doorway, and taking hold of Mariana's hand, they ran away from the hated cloister of Santa Cruz. Unfortunately, the freedom of the lovers did not last long. Their flight was noticed by one of the teachers who, with the help of the guards of the nearby Royal Tobacco Factory, went in pursuit. The lovers were caught, Mariana brought back to the school and thrown into jail, confined by wrists and ankles to the stocks. On December 23, 1776, the inquisitor Don Bartolomé López informed his colleagues in the Holy Tribunal of Mariana's latest escapade. Acting as the board of directors of Santa Cruz, the inquisitors deprived Mariana of her dowry and expelled her from the school.[26]

The rebelliousness and disciplinary problems exemplified by Rafaela de Atocha, María Josefa de Atocha, and Mariana de Atocha y Zurvarán should not obscure the fact that the majority of the students accepted the discipline of Santa Cruz and spent an average of ten years in the school in a life of prayer, study, and work, without ever creating any major problem. One hestitates to think what the future of those foundlings would have been without the School of Santa Cruz. Life would have thrown them into the underworld of thieves, prostitutes, campfollowers, beggars, or exploited servants, who formed the coarse, seamy side of colonial society. Santa Cruz rescued them from that almost certain future.

It shaped their young lives along the norms and values accepted in their society, and gave them the basic tools for future mental and spiritual growth. It also furnished them with a generous dowry to become useful individuals, either as consecrated virgins or as wives and mothers. Regardless of what we may think of the School of Santa Cruz, the intellectual leaders of colonial Peru were truly proud of the institution. Even after the Enlightenment had begun to destroy the old academic and intellectual foundations of Peru, some of those intellectuals were still extolling the accomplishments of the school. In an article published in the important *Mercurio Peruano* on March 6, 1791, the publishers of this paper sounded almost rhapsodical on the subject of Santa Cruz. To them the school was an excellent example of the humanism that permeated Peruvian academic circles, and of the generous philanthropy, "which the philosophers of our days so much extol and practice so little."

Scanning the academic landscape of Peru to determine the existence and nature of female education in the Spanish viceroyalty, one draws several general conclusions. In colonial Peru, there was a widespread interest in, and at times an almost obsessive concern with, the training and education of young women. Kings, viceroys, governors, city fathers, families, and public and private agencies showed that interest and concern at one time or another during the three hundred years of colonial rule. The results of that interest and concern were a great number of institutions dedicated to the education of women. Rare would be the city or important town of Peru that could not boast of one or two schools for girls. Lima, of course, had almost a dozen institutions where the young ladies could receive an education. Most of the schools scattered throughout Peru were not "public" institutions founded and controlled by the Spanish government but "private" schools, founded and governed by individuals or corporations, which in no way were answerable to the official representatives of the Spanish crown.

It would be absurd to distinguish between "religious" and "secular" schools in a society in which the Catholic church was ubiquitous. In a certain sense, all women's schools in colonial Peru were religious schools. Yet, there was a clear distinction between the schools controlled by female, religious orders, housed in the colonial nunneries, and the schools run by lay individuals, who had no official status within the hierarchical structure of the Catholic church. The former were rather expensive and exclusive institutions, where only the powerful colonial elites could afford to educate their daughters. The latter were more popular schools open to the lower Spanish classes, and even to mestizo and mulatto girls.

Regardless of the juridical structure of those schools, all of them had a profound similarity in their goals, curricula, and methods of education. The girls' schools of colonial Peru, like their counterparts for boys, were not concerned with preparing students for specific social roles or professions. Their goals were more humanistic in nature, namely the inner development of the spirit and mind of individuals, the acquisition of aesthetic and moral values and of basic intellectual skills that would enable the students to lead richer and more fulfilled lives. In fact, these goals reflected the ideals of that Christian humanism which, under the influence of Cardinal Cisneros, had become the cornerstone of the University of Alcalá. The ideals of Christian humanism had been applied to the education of women in the works of two of the most outstanding Spanish intellectuals of the sixteenth century. Luís Vives, in his *De Institutione Feminae Christianae* (On the education of the Christian Woman), Fray Luís de León, in his *La Perfecta Casada,* gave the educators of the period a blueprint of how to develop the perfect woman within the ideals and values of humanism and Christianity. These works reached Peru shortly after their publication in Europe and were read by those concerned with the education of women. We are not interested in establishing a relationship of cause and effect, but the goals and methods of Peru's girls' schools resemble intimately those contained in the works of Luís Vives and Fray Luís de León.

Like Spain, Peru was deeply affected in the sixteenth century by waves of popular marianism, the cult of Mary as the epitome and symbol of perfect womanhood. It is not surprising then that the educators of women in the viceroyalty of Peru used the figure of Mary to make more understandable and accessible the ideals and values of their educational system. A great number of the girls' schools of Peru were given marian names: Our Lady of Mount Carmel, Our Lady of Atocha, Our Lady of Charity, School of La Concepción, School of La Asunción, and School of La Encarnación. Statues and paintings of the mother of Christ presided over the chapels, classrooms, and dormitories of those schools. The prayerful recitation of the marian rosary was one of the most important religious practices observed daily in all the girls' schools. Twice every day the girls assembled in the chapel and, while contemplating a statue or painting of Mary, they slowly and rhythmically recited fifty "Hail Mary's," the salutation of the angel to the mother of Jesus. Thus, twice every day the girls reviewed the happenings in the life of Mary and learned to accept her as "full of grace" and chosen by the Lord. No wonder that a marian atmosphere seemed to envelop their lives, and that the girls were rewarded for imitating the great marian virtues of purity, unselfishness, humility, hard work, discipline, silence, and, above all, love and charity.

Perhaps it was never expressed in words, but the educators of women in colonial Peru were obviously striving to produce madonnas—living replicas of the sinless Mary, who later in life could become the leaven of a sinful world. In our modern secularized societies, amidst the sexual revolution of our time, we may reject those goals and ideals, but in the society of colonial Peru, they shaped the lives of countless young women.

5

⟨⟨✿⟩⟩

Marriages,
Dowries, and
Annulments

ALTHOUGH, AS WE SHALL SEE LATER, an incredible number of women in colonial Peru chose to lead the lives of consecrated virgins, a majority of girls of Spanish Peru became wives and mothers. The young girls, who had spent long years in the cloistered world of schools and nunneries, were suddenly returned to the city of men and, attached to a male not always of their own choice, began their new lives within the institutional framework of marriage.

Marriage, a universal institution, exhibited in colonial Peru some peculiar and specific differences, affecting the lives of countless women. The element of individual choice and personal, romantic love was frequently absent in the process of marriage. The church, the state, the family, the schools, the religious orders, the many lay sodalities, and, at times, some of the guilds had a vested interest in the institution of marriage, and most of the time controlled it, imposing conditions for its validity and influencing the choice of partners for political, economic, social, and theological reasons. Devoid of personal love and commitment, many Peruvian marriages ended in "divorces" or legal annulments, and the custom of concubinage became almost universally accepted as an outlet for romantic love and sexual attraction.

Hardly a better example of the exploitation and manipulation of women at the hands of self-centered males could be offered than the marriages of colonial Peru. That many women made those marriages work for their own personal fulfillment and advantage speaks very highly of their shrewdness and strength of character, not of the justice and benevolence of the institution itself.

Even before the discovery and conquest of Peru, the church had a strong hold on marriage within Catholic countries such as Spain. The case of Ferdinand and Isabella is a good example. The marriage of Queen Isabella to the Prince of Aragon, Ferdinand, was found null and void by the ecclesiastical authorities of Rome, and the young couple was threatened with excommunication. Until all the conditions imposed by the Holy See had been fulfilled, Isabella could not be officially recognized as Ferdinand's lawful wife. As a result of the legislation issued by the Council of Trent, the church's hold on the institution of marriage grew even stronger in the second half of the sixteenth century. The Council of Trent, although "ecumenical and universal" in its official title, was, in substance, a very Spanish council which reflected the values and ideals of Spanish society. It had been imposed on a reluctant pope by Emperor Charles V, the Spanish king, and was dominated from its inception in 1545 by Spanish bishops and Spanish theologians.

In its twenty-fourth session, the council defined the doctrine of marriage and declared it binding on all Catholics. This new legislation soon found its way into Spanish Peru. It affected the form of marriages in the viceroyalty, and was faithfully reflected in the legal and ethical treatises written by Peruvian authors and in the canons of the councils of Lima. For three hundred years, the Peruvian church, based on the legislatin of the Council of Trent, claimed the sole right to approve and bless marriages, declare their nullity, and issue decrees of dissolution. That claim was recognized by king and viceroy, and generally accepted by the people.[1]

Armed with the authority granted by the Council of Trent, the ecclesiastical authorities of Peru took firm control of the institution of marriage. The intended groom and bride began by presenting themselves to the parish priest, who opened a semilegal inquiry on their juridical capability to marry. It was not enough to prove that they were single and willing to marry. Canon IV, session twenty-four, of the Council of Trent recognized the authority of the church to create certain legal impediments that would render the subsequent marriage null and void. Certain degrees of consanguinity, a previous vow of chastity, some religious and spiritual relationships, like the one between godfather and goddaughter, could render the marriage null. The priest, therefore, had to ascertain that those impediments did not exist before approving the intended marriage. If the impediments existed, the parties had to petition the bishop, and in certain cases the pope himself, for a dispensation of the impediments. These petitions could be lengthy affairs involving dozens of faceless, ecclesiastical bureaucrats. Cheating, lying, and bribing were not uncommon means used to break through the ecclesiastical barrier.

Clearing the issue of impediments was only the first step in the long march toward the altar. The second step was the solemn proclamation of the marriage banns. A public announcement was made in church on three consecutive Sundays to notify the congregation of the proposed marriage. All members of the community were urged to come forward and report to the priests any reasons that could possibly invalidate the marriage. These solemn announcements were, of course, intended to underscore the social character of marriage and to stress that matrimony was not just a private, personal arrangement, but a public and social one. The community had to be involved, if not to approve, at least not to object seriously to the intended marriage. That the proclamation of banns could lead to new, lengthy legal inquiries is a matter of record both in Spain and in colonial Peru.

After all the above proceedings had been completed, and again following the directives of the Council of Trent, the marriage ceremony took place *in facie ecclesiae,* in the presence of the church. That meant that the parish priest or a cleric delegated by him had to preside over the ceremony, or else the marriage would be considered invalid by the church. In colonial Peru, the ceremony took place either in the church or in a private home. The priest, accompanied by at least two official witnesses, interrogated the bride and groom about their willingness to marry. After their mutual consent had been obtained, the priest pronounced the solemn words which made them husband and wife: *"Ego vos in matrimonium conjungum,"* "I join you in matrimony."

From that moment on, the official doctrine of the church considered that marriage a sacramental union, which could not be dissolved by any human authority. The religious ceremony was followed by a wedding feast with music, dances, food, and drinks.

The month following the ceremony was usually one of seclusion for the bride. A society deeply immersed in the marian doctrine of the virgin-mother considered it improper for a young virgin, in the process of becoming a "deflowered" woman, to expose herself to the curious gaze of relatives and friends. After the month of seclusion was over, the Peruvian social customs required that the newlyweds pay a formal visit to all the relatives and friends who had honored them by being present at the wedding. Depending on the social status of the family, this elaborate cycle of visits could take almost a year to complete. Although a heavy burden on the young bride, these visits gave her an opportunity to move freely around the city without parental consent or the constant vigilance of a chaperone.[2]

The legislation of Trent, so heavily influenced by Spanish theologians, reflected in a high degree the new social conditions that were taking shape in the expanding frontiers of the Spanish empire. While the Council of Trent was in session, a new society was being born in Peru and Mexico whose needs not always corresponded to those of Europe. It was a multiracial and multiclass society of a degree yet unknown in Europe, with a moving frontier and hundreds of new towns and mining camps being established along the length of the continent. Peruvian society was extremely mobile compared to the almost frozen stability of many Castilian communities. Local viceroys and governors, far removed from the moderating power of the crown and of the royal councils, at times became ruthless dictators. Hundreds of clerics, loose from the protective moorings of their ecclesiastical communities, roamed the lands of Peru following in the path of conquerors, merchants, and miners. The sounds of this new life-style resounded in the halls of Trent when the council fathers wrote their legislation of marriage.

One of the more clear cases of the mutual relationship between social conditions in colonial Peru and the marriage legislation of Trent can be seen in the case of *vagi*, the Latin juridical term for persons without an established residence who constantly moved from one place to another. In 1551, more than ten years before Trent issued its legislation on marriage, the bishop of Lima, Fray Gerónimo de Loayza, called the First Provincial Council of Peru into session. The Peruvian council sounded a strong warning in its constitution: sixty-three against the marriages of aliens, transients, and nonresidents. Local priests found it almost impossible to investigate the marital status of such highly movable individuals, who could easily enter into multiple marriages to take possession of the dowries of unsuspecting brides.

The words of the First Council of Lima are unmistakable. Many aliens and transients had entered the provinces of Peru and, pretending to be single, had married for a second time. To prevent this in the future, the fathers of the Council of Lima issued several orders and guidelines: no cleric, either secular or regular, could perform the wedding of a transient without the bishop's approval; testimonies had to be gathered from all places the transient had resided to ascertain he was not married there; the banns of marriage had to be published in all those places; the priests who ignored these directives were immediately suspended from their ecclesiastical functions. In 1563, the Council of Trent reflected this concern of the Peruvian church in chapter seven of its session on marriage: *Vagi matrimonio caute jungendi.* Four years later the Second Council of Lima, this time quoting the legislation of Trent, raised its voice once more against the marriage of transients and nonresidents. The fathers of the Second Council of Lima were shocked by the increasing numbers of people who entered into a second marriage while their first spouses were still alive.

By 1567, the council fathers wrote, the women of Peru were not always the innocent, unsuspecting victims of unscrupulous males. At times they were the instigators of these unlawful marriages. The words of the Second Council of Lima of 1567 are crystal clear: "plures *mulieres, quae propiis relectis viris, aliis nupserunt . . . ,*" "[there were] *many* women, who abandoning their own husbands, married others. . . ." The adventurous and manhunting female Don Juan was still very much visible in the Peru of 1560s.[3]

In spite of the constant efforts of the Peruvian ecclesiastical authorities, the problem of multiple marriages would not go away. In 1582, when the saintly bishop of Lima, Toribio Alfonso de Mogrovejo, called into session the Third Provincial Council of Peru, the assembled fathers again had to face the disruptive social effects of multiple marriages. The bishops gathered in Lima in 1582 were Antonio de San Miguel, bishop of Potosí; Sebastián Lartaún, bishop of Cuzco; Diego de Medellín, bishop of Chile; Alfonso Guerra, bishop of Rio de La Plata; Pedro de la Peña, bishop of Quito; Francisco de Vitoria, bishop of Tucumán; and

Alonso Granero de Avalos, bishop of La Plata. All of them agreed that the monogamous character of the marriage was still threatened in the viceroyalty of Peru by many unscrupulous individuals. Once again they gave orders to all the clergy of Peru not, under any circumstances, to join in matrimony "unknown persons, aliens, and transients." This decree was renewed again in 1591 and 1601 during the Fourth and Fifth Councils of Lima.

Since the Peruvian bishops could not eradicate the problem, the independent Tribunal of the Holy Inquisition took upon itself to chastise the offenders. Almost every year during the seventeenth century, the Inquisition of Lima detained and sentenced individuals who were convicted of polygamous marriages. One of the most notorious cases occurred in 1686. In the *auto-da-fé* celebrated on September 28, eight men were condemned for being "married two, three, four, and five times." The Inquisition fined and imprisoned them and, of course, declared null all their marriages except the first one. Three of the men, who had married more than twice, were taken through the streets of Lima amidst the insults of the crowd, while the crier proclaimed their sin and the executioner whipped their stripped backs. The rejection by the inquisitors of Lima of the suitor of Mariana de Atocha y Zurvarán in 1776 was partly based, as we saw in the preceding chapter, on the fact that the young man was not a resident of Lima and was suspected of trying to run away with Mariana's dowry.[4]

If the church took a dim view of the proposed marriages of persons without an established, permanent residence, it also took a strong stand in defending the marriage bond. Even when one of the partners had been lured by the frontier and long years of absence had rendered marital life impossible, the Council of Trent and the councils of Lima took the stand that only death could dissolve a consummated, sacramental marriage. Peruvian ecclesiastical authorities were well aware of the heartbreak and agony of countless abandoned wives, and yet they reaffirmed the letter of the law as proclaimed by Trent. On the other hand, many new lovers could never formalize their unions because one of them still had a living spouse they may not have seen for decades. Inés Suárez, the first lady of the frontier of Chile, had to suffer for years the ignominy of being the concubine of Captain Pedro de Valdivia, whose wife was still living in Spain.

Instead of changing the law of the indissolubility of marriage, the church used all its moral authority to bring about the reunion of separated spouses. Bishops and priests pressured individuals and civil authorities to put an end to the prolonged separation of spouses. One of the most eloquent voices raised against this abuse was that of the Jesuit Diego de Avendaño, who in the second half of the seventeenth century was the professor of moral theology in the College of San Pablo in Lima. In his massive Latin encyclopedia *Thesaurus Indicus,* he wrote that the civil authorities of the viceroyalty had a serious moral obligation to force husbands to bring their wives from Spain or from wherever they may have abandoned them. Avendaño gave as a reason for this serious moral duty *quia divortium istud contra uxorum iura inhumane protractum, crimen est* (because these long, inhuman separations are a crime against the natural rights of wives). Then he went on to explain that the absence of a husband deprived a wife of her basic right to sexual fulfillment and to the companionship and protection of a man, and could easily place her in a situation to break her marital vows and conjugal fidelity. That, according to Avendaño, was a crime which could not be tolerated by either civil or ecclesiastical law.[5]

Another problem concerning marriage, which for days occupied the attention of the bishops and theologians congregated at Trent, closely reflected the social and political situation of colonial Peru. Chapter nine, session twenty-four, of the Council of Trent was a strong appeal to civil authorities on the part of the church not to interfere with the institution of marriage, and not to pressure individuals to marry for political, social, or economic reasons. The council was concerned that, in the case of individuals with political power, great wealth, or the hope of an ample inheritance, the state would be tempted to manipulate their marriages. The fathers of the council were, of course, talking in general, theoretical terms, but they could very well have been describing conditions in the viceroyalty of Peru.

When it came to the marriages of royal officials, encomenderos, rich merchants, wealthy miners, and members of the nobility, viceroys and governors could hardly accept the role of passive, respectful spectators. Their manipulations and pressures, at times blatant and at times subtle, raised the question of the freedom of choice in many marriages of colonial Peru. The concern of the Council of Trent with the freedom of marriage echoed within the

Peruvian church. As early as 1567, during the Second Provincial Council of Lima, the bishops of Peru felt compelled to declare, against the encroachment of civil authorities and relatives, that *contrahentium libera debet esse voluntas,* the will of the contracting parties must always be free. Without that freedom to choose, the subsequent marriage would be null and void in the eyes of the church, even if blessed by a priest.

The church, which had itself placed so many restrictions and conditions on the institution of marriage, did not tolerate the interference and pressures emanating from civil authorities, families, and private corporations. And yet, from the very early days of the discovery and settlement of the New World, the Spanish crown had taken a very active role in the affairs related to colonial marriages. Thousands of young orphan girls had been sent from Spain to be married in the colonies by the arrangements of local authorities. Legal pressures were imposed on the early conquistadores and settlers either to marry or loose the rights and privileges they enjoyed in the emerging societies of America. Marriage was made a condition for eligibility to certain civil offices, and for membership in certain guilds and corporations. Some ruthless viceroys forced specific marriages on reluctant partners for purely political reasons. The already mentioned case of Viceroy Marquis de Cañete is but one of the many that could be mentioned.

Shortly after his arrival in Peru in 1556, he forced two wealthy ladies, Doña Beatriz de Santillana and Doña Bernardina de Heredia, to marry husbands of his own choice. Cañete also forced a young, ten-year-old daughter of Doña María de Sandoval to marry a young boy, also ten years old, who had come to Peru in the entourage of the viceroy. The viceroy count of Lemos singled out an entire class of people and presented them with a draconian edict to marry. On August 9, 1669, the town crier of Lima stood in the main plaza and read to the gathering crowd the edict of the viceroy: All the owners of *pulperias* (the combination of liquor and drug stores of colonial Peru) had to be married or loose their *pulperias.* Unmarried *pulperos* were given six days to find a spouse or lose their places of business.

The count of Lemos was a very religious and moral man, and he was worried that the *pulperias* were becoming a favored gathering place for drinking rogues and loose women and therefore a menace to public morality. He undoubtedly thought that the presence of a wife would give respectability to the *pulperia* and forced the *pulpero*-husband to maintain a decent and respectable establishment. But decrees like the one issued by Lemos resulted in thousands of marriages of convenience, utterly devoid of love, and lacking the degree of personal freedom required by natural and ecclesiastical law for the validity of the marriage contract. No wonder that hundreds of women, as we shall see later, flocked to the ecclesiastical tribunals demanding the annulment of their marriages.[6]

If the pressures exercised by civil authorities brought into question the validity of many colonial marriages, the ones applied by parents and relatives made many women pawns in the political and economic games played by ambitious families. The daughter of Doña María de Sandoval was not the only child who was forced to marry before she could comprehend the full implications of a matrimonial life. In fact, child brides between nine and twelve years old were a common sight in all the cities of colonial Peru. Their marriages had been arranged in family councils, and usually to older and wealthier men whose social positions brought prestige and recognition to the family of the bride. Although most of those children were easily manipulated by their families, the reluctant child bride, who fought the will of her parents, was also present in the colonial cities. The young women, who refused to be forced into unwanted marriages, were simply asking with their actions to be treated as free and independent human beings. Three of those independent women were Doña Mariana de Torres, Andrea de Berrio, and the darling of Lima, the beautiful and witty Doña Marianita Belzunce. Mariana lived in the sixteenth century, Andrea in the seventeenth, and Marianita in the eighteenth, but they had a common bond in their efforts to preserve their freedom and independence.

Doña Mariana de Torres was only twelve years old in 1597, when her family decided to marry her to Don Hernando de la Concha Marríquez. He carried two of the most illustrious surnames of the viceroyalty and was a gentleman of means. Once the decision had been made in the family council, a web of subtle pressures was woven around the unsuspecting child bride. Since she was not yet of canonical age to marry, a dispensation was obtained by her parents from the ecclesiastical authorities. One of the best-known and most respected priests of the viceroyalty, the Jesuit Juan de Avila, was brought to the house to counsel and instruct the young child on her future duties as a wife. They met alone, and one can only imagine the fearful respect of Mariana in the presence of a man who represented to her the authority of God on earth. Juan de Avila emerged from the counseling session with a cautious report. Mariana was an intelligent and mature child, who seemed to understand the nature of the marital relations between a man and a woman. But the Jesuit cautioned the family that, owing to Mariana's tender years, she may not yet be *apta viro,* physically capable of sexual intercourse.

The family was obviously so eager to have the marriage performed as soon as possible that they summoned the family doctor, Juan de Texada, to determine if Mariana was *apta viro.* The historical records do not detail the physical examination of the young child. We are only told that Dr. Texada determined to the satisfaction of the family that Mariana was physically capable of sexual intercourse. With these preliminaries out of the way, the wedding date was set for October 4, 1599. To emphasize the social prominence of the family, one of the highest-ranking prelates of the Peruvian church, the bishop of Popayán, Don Juan de la Roca, was invited to perform the ceremony. Any twelve-year-old girl, regardless of time and place, would have been intimidated by this blatant display of manipulation. In the society of colonial Peru, it was practically impossible to free oneself from this constraining web of family pressures. It is to the credit of Mariana that she did not acquiesce to the family arrangements.

There was very little she could do to prevent the marriage, but a few months after the bishop of Popayán had solemnly pronounced her the wife of Hernando de la Concha, Mariana challenged the validity of her marriage before the ecclesiastical tribual of Lima. She retained one of the best lawyers of Lima, Don Benito de Salvatierra, and the case opened in the winter of 1599. Several witnesses summoned by Salvatierra swore under oath that Mariana did not freely consent to the marriage, and that in fact she did not fully understand before the wedding the substance of the marital contract. This testimony was contradicted by another group of witnesses presented by Mariana's family. Caught in the maze of these sworn, contradictory testimonies, the ecclesiastical judges could not resolve the quandary. Their feelings of uneasiness and hesitation must have been increased by the fact that the wedding was performed by a prominent bishop, Don Juan de la Roca of Popayán. To break the impasse, Doña Mariana's lawyer shifted strategy. He now demanded a decree of annulment on the grounds that Doña Mariana had not been at the time of the wedding, and still was not *apta viro,* and that, in fact, after several months of marital life she was still a virgin. Two expert and independent witnesses, the midwives Leonor de Vargas and Ana de Santiago, were summoned by the tribunal. Their report to the ecclesiastical tribunal was conclusive. After a thorough physical examination, they had found that Doña Mariana de Torres was still a virgin and that indeed she was not yet *apta viro.* After several weeks, the ecclesiastical judges declared the marriage null and void, and Doña Mariana totally free from any marital bonds.[7]

A few years later, in 1604, the same ecclesiastical tribunal handled the case of Andrea Berrio, a young girl of a modest family who had just turned twelve years old. The story told by several witnesses before the ecclesiastical judges reveals a texture of colonial life coarser than the one exhibited in the case of Doña Mariana de Torres. The subtle and diplomatic pressures of the de Torres family gave way this time to insults, violence, and physical abuse. Andrea's mother had arranged a marriage between her daughter and a certain gentleman by the name of Gerónimo Ufano. When Andrea was notified of the family decision, she adamantly refused to accept her mother's choice for a husband. When the initial maternal pleadings were ignored, Andrea was insulted and repeatedly beaten by her family. The young girl was threatened with death if she would not consent to the marriage. Her own mother called her "a rotten woman who refused to marry because she wanted to become a whore."

Physical pain and fear finally broke the will of the courageous girl, who went through the motions of getting married to Gerónimo Ufano, but determined not to consummate the marriage. With a strength beyond her years, Andrea resisted the sexual advances of Gerónimo, and once again she was insulted and beaten. When she finally lost her virginity, it was not an act of love, but a brutal and monstrous act of rape. A brother of Gerónimo forced her into the bedchamber and tied her to the bed, where Gerónimo raped the terrified child. Obviously, the family thought that once she had lost her virginity, Andrea would settle into the role of a wife. Instead, the girl appealed to the ecclesiastical tribunal to demand a decree of annulment. Several witnesses confirmed under oath the tale of horrors, including the rape, and the judges issued a decree of nullity for lack of freedom and consent.[8]

Perhaps the most famous child bride of colonial Peru was Doña Marianita Belzunce, a *limeña* of beauty, wit, and charm. She was born around 1742, when her father, Don Juan Bautista Belzunce, a gentleman of French origin, was the president of the powerful and prestigious merchant's guild of Lima. Her mother, Doña Rosa Salazar y Muñatones, was related to the best society of colonial Peru. Marianita never knew her parents. Don Juan Bautista died a few months before her birth, and Doña Rosa died as a result of the birth of the girl. Marianita was raised by a spinster aunt, Doña Margarita de Murga y Muñatones, the indisputable queen of a rural empire, the large estate of Casa-Blanca in the fertile valley of Cañete. By herself, Doña Margarita ruled a vast estate, four hundred black slaves, Spanish and Indian servants, and a few tenant farmers. Marianita Belzunce became the princess of this rural kingdom, where she grew without the restrictions imposed on urban children.

Her education was informal, to say the least. With a keen and gifted mind, she learned mostly from nature, from the songs of the slaves, and from the fascinating stories and legends told by the fireplace in the long winter evenings by the maids of the hacienda. Somehow Marianita learned to read and write. In the gorgeous setting of Casa-Blanca, Marianita led a happy existence filled with games and laughter, and enjoyed all the luxuries common to the landed aristocracy of the viceroyalty. She was the sole heiress of Casa-Blanca, and her future should have been a happy one. Yet, around 1755, when she was thirteen years old and had grown into a charming and beautiful young lady, Marianita's safe world collapsed. For the first time she knew fear, anguish, and heartbreak. But her behavior in the crisis caused Marianita to capture the heart and imagination of the popular masses and to be remembered in their songs and poems.

In 1755, the neighboring estate of Cali was getting ready to receive its absentee landlord, Don Juan Dávalos y Rivera, count of Casa Dávalos. The count had just become a widower and was coming to Cali to retire peacefully in his rural dominions. One of his first duties after settling at Cali was to pay a courtesy visit to his neighbors, the landlady of Casa-Blanca, Doña Margarita de

Murga y Muñatones. The count arrived at Casa-Blanca riding a superb Peruvian horse called *paso fino* because of the balletic quality of its stride. He was accompanied by the administrator, the chaplain, the butler, and the doctor of his hacienda of Cali. Captivated by the charm and wit of Marianita, the count of Casa Dávalos soon became a regular visitor at Casa-Blanca. Soon the sixty-year-old count realized that he had fallen in love with a thirteen-year-old child-woman. His visits to Casa-Blanca became more and more frequent and, before Marianita could suspect anything, the young heiress of Casa-Blanca had been formally promised in marriage by her aunt Doña Margarita to the lord and owner of Cali. Doña Margarita saw the arrangement not so much as a marriage between her niece and the aging count, but as a marriage between Casa-Blanca and Casa Dávalos.

Weeks of pleading, threats, and even physical abuse finally forced Marianita Belzunce to go through the motions of marrying the count. But she never gave her inner consent and was determined to die rather than consummate the marriage. The ceremony took place in the large living room of Casa-Blanca, and was performed by a priest who was a close relative of the count. To his questions Marianita only answered with tears. Her silence was taken for assent, and she was pronounced wife of the count and the new countess of Casa Dávalos. The ceremony was as far as Marianita was ready to go, and months of pressures on the part of the count and of her aunt failed to persuade her to consummate the marriage. The frustrated count finally sent the child bride back to the hacienda of Casa-Blanca, to the abusive anger of her spinster aunt, but also to the loving sympathy of slaves and servants.

Many persons had been shocked by the callous behavior of Doña Margarita de Murga y Muñatones, and when she died sometime before June 1756, they helped Marianita to challenge the validity of her marriage before the ecclesiastical authorities of Lima. One of the most prestigious legal scholars of eighteenth-century Peru, Don Pedro José Bravo de Lagunas y Castilla, professor of law at the University of San Marcos, took the case directly to the archbishop of Lima, Don Pedro Antonio de Barroeta. While the ecclesiastical judges took their time studying the case and calling witnesses, the popular masses of Lima returned a quick verdict. In *pulperias,* markets, plazas, and street corners the consensus was universal. The count of Casa Dávalos was a senile, old fool, and the dead Doña Margarita de Murga a heartless woman. Overnight, Marianita Belzunce became the adored heroine of the common masses, who saw her as a successful symbol of rebellion against social and political manipulation. Jokes, poems, and songs ridiculed the poor count and praised Marianita for not surrendering her virginity. One of those poems was still remembered by the popular masses at the end of the nineteenth century:

> *With a rusty sword*
> *which has already lost its point and edge,*
> *you should not think anything else, dear Count,*
> *but to spend your life at ease.*
>
> *All your courage miscarries*
> *when you try to test your sword*
> *which, not being new any more,*
> *neither pricks nor pierces.*
>
> *The best thing I can advise*
> *is that you become an abstaining recluse*
> *since rich food damages*
> *the stomach of old men.*
>
> *For Mariana to accept*
> *certain parts of your marital rights*
> *you would have to be armed*
> *with a sword forged in Toledo.*

Finally the ecclesiastical tribunal declared the marriage of Casa-Blanca null and void and Marianita free to marry again. Years later the beautiful Marianita Belzunce married a man of her choice, Don Agustín Hipólito de Landaburu y Rivera, and lived a happy life, loved and admired by the people of Lima. She died in the last decade of the eighteenth century.[10]

Dowries

Mariana de Torres, Andrea de Berrio, and Marianita Belzunce were three brides who revolted against a system of arranged and forced marriages, based only on the social and economic conveniences of their families. But countless of their colonial sisters were caught for life in marriages imposed on them by parents and relatives without regard to personal preference and fulfillment. The families of colonial Peru had at their disposal a powerful legal instrument, which enabled them to shape and manipulate the marriages of their daughters at will. The traditional system of dowries, recognized and reinforced by Castilian law, could be and was used in colonial Peru to force young brides into marriages arranged or approved by their families. A marriage without some sort of a dowry was socially and even legally unthinkable, and therefore, those who controlled the dowry could also control the marriage. The need to provide a dowry made those colonial marriages a family and community affair to a degree unknown in our own society, and the decision to marry or not to marry a specific person could not be the sole and exclusive decision of the bride.

By the time Peru was conquered and settled by the Spaniards, the system of dowries had been part of the legislation of Castile for more than two centuries. Introduced in Iberia by the Romans, the dowry was defined in Roman law as "a donation made to the husband in order to sustain the burdens of matrimony." It was supposed to symbolize that the woman was not a servant, but an equal partner in the new shared life. Roman brides were not "bought" by the groom as was customary in some of the germanic tribes of central Europe. Instead they could, depending on the size of their dowries, "buy" a suitable and convenient husband. Alfonso X, "El Sabio," introduced this Roman custom into the legislation of Castile, when he wrote the first great Castilian code of laws, *Las Partidas,* between 1256 and 1263. The dowry laws were reaffirmed by the famous *Leyes de Toro* issued by the Castilian parliament in 1505, shortly after the death of Queen Isabella. They were revised during the reign of Philip II, and finally found their way into the *Novisima Recopilación,* the new codification of all the laws of Spain. Peruvian legal scholars, like Diego de Avendaño in his massive *Thesaurus Indicus,* years later would explain how the legal system of dowries affected the colonial marriages of Peru.[11]

This legislation reveals the following characteristics of the Castilian-Peruvian dowries. The dowry was a donation, which could be provided either by the family of the bride or by any donor so inclined. In families of means, the parents had a moral and legal obligation to provide a dowry equivalent to at least half of the expected inheritance, if the daughter married with their consent. The implications of this condition are easily imaginable. The dowry could be established either by a formal, notarized, legal document, or simply by a *carta dotal*, a private letter given to the groom with the specific details of the dowry. After the marriage, the administration of the dowry was in the hands of the husband, but the dominion could legally be held by the wife. If the marital bond was dissolved either by death, or divorce annulment, the dowry and the income produced by it had to be returned to the wife or her legal heirs.

By giving the reader a fictitious case in the tradition of colonial, legal casuistry, Diego de Avendaño in his *Thesaurus Indicus* provides a magnificent insight into how seriously Peruvian colonial society took the system of dowries. Avendaño imagines a man who has solemnly and in the eyes of the church been betrothed to a woman, who in turn has legally bound herself to bring a certain dowry to the marriage. To make the case more extreme, Avendaño imagines that after the betrothal the woman has willingly and in view of the upcoming marriage surrendered her virginity to the man, and this fact has become known. After explaining these circumstances of the case, Avendaño asks the following moral and legal question: If in the last minute and for reasons beyond the control of the bride the dowry cannot actually be transferred to the groom, does he have any moral or legal obligation to proceed with the marriage honoring the previous solemn betrothal? Diego de Avendaño, the undisputed moral and legal guide of the Peruvian conscience, does not hesitate in his answer: Without the actual possession of the dowry and in spite of the fact that the bride has already lost her virginity, the groom has no legal or moral obligation to honor the betrothal. He is free to walk away from his previous promise to marry. Avendaño seems to be saying that the dowry was such an essential element in the structure of colonial marriages that without it even the most solemn promise could be legally and ethically broken.[12]

Even without the writings of Diego de Avendaño, there are enough specific cases of wealthy heiresses, middle-class women, and poor maidens to illustrate the universality and importance of the Peruvian dowries. We have already encountered in a previous chapter the powerful Chilean family, de los Rios y Lisperguer, whose daughter Doña Agueda married Don Blas de Torres Altamirano, a judge of the audiencia de Lima. It was a marriage of convenience between the wealth of the Lisperguers and the political power of Don Blas. In the delicate negotiations leading to the marriage, the question of the dowry was of paramount importance. As a judge, Don Blas knew well all the subtleties of the law and did not leave anything to chance. On July 24, 1616, and before the notary public Bartolomé de Maldonado, he drew a legal document concerning the dowry of his future wife Doña Agueda. The document was sent to Chile to be signed and accepted before witnesses by the parents of the bride, and it specified what Don Blas expected for a dowry before celebrating the marriage ceremony. The judge of Lima expected that the heiress of Chile would bring a dowry of 50,000 pesos, and that 30,000 of them in cash should arrive in Lima with the bride, to be handed to him before the wedding. The remaining 20,000 pesos had to be paid in three installments in the three consecutive years following the marriage, and at the time the crops were gathered and sold in the extensive rural properties of the de los Rios y Lisperguers. Not only the parents of Doña Agudea, General Don Gonzalo de los Rios and Doña Catalina de Flores, but also her uncle, General Don Pedro Lisperguer, and Doña Catral de Flores obliged themselves to pay in the term of three years the remaining 20,000 pesos and offered as a guarantee of this pledge their haciendas and encomiendas in Peru and Chile. The dowry of 50,000 pesos was such an essential element in the engagement of Doña Agueda and Don Blas that without it the marriage would have never taken place.[13]

Considering the incredible amount of wealth transferred by some Peruvian families to the legal control of their future sons-in-law, one understands why many of those families could not easily yield to the mere romantic attachments of their daughters. The brides were not simply giving themselves in marriage; they carried with them such a substantial amount of the family wealth that their marriages became, almost by necessity, a family affair.

For example, one can hardly blame the Pastene family of Chile for taking a strong interest in selecting a husband for their daughter Doña Lucía, whose dowry represented a veritable fortune. The *carta dotal* or "dowry letter" of Doña Lucía de Pastene was signed in Lima February 5, 1635, and given to the groom, Maese de Campo Don Bernardo de Amara Yturigoyen, who took possession of the property specified in the letter. Doña Lucía gave Don Bernardo as a dowry 7,000 pesos in cash and the ranch of La Quillota with 1,200 heads of cattle, 1,000 goats, 6,500 sheep, and 12 pairs of oxen, all of them valued at 18,190 pesos, without counting the value of the land. The agricultural yield of La Quillota was valued at 23,231 pesos per year. Doña Lucía's dowry also included several houses in Santiago de Chile, which were valued at 8,300 pesos, and twenty-seven slaves whose price in the slave market was 10,300 pesos. Doña Lucía brought also as a part of the dowry silverware and silver luxury objects with a combined weight of 277.12 kilos, a personal wardrobe worthy of a queen, jewelry, a collection of paintings by colonial artists, and exquisite linens for beds and tables. If all the above was not enough, Doña Lucía de Pastene owned a small encomienda of twenty-five Indians which also became part of the dowry transferred to Maese de Campo Don Bernardo de Amara Yturigoyen. Again, colonial wealth married the power and prestige of a royal appointee, and the personal feelings of Doña Lucía and Don Bernardo for each other probably had very little to do with the wedding arrangements.[14]

Dowries were not restricted in colonial Peru to wealthy heiresses or to daughters of prominent families. They were also common among families of modest means, and a myriad of public and private agencies offered dowries to the daughters of the poor, to orphans, and to foundling girls in an effort to place them "in honest and respectable marriages." In fact, the offering of dowries to poor maidens seems to have been one of the favored charities practiced in colonial days by the devout people of Lima. Many religious sodalities, like the famous Marian Sodality of La O directed by the Jesuits of the College of San Pablo, collected money from the faithful all year round, and on the feast day of their patron saints offered modest dowries to the daughters of the poor.

The membership of La O was composed of wealthy merchants, nobles, and royal officials, and by the middle of the seventeenth century, the sodality enrollment fluctuated between 800 and 1,000 prominent persons of the best society of Lima. By the end of that century, when Don Juan de Murga was the treasurer, the Sodality of La O had become one of the wealthiest religious corporations of Peru. It had a yearly income of more than 59,000 pesos, which was used for charitable purposes. Among the favored charities of La O was the granting of dowries to the daughters of the poor.

The sodality chose only poor girls who showed promise of being good Christian wives and mothers, and whose intended husbands had been examined and approved by the directors of the sodality. It must have been clear to all those involved in this process that, without the approval by the sodality of both bride and groom, the dowry would have never been granted. In this way the dowries of La O became a powerful tool in determining who married whom and when. The pressures exercised by parents in the case of wealthy heiresses could, and were, exercised by dowry-granting agencies in the case of the poor.[15]

This kind of control and pressure is extremely clear in the case of the School of Santa Cruz which, as seen in a previous chapter, not only educated foundling Spanish girls, but also provided them with a dowry upon graduation. From its foundation in the closing years of the sixteenth century until the end of the colonial period, the School of Santa Cruz granted hundreds of dowries ranging from 400 pesos to 2,000 pesos. The judges of the Holy Tribunal of the Inquisition, acting as a board of trustees of the school, investigated the backgrounds of all prospective husbands, and granted or withheld the dowries accordingly. In fact, the alumnae of Santa Cruz had very little chance of marrying unless they accepted the men approved by the inquisitors, and even when that approval was forthcoming, there was practically no room for personal choice on the part of the brides.

Since the girls led a cloistered life within the walls of Santa Cruz, no personal, continuous contacts with eligible males were ever possible. The prospective brides played a completely passive role in a rather cold and businesslike process leading into marriage. The prospective husbands took the initiative of contacting the school authorities and requesting a bride, whom they may have never met personally. Custom dictated that, when such a petition was received and approved, the most senior girl in the school should be the designated bride. By the time the marriage took place, the bride and groom had met several times in a formal setting under the eyes of a chaperone. It is very doubtful that they had been able to develop any links of true friendship, affection, and romantic love.

The partial, extant records of the School of Santa Cruz give us a good insight into the kind of men who came to the school looking for a bride. Almost without exception, they were of Spanish origin and belonged to a rather low social class. We find among them tenant farmers like Rosendo Carro, who married Juana de Atocha y Azcona in 1784; *pulperos* like Francisco de Oro to whom the school authorities gave in 1781 Paula de Atocha Inclán as a wife; bakers like Francisco Ocelli, who married María Casimira de Atocha y Cáceres in 1776; village teachers like Cristobal de Mora, who married María Josefa de Atocha y Machado in the same year; small merchants like Blas Rodríguez, who married María de la Asunción Atocha in 1781; debt collectors like Agustín Morales, who married María Florentina de Atocha y Ayamar in 1787; street sellers like Gabriel Solís, who married María Josefa Petronila de Atocha y Pacheco also in 1787; and a myriad of lesser employees in the complex colonial bureaucracy, people like José Aguilar, Gregorio Caycedo, and Juan Seguando Valencia, all of whom requested and obtained brides from among the foundling girls of the School of Santa Cruz, Gregorio Caycedo seems to have been one of the few suitors who approached the school authorities to ask for the hand of a specific young lady. As his petition shows, through a priest friend he had heard great things about María Dolores Atocha y Coronel, and the headmistress had informed him that María Dolores was a young lady "of good life and excellent behavior." On the basis of this information, Gregório requested her hand from the inquisitors. In view of the fact that Gregório was a well-established employee of the royal treasury, the petition was granted, and the marriage took place in 1772. Occasionally, men of a better economic position also came to Santa Cruz, but most of them were older widowers. A typical example was Gregorio Palacios, a resident of the northern city of Piura. He was an officially recognized master silversmith who owned a prosperous store in Piura. In 1782, sad and lonely after the death of his wife, Gregorio came all the way to Lima to find a wife among the girls of Santa Cruz. He eventually married María Vicenta de Atocha y Palomino.

The trustees of Santa Cruz considered the dowries given by the school as an investment in the future of stable, Christian marriages, and in the security of the foundling alumnae of the school. They obviously saw no relationship between the personal feelings of love and affection and the stability of marriage and the security of the girls. Once the students had expressed the general intention of becoming wives and mothers instead of taking the veil in a convent, the important thing was to find for them honest and decent men who were permanent residents of Peru and held good, steady jobs. Mutual and personal feelings of affection and love may have been expected to grow after the marriage, but they certainly did not play any discernible role in arranging the marriage. The school authorities did not hesitate to reject suitors who were unknown drifters or who did not have a steady, decent profession. On the other hand they did not hesitate to approve as acceptable husbands men whose motivation was totally selfish. They approved, for instance, old widowers who were looking more for an efficient housekeeper to cook and clean than for a wife to love and cherish. They also approved men who were clearly more interested in the amount of the dowry than in the girl they would marry.

Both Tomás Arcos in 1753 and Antonio Barón in 1772 obtained wives from Santa Cruz, although both of them were clearly after the dowries. Neither of them hid their feelings, and Antonio even wrote to the inquisitors that he would marry María Pascuala Alvarez de Atocha right away if her dowry was available and immediately transferrable. If the dowry was not yet available, Antonio would wait. The inquisitors did not feel that his attitude was unacceptable or unreasonable and, when the dowry became available, they gave their blessing to the marriage of Antonio and María Pascuala.[16]

Most of the dowry-granting agencies of colonial Peru tried to help the daughters of the very poor, and foundling and mestiza girls. A few of them, however, chose to grant dowries to daughters of middle-class families who could not afford to place all their daughters in "convenient" marriages for lack of sufficient funds. One such agency was the Sodality of the Immaculate Conception directed by the Franciscan friars of Lima. Respectable families of scarce means could present their daughters to the Franciscan sodality as candidates for a dowry, and once a year on the feast day of the Immaculate Conception, twelve candidates were chosen by lot and granted a dowry. This enabled them to marry well above their own social station. A typical case of this kind was the family of Don José de Mugaburu, a military man of low rank in the royal militia of Peru. Don José had a family of at least twelve children, of whom five were girls: Doña Damiana, Doña Antonia Marcela,

Doña Ana Josefa, Doña María Josefa, and Doña Margarita. One can easily imagine how Don José worried about finding suitable husbands for so many girls. In 1647, he presented his daughter Doña Damiana to the Franciscan Sodality of the Immaculate Conception as a candidate for a dowry. The following year, on November 30, a week before the feast, the Franciscans and the lay members of their sodality gathered in the convent to draw lots and award that year's dowries. Doña Damiana, at the time about thirteen years old, was one of the twelve maidens chosen in 1648, and was given a dowry of 450 *patacones,* a silver coin of one ounce. At the feast, Doña Damiana and the other eleven chosen girls took part in the solemn procession of the Immaculate Conception, which left the Franciscan convent and went through the main streets of Lima. Each girl was escorted by a gentleman of the sodality and, as they followed the float of the Virgin Mother, they were presented to the public of Lima as the worthy recipients of the Franciscan dowries. As sterling examples of Christian maidenhood, the girls were expected to follow in their married life in the footsteps of the mother of Christ, just as they followed in the procession the float of Mary under the curious gaze of relatives and friends.

Thanks to the dowry of the Franciscan sodality and to a supplement of 700 pesos received from her father, Doña Damiana was able to marry well. The groom was Don Agustín de Iparraguirre, a young and promising miner in the silver mines of Potosí. The wedding took place in Lima, on March 1, 1652, when Doña Damiana was seventeen years old, and by that marriage she entered into the prosperous class of merchants and miners of Potosí. Unfortunately, that marriage did not last long. Don Agustín died on March 1, 1658, when Doña Damiana was only twenty-two years old. The young widow did not spend much time in mourning, and less than a month after the death of her husband she married for a second time. The new husband was Don Francisco de Ribero who, for reasons which are not clear, did not prove to be acceptable to Doña Damiana. After a short marriage, Doña Damiana petitioned the ecclesiastical authorities for a decree of annulment, and her marriage to Don Francisco was dissolved.

Still in her early thirties, enjoying the fruits of her dowry, the inheritance of her first husband, and the settlement of her second marriage, Doña Damiana was ready in the late 1660s to marry for a third time. This marriage brought Doña Damiana into the upper strata of Peruvian colonial society. Her third husband was Don Diego Pardo, a maestro de campo (a high military rank), protegé of the viceroy count of Lemos, and appointed by him to the prestigious position of corregidor of Yauyos. The wedding took place on July 25, 1668, and the following month the couple left for the corregimiento of Yauyos, where Doña Damiana became the first lady of the province. She had come a long way indeed from the innocent child of a modest family, who in 1647 had applied to the charity of the Franciscans for a dowry to be able to enter into an honest and decent marriage.[17]

The availability of so many dowries clearly gave some unscrupulous males a golden opportunity to manipulate the system for their own selfish, economic motives, as evidenced by the men mentioned above, who were condemned by the Inquisition for attempting two, three, and even four marriages. Those men did not break the civil and ecclesiastical laws just for the sake of female companionship and sexual fulfillment, which were readily available in colonial Peru without marriage. In breaking the law, they were undoubtedly seeking to obtain legal control of their deceived brides' dowries.

A case that occurred in the provincial town of Huamanga in 1593 illustrates this type of unscrupulous male. The man, Diego Alonso Hermoso, had come to Peru from the viceroyalty of New Spain (Mexico), where he was already married. Diego Alonso settled in Huamanga and posed as an unattached male looking for a bride with a good dowry. Obviously the distant provincial town of Huamanga was a much better field of operation than the viceroyal capital of Lima, where he could have been easily recognized by the many merchants and royal officials who visited there from New Spain. In Huamanga, Diego Alonso finally chose his victim, Lucía Aguilar, daughter of Don Antonio de Aguilar Guerrero. After deceiving Don Antonio, Diego Alonso was granted the hand of Lucía and the wedding preparations got under way. The ecclesiastic in charge obviously ignored the directives of the councils of Trent and of Lima concerning the marriage of nonresidents, and no serious investigation was made of the previous marital status of Diego Alonso. The wedding took place, and Diego

Alonso took legal possession of Lucía's dowry: twenty mules with their harnesses, valued at 2,000 pesos; a house in Huamanga valued at 300 pesos; a city lot half a block worth 200 pesos; jewelry valued at 150 pesos; the bride's wardrobe and household furnishings; and finally a legal document empowering Diego Alonso to demand payments of debts from the creditors of the Aguilar family. It was indeed a handsome dowry for a provincial city. But the happiness of the Aguilar family turned soon to shame and sorrow, when the groom disappeared with the fruits of Lucía's dowry.

Don Antonio, Lucía's father, appealed to the tribunals of justice, and a legal inquiry was opened, which established beyond doubt that the groom had been married previously in New Spain. Diego Alonso stood now accused of theft, bigamy, sacrilege, and perjury and was sought by civil and ecclesiastical authorities. He was last seen fleeing on the road of Cuzco, attempting to vanish into the trackless backlands of upper Peru. The many cases of bigamy tried by the Inquisition of Lima are a clear indication that Diego Alonso was not the only one to engage in snatching dowries from unsuspecting brides.

Juan Antonio de Morales was another who, lured by the glitter of a new dowry, attempted a bigamous marriage and ended in the clutches of the Peruvian Inquisition. He was an Andalusian from Ecija or Seville, who had settled in Quito early in the seventeenth century, and had married Juana de Aroza. Tired of the conservative, slow pace of Quito, Juan Antonio abandoned his wife and moved to Potosí, in Upper Peru, which, because of its boundless silver mines, was becoming a great metropolis. In one of the greatest urban booms in history, Potosí was crowded with thousands of miners, merchants, silver brokers, speculators, royal officials, and countless Indian laborers. There, Juan Antonio de Morales, claiming to be single, married Marcela de Aguirre and took control of her dowry, while his lawful wife was still living in Quito. An anonymous informant accused the bigamist to the inquistadors, and Juan Antonio was taken into custody, tried, and found guilty. The Inquisition declared the marriage to Marcela null and void, exposed the bigamist to public shame in the streets of the city, and imposed on him the customary corporal punishment of a public lashing.[18]

Annulments

The church in colonial Peru always maintained and defended the Catholic doctrine of the absolute indissolubility of the marriage bond among baptized Christians. Yet, through its ecclesiastical tribunal, the Peruvian church granted thousands of "divorces" or dissolutions of marriages, which, to the eye of the layman, may have appeared as sacramental and indissoluble. The tangle of ecclesiastical legislation concerning marriage was so abundant and complex that a good lawyer, trained in canon law, could easily find enough loopholes to have any marriage declared null and void, sometimes on pure legal technicalities. A review of the data contained in the archives of the ecclesiastical tribunal of the bishopric of Lima gives the distinctive impression that, with a good lawyer, enough money, and a great deal of patience, almost any couple could obtain a decree of nullity or at least a legal separation. In the case of annulment, the parties were allowed to marry again as did Doña Damiana Mugaburu in the seventeenth century and Doña Mariana Belzunce in the eighteenth.

As early as the mid-sixteenth century, the always increasing numbers of people who flocked to the ecclesiastical tribunal in search of a dissolution or a separation began worrying the bishops of colonial Peru. In 1567, when they gathered in the viceroyal capital to attend the Second Council of Lima, the bishops issued a stern warning against the easy granting of marital dissolutions:

> *Many persons, especially women, for extremely shallow reasons and with the intention of regaining their freedom, fulfilling their lust, and avoiding the burdens of marriage, are too quick to initiate divorce proceedings. . . . We order that from now on nobody, but the bishop himself, may be allowed to hear divorce cases. The bishop may do so only for absolutely certain, rational and manifest causes. . . .*[19]

It is clear from the repeated warnings of bishops, the learned treatise of moral theologians like Avendaño, and from the sermons of colonial preachers that the problem of marital dissolutions would not go away. In fact, by the eighteenth century, the problem seems to have grown out of control. In 1711, a young French military engineer by the name of Amadée François Frézier arrived in Peru to conduct military-scientific observations. The new Bourbon rulers of Spain were concerned with the outdated fortifications and defenses of the Peruvian ports, and they expected the French military engineer to make recommendations on how to improve those defenses. Frézier also took advantage of his visit to Peru to make keen observations on the social and economic status of the viceroyalty. Although he was a rather wordly man and familiar with the changing intellectual and religious climate of Europe, Frézier was shocked and dismayed at the corruption of the institution of marriage in Spanish Peru.

It is incredible to which degree of excess they have been brought by this abuse [of easy marital dissolutions]. One sees every day people being divorced with the same easiness as if marriage were nothing more than a civil contract, [which can be dissolved] for the simple complaints of misunderstanding, lack of health, or unhappiness. Even more shocking still is that they remarry right away. This abuse has come to them from Spain. . . . The contacts experienced there with the moslems had rendered [separation and divorce] a very common occurrence. . . .[20]

A cursory examination of the records faithfully kept by the ecclesiastical tribunal of Lima substantiates Frézier's observations. Dissolutions of marital bonds were indeed common occurrences in colonial Peru and, as already observed in 1567 by the bishops of Peru, the initiators of divorce proceedings were often women— probably because they were more frequently the victims and injured parties in bad marriages. Women were also more prone to influence by religious confessors and ecclesiastical counselors, who would naturally advise them to go through regular channels in trying to solve or alleviate their marital difficulties. Many men did not seem to have cared much about the legal judgment of the ecclesiastical tribunal. When a marriage became intolerable, some of the men would simply walk out, abandon their wives, and start living with a mistress or concubine. Women, on the other hand, more loyal to the doctrine of the church and more influenced by it, would appear before the ecclesiastical tribunal and request an annulment or a legal separation.

No class of Peruvian colonial society seems to have been immune to the disruptive forces, which strained and destroyed many marriages. The ecclesiastical tribunal handled marital cases from all levels of society. Nobility, royal officials, advisors to the viceroy, judges, middle-class couples, poor Spaniards and criollos, mestizos, Indians, and black slaves can be found among those who initiated divorce procedures in the ecclesiastical tribunal of Lima. Since the wealthy could hire the best lawyers in the viceroyalty, and had the economic means to keep a case alive through years of tangled court procedures, they stood a better chance of obtaining a positive resolution to their cases. Yet, the poor, the Indians, and the slaves could always find a charitable lawyer to take their cases or have the tribunal appoint one for them. Besides, the ecclesiastical judges were expeditious and sympathetic in cases of marriages, that, unless dissolved or annulled, could present an occasion for the parties to live in sin. Once a case was brought to the tribunal, there were three possible resolutions. First, the marriage could be declared null and void and the parties free to remarry. Second, a legal separation could be granted and, although the parties could live apart, they could not remarry. Third, the marriage bond was upheld, and the married couple was urged to reconcile. Sometimes, in this third instance, the ecclesiastical tribunal, aided by the state, imposed either a fine or some other punishment on the party found guilty of disrupting the marital peace.

The most curious cases, and to Frézier and other observers the most "shocking," were the ones that ended in annulment and left the parties free to remarry. The most common ground to petition the tribunal for an annulment was the lack of consent and freedom of choice. As we have already seen, the Second Council of Lima in 1567 reaffirmed the common Catholic doctrine that for the validity of a marriage, *contrahentium libera debet esse voluntas*, the will of the contracting parties must be free. It was therefore sufficient to have a marriage annulled if one could prove to the satisfaction of the judges that one of the parties had not freely entered into the marital contract. This was the legal reasoning followed by the lawyers of Doña Mariana de Torres, Andrea de Berrio, and Doña Marianita Belzunce, when they successfully challenged the validity of their marriages before the ecclesiastical tribunal.

Hundreds of other women from all social classes used the same argument to obtain annulments, in some cases even after many years of marriage. Juana Rossa, for instance, presented her case to the tribunal in 1605. She was an Indian and married to an Indian by the name of Tomás José. Juana explained to the judges that, when she was hardly twelve years old, her father Francisco Domingo forced her, through punishments and physical abuse, to marry Tomás José. She swore that she had not freely consented to the marriage and had gone through the ceremony to avoid the paternal violence. Witnesses were called to verify the story, and finally Juana Rossa was declared free to remarry since her so-called marriage to Tomás José was null and void. Again, early in the seventeenth century and on the same grounds of lack of consent, the ecclesiastical tribunal dissolved the marriages of Catalina Rodríguez de Vargas, Catalina de León, Leonarda de las Casas, Juana de Almansa, and María de Sierra. The case of María de Sierra reveals the degree of brutality of which some relatives were capable to force a young child to marry. After María had resisted punishments and pleas, she was locked in a room with the intended groom, a man by the name of Juan Alvarez. The young girl was raped and then informed that marriage was the only way to avoid the shame of going through life as a "deflowered" maiden. When she appealed her case to the ecclesiastical tribunal, Juan Alvarez was in jail convicted of murder—a fact that hastened the resolution of her case with a decree of annulment.[21]

Although the most common, the lack of consent was by no means the only grounds to dissolve a marriage. When the legal impediment, called in canon law *"impedimentum criminis,"* was discovered and was proven in court, many other colonial marriages were dissolved by the ecclesiastical tribunal. The *impedimentum criminis,* as explained by the Peruvian moralist Diego de Avendaño, affected the validity of a marriage when the following circumstances took place: a married person had adulterous, sexual relations with a third party and promised to marry that party if the injured spouse died. If this occurred and the two persons guilty of adultery married according to the previous promise, their marriage was null and void and must be terminated by a legal action of the ecclesiastical tribunal.[22]

In 1608, a textbook case of the *impedimentum criminis* occurred in Lima. As explained by Avendaño, a society lady, Doña María Cortés, was married to Captain Don Rodrigo Martínez, but some time around the turn of the century she fell in love with Don Diego de Robles, a gentleman married to Doña Leonor de Amaya.

Doña María and Don Diego became lovers and for more than
three years carried on a secret, adulterous love affair. During that
period they promised each other that they would marry should
they ever become free by the deaths of their spouses. Doña María's
husband died early in the seventeenth century, and a few months
later Don Diego's wife died in childbirth. The adulterous lovers
spent little time in mourning. Five months after the burial of Doña
Leonor de Amaya they married in the church, hiding from the
priest the fact that they had been lovers and had given each other
the promise to marry. As far as friends and relatives were concerned, their marriage was a happy ending to a double family
tragedy, and the newlyweds began their life together with the
blessing of the church and the best wishes of their families and
friends.

The marriage may have endured except for the pangs of conscience on the part of Doña María. One day, in the secret of
confessional, she revealed to her confessor her long story of adulterous relations with Don Diego while their spouses were still alive.
Prodded by the confessor, Doña María also revealed the mutual
promise to marry, and was then informed that she had incurred
the *impedimentum criminis,* that her present marriage to Don
Diego was null and void and therefore she was living in sin. She
was advised to present her case to the ecclesiastical tribunal and
obtain a decree of nullity. Doña María followed the advice of the
confessor, and the case opened with her sworn deposition. Don
Diego was confined in the ecclesiastical jail and Doña María in her
own residence until the judges issued the decree of nullity declaring them free to remarry, but never to each other again.[23]

Other Peruvian marriages were dissolved by the ecclesiastical
judges on grounds of either total or partial impotence. The primary aim of marriage according to the doctrine of the church was
procreation. If this aim could not be fulfilled because of male
impotence, the marriage should be terminated. The ecclesiastical
authorities also considered "partial impotence" sufficient grounds
for dissolution of the marriage. Partial impotence occurred when
two specific individuals were incapable of sexual intercourse, although they may have been capable of performing the sexual act
with different partners. The case of Doña Mariana de Torres,
already described above, may have been a case of partial impotence since she was declared *non apta viro,* physically incapable of

sexual relations at that particular time and with that particular man.

In 1635, Ana Rebelledo requested a dissolution of her marriage to Martín de Montellano and gave as a reason her physical incapability to accommodate her husband sexually. From Potosí, where they lived, Ana appealed to the ecclesiastical tribunal of Lima, and through her lawyer presented her case to the ecclesiastical judges. She had been married ten years, and was only ten years old when the family married her to Martín. Their first attempt with sexual intercourse ended in excruciating pain for Ana, who became seriously ill and nearly died. The same effects had followed every time that Martín attempted to consummate the marriage. Although the records do not say so, it is clear from Ana's deposition that she was *non apta viro*.

In 1606, the ecclesiastical tribunal heard the case of Florencia Giménez, who asked for a dissolution because her husband Gaspar Durán had been impotent all his life. Gaspar Durán contested the petition of his wife, and through his lawyer explained to the tribunal that they had been married for three years, that Florencia was sixty-three years old and he himself was in his mid-fifties. The lawyer never denied the impotence of Gaspar, but tried to win the sympathy of the judges. In view of their advanced years, he said, "It was an obvious and plain thing that in getting married they were not trying to satisfy the desire for such a thing [sexual intercourse], but rather to live and cohabit in the face of Holy Mother Church." Florencia's counselor retorted that Holy Mother the Church recognized that total impotence was an impediment, which automatically annuls any marriage, and that Gaspar had always been impotent. Then, using a very graphic language that must have made the celibate judges blush, he went on to explain that Gaspar had fallen from a tree in his early youth and, as a result, "the genital organ lacks potency and strength in such a way that it cannot get an erection, and therefore the marriage cannot be consumated since the organ cannot penetrate the woman's vagina." This contention, if true, would have nullified the marriage, but the records of the case are incomplete. Perhaps Gaspar's impotence was not sufficiently proven in court, or perhaps one of the parties died before the resolution of the case.[24]

Prior to the conquest and settlement of Peru, the church had enacted a body of complex legislation prohibiting the marriage of persons related by certain degrees of consanguinity and affinity. The Council of Trent and the provincial councils of Lima had reaffirmed most of the traditional legislation that would affect the validity of the marriages of colonial Peru. Since the legislation was so abundant and complex, often only experts in canon law could determine whether some intended marriages could legally be performed or whether a dispensation from the Holy See was required. As a result of this legal complexity, it was not uncommon for some couples to discover a few months or a few years later that their marriage was null for reasons of consanguinity or of affinity. A common example was first and second cousins who had married without a dispensation and had hidden their consanguinity; they often saw their marriages annulled as soon as the impediment of consanguinity became known and proven in court. Affinity, relations by marriage, or some spiritual bonds established by the church were harder to determine. A good lawyer could find or fabricate arguments to prove affinity between spouses who wanted their marriage nullified by the ecclesiastical tribunal. In fact, in reading the documents of dissolution of marriages, it seems that a great deal of cheating and twisting of evidence was possible in handling cases affected by the ecclesiastical laws of affinity.

Around 1608, Juana Bautista asked the ecclesiastical tribunal for a dissolution and termination of her marriage to Fernando de Aguilar. They had married in the church, but the officiating priest was not aware at the time of the ceremony that Juana and Fernando were *compadres*, the spiritual relationship which, according to ecclesiastical law, tied parents and godparents of the same child. The judges were not convinced that the spiritual relationship existed between Juana Bautista and Fernando, and did not seem inclined to annul the marriage. Juana was so eager to obtain an annulment that, following a pattern already seen in other cases, she changed legal strategy. She argued through her lawyer that, if the affinity of *compadrazgo* was not conclusive, she should still obtain an annulment on grounds of *impedimentum criminis*. Juana testified under oath that during the life of her first husband, she had committed adultery with Fernando and had promised to marry him, should she become free by the death of her husband. The lady did not hesitate to have her adultery entered into the record to free herself of an unwanted marriage. The judges were more moved by this second argument, and the marriage ended in a legal separation. Eventually it was declared null and the parties free to remarry.[25]

In 1635, the ecclesiastical tribunal of Lima handled a case that reveals not only how intricate and obscure the laws of affinity could be, but also the loose moral behavior of some of the men and women in colonial Peru. The case involved a married couple, Gonzalo de Bustamante and Agustina de Ribera, who had contracted an impediment of affinity because of Gonzalo's adulterous relations with a married first cousin of Agustina's prior to their marriage. As in other cases, the sexual relations of a man with his intended wife's daughter, sister, or first cousin created, according to the legislation of the church then in force, an impediment that would automatically nullify the subsequent marriage. In 1635, Gonzalo de Bustamante appeared before the ecclesiastical tribunal and, pretending to be tortured by his conscience, requested an annulment of his marriage to Agustina de Ribera. He declared in his deposition that two years ago, before the marriage, he had frequently engaged in sexual relations with a married woman who lived in El Callao, the port city of Lima. Only recently, Gonzalo claimed, had he found that his wife and his former lover were first cousins, and that an expert in canon law had explained to him that his marriage to Agustina was null because of the blood relation between the two women. As a good, devout Christian, Gonzalo said he had no other choice but immediately to abandon his marital life and to request from the Holy Mother Church a decree of nullity. The experienced judges of the ecclesiastical tribunal did not believe Gonzalo's story or his phony scruples of conscience, and they opened an official inquiry, which lasted more than three years.

The first witness called was Agustina de Ribera herself. As the injured party, she insisted that the words of Gonzalo should not be accepted unless corroborated by independent witnesses under oath, and that Gonzalo should be legally forced to support her financially until the resolution of the case. The second witness was Agustina's first cousin, the alleged adulteress, whose name was never mentioned so that her reputation as a married woman would be protected. She confirmed that Gonzalo de Bustamante had been her lover, and that "if she would have known that Doña

Agustina de Ribera, her first cousin, was going to marry the said Gonzalo de Bustamante, she would have impeded the said marriage."

After some delays, five independent witnesses were called to testify. The first witness was the Indian Francisco de Nola, shoemaker by trade and former servant of Gonzalo de Bustamante. He testified that he used to bring the mysterious woman of El Callao to Gonzalo's house, and saw them bedding together, but did not know that the lady was married or related by blood to the future wife of Gonzalo. The second witness, the widow Doña Isabel de Guzmán, who lived for a time in the house of the alleged adulteress, testified that she used to see Gonzalo's servant come to the house with a mule and carry her friend away. Doña Isabel also testified that she was told by her landlady and friend that the mule and servant belonged to Gonzalo and that she went to his house "to sleep with him because he gave her anything she wanted." The widow finally testified that the alleged adulteress was a first cousin of the present wife of Gonzalo. The next witness, Doña Gerónima de los Angeles, confirmed the testimony of Doña Isabel de Guzmán, stressing that the love affair took place before the marriage of Gonzalo. The last two witnesses were sisters, Doña Leonor and Doña Ana de Ribera, who happened to be first cousins of both Agustina de Ribera and the lady of El Callao, with whom, as cousins and friends, they had shared confidences. Several times they heard her talking about her love affair with Gonzalo, and they were sure that the affair took place before Gonzalo's marriage to their other cousin Agustina Ribera. Moreover, the two sisters were also sure that Gonzalo had known all along the blood relationship between his present wife and his former lover. The final witness was the lady of El Callao. Once again she confirmed under oath her adulterous relationship with Gonzalo de Bustamante, but insisted that he had known all along that Doña Agustina Ribera was her first cousin.

At this point in the case, Dr. Gabriel de Alvarado the defender of the marriage bond, conceded that an impediment had existed and, therefore, the marriage should be declared null and void. Yet, he went on to accuse Gonzalo of duplicity and bad faith since, according to the testimony of several witnesses, Gonzalo had known all along of the impediment. Gonzalo's bad faith was confirmed by the fact that, even after requesting an annulment, he had tried several times to have sexual relations with Agustina de Ribera, who by his own admission was not his lawful wife. On January 7, 1639, the ecclesiastical judges issued an official decree nullifying the marriage of Gonzalo and Agustina. At the same time they found Gonzalo guilty of deceit, perjury, and adultery, and requested the help of the state to confiscate all his properties and place him under arrest.[26]

The reasons for dissolving marriages in colonial Peru were not limited to lack of consent, impotency, relationships of affinity and consanguinity, and to the notorious and frequent *impedimentum criminis*. Many other ecclesiastical laws, if not faithfully observed, could render a marriage null and void in the eyes of the church. If the officiating priest, for instance, did not have the proper license or if the attending witnesses lacked the required legal capability, the subsequent marriage was both illegal and invalid. If such a case was proven in court, the parties were declared free of any marital bonds and could remarry. The case of Ana Rodríguez, heard by the ecclesiastical tribunal of Lima in 1660, showed how the most unsuspected causes could nullify a marriage, which had appeared to be valid and to conform to all the requirements of the law.

Ana had married a mestizo, Andrés de Arébalo, after the banns of marriage had been proclaimed and no impediment had been discovered. They were both adults and freely consenting to the marriage. No affinity of consanguinity existed between them; they were physically capable of sexual intercourse; and they had not incurred the *impedimentum criminis*. Yet, after a few years of normal marital life, the ecclesiastical tribunal nullified their marriage. It turned out that Andrés had been born out of wedlock in a secluded and distant hacienda the child of a Spanish father and an Indian mother. He was raised by Indians, who never thought to have the child baptized by a priest. Andrés was therefore an "infidel and pagan," and as such legally incapable of entering into a sacramental marriage with a baptized Christian.

Other colonial marriages ended in annulments when a substantial error had been committed in clarifying the legal and social status of one of the parties. Two cases taken from the top and bottom of the social pyramid illustrate this type of annulment. In 1661, Juan Bazarrete, a mulatto and freeman, appeared before the ecclesiastical tribunal to request an annulment of his marriage to Ana María, a black woman. They had been married fourteen years, but Juan claimed that he had been deceived about the legal status of Ana María. In 1647, when the marriage took place, Juan was told that she was a free black. In fact, she was at the time, and still was in 1661, a slave owned by Doña María de Arcos, a professed nun in the convent of La Concepción. This serious deception was compounded by another. Ana María's mother, the black slave María Conga, had assured Juan that her daughter would bring to the marriage as a dowry a big jar filled with silver coins "to support him and give him a life filled with all comfort." But, during the fourteen years the jar of silver coins never materialized, and life had been far from comfortable. In fact, Juan testified that their marriage had never been consummated.

The second case of this type was brought to the tribunal by Doña Juana de Almansa in the opening years of the seventeenth century. Doña Juana, a lady of the upper class, had married Don Rodrigo Niño de Guzmán, when she was only ten years old. Her family had been eager to finalize this marriage because Don Rodrigo claimed to be the oldest son of a prominent Spanish father, Don Fernando Niño de Guzmán, and the holder of a substantial *mayorazgo* or entailed estate. Later events showed that Don Rodrigo was neither the son of Don Fernando nor the holder of a *mayorazgo,* but an unscrupulous dowry hunter ready to buy colonial wealth with his Spanish blood and name. In 1607, the ecclesiastical tribunal decided that the deception, coupled with the fact that the bride was only ten years old and unaware of the substance of the marital contract, dissolved the marriage of Doña Juana and Don Rodrigo.

The prearranged nature of most marriages, the long distances between Spanish towns, and the frequent mobility of many males created the need to perform the wedding ceremony by proxy. These marriages by proxy were subject to a series of legal conditions which, if not carefully observed, could render the marital contract invalid. In 1633, there was an elegant society wedding in Lima performed by proxy. The groom was Don Juan de Baca de Avila, a gentleman and courier attached to the household of the viceroy count of Chinchón. The bride was Doña Petronila López, a society lady. Don Juan was absent from Lima in affairs of state, and from the northern city of Paita sent a power of attorney to his friend Don Pedro Loarte to marry Doña Petronila as his proxy agent. The wedding took place June 22, 1633, with the solemnity and fanfare befitting a gentleman of the court of the viceroy and a lady of the best society of Lima. A few days after the wedding, a courier from Paita arrived in Lima bringing a new document sent by Don Juan de Baca. This new document, signed by Don Juan in Paita on April 22, two months before the wedding, revoked the power of attorney granted to Don Pedro Loarte and instructed him not to marry Doña Petronila. The bride's family was embarrassed and indignant, while lawyers and judges clashed in a long and tedious legal battle. The records of this case do not clearly show what the final resolution was, but their bulk and complexity indicate that a marriage by proxy could lead into an unmapped forest of legal contradictions, where one could be lost for years.[27]

Conclusion

It is quite clear that in colonial Peru the institution of marriage was placed under total and absolute control of the church, and that both the civil authorities and the general public accepted that control as a matter of course. The natural right to marry could not be exercised until all the conditions imposed by celibate priests and bishops were fully met. The church was indeed the sole, unchallenged judge of who could marry whom, when, how, and under what conditions. The church legislation on marriage was so abundant, so complex, and at times so esoteric and illogical that hundreds of legal loopholes could be discovered by clever attorneys to serve as escape hatches from the constraints and agonies of bad marriages. The testimony of European visitors, who were shocked by the amount and easiness of marital dissolutions in colonial Peru, is fully backed by the records faithfully kept for three hundred years by the ecclesiastical tribunal of the bishopric of Lima.

Peruvian marriages in the colonial period were also social and public agreements usually dictated by family interests, and in which the personal feelings of bride and groom barely played any discernible role. The dowry system, so entrenched in the customs and laws of the period, gave parents and relatives a unique tool for manipulating the marriages of their daughters. The child bride, neither physically nor emotionally capable of marriage, was a common and well-documented figure in colonial Peruvian society. Some Peruvian girls were used by their families like a check or a commercial letter of exchange to merge properties or to secure social and political power. Women of character and personality revolted against this intolerable situation and fought for their freedom in the ecclesiastical tribunal until they obtained a dissolution for their prearranged marriages. These pressures, exercised by relatives in the case of girls of the middle and upper class, were exercised by schools, orphanages, and private, dowry-granting agencies in the case of orphans, mestizas, and poor Spanish girls.

In Peruvian society, marriage did not serve as the normal outlet for love and romantic attachment. When it came to the affairs of the heart, the illicit lover, the mistress, and the concubine replaced the wife. Concubines, as we shall see later, were ubiquitous in colonial Peru. Yet many strong and independent women must have found the choice between a prearranged marriage and an illicit love life revolting. Thousands of them, as we shall also see later, fled the world and chose to lock themselves in the cloisters of the colonial nunneries for life. Those thousands of nuns, together with the mistresses and concubines, present perhaps the best testimony that something, at least from a female point of view, was deeply wrong with the institution of marriage in colonial Peru.

6

❦

Divorcees,
Concubines, and
Repentant Women

THE GREAT NUMBERS OF ANNULMENTS granted by the ecclesiastical tribunal of Lima was not the only sign that many women found marriage an impossible burden to bear. Thousands of other women, besides those who obtained annulments, flocked to the ecclesiastical tribunal. Knowing that they lacked the legal grounds for a complete dissolution of the marriage bonds, they petitioned the judges for a *divorcio*, which, in the legal terminology of the period, meant a legal separation. A divorcee was allowed by the church to abandon marital cohabitation while recovering the legal control of her dowry, and her husband was legally bound to pay a monthly amount for her personal support and for the support of her children. The divorcee could never remarry "in the face of the church," but at least she could lead an independent life, free from the daily constraints of an intolerable marriage.

Even a cursory review of the records of the ecclesiastical tribunal would reveal that the overwhelming majority of petitioners for *divorcios* were women, who took the responsibility of terminating their marriages upon themselves. Many of those divorcees had been forced by their families into marriages devoid of tenderness and love. They had been pawns in the social, political, and economic games played by their parents and relatives. But life gave them the courage to be themselves and terminate an arrangement not of their choice. It took indeed a great deal of courage in colonial Peru to petition for a *divorcio*. Regardless of how just and reasonable that petition was, the divorcee, as we shall see later, was wrapped in a cloud of suspicion, was subjected to harsh humiliations, and in many instances lost her status as a "respectable woman" for life. Yet thousands of women took that courageous step and chose to become *divorciadas* instead of remaining abandoned wives, battered spouses, or the second women in the lives of their husbands.

The life-style created in colonial Peru by the need to populate and colonize a vast continent did not provide a very conducive atmosphere for the stability of the family and the unity between husbands and wives. Many men were lured away by instant wealth found in distant mining camps. As early as the sixteenth century, bishops and theologians pointed out the increasing numbers of deserted wives and pleaded with the civil authorities to force husbands to return to the common, marital life. Things changed for the worse in the next one hundred years, and in the second half of the seventeenth century Diego de Avendaño had to raise his voice against an abuse, which to him was an unforgivable "crime" against the natural rights of women. Those abandoned wives, Avendaño thought, should appeal to ecclesiastical and civil authorities to force their husbands to return or to otherwise alleviate with some legal measures their ambivalent status. One of the legal avenues open to the deserted wife was to petition the ecclesiastical tribunal for a divorce, which gave her back the legal control of her dowry and forced the husband to provide suitable financial support. Hundreds of women followed this course of action, and the ecclesiastical tribunal did not hesitate to grant the divorce when all other means to bring about the reunion of the spouses had failed. A few specific cases of *divorciadas* may serve to illustrate the mechanics of obtaining a *divorcio* in the colonial days.

Doña Beatriz de Vera and Doña María Josefa Duarte lived in the seventeenth century on the fringes of the viceroyalty of Peru in Santiago del Estero and Asunción, respectively. Both had suffered years of desertion and loneliness, and both had tried to persuade their husbands to return to marital life. The letters they wrote to their absent spouses are filled with tenderness and affection, with loving allusions to the home and to the small, daily events of the family. They revealed that Doña Beatriz and Doña María Josefa were both well-educated and refined women. Yet, their letters failed to move the husbands to return home. Unable to resolve their problems by themselves and, probably advised by their confessors, the women turned to the ecclesiastical authorities. Doña María Josefa was quite specific and clear in a letter written to her husband from Asunción on July 31, 1686: "If in spite of the affection with which I write this letter, I fail to persuade you to return; I shall have resource to the censures of His Lordship the Bishop. . . ." Doña María Josefa knew well that in the legal system of the Spanish colonial empire only the bishop's tribunal had the authority to handle cases related to the institution of marriage. One may assume that with that warning the process of her divorce was begun by the bishopric of Asunción.

A much more interesting and revealing case is the marriage and subsequent divorce of Doña Juana Maldonado de Aro and Don Juan Andrés Picón y Bicueta. Both of them came from prominent, wealthy families, and their case dragged through the ecclesiastical tribunal for more than twenty years. They must have married by family arrangement around 1610, when Juana was in her early teens. She brought to the marriage a dowry of more than eight thousand pesos, and Juan Andrés had the authority and prestige of an important royal position in the government of the city of Panamá. Shortly after the marriage, Don Juan returned to Panamá, and for reasons that are not clear Doña Juana remained in Lima. The absence was prolonged for several years, during which Don Juan's career prospered in Panamá. He was chosen as a member of the city council and was appointed *procurador general* of the isthmian town to represent Panamá officially in all its dealings with the Spanish crown and with the viceroyal authorities. As the years went by, it became clear that in spite of the pleas of his wife, Don Juan had no intentions of returning to Lima or of giving up his successful career in Panamá. The abandoned wife finally appealed to the ecclesiastical tribunal and asked for a decree of annulment, which was denied by the ecclesiastical judges because of lack of proper legal grounds. Doña Juana then changed her petition and requested this time a *divorcio* or legal separation. The slow wheels of the ecclesiastical bureaucracy then began moving in a lengthy process of depositions, examination of witnesses, appeals, and counterappeals. The need to coordinate the process in Lima with the ecclesiastical authorities of Panamá, and the powerful friends of Don Juan in the isthmus explain, in part, why the legal battle was waged across half a continent for two decades without reaching an agreement satisfactory to both parties. Then, around 1634, a breakthrough occurred which brought about the final resolution of the case.

Don Juan Andrés Picón y Bicueta arrived in Lima in official business in the mid-1630s. His presence in the city gave the ecclesiastical tribunal the opportunity to force him into an agreement with his estranged wife. First of all, the ecclesiastical judges issued orders to all ship captains in the route Callao-Panamá not to give passage to Don Juan Andrés until his marital case was resolved to the satisfaction of the tribunal. The judges also appealed to the civil authorities not to allow Don Juan Andrés to leave Lima by any other means. Once his presence in the city was secure, the tribunal heard a new appeal by Doña Juana Maldonado de Aro. Her demand this time was crystal clear: Don Juan Andrés should resume immediate cohabitation and marital life with her, or else agree to a *divorcio* by which she would recover the control of her dowry. In addition, she was to receive two thousand pesos to enter as a nun in the convent of La Concepción. The tribunal acquiesced to this petition, and ordered Don Juan Andrés "within twenty-four hours . . . [to] begin marital life with Doña Juana Maldonado, his wife, and that he should do this in virtue of holy obedience and under penalty of major excommunication. . . ." Then the tribunal softened its order by presenting the alternative of a *divorcio* under the conditions requested by Doña Juana. Don Juan Andrés chose the *divorcio* and, after signing a legal document transferring two thousand pesos to Doña Juana, was allowed to return to Panamá. His now divorced wife entered the cloister of La Concepción to lead the celibate life of a nun.[1]

Another example of *divorcio* or legal separation brought about by the desertion of the husband was the case of Doña María Fernández de Zuñiga, also a prominent and well-known lady of Lima. Doña María had married Don Lorenzo de Ulloa y Cabrera, corregidor or governor of Parinacocha, under circumstances which reveal how the "virtue" of a woman was a matter of *pundonor* or point of honor for an entire family, and how a woman's life could be manipulated by the male relatives in order to maintain the family honor and reputation. Some time in the first half of the sixteenth century, the father of Doña María, Don Pedro de Zuñiga, was appointed the new corregidor of Parinacocha to succeed in the office Don Lorenzo de Ulloa y Cabrera, his future son-in-law.

One of the first duties of the new corregidor was to open the residencia or legal review of his predecessor's term of office. Like most corregidores, Don Lorenzo was probably guilty of abuses against the Indians and of misappropriation of funds because he began a subtle campaign to neutralize the judicial inquiry of his residencia.

Almost daily he dropped by the house of Don Pedro de Zuñiga to play cards and to entertain him with his witty conversation in the long hours of that remote province. Don Lorenzo also began paying special attention to the young Doña María de Zuñiga, bringing her presents, amusing her with the tall tales of his adventures in Parinacocha, and hinting in a flirtatious way that she could make somebody a perfect wife. Eventually Don Lorenzo and Doña María had an affair, and Doña María gave birth to a girl, who died shortly after. The Zuñiga family was stunned. The father, Don Pedro de Zuñiga, and two brothers, Don Juan and Don Luís de Zuñiga, took custody of Don Lorenzo de Ulloa and threatened his life unless he cleanse the stain on the family honor by marrying Doña María immediately.

Knowing well that it was either marriage or death, Don Lorenzo agreed to marry Doña María under two conditions. First, Doña María should bring a dowry sufficient to cover all his debts in the amount of fourteen thousand pesos; second, the judicial inquiry of the residencia should be suspended or whitewashed. Don Pedro de Zuñiga had no problem with the first condition, but he was furious about the second, which to him was clearly against his honor as a royal official. Only the intervention of some Dominican friars, friends of the Zuñiga family, saved a new confrontation and helped the two parties to reach a compromise. The marriage of Doña María and Don Lorenzo was finally celebrated and blessed by the church around 1628.

The Ulloa-Zuñiga marriage was obviously an economic and political deal arranged by family males with the help of a group of zealous friars. From the very beginning, it had all the characteristics of a marriage bound to end in failure. As soon as his affairs in Parinacocha were settled, Don Lorenzo abandoned his wife and went to live by himself in the booming mining town of Huancavelica. Huancavelica was producing a river of mercury, and great fortunes were being made in the mining of quick silver. Don Lorenzo de Ulloa became a royal official and prosperous miner in Huancavelica and tried to forget all the unpleasant events of Parinacocha. Six years had passed since the celebration of the marriage, when in 1634 Doña María de Zuñiga asked the ecclesiastical tribunal of Lima for a legal separation on grounds of desertion. The tribunal issued orders to Don Lorenzo immediately to resume his marital life with Doña María and, when Don Lorenzo failed to obey, imposed on him the harsh, ecclesiastical penalty of excommunication. After its failure to reconcile the spouses, the ecclesiastical tribunal went on with the legal process of arranging a *divorcio*.

A decree of annulment seems to have been possible at that point, but Doña María insisted that she was "a lawful wife of high social status," and that her estranged husband should agree to an equitable financial arrangement with her. The judges went along with the desires of Doña María, and a sentence of separation was finally issued. Don Lorenzo and Doña María were allowed by the church to lead their own separate lives but could not remarry as long as one of them was alive. Don Lorenzo was bound by the decree of separation to provide a house for Doña María to live in, a slave girl to serve her for life, and seven hundred and fifty pesos a year for her support. With this agreement, the daughter of the corregidor of Parinacocha became a *divorciada* and led a rather lonely and secluded life in a society where only the housewife and the consecrated virgin were considered "normal."[2]

Desertion was not the only, or even the most frequent, cause of colonial divorces. Family violence and physical abuse appeared with monotonous regularity in the records of the ecclesiastical tribunal as one of the main reasons for requesting a legal separation. Spanish Peru was born out of the violence of the conquest and of the civil wars; the ever-expanding frontier had an edge of harshness and brutality noticed by many colonial observers; many mining towns like Potosí exploded periodically into orgies of senseless violence; thousands of Indians were kept submissive by brute force; and even the church and the schools approved physical punishment as an acceptable means of teaching youngsters and keeping the purity of the faith among the general population. Within this general climate, the stability of the family was frequently threatened by the onslaughts of violent behavior. No social class seems to have been immune to this problem, and the ecclesiastical judges granted *divorcios* on grounds of physical abuse to members of the nobility, royal officials, middle-class criollos, poor Spaniards, Indians, and blacks.

Two noble families who were destroyed by violence and physical abuse were the familes of the admiral of the fleet Don Juan de Reynoso and the family of Don Antonio de Leyba, father of the marqués del Lago. Admiral Don Juan de Reynoso was brought to court in 1612 by his wife Doña Ana de la Torre, who under oath and backed by the testimony of witnesses told the judges the following tale of horrors. Don Juan did not share the marital bed and even refused to sit at the family table with Doña Ana, and he frequently struck and kicked her. Several times, blind with hate and anger, the admiral had run after her with a rapier in his hand, and only the intervention of relatives and servants had saved her life. Don Juan had also thrown the children out of the house, and in the process had seriously wounded one of them. A notorious scandal was caused in the city. He had sworn, moreover, to kill Doña Ana and had stolen her jewels and wardrobe, disposing of them without her permission.

The presiding ecclesiastical judge, Dr. de la Vega, knew that the life of Doña Ana was in danger and acted immediately. He summoned the *alguacil*, a royal official in charge of public order, and gave him instructions to proceed without delay to the house of the admiral and take Doña Ana under his protection in the name of the king and of the church. He was to bring her to the house of a friend, Doña Elvira Bravo, where Doña Ana was to be sheltered until the process of divorce was finished. Dr. de la Vega also imposed the penalty of excommunication on Don Juan and forced him to send sixty pesos every month to his wife and provide her with the services of two of the family slaves. Once these urgent measures were taken, the legal action continued with the slowness typical of the colonial bureaucracy. Doña Ana de la Torre, worn out by her sufferings, passed away in the house of her friend Doña Elvira Bravo a few months later, before her divorce proceedings were finalized by the ecclesiastical tribunal.[3]

In a similar case a century later, the nobleman Don Antonio de Leyba was accused in 1701 of physical abuse and had to face a demand of divorce presented by his wife Doña Costanza Rojas. After years of conflict within the family, Don Antonio was ready to abandon his wife and children and exile himself to the kingdom of Chile. When Doña Costanza objected, she was physically abused by her husband. Soon a pattern of verbal and physical abuse developed in the behavior of Don Antonio, who, at times, exploded even in public. Eventually, in anger Don Antonio ransacked the private rooms of Doña Costanza, ruining the furniture, throwing out her dresses, and stealing her jewelry and silver. Convinced that a peaceful solution was impossible, Doña Costanza chose to become a *divorciada* and took all the steps required by the ecclesiastical tribunal to obtain a decree of legal and permanent separation from Don Antonio.[4]

As one moves from the upper class into the middle and poor Spanish class and into the *castas* of mestizos, mulattos, and blacks, the frequency and intensity of physical violence as a justification for divorce seem to increase. It also becomes apparent from the testimony of many battered wives that physical abuse was more a symptom than a cause in the break up of many colonial marriages. Testifying in her divorce proceedings in 1609, Isabel de Zamudio explained to the judges that she had been married for four years and had been constantly beaten by her husband Cristóbal de la Barrera, an employee in one of the city pastry shops. She brought to the marriage a dowry of 2,546 persos, which Cristóbal had been squandering in gambling, drinking, and perhaps in other women. When Isabel objected and tried to stop the dissipation of the family income, Cristóbal beat her, inflicting serious injuries.

Cristóbal's answer to these accusations, an answer never challenged either by the prosecutor or by the judges, reveals the cavalier attitude of some husbands toward the occasional physical punishment of a wife. Cristóbal did not deny that he had beaten Isabel, but tried to justify his actions by saying that "if some times I had put my hands on her, it would had been with moderation and in the spirit of correcting some of her imperfections and trying to scare her a little, which is permissible to a husband according to the law." By not challenging such a statement, the men involved in the case seem to have agreed that an occasional, "moderate" beating of a wife was, after all, perfectly all right.

Catalina Daza, who asked for a divorce in 1608, had the same problem as Isabel de Zamudio. She was beaten by her husband Alonso de Avila, and again the cause was money. Catalina was fifty years old and very well off when she married Alonso, a younger and poor Spaniard. He began to misuse his wife's wealth. When Catalina tried to stop his reckless spending, she was slapped, kicked, knocked about, and beaten with a cane. Lucía de Cárdenas was also a battered wife whose money was the root of her problem. Her husband, Antonio de Cevallos, did not support the family, and Catalina kept a small store in Lima to make ends meet. He was always demanding money and tried to steal merchandise from the store. Lucía was beaten every time she refused to give him money or tried to stop him from taking merchandise out of the store.[5]

Although money disagreements between the spouses were frequently the origin of violence and physical abuse, they were by no means the only cause of this type of disruptive behavior. The testimonies and depositions of many battered wives showed that, at times, the problem was caused by the husband's excessive drinking, by sexual problems and incompatibility between the spouses, by marital infidelities, by the disruptive influence of in-laws, and by deep disagreements on how to deal with children and servants and how to govern the household. Whatever the causes of physical abuse within the family, once a case was proven, the ecclesiastical tribunal always acted quickly to protect and shelter the victim of the violence and always considered physical abuse sufficient grounds to grant a divorce. The battered wife always found a sympathetic ear in the ecclesiastical tribunal, which seldom raised any major objection to the legal separation of the spouses. With the help of the civil authorities, the tribunal went even further by frequently throwing the aggressor into jail, by imposing on him the feared penalty of ecclesiastical excommunication, and by forcing him to support his estranged wife.

The above comments on battered spouses would be incomplete without pointing out that colonial Peru had also its own cases of husbands physically abused by their wives. The strong and unscrupulous female Don Juans, who in their private life ignored the accepted social customs, the doctrine of the church, and the laws of the state, did not disappear from Peru with the soldaderas and campfollowers of the conquest period. Some of those women, in their eagerness to live their own lives without restraint, did not hesitate to abandon their husbands. These abandonments sometimes led to violent confrontations. Two such women were Feliciana Barreto de Castro and Antonia de Solorzano, both of whom were accused by their husbands before the ecclesiastical tribunal of infidelity and physical abuse.

The husband of Feliciana was Francisco de Velasco, who in 1703 presented a demand for a legal separation claiming that marital life with Feliciana had become unbearable. His deposition under oath reveals the sad story of a man almost driven to despair. Feliciana, it seems, hated him and their life in common and consistently denied him his marital rights. She had destroyed his honor and reputation in the city so that Francisco was ashamed to present himself in public. Feliciana had established a liaison with a local man, Juan de Dios de Lumbreras, and both of them had attacked Francisco on the road from Lima to Callao. Francisco was beaten and left wounded by the roadside. Feliciana had tried to stone him to death, and on another occasion, with the help of her friend, had attacked Francisco with a sword and had unleashed a pack of wild dogs on him. After this last experience, which almost caused his death, Francisco pleaded with the ecclesiastical judges to grant him a quick divorce from Feliciana.

The case of Antonia Solorzano is very similar to the one of Feliciana but with the added complication that Antonia was a slave and her husband Francisco de Añasgo was a free man. Thanks to the help and protection of her master and owner Don Francisco de Solorzano, Antonia got away with violence and abuse for years. In 1703, Francisco de Añasgo put an end to his misery by accusing Antonia before the ecclesiastical judges and requesting an immediate divorce. His frustration was obvious when he explained to the judges that, if the divorce was not granted soon, he may have to kill Antonia and thus jeopardize his eternal salvation.[6]

Concubines

Although hundreds of divorces were granted by the ecclesiastical authorities because of desertion, physical abuse, and total incompatibility of the spouses, marital infidelity was also extremely prevalent and seemed to have permeated all other grounds of divorce. There is nothing unique about those Peruvian marriages destroyed by marital infidelity. What makes the case of colonial Peru peculiar is that the illicit sexual relations between the sexes were perceived and reported by the church, by civil authorities, and by many European observers as a widespread social disease, which was so common and habitual that it was accepted as normal by a large segment of society. The problem was, as seen by the defenders of the monogamous character of marriage, not the human weakness of spouses who may have occasionally indulged in illicit, extramarital affairs, but the many men and women who "kept" unlawful sexual partners and lived with them in an imitation of a legal marriage. The problem, in other words, was not the lover, but the concubine.

The concubine was even more visible in the colonial cities of Peru than the child bride, the deserted spouse, and the battered wife. Frequently a sensuous mulatta or mestiza, occasionally an exotic morisca or a black slave, the concubine ignored the religious and legal tenets of her society and flaunted her dubious status without shame. She captured the heart and fired the imagination of hundreds of men, whose marriages were, at best, dull, stultifying social arrangements. The ubiquitousness and acceptance of the concubine does not need to be explained, as some European critics tried, by some inner, moral decadence prevalent in the new world. Rather, it is explained by the unique cultural and social characteristics of Spanish Peru.

Most colonial marriages began as social and political deals arranged by families, not as the normal outlets for sexual attraction and personal affection. Art and literature had exalted romantic love and, in the minds of many men, had transformed women into elusive creatures of unearthly perfection and beauty. When the longings for love, affection, and sexual satisfaction were not, or could not be, realized within the structures of marital life, individuals tended to look elsewhere for that fulfillment. In Spanish Peru, there was a large population of mestizas, mulattas, Indians, and black women with a low social and economic status. These women were easily manipulated by aggressive and wealthy males and provided the perfect outlet for the romantic and sexual longings of many frustrated men. The wives were the mothers and the social companions. The concubines were, to use an expression often repeated in colonial documents, the "women of love."

In the 1560s, only thirty years after the conquest, the ecclesiastical authorities of Peru were shocked and amazed by the widespread practice of concubinage. In 1567, the prelates that gathered in Lima under the leadership of Archbishop Don Gerónimo de Loaysa to open the Second Council of Lima, agreed that concubinage was one of the most common and most serious moral

problems in the emerging Spanish society of Peru. They also took
notice that women were not always the victims of this unethical
practice, but that in many instances women were the originators
and defenders of a way of life seen by the bishops as contrary to
the ideals of Christian womanhood. Their words, taken from the
twenty-second chapter of the Council Acts and already quoted
above, merit a further reflection on our part:

> . . . *similiter quam plures mulieres quae propiis relictis viris, aliis
> nupserunt, et ut licentiose and impudice vivere possint, hominem
> eligunt, quem nunc virum, nunc fratrem, aliquando consanguineum,
> numquam tamen concubinum appellant.*[7]

What the bishops of Peru are saying in describing the conditions
of the viceroyalty in 1567 is that "many women had abandoned
their own husbands and joined themselves to others. In order to
live licentiously and shamelessly they had chosen themselves a
man, whom they call either spouse, or brother, or blood relative,
but never lover or male concubine." The Peruvian bishops, following strict interpretation of the Catholic doctrine on marriage,
dreamed of a permanent, monogamous marriage, in which sexual
relations were justified only in order to procreate, and in which
the wives would strive to combine their motherhood with a saintly
way of life. By their beliefs and celibacy, the bishops were not able
to understand, much less to condone, the many female Don Juans,
who chose a man with whom to live a life of love and sexual
fulfillment. The bishops took the only course of action open to
them within the strict moral standards of the church: they forbade
concubinage under severe ecclesiastical penalties, including excommunication. The council also appealed to the state to use force
to break up those illicit unions and to induce the concubines to
return to their lawful husbands or to lead continent lives. During
their meetings in the council, those intelligent men of goodwill
did not show any awareness of the psychological and social forces
that made concubinage flourish in Spanish Peru.

The warnings and threats of the Second Council of Lima against
concubinage were repeated by ecclesiastical authorities and echoed
by the preachers and confessors of the viceroyalty in the seven-

teenth and eighteenth centuries with little visible result. In their reports to the Spanish crown on the status of the viceroyalty, not only the bishops, but the viceroys themselves kept referring to the widespread phenomenon of concubinage and its adverse effects on the moral fabric of colonial society. Some viceroys, like Don Juan de Mendoza in 1615, tried to find an explanation for a practice they were unable to endure.

Don Juan de Mendoza, marqués de Montesclaros, thought that the lack of enough Castilian women in the early years of colonial Peru, and their excessive numbers shortly thereafter had something to do with the problem of concubinage. At the beginning, the marqués thought, many Spanish men took Indian and black concubines simply because they could not find suitable Castilian wives. Later, the overabundance of Castilian women elicited in the men a feeling of boredom, while the Indian and the exotic mestiza and mulatta appeared to them as much more desirable sexual partners. Other viceroys, like Don Baltasar de la Cueva, count of Castellar from 1674 to 1681, limited themselves to fighting the type of concubinage which was both "public and scandalous." In other words, the problem was large and complex, and, although the church rightly condemned all kinds of concubinage, the royal officials concentrated on suppressing those cases that caused public scandal. Since a great number of people accepted concubinage, the royal officials were undoubtedly hard pressed to make a case of public scandal.[8]

It is clear from the testimony of the French scientist Amadée Frézier that in the eighteenth century concubinage was still very common in the viceroyalty of Peru and was accepted by most people as a normal way of life. The sophisticated Frenchman was amazed to observe the loose sexual mores prevalent in colonial Peru, and to see that the average man was "generous without measure" toward women. Writing more specifically about concubinage, Frézier informed his countrymen that:

> . . . *ils se marient generalement tous derrière l'Église, c'est à dire sont tous engagez dans un honnête concubinage, qui chez eux n'a rien de scandaleux: bien loin de lá c'est une honte de n'être pas amancebé. . . .*[9]

(. . . they all get married generally behind the back of the Church, which means that they are all involved in an honest concubinage, which among them is not considered scandalous. On the contrary, it is considered a shame to live without a concubine. . . .)

As if trying to explain why he calls that common arrangement "an *honest* concubinage," Frézier goes on to say that in Peru this illicit arrangement has the stability and mutual fidelity one would except in marriages approved and blessed by the church. The Don Juan-macho mentality is obviously implied, when Frézier notes that in colonial Peru, it was considered some kind of social shame to be without one's own concubine. The French observer also noted, as many others had before him, that the majority of the concubines were women of the lower classes: mestizas, mulattas, and black women.

In the closing years of the eighteenth century, the issue of concubinage was still eliciting the attention of the Spanish crown and of the leaders of the viceroyalty. As late as 1789, the Spanish king, always concerned with the spiritual welfare of his distant subjects, directed the viceroy, the governors, and the royal judges to use all the authority of the secular arm in helping the church to eradicate the vices of poligamy and concubinage. The royal orders were sent to all the tribunals of Peru and were duly acknowledged by the presiding judges, but they probably had little visible effect at that late date.

Two years later, in 1791, the intellectual leaders of the Peruvian enlightenment and editors of the *Mercurio Peruano* held a discussion in their editorial office to clarify the nature of love and its relationship to marriage and to concubinage. The discussion reveals a new enlightened understanding of the dignity and rights of women, while rejecting the Don Juan mentality as demeaning to both men and women. The editors of the *Mercurio* concluded in their discussion that concubinage and true love were two incompatible realities and therefore, could not exist together. In an article published on January 23, 1791, the editors commited themselves to defending and upholding the honor and dignity of women. They poked fun at the Don Juans who dressed in silks, covered themselves with perfumes, and flaunted their machismo through the streets and plazas of Lima, and finally concluded that:

the love born in an illicit environment or from any other criminal source is not love: it is rather a savage and despicable passion, which will never find a place in an honest and refined heart. An infamous concubinage is incompatible with true tenderness because true tenderness can not rest unless on an object of esteem. The concubine elicits contempt even at the moment of drawing you to her. Would it be possible to love a person, whom one must see from a disgusting point of view, contrary to religion and honor? Vice, human weakness, and at times too much leisure draws us to such creatures but, as soon as reason resumes its command over the senses, we despise them.[10]

This quotation shows that concubinage was still common at the end of the eighteenth century. Yet, the best secular minds of the viceroyalty had begun to realize that concubinage was a social malaise and should not be accepted as a matter of course. The words of the editors of the *Mercurio Peruano* unfortunately came too late to alter the over-all picture of Peruvian colonial society, where concubinage was already an established pattern.

The presence of a concubine, as indicated above, was frequently the hidden cause of all kinds of marital problems. These problems led many colonial wives to request and obtain a divorce. A careful examination of the records of the ecclesiastical tribunal in divorce cases reveals that in many instances physical abuse, desertion, lack of support, and irreconcilable differences concerning family finances could be traced back to the presence of another woman in the lives of many husbands. Yet, divorce records also reveal that the words of the Peruvian bishops in 1567 were well grounded in facts: many women of the lower class did indeed abandon their lawful husbands to become the concubines of more powerful and wealthier men. Margarita de Argandona, Francisca Gómez, Isabel Vela, Luísa Conga, and María de Salas were a few of those wives-turned-concubines who, accused by their own husbands, found themselves in trouble with the ecclesiastical tribunal.

Margarita de Argandona was an attractive mulatta and a slave owned by Juan Antonio Serisa, a small merchant of Lima. She married Marcos de Rosso, who bought her freedom for eight hundred pesos. The marriage fell apart when Margarita abandoned her husband and went to live as the concubine of her former owner. The heartbroken husband appealed to the ecclesiastical tribunal, which with the help of the state took Margarita into custody and placed her in the Hospital of La Caridad as ward of the tribunal. That same night Margarita fled the hospital and met Juan Antonio in the outskirts of Lima, and the two lovers went to live together in the town of Pisco, far from the reach of the Lima authorities. When they returned to Lima several months later, hoping that their case had been forgotten, Margarita was recognized and taken again into custody. This time she was thrown in the women's jail, but by the goodness of her husband, Marcos de Rosso, she was transferred to the more confortable convent of Santa Catalina. This time the ecclesiastical tribunal imposed an automatic penalty of excommunication should she abandon the convent without permission.

Neither the kindness of her husband nor the severity of the tribunal made an impression on Margarita. Days later she climbed the fence of the cloister and disappeared once more with her lover Juan Antonio into the backlands of Peru. Condemned by the church and sought by the state, Margarita de Argandona exemplified the Peruvian concubine, fearless and aggressive, who defied civil and religious authority to live her own life as she saw fit.[11]

Francisca Gómez, also a mulatta, had been the lawful wife of the bricklayer Cristóbal Gómez for twenty years. She drank in excess, was known as a borracha, and had a history of more than a decade of concubinage with different men. Luísa Conga was also, like Margarita de Argandona, a black slave and the concubine of her master Don Lorenzo de los Rios. Through the years their illicit relationship had caused all kinds of problems in the marriage of Don Lorenzo to Doña Juana de Mora. In 1637, she appeared before the ecclesiastical tribunal with a demand of divorce. The legal separation was granted, and the concubine Luísa Conga ended up in jail while the wife Doña Juana was allowed to enter one of the nunneries of Lima as a divorcee. For eight years Isabel de Vela was the concubine of her own brother-in-law, the silk merchant Lorenzo Guarnido. The wronged wife and sister of Isabel, Ana María de Vela, began divorce proceedings in 1637 and obtained a legal separation after having the two lovers placed in jail. María de Salas was the wife of the furniture maker Marcos Ramírez. She had abandoned her home more than twelve times to live freely with different lovers and had been caught in adultery by her own husband. In 1703, when she robbed her husband's shop with one of her lovers, María was accused before the tribunal, which took steps to grant Marcos a legal separation.[12]

Peruvian colonial society may have had a rather sympathetic and lax attitude toward concubinage, but when a case had become "notorious and scandalous," the civil and ecclesiastical authorities had no other choice than to intervene and to impose all the force of the law. Scandal and notoriety tended to occur more frequently when married women, like the five just mentioned, abandoned their lawful husbands and went to live openly with their male lovers. Another concubine, whom the church and the state could hardly ignore, was the "clerical concubine," if one may use such an expression, who was more prone to raise eyebrows, to cause serious scandal, and to become the target of social criticism. The widespread nature of clerical concubinage in the viceroyalty of Peru was not an invention of the enemies of the church, but a fact sadly recognized by the ecclesiastical authorities themselves. Although the regular clergy (members of the religious orders) seem to have been generally faithful to the vow of celibacy, the secular clergy produced, with disturbing consistency, clerics who habitually lived in concubinage.

Yet, one must not be too harsh in condemning those men. For the most part, the secular cleric of colonial Peru had received little education and training, lived most of his life by himself without the protective aid of a community and cloister, and celibacy was for him not an obligation emanating from a religious vow, but a legal condition imposed by the church in order to become a cleric. While the regular clergy usually led comfortable lives, the secular cleric was poor and tended to see his clerical office as the only road open to him to economic well-being and social acceptability. When such a cleric was discreet about his concubinage and led otherwise a responsible life, most people, and even at times his religious superiors, tended to ignore the presence of the concubine. Unfortunately, there were exceptions to the discreet and responsible cleric. The secular clergy produced many clerical Don Juans, who made a mockery out of clerical celibacy by flaunting their concubines in public, becoming involved with married women, or forcing young maidens to live with them. In such cases, ecclesiastical authorities could be extremely harsh. All kinds of severe penalties were imposed on them, including long periods of incarceration. The clerical concubine could also suffer a great deal of social rejection and seldom escaped without some ecclesiastical penalty, usually a period of internment in a reform institution.

Juana Delgado, Antonia de Espinosa, Ana María de los Reyes, María de Alarcón, Francisca "China," Juana de Lasarte, Ana de Escobar, María Cabezudo, Luísa de Revelo, and Yolanda Messias were all clerical concubines of the seventeenth century. Juana Delgado was a single woman, twenty-six years old, and since she was allowed to use the honorific title of Doña, obviously from a prominent family. In 1630, she was accused of being the public concubine of the cleric Gerónimo de Antesana, and the accuser specified that it was public knowledge that Juana and the cleric "slept in one bed, and ate at one table." The testimony of several witnesses unfolded before the ecclesiastical tribunal the story of the love between Juana and Gerónimo. Gerónimo de Antesana was, at the time, thirty-three years old, and a poor cleric without any means of self support. A morisca named María de Antesana, who was a former slave of the cleric's father and owned at the time a small boardinghouse in Lima, took Gerónimo in and provided him with free room and board. Doña Juana Delgado was also a boarder in the morisca's house, and there she became the lover and companion of Gerónimo. She had the tacit and sympathetic approval of María de Antesana, who probably had some kind of motherly attachment to the son of her former master. In spite of the suspicious arrangement, Gerónimo denied any immoral behavior, but the ecclesiastical judges found him guilty of concubinage and incarcerated him in the diocesean jail. Doña Juana was also removed from the boardinghouse and placed under custody in a cloister founded for the reformation of loose women.[13]

Another case, that of Antonia de Espinosa, was brought to the attention of the ecclesiastical judges by her own husband Francisco de Espinosa. He was a tributary Indian of the village of La Concepción de Paucartambo in the distant province of Tarma. Francisco explained to the tribunal that the parish priest of Paucartambo, Don Juan Tamayo, had taken his wife Antonia away and had been living with her for more than four years. The sinful concubinage between Antonia and the priest was well known in the region of Tarma and had caused a great deal of scandal among the Indians of the village. Unable to persuade Antonia to break the relationship and return to him, Francisco de Espinosa appealed to the ecclesiastical authorities of Lima to take legal action against Don

Juan Tamayo and against the adulterous wife. After months of delay, Antonia was finally taken from the home of the priests of Paucartambo to be "deposited in a safe location" unknown to Don Juan.

Ana María de los Reyes was a young mulatta and daughter of Catalina María de Medina. In 1650, the mother denounced the priest Matías de Vicuña for having an illicit relationship with her daughter. According to her deposition to the tribunal, Catalina María had been making plans for her daughter Ana María to enter a nunnery as a maid of one of the professed nuns of the convent. Under the pretext of helping the girl to obtain admission into the convent, and with the help of some of his friends, the priest befriended Ana María and tried to persuade her to move into his house. He obviously succeeded; by 1650, Catalina María could affirm under oath that Matías "has stolen my daughter from me, took her into his house and under his power, has deflowered her, and has robbed her of her virginity. . . ." When the ecclesiastical judges conducted an investigation of the case, they found Ana María living as the concubine of Matías de Vicuña. They had no choice but to place the priest in jail and Ana María into a convent.

Francisca "China" was a young woman of oriental descent, who had probably been brought to Lima by some merchants in the famous Acapulco-Manila trading route. In 1667, she had been living for eight years as the concubine of the cleric Bernardo López de Urteaga and had at least two children by him. Bernardo made no secret of their relationship. He was frequently seen taking his children for walks through the streets and plazas of Lima. The notoriety and scandal of this concubinage had reached a point that the tribunal had no choice but to take judicial action against Francisca and Bernardo.[14]

María de Alarcón was the beautiful black concubine of the cleric Martín de Medrano, by whom she had a daughter. María was not only black, but also a slave owned by Captain Don Cristóbal de Alarcón, who in 1642 reported to the ecclesiastical authorities that the cleric had had for seven years "an illicit friendship" with his slave María. What prompted the captain to come forward and accuse the cleric was not the illicit friendship, but the fact that Martín de Medrano had stolen the slave and was keeping her in hiding. The judges called six witnesses in the case, all of them also slaves of Don Cristóbal. The first witness was a female slave

by the name of Mariana, who confirmed under oath the illicit,
sexual relationship between the cleric and María de Alarcón and
the existence of a daughter. She went on to say that the cleric was
in the process of mortgaging his chaplaincy to obtain the money
needed to buy the freedom of María and her daughter. This fact
seems to indicate that Martín de Medrano saw in María something
more than an easily available sexual partner. The other five witnesses, María and Juan Barreto, Juan Ignacio, Isabel Terranova,
and Antonio Biafra, confirmed the story in their testimony before
the tribunal. Isabel Terranova must have been a close friend of
María de Alarcon's and perhaps an accomplice of the two lovers,
because she was the only one to assure the judges of having seen
with her own eyes Martín and María sleeping together in the same
bed.

After taking the testimony of all the above witnesses, the judges
issued an order for the imprisonment of Martín de Medrano. He
ended up in the episcopal jail. He was nevertheless allowed to tell
his own side of the story and to present his own witnesses. Martín
finally escaped with a slight slap on the wrists, perhaps because
all the prosecution witnesses were slaves of the accuser, and Don
Cristóbal himself had complained not of the illicit friendship, but
of the stealing of the slave. The cleric was set free after returning
the slave, and he was given a stern warning: "from now on he
should never be together, deal, or communicate neither in public
nor secretly with the said mulatta María."[15]

Juana de Lasarte, Ana de Escobar, María Cabezudo, Luísa de
Revelo, and Yolanda Messias all shared the dubious distinction of
having been, at one time or another, the lovers or concubines of
the same priest. He was Don Diego Ormeno de Cabrera, one of
the most notorious clerical Don Juans of seventeenth-century Peru.
Don Diego had been expelled from the Augustinian order because
of immorality and incorrigible behavior. He lived for more than
eighteen years in the town of Ica, where he constantly made a
mockery of civil and ecclesiastical laws. Nothing secular or divine
seems to have been able to contain his boundless ego. He went
around the valley of Ica in secular garb, usually accompanied by
women friends—some of them described as "public women." He
became the ruthless cacique or political boss of the valley. He
engineered the election of his friends to public office, bought

votes, and bribed and blackmailed royal officials. He bought the position of collector of ecclesiastical tributes and taxes to exploit Indians and Spaniards alike. He became a mule and horse trader, owned one hundred mules which he rented out to bring mineral and silver from the mines of upper Peru, bought and sold cattle, and acted as agent for "respectable" merchants in many illicit commercial operations. He was also well known as an efficient collector of debts which others had thought to be uncollectable. As a skillful swordsman, he never shrank from a fight and had participated in quite a few formal duels. Yet, what became a legend in the valley of Ica was his love life and his unquenchable sexual appetite. As an eyewitness reported in 1679, more in awe than in shock, if one could possibly count all his love affairs, it would be found that Don Diego Ormeno de Cabrera "had more girl friends than King Solomon had concubines."

Doña Juana de Lasarte was one of his first concubines, but she had a powerful rival in a society lady of Ica, whose name is concealed in the record because of the "quality" of her family. Jealousy between the two women erupted in fights, and in one of those clashes, Don Diego stabbed Doña Juana with his sword. Doña Ana de Escobar, also a well-born lady, was the lawful wife of Don Juan de Espinosa. She was a cousin of the cleric Don Diego who, because of the blood relationship, had easy access to the household of Doña Ana. The cousins became lovers, but their illicit affair ended in tragedy. The deceived husband "caught them past midnight naked in his own bed and drew his sword to kill them." Don Diego, using his lover's body as a shield, managed to escape while poor Doña Ana was stabbed nineteen times and almost died of her wounds.

Doña Luisa Revelo was an older woman, who had a married daughter and whose son-in-law was Juan Sotil, a well-known gentleman of Ica. She became the willing lover of the cleric Don Diego, who used to take her to his nearby hacienda, where she lived as "if she were his wife." Two other known concubines of Don Diego were Doña María Cabezudo, the widow of Diego Pacheco, and Doña Yolanda Messias, a first cousin of the cleric. She lived with him in Ica and had his child. Besides these women, who were obviously members of "good" families and could use the title of Doña, there were many others in the life of Don Diego. The judicial process filed against him in the bishopric of Lima also revealed that some unnamed mestizas, mulattas, and blacks had been at one time or another his lovers or concubines.

Repentant Women

It is an illogical and tragic-comic quirk of life that the shameless concubine and the wronged, divorced wife could end up being detained by society under the roof of the same institution. The divorced woman, although by no means rare in colonial Peru, was nevertheless an anomaly from a religious and a legal point of view. Colonial society could understand the daughter, the sheltered schoolgirl, the consecrated virgin, and the wife-mother, all of whom fit well into clearly defined social niches. In a sense, colonial society also knew how to handle the criminal woman, the prostitute, and the habitual concubine, whose final destinations were a house of detention for women. But that society was confused by the divorced woman. According to tradition, she was, after all, a member "of a sex subject by order of the Creator to subordination and dependence," and by her divorce she had lost the man to whom, in the natural order of things, she should be subordinated and upon whom she should be dependent.

If the divorcee could not, for whatever reason, reattach herself to a living parent or to a male relative, her social and ethical status suddenly became a problem for colonial society. In the case of divorcees without any means of support, the problem was compounded by the urgent need to find food and shelter for them. The ecclesiastical judges usually resolved this quandary by treating the female applicants for divorces as wards of the tribunal and by ordering the civil authorities "to deposit" them under protective custody in some trusted institution, which must have been painfully humiliating for grown women. The situation was truly tragic for poor women without money and without powerful friends, who ended up in an institution where repentant women were sheltered and prostitutes and concubines were incarcerated.

The divorcee of the upper class could always persuade the tribunal to place her in seclusion in the house of a wealthy friend, as was the case of Doña Ana de la Torre who went into the house of Doña Elvira Bravo. If the divorcee had sisters or female relatives who were professed nuns in one of the city convents, she could be placed in the nunnery to hide her sorrow and shame among the consecrated virgins. The ecclesiastical judges also used another colonial institution, the Hospital of La Caridad, to shelter divorcees. La Caridad had been founded as a public hospital for poor Spanish women, and it became a convenient place where the ecclesiastical authorities could provide room and board for deserted and battered wives during the process of obtaining a divorce. Yet, the most widely used shelter for divorced women of the poor classes was an institution originally conceived as a cloister for repentant and reformed prostitutes and concubines, and where eventually some women of ill repute were detained against their wills. This institution was named by the founders La Casa de las Amparadas de la Concepción, and the Peruvian public, with no pun intended, referred to the inmates as "protegées of the Conception." Every year, a group of divorcees lived there waiting for the ecclesiastical judges to find a better solution to their uncertain futures.

The foundation and history of La Casa de las Amparadas are important not only in understanding the type of life led by some of the divorcees, but also in gaining some insight into the shadowy, often invisible world of the prostitute and the woman of ill repute. In the second half of the sixteenth century, there was already talk among some clerics and pious gentlemen of Lima about the need to open a women's shelter. This shelter was needed, as Fray Juan de Bivero informed the king on January 24, 1572, because many loose women in the city, lacking honest means of support and not wanting to be servants, had become *mujeres perdidas,* and lived on the fringes of social respectability. At the end of that year, on December 30, Don Francisco de Arcaín left in his will an endowment of seven thousand pesos for the foundation of a shelter of repentant women to be named La Concepción, and a wealthy woman of Lima donated a house for that purpose next to the Hospital of San Diego.

These early efforts did not have the desired results. It was not until the first decade of the seventeenth century that the viceroy marqués of Montesclaros began gathering repentant women in the hope of reforming them. With pride, Montesclaros wrote to his successor on September 12, 1615 that it was he who "finally populated the pigeon coop" and supported the inmates with donations and with Indian tributes not earmarked for other causes. The successors of Montesclaros either did not share his zeal for public morality or could not find the means to support the work, and La Concepción was almost forgotten after a few years of dormant life.[17]

The idea of a shelter for women was revived in 1668 by two remarkable men, the viceroy count of Lemos and the Jesuit Francisco del Castillo. Francisco del Castillo had worked for several years in the ministry in an attempt to convert the "fallen women" of Lima and, when he was chosen confessor of the count of Lemos, the priest persuaded him to reestablish the women's shelter. The count of Lemos, whom his enemies accused of trying to convert the entire city of Lima into a religious cloister, accepted the suggestions of Francisco del Castillo with enthusiasm, and spent 11,000 pesos to buy a convenient property for the shelter. For two years, Lemos and Castillo worked diligently to build a chapel, a cloister and cells, and all offices and workshops needed for the institution. They spent 10,200 pesos, and finally La Casa de las Amparadas de La Concepción was ready to reopen its doors on March 19, 1670.

A few weeks before that date, large posters had been placed in the churches and public buildings announcing the opening of La Concepción and explaining its purpose and its rules. The institution was meant to be, according to the posters, "a voluntary and free retreat" for repentant women and for girls in danger of losing their virtue. For any woman to come forward and freely request admission in La Concepción was, of course, tantamount to declaring herself a fallen woman or a woman on the brink of loosing her virtue, so, unsurprisingly, on the day of the opening no candidates for admission could be found.

The disappointment of Lemos and Castillo must have turned to panic when weeks went by and still no candidates came forward. For two months La Concepción stood empty, while Francisco del Castillo went through the lower quarters of the city recruiting women of ill repute. Finally nine women, whose names are not known, were persuaded to enter La Concepción on May 28, 1670. To mark the occasion, a solemn procession marched from the cathedral to La Concepción "in the middle of an innumerable gathering of people." Colonial Lima loved parades and processions for any reason and on any occasion, and the best society of

Lima took part in the procession of May 28, 1670, to celebrate that nine fallen women were about the enter the cloisters of La Concepción. The viceroy count of Lemos and his wife, Doña Ana de Borja, accompanied by gentlemen of the court and ladies-in-waiting, Archbishop Don Pedro Villagómez, the civil and ecclesiastical tribunals, the city council and the cathedral chapter, the university and the colleges, and the secular and the regular clergy, all took part in the festivities of the day.[18]

The difficulties experienced by Francisco del Castillo in recruiting repentant women remained unchanged in the last three decades of the seventeenth century, and the need to fill all the vacancies of La Concepción began to change the nature of the institution. Very soon the ecclesiastical tribunal took advantage of the available space and began interning divorcees in the secluded retreat. In 1690, the viceroy count of La Monclova, "in order to eradicate from public life the motives of prostitution and criminal disorders, added [to La Concepción] a new jail for public and scandalous women. These women would live segragated from the other inmates but subject to the same warden in charge of correcting their bad habits." It must have been obvious to the viceroy that, although prostitutes and scandalous concubines were as numerous as ever, few of them were truly repentant, and fewer still were willing to apply for admission in La Concepción. If the scandalous women of Lima did not come of their own will to be reformed at La Concepción, the viceroy count of La Monclova was determined to compel them.

This decision represented a return to a practice that had been common in the old La Concepción during the days of the viceroy marqués de Montesclaros. We even know the names of some of those early prostitutes. In 1631, four prostitutes, the mulatta Pascala de Cabeza, Melchora García, described as *"quarterona de mulatta,"* a mestiza known as Marota, and the mulatta Dominga were brought to and incarcerated in La Concepción. The four of them had kept a house of ill repute on Las Cruces Street "to give themselves to all men, who wanted to have illicit relations with them. These men come and go, in and out of the house day and night and at all hours, without any shame and restraint. . . ." The four women were also accused of serving drinks and organizing lascivious dances in the house. They finally got in trouble with the law on December 8, 1631, the feast of the Immaculate Conception when the four prostitutes erected a small altar on the patio of the house, placed on it a statue of the Virgin Mother, lit candles in her honor, and gathered in front of the altar to pray to the Virgin Mary. This was too much for the Lima authorities, who were shocked to discover such an altar in a house of ill repute. Pascuala, Melchora, Dominga, and Marota were taken into custody to become "protegées of the Conception."[19]

Before the end of the century, another change, not envisioned by the founders, took place at La Concepción. The doors of the institute were opened to poor and abandoned young girls whose education could not be attended to in other schools and orphanages of the city. By 1708, La Concepción had two hundred women interned there for many different reasons. They were repentant women, incarcerated prostitutes and concubines, women in the process of obtaining a legal separation from their husbands, young students of the very low class and their female teachers, about a dozen female servants, and a handful of black slaves engaged in menial work.

In the second half of the eighteenth century and as a result of the devastating earthquake of 1746, La Concepción was moved several times to new and better facilities. The changes introduced since the days of the count of La Monclova became entrenched and institutionalized. By 1771, without counting the incarcerated women, La Concepción had 167 inmates divided into the following groups: 79 young girls, 15 repentant women, 11 divorcees, 36 servants, 14 ladies in retirement, and the rest were administrators and teachers.

Because of a lack of sufficient funds to support so many women, the conditions of life in La Concepción were deplorable. There was a shortage of food and clothing; clashes between the inmates occurred frequently, and the administrators had their hands full trying to maintain a minimum of discipline and order. By the end of the century, ecclesiastical and civil authorities knew that La Concepción could not survive unless the number of women was reduced and the institution returned to the original purpose. In 1801, the archbishop of Lima advised the viceroy to limit the inmates of La Concepción to repentant women, women in the process of obtaining divorces, and those jailed because of their immoral behavior. Three years later, the new viceroy marqués de Avilés put that advice into effect by dispersing all the women who could not be classified as repentant, divorced, or incarcerated. At the same time, Avilés had the building repaired and the walls of the cloister erected higher to prevent the escapes that had occurred in the past.[20]

This last action points out a problem that had existed in La Concepción since the days of the count of Lemos and Francisco del Castillo in 1668. The problem was the reluctance of most women to be interned in La Concepción; once forced to live there, they made every effort to get out, including a risky jump over the fence of the cloister. This attitude of reluctance and unhappiness was most prevalent among the divorcees, who, although innocent of any crime, were forced to live for months in the close company of prostitutes and concubines. As mentioned above, the colonial divorcee knew that the ecclesiastical tribunal would confine her somewhere until her status was clarified, but she tried to go either to a private home, or a nunnery, or even the Hospital of La Caridad. She hoped to avoid La Concepción altogether. If forced to go there, the divorcee made all kinds of appeals to the tribunal to be transferred somewhere else. Although hundreds of such cases can be found in the records of the tribunal, the case of María Poblete will suffice to illustrate the point.

María Poblete was married to Melchor García, a small merchant, and the couple had lived a seemingly uneventful marital life for several years in the Valley of La Barranca. Some time in the early 1630s, in order to improve his business opportunities, Melchor had decided to move to another location not mentioned in the record. María, his wife, may not have been very happy about the move, but for a while, at least, she went along with the desires of her husband and began preparations to move their belongings to the new residence. Everything seemed to be going well until Melchor's mother-in-law, Doña Isabel de Carvajal, intervened. She was as stubborn as a Castilian mule and, after years of personal frustrations, had developed a great need to control the lives of those around her.

It was not rare for some women, after years of domination by parents as young girls, by teachers in the convent schools, and by husbands in an unequal marriage, to become ruthless tyrants in their widowhood. Doña Isabel de Carvajal was one of them, and she made very clear to Melchor that her daughter María was not going to leave her and the Valley of La Barranca. Unfortunately

for Melchor, María had been persuaded by her mother and refused to follow her husband to the new family residence. When
his pleas with his wife failed, Melchor tried to appeal to his rights
as a husband and to pressure the two women through relatives
and important people of the community. Doña Isabel de Carvajal
did not like to be pressured, and one night she disappeared from
La Barranca, taking her daughter María with her. The two women
reappeared a few weeks later in Lima.

At this point, Melchor García knew that the only recourse left
to him was a formal appeal to the ecclesiastical tribunal of the
archbishopric of Lima. He filed a petition with the court explaining all the events that had transpired in La Barranca, the unreasonable stand of his mother-in-law and the flight of his wife. The
ecclesiastical judges ordered the *alguacil* to take María Poblete under custody, and to bring her by force "to the house and retreat
of the divorcees to remain there in charge of the warden." After
being detained within the walls of La Concepción, María Poblete
counteracted with a petition of her own requesting to be set free
on grounds that she was not the lawful wife of Melchor García.
In her eagerness to get out of the house of detention, María
claimed that her marriage to Melchor should be immediately annulled because she did not freely consent to the union and had
gone through the ceremonial formalities pressured "by the force
and violence of her parents."

María also planned an alternative course of action to get out of
La Concepción: She would obtain a quick legal separation and be
allowed to live as a divorcee in the household of her mother Doña
Isabel. Since she could not prove either desertion or infidelity on
the part of Melchor, she presented physical abuse and violence as
her reason. Her story, if true, shows that her life in La Barranca
had not been as uneventful as it first appeared. María testified
that she had been thrown out of the marital bed by Melchor and
forced to sleep on the bare floor without any covers. She had been
pulled by her hair and dragged all over the house, and she had
been kicked many times, and once attacked with a sword. On one
occasion, María claimed, Melchor bit her in the face, and she
carried the teeth marks in her left cheek for a whole month.

The ecclesiastical judges took María's deposition under advise-
ment, while upholding their previous order to keep her detained
in La Concepción. The legal process went slowly, but to María,

the outcome was not as important as finding a way out of La Concepción. She finally succeeded; living conditions in La Concepción, as suggested above, were extremely harsh and unhealthy, and María Poblete fell sick and asked permission of the tribunal to abandon the cloister for reasons of health. Commissioned by the judges, the surgeon general officially stated that María was truly ill and had little hope of recovering in the wretched conditions of the cloister. He recommended that María be placed where she could be cured. The ecclesiastical judges accepted the medical opinion, but they refused to release María to her mother. Instead, they ordered her to the house of Doña María de Fuentes, making clear that the new residence was still a house of detention and that María was not allowed to leave at will. To deter her, the tribunal imposed a penalty of automatic excommunication in case María went out of the house without permission.

While María Poblete recuperated, the tribunal went on deliberating. After long months of legal battles, the judges pronounced the marriage of Melchor and María null and void. They found that the ruthless matriarch Doña Isabel de Carvajal had indeed used "force and violence" to pressure her daughter María into a marriage. María was now not only free of her detention but also free to remarry. She wasted no time, and soon began preparations to marry Alonso Vázquez. Melchor García moved even faster to reach the altar. He married Leonor Pedrero, whom he probably had kept as a concubine during the lengthy process against María.

This should have been the end of the story of Melchor and María, but an unexpected event again threw their lives into utter confusion. Some priests who had testified in the process and now felt guilty went back to the tribunal to assure the judges that the entire testimony in the annulment suit had been vitiated by lies and perjuries. According to those priests, Melchor and María were still husband and wife. Regardless of his approved second marriage, Melchor was living in sin with Leonor, and María could never be allowed to marry Alonso Vázquez in the face of the church.[21]

It is not known if María went back to the house of divorced women, but her sad story shows that it was not easy for a woman to play by the rules of the church in her efforts to terminate an unbearable marriage. It was easier to ignore the ecclesiastical channels and become somebody's "honest concubine." If, as a concubine, she maintained a low profile and avoided public scandal, a woman had a very good chance of leading a fairly normal life without ever being in serious trouble with the law. Perhaps this explains why hundreds of women of colonial Peru followed the path of honest concubinage in their quest for personal fulfillment and marital happiness. The records of the period show that it was easier for an honest concubine to obtain social acceptability than it was for a divorcee who had been in and out of institutions, and whose marital problems had become the gossip of the community. The editors of the *Mercurio Peruano* may have claimed that concubinage was incompatible with happiness and love, yet it is hard to believe that a way of life so prevalent and so widespread could have been entirely devoid of happiness and love.

Despite these stories of divorcees, concubines, and repentant women, the consecrated virgin was perhaps the most remarkable woman of Peru, and the one who exhibited a greater independence from the world of men. The characteristics of Peruvian, female monasticism were unparalleled in other Catholic countries. The great numbers of women who fled to the cloisters worried both civil and ecclesiastical authorities, who feared that a healthy social balance between the cloister and the secular city was being broken in Peru. One can only speculate about the great female exodus into the cloisters, but perhaps the subconscious longings on the part of many women to liberate themselves from the overwhelming dominance of the male is part of the explanation. The ideals of marianism and the ever-present figure of the Virgin Mother may have also impelled many women to enter the colonial nunneries, which were true and independent islands of women in the midst of a male-dominated society. The colonial nunnery was undoubtedly the most important institutional contribution made by and for women in the three hundred years that Peru was under the dominion of the Spanish crown.

7

(❀)

Islands
of Women

IN THE CLOSING YEARS of the fifteenth century, Spain and Portugal both founded two great overseas empires. A variety of cultural, economic, political, and technological forces filled the sails of their ships as they sought to penetrate the hidden mysteries of the *mare incognitum*. New technologies in the art of navigation and ship-building, incipient nationalism, mercantilistic theories, the struggle for new trading routes, the intellectual curiosity unleashed by the Renaissance, and the religious fervor of an expanding Christianity were some of those forces.

Yet, there were other forces—legends and myths— that spurred discoverers and conquerors toward the shores of the New World. The Fountain of Youth, El Dorado, the New Jerusalem, the Noble Savage, sunken Atlantis, the mysterious tribes of the Antipodes, and the islands of the Amazons are but a few of those legends. In a curious way, some of those dreams, although changed and transformed, were realized in the New World. The Fountain of Youth was never found, but the quinine of the mountains of Loja rejuvenated many bodies ravaged by fevers. El Dorado may never have materialized, but the mountain of silver of Potosí brought untold wealth to many Spaniards. The Noble Savage was never seen, but many Indian communities impressed the Europeans with the civilized nobility of their way of life. Atlantis was never salvaged, but new continents did emerge from the ocean. The Amazons, women warriors who had inspired the imagination of

Europe since the days of Herodotus, did not clash with the new conquerors of America. Yet, Francisco de Orellana thought that he had seen them fighting in the rain forest; from then on the forest and its river were known to the Spanish as the Amazon forest and the Amazon River. Islands of women eventually appeared in the New World, inhabited by "divine amazons." These women cut themselves off from the world of men to form autonomous and hidden kingdoms. The colonial nunneries were refuges for women in the midst of a society shaped and controlled by men.

No detailed and comprehensive map of these nunneries has yet been produced by scholars, but hardly any city of importance existed in the viceroyalty of Peru which did not have at least one or two. Lima alone had thirteen convents at one time, canonically established and recognized by the church. This figure does not include half a dozen beaterios or retreat houses for women, which lacked canonical recognition. The thirteen nunneries of Lima were La Encarnación, La Concepción, La Trinidad, Santa Clara, El Prado, Las Descalzas, El Carmen, Las Trinitarias, Las Nazarenas, Las Mercedarias, Las Capuchinas, Santa Rosa, and Las Agustinas Recoletas. They formed a widely scattered archipelago of women, which at its peak occupied a fifth of the area of Lima and contained more than a fifth of the female population of the city. Six of those nunneries were popularly called *los conventos grandes,* and one could hardly move in any direction through the streets of colonial Lima without coming upon the blocking walls of their cloisters. Because of the great extension of their physical plants and the large female population within the six cloisters, colonial observers frequently mentioned the presence of *los conventos grandes.*

The six *conventos grandes* and their founders were: La Concepción founded in 1561 by Doña Leonor de Portocarrero, widow of the royal treasurer of Peru; La Encarnación founded in 1573 by Doña Inés Muñoz de Rivera, the already mentioned sister-in-law of Francisco Pizarro and one of the most remarkable women of colonial Peru; La Santísima Trinidad founded by Doña Lucrecia Sansoles in 1584; Las Descalzas, which opened its doors in 1602 and whose first abbess was Doña Inés de Rivera, sister of the marqués de Mortara; Santa Clara founded two years later in 1604; and finally Santa Catalina, which began receiving novices in 1624 and was founded by two noble sisters, Doña Lucía and Doña Clara de la Daga.[1]

In Cuzco, the imperial capital of the Incas, there were three *conventos grandes* and half a dozen beaterios and minor nunneries. The three important convents of Cuzco were Santa Clara, Santa Catalina, and Las Carmelitas. In the closing years of the sixteenth century, Santa Clara was founded as a female branch of the Franciscan order, and the nuns wore the Franciscan robe, followed the rule of St. Francis, and were subject by their vows to the superiors of the Franciscan order. Santa Catalina was a convent of Dominican nuns who, like their male counterparts, followed the monastic rule of St. Dominic. However, the nuns were under the direct jurisdiction of the bishop of Cuzco and owed no obedience to the Dominican friars. Las Carmelitas were also under the jurisdiction of the local bishop, and its nuns followed the strict rule of St. Theresa of Avila, the great Castilian mystic. The foundation of Las Carmelitas was begun in 1644 by Doña Leonor Costilla y Gallinato, widow of Don Diego López de Zuñiga, and one of the wealthiest women of Cuzco. According to reports sent to the king by the civil and ecclesiastical authorities of Cuzco, the new foundation was needed because by 1644 the other two convents were already filled with more than 220 professed nuns.[2]

On the frontier of Chile, there were also several convents of nuns; the two most important ones were Las Agustinas and Santa Cruz. Las Agustinas was founded in Santiago around 1575 by a group of "heroic and Christian ladies, all of them widows of the captains who accompanied Pedro de Valdivia in the conquest of Chile." The founders of Las Agustinas had experienced the perils and dangers of the early frontier and the Indian wars of Chile, had been matriarchs of extended families, and had all outlived their husbands.

The nunnery of Santa Clara was founded in 1553 by Doña Isabel de Plasencia in the provincial town of Osorno. In 1603, owing to revolts and upheavals in the provinces, the nuns abandoned Osorno and went on foot through fields and towns ravaged by war to Santiago. Santa Clara prospered in Santiago; it had four hundred professed nuns by the end of the seventeenth century. There were also nunneries in Arequipa, Potosí, La Plata, Cordoba, Santa Fe, Buenos Aires, and even in some smaller towns and villages. Tunja, for instance, a small town in the northern region of the viceroyalty, had two nunneries: La Concepción founded in 1599 by Doña Beatriz and Doña Catalina de los Rios, and Santa Clara where for fifty-three years, from 1689 to 1742, the remarkable Doña Francisca Josefa del Castillo lived. She was compared by some to Sor Juana Inés de la Cruz in Mexico and to St. Theresa of Avila in Spain.[3]

Los Conventos Grandes

The physical plant of these Peruvian nunneries gave them an appearance totally unlike that of a modern convent. The Jesuit Bernabé Cobo, who as a priest and confessor of nuns had many opportunities to visit the nunneries, has left us a description of the large size of colonial convents of Lima as they appeared in the first half of the seventeenth century. La Encarnación alone occupied an area of two and a half city blocks. Santa Catalina encompassed more than two city blocks within its walls. La Concepción and Santa Clara extended for a block and a half each, while La Trinidad owned as conventual residences an entire city block. Cobo assured his European readers that within the walls of those convents "the amount of buildings is such that the nunnery resembles a developed town, and in fact is truly a town. . . ."

The occasional visitor who stepped into the nunnery from the noisy and often crowded city streets must have been dazzled by the uniqueness of this city within a city. Moving along beautifully designed and silent cloisters, the visitor would come upon the imposing structure of the conventual church, often luxuriously decorated and always kept spotlessly clean by the devoted nuns. Well-tended gardens, filled with trees and flowers, crossed by acequias of running water, and whose silence was broken only by the jets of an occasional fountain, muffled the sounds of the city beyond the walls and surrounded the convent with a green belt.

The common offices and workshops of the nunnery, kitchens, laundry rooms, bakeries, sewing rooms, storage space, and other facilities usually stood together in a secluded corner of the extended property. They were beehives of activity, where the maids and black slaves toiled in the daily menial work of the convent. The *seglarado* or building for secular girls housed the youngsters being educated in the convent and was furnished with classrooms, workshops, a dining room, a common dormitory for the students, and a few private rooms for teachers and supervisors. The novitiate was a similar construction, where the candidates for the veil lived in segregation for a whole year under the exclusive care of a mistress of novices. Less elaborate than the two last buildings, but similar to them in size, were the dormitories and common rooms of the many maids and slaves who lived within the cloister. The nunnery also had an infirmary or tiny hospital, usually furnished with a small pharmacy, and a conventual jail, where not only maids and slaves but also professed nuns were occasionally detained.

Perhaps, from our modern point of view, the *celdas* or cells of the professed nuns constituted the most remarkable feature in the physiognomy of the colonial nunnery. The word *cell* is, in fact, a misnomer, and refers to the private dwellings of the professed nuns. The cells were usually located toward the center of the property in one of the best locations within the nunnery. Seen from the tall towers of the nearby churches, they resembled a miniature Andalusian village of small houses, narrow, twisting streets, and whitewashed walls. Some of the cells had *altos y bajos,* a groundfloor and an upstairs, and a good number of them had their own patios and a private, tiny garden. In some convents, the narrow streets formed by the cells led into a small plaza adorned with a fountain, which provided the nuns with an abundance of fresh water. Bernabé Cobo accurately described the nunneries as *pueblos formados,* developed towns.

The cells were owned, as we shall see later, not by the convent, but by the individual nuns. Many of them were large enough to house several persons comfortably. Within her cell, each nun was queen and, if she came from a well-to-do family, as most of them did, she was allowed to furnish it with the luxury and comforts she would have enjoyed in her parents' home. The professed nuns spent a great deal of their time in this miniature town, where they could lead fairly independent lives, not only from the outside city, but even from the rest of the convent. In their private cells they rested, read, worked on personal projects, and frequently gathered their close friends within the community for evenings of long conversations and even music and songs. Not far from the cells of the professed nuns were the small houses or apartments of the *señoras seculares,* the lay women who had retired to live within the nunnery. There one could find also an occasional divorcee waiting for the ecclesiastical tribunal to grant her a legal separation from her husband.

One could not visit one of the *conventos grandes* of Peru without lingering in the *porteria* and in the *locutorios* of the nunnery. The *porteria* was the main door and large entrance hall of the convent, and the *locutorios* were the parlors and private offices, where the nuns could receive outside friends and relatives and where the officers of the nunnery could conduct business with their outside agents. Forming a rather large building with an elaborate facade facing the city street, the *porteria* and the *locutorios* were the busiest and most visible places in the convent. Merchants arrived there with their wares, judges and royal officials came on official business, ladyfriends paid their visits to show the latest fashions and to share the latest gossip of the secular city, parents came to see their daughters, confessors and priests were entertained with music and songs, maids and black slaves delivered written and verbal messages, while young caballeros were drawn by their romantic, platonic attachments toward some of the most beautiful and charming nuns.

The *porteria* and *locutorios* were windows through which the nuns could watch the outside world, and through which outsiders could peep hastily into their mysterious and hidden world. The *porterias* and the *locutorios* were like a constantly revolving stage, where some of the most unique social rituals of colonial days were performed. Hundreds of incidents occurred in the *locutorios,* which both amused and shocked the secular city.[4]

Population of the Convents

The female population in the nunneries of colonial Peru constantly increased throughout the seventeenth century until, in the opening years of the eighteenth century, the numbers of consecrated virgins in the viceroyalty sharply decreased. From the modest beginnings of perhaps a dozen women, the *conventos grandes* reached a population of more than one thousand women within each one of their cloisters. In 1561, when Doña Leonor de Portocarrero opened the doors of La Concepción, only nine women accompanied her in taking the vows. By the late 1630s, La Concepción had seven hundred women living within its cloister. La Encarnación was founded in 1573 by Doña Inés Munoz de Rivera with about twelve nuns. Three years later, the convent had thirty professed nuns, plus novices, students, and servants. In 1594, the year Doña Inés died, about two hundred women were living in La Concepción, which reached a population of five hundred in 1639. In 1700, when the viceroy count of La Monclova took a census at the convent of La Concepción, he found, to his surprise, 1,041 women there. The convents of Santa Clara and La Santísima Trinidad had also reached a population of five hundred women each before 1650. Even the convent of Las Descalzas, which, following the rule of St. Theresa of Avila, was bound by its constitution to limit the community to thirty-three members, had sixty-two professed nuns by 1650. Counting the servants, secular women, and young girls, their numbers were close to two hundred.[5]

With the increasing numbers of women, the convents could not handle and accept all the women who knocked at their doors, and efforts were made to open new convents and *beaterios*. In fact, the Spanish crown had to intervene to stop this incredible exodus into the colonial nunneries. Orders were repeatedly sent to the Peruvian viceroys not to allow the opening of new convents and to control the numbers of women accepted into those already established. In 1641, the viceroy marqués de Mancera was severely reprimanded by the Royal Council of the Indies for allowing the opening of the convent of Las Recoletas. In a humble and apologetic tone, the viceroy tried to explain and justify his action: the new convent had been opened only as a branch of La Encarnación to take care of the overflow of candidates. The founders, Doña Angela and Doña Francisca de Zárate, intended to limit the new community to thirty-three nuns and had a capital of 156,800 pesos, more than enough to support the new foundation "without any burden to the republic." The council was not impressed and sent a stern letter to the audiencia of Lima:

There are no grounds to grant confirmation and approval of this foundation. The Viceroy should be told that he went a great deal beyond the limits of his authority in granting the said license, and he should be aware that his action was taken against the law. . . . With so many convents already in Lima, there is little need for this new

one, and it will cause great inconveniences to make any exceptions.
In view of the above, we order that the Royal Officials pay 2,000
pesos from their salaries as a fine for this excess. . . .[6]

This type of order was often issued by the crown during the second
half of the seventeenth century. While hundreds of women waited
to enter the cloisters, the crown erected all sorts of legal barriers
to prevent them. Was the crown afraid that the pool of potential
brides from good families was decreasing dangerously? Was it
concerned with the fact that many of the *conventos grandes* were
becoming unruly, independent kingdoms of women, which flaunted
their freedom and self-sufficiency in the face of a male-controlled
society? Was the king worried that a great number of those women
were entering the cloisters without a true supernatural vocation,
moved by very worldly reasons? Perhaps somehow all these reasons influenced royal policies, but the real reason may have been
fear that the proliferation of nunneries was becoming "a burden
to the republic."

Through dowries and donations, some of the convents had
accumulated a large amount of capital and a great deal of prime,
urban real estate. All those assets were frozen in the hands of a
religious community, did not contribute to the normal flow of
wealth within viceroyal society, and moreover were not subject to
royal taxation. Other convents had overextended themselves by
accepting too many nuns, and constantly had to beg to feed so
many mouths. This condition created an unfair burden for the
productive members of the colonial society.

The restrictive policies of the crown, the increasing seculari-
zation of the culture in the eighteenth century, and the deteriorating economic conditions of the viceroyalty did considerably
reduce the number of nuns by 1750. In the 1780s, Viceroy Don
Agustín de Jauregui informed his successor that "the number of
nuns had decreased noticeably if compared with their numbers
in the previous century," a fact clearly confirmed by the statistics
compiled by royal officials in 1790. The census of the convents,
taken by orders of Viceroy Don Francisco Gil Taboada y Lemos
and published in the *Mercurio Peruano,* shows that the nunneries
of Lima had a combined female population of only 1,585, while
the beaterios housed 310 women. Considering that at one time
La Concepción alone had more than one thousand inmates, and

that in Lima there were more than ten thousand cloistered women at the end of the seventeenth century, the decrease reported in 1790 by Gil Taboada y Lemos was not just "noticeable," it was dramatic.[7]

Although much more quantitative data are still needed for a full description of the Peruvian nunneries, the abundant qualitative data contained in the conventual records are perhaps more important for a full understanding of women's life in the viceroyalty of Peru. Regardless of exact numbers, the female population of the nunneries did not form a democratic society of equal members who enjoyed the same rights and privileges. The nunnery was, rather, an aristocratic pyramid of unequals, clustered into rigidly defined and mutually exclusive social classes: nuns of the black veil, nuns of the white veil, novices, *donadas*, whose nature and role shall be explained later, secular ladies in retirement, schoolgirls and babies, servants and maids, and at the bottom of the pyramid, the slaves of the convent. The headcount of all the women in the convent of La Concepción taken in 1700 by the count of La Monclova may give an idea of the proportional sizes of those different classes.

As we have already seen, the community numbered 1,041 persons; the 271 nuns included the three subclasses of nuns. The *donadas* were only 47. The secular population of the convent, including ladies, schoolgirls, and babies, had a total of 162 persons. Servants and maids of a free juridical condition numbered 290, while the slaves living in the cloister numbered 271. The four or five women not included in the above numbers were probably divorcees housed temporarily in the convent by orders of the ecclesiastical tribunal. It is difficult to comprehend that 561 women, either free or slaves, lived in a single nunnery as servants and maids of 271 nuns who had vowed themselves to a life of evangelical perfection.

The *monjas de velo negro*, or nuns of the black veil, constituted the closed aristocracy of the convent. Only they had the right to vote in conventual elections or to be elected to office within the nunnery. As we shall see later, the community was governed by a complex system of hierarchical offices with well-defined power, but access to that power was restricted to nuns of the black veil. These nuns were free from menial and servile work, and their main daily duty was the singing of the canonical hours in the choir of the convent. Therefore, they were also called *monjas de coro* or nuns of the choir. Their educational level was among the highest in the female world of colonial Peru. Most nuns of the black veil had attended the convent schools, where they had been taught reading, writing, arithmetic, music, drama, plus all the manual skills and social graces expected of young ladies of good families. Some of them, like the already mentioned Doña Francisca Josefa del Castillo, learned enough theology and Latin to follow the liturgy and sing the psalms with understanding.

On the rare occasion when a candidate to the black veil had not yet reached a minimum level of education, the community felt compelled to request a dispensation to accept her with a commitment that she would be taught before her profession. In 1621, for instance, the young Isabel de Burgos, who could neither read nor write, asked for admission in La Concepción as a candidate for the black veil. After consulting with the community, the abbess of the convent wrote to the bishop of Lima requesting a dispensation to accept Isabel, and assuring his lordship that once in the convent, Isabel "will be able to learn very easily (reading and writing) and many other worthy disciplines." The bishop granted the dispensation but insisted that "care should be taken that she should be taught how to read so that she knows how at the time of her profession." In other words, an illiterate novice could be tolerated now and then, but a professed nun of the black veil needed to know how to read and write before taking the vows.

A similar case occurred in 1681 in the convent of Las Trinitarias with Ventura María de la Encarnación, "who could hardly read." The case was sent for dispensation to the archbishop, Don Melchor de Liñán y Cisneros, who granted permission to accept Ventura María under the same conditions as in the case of Isabel de Burgos. An illiterate nun of the black veil was simply unthinkable; one can rightly assume that those nuns were, as a group, among the best-educated women of the viceroyalty.[8]

Although the educational level of the candidate was very important in becoming a nun of the black veil, the economic and social status of the candidate's family was even more important. All the nunneries required a sizable dowry to become a nun of the black veil, and only families of certain means could afford to provide their daughters with the dowry that was supposed to support them during their entire lives in the convent. During the seventeenth century, the required dowry fluctuated between 2,000 and 2,500 pesos, depending on the convent. In 1627, for instance, Don Alfonso de Hita paid 2,000 pesos to the nunnery of Santa Catalina as the dowry of his daughter Doña Antonia de Hita, who was not formally accepted until that financial transaction was finalized. By the eighteenth century, the amount of money required had gone up, and Doña Bernarda Vazques had to bring a dowry of 3,515 pesos. The dowries represented, nevertheless, a fraction of the money provided by the families to secure a position for their daughters among the nuns of the black veil.

On the day of acceptance into the novitiate and the day of the solemn profession, the parents of the nun had to give the convent a *donación* of several hundred pesos and a specified number of candles for the illumination of the church and cloisters. The greater expense, apart from the dowry, came on the day of the profession, when the young nun moved from the communal building of the novitiate into her own cell, which had to be bought or built for her.

One example may illustrate this process. On May 20, 1626, Don Francisco Ramos Galbán, a prominent judge in the audiencia of Lima, bought a plot within the nunnery of La Santísima Trinidad to build a *celda* for three of his daughters, who were about to take the vows. The price of the plot was 1,200 pesos, and the sales document, which made the Ramos Galbán girls owners of the conventual plot, was signed by their father, Don Francisco, and by the abbess, Doña Juana de Cisnero, in the presence of three witnesses, Diego Diaz de Tapía, Alonso Sánchez Galindo, and Antonio Rodríguez Galindo. The formidable legal document was also countersigned by forty-eight nuns of the black veil, who formally approved the sale, and was certified as valid by the notary public Don Juan Bernardo de Quirós.[9]

Obviously, not all colonial families were able to offer their daughters a substantial dowry, to buy and build their cells, and to make the required donations to the convent. On rare occasions and for very special reasons, some girls were accepted without a complete dowry as nuns of the black veil, but first they had to establish their "right" and "proper" social background. One of the most common reasons for waiving the complete dowry was the musical talents of the candidate. Since the nuns of the black veil spent a great deal of their time singing the psalms accompanied by the organ and other musical instruments, a remarkable voice or the ability to play the organ, the harp, or the violin was considered sufficient reason to waive full payment of the dowry. The documents of admission reveal that in almost every decade several girls were accepted in different convents without a full dowry because of their artistic talents as singers and musicians.

In 1708, for instance, Doña Andrea Cortés and Doña Francisca Valdez were accepted in La Encarnación without a full dowry to assist the other nuns of the black veil "with the music and with the organ." When their case was submitted to a secret vote of the community, 118 nuns voted without dissent to accept them into their exclusive rank without a full dowry.

The same exception was made in 1714 in favor of three sisters, Doña Andrea Teresa, Doña Melchora Olaya, and Doña María Margarita de Soria, who had been in the convent of La Encarnación since they were three years old. Their father, Don Melchor de Soria, had thirteen children and could not provide them with the full dowry required to become nuns of the black veil. A wealthy aunt, Doña María Falcón, who was the wife of General Don Manuel Lorenzo de los Montes, tried to help the Soria sisters by donating a house to the convent as part of the dowries of her nieces. Although the house was valued at more than 7,000 pesos, it was not enough to cover the full dowry of the three sisters.

At this point, a formal petition was made to the abbess to waive the remaining amount and to accept the three young girls. The reason for the petition was that the three Soria sisters were among the best instrumentalists and vocalists in the nunnery. One of them was a recognized artist with the violin and the viola, while the other two sisters were excellent at playing the harp. The three of them were gifted with beautiful singing voices, and for two years they had distinguished themselves among the soloists of the conventual choir. The petition was granted. Their musical talents, plus the fact that they were nieces of a general, opened the rank of the black veil to the Soria sisters.[10]

If occasional exceptions were made of the economic status of some candidates, none appeared to have been made of their social background. The nuns of the black veil came invariably from wealthy, or at least socially prominent, families. They were related by blood to royal officials, members of the powerful merchants' guild, officers in the royal militias, judges, prominent clerics, university professors, prosperous miners, encomenderos, and inquisitors. In other words, the nuns of the black veil belonged, if not always to the economic elite of the viceroyalty, certainly to the upper social strata of colonial Peru. This is perhaps one reason why they carried the aristocratic title of Doña. In the thousands of nunnery documents kept in the Peruvian archives, there are hardly any cases in which nuns of the black veil were given the most religious and most humble title of "mother" or "sister." If they were nuns of the black veil, they were always addressed as Doña as if to underscore their social prominence within the convent and vis-à-vis other women of the viceroyalty.

Two cases occurred early in the seventeenth century which dramatically illustrate the requirement of social prominence, regardless of economic status, to become a nun of the black veil. One girl, socially prominent but without money, was accepted into the convent as a nun of the black veil. The other, with enough money to pay her full dowry but of low social class, was not even considered.

The first case took place in 1612 in the convent of La Concepción and involved Doña Tomasa de Polanco. Although Doña Tomasa's relatives were unable to furnish even part of her dowry, the nuns of La Concepción were determined to find her a dowry through donations because she belonged to one of the most prominent families of Lima, the Ampuero family. Doña Tomasa was "a granddaughter of Captain Martín de Ampuero and a great-granddaughter of Captain Francisco de Ampuero, one of the first and most prominent conquerors of these kingdoms, married in legitimate marriage to Doña Inés Yupangui, daughter and sister of the Incan Emperors." Doña Tomasa was related to the Incan imperial family and to a Spanish conquistador, friend and companion of Pizarro, and that in itself made her a prime candidate for the black veil. The nuns of La Concepción found some pious donors, perhaps one of the many dowry-granting agencies, and enough money was collected.

The reverse case occurred a few years before, in 1609, in the convent of La Encarnación. The abbess of La Encarnación, Doña Mencia de Sosa, handled the official correspondence of the convent with the ecclesiastical authorities. In a letter, Doña Mencia informed the bishop of Lima of the case of María de los Reyes, a young girl who wanted to enter the convent as a nun. She also explained that the girl in question was an orphan and a mulatta, who in 1605 had been allowed to enter the nunnery as the maid of one of the most senior nuns of the black veil. For four years María de los Reyes lived in the cell of her lady, serving her faithfully, but now she wanted to take the vows and tie herself more closely to the religious community of La Encarnación. María de los Reyes had enough money for a full dowry: she had one thousand pesos of her own, and her "old and sick grandmother" appeared ready to give the girl between four or five thousand pesos more, an amount more than sufficient to pay a full dowry and to buy or rent a small cell within the nunnery. Yet, María de los Reyes was considered an acceptable candidate neither for the black veil nor for the next conventual rank, that of the white veil. The abbess Doña Mencia de Sosa informed the bishop that María de los Reyes, in spite of her money, was going to be accepted as a *donada,* the lowest rank of the religious community and a buffer between the nuns and the world of servants and slaves of the convent. In that period, a little mulatta, (*mulatilla* was the word used patronizingly by Doña Mencia), with little or no education, known to all as a *criada* or maid, could not possibly fit into the aristocratic world of the donãs of the black veil, as even María herself had to accept.[11]

The nuns of the next lower order, white veil, formed within the nunnery an auxiliary body similar to the lay brothers within a religious community of priests. They were usually Spanish or criollo women of very little education and modest financial means, whose families did not belong to any of the prestigious professions. Among them were also mestizas, who had either moved into the convent from some of the orphanages of the city or were sponsored with a modest dowry by one or another of the pious sodalities of Lima. The nuns of the white veil were known by their first names and never by the title of Doña; they did not have a vote in the frequent conventual elections and were not juridically capable of being elected to office; they were excluded from the main duty of the nuns of the black veil, namely the singing of the canonical hours in the choir; and they usually assumed the chores of housekeepers. More commonly they were gardeners, infirmarians, bakers, jailers, supervisors of kitchens and laundry rooms, buyers, aids to the different officers of the nunnery, and directors of *donadas,* maids, and slaves.

Very seldom, if ever, did nuns of the white veil own their own private cells; they lived either as guests of nuns of the black veil or in the communal rooms of the nunnery. Yet, in the canonical sense, they were true nuns, bound by the religious vows and subject in virtue of them to all the rules of the nunnery. The difference between the nuns of the white and the black veil was more social and economic than legal and canonical.

Catalina Maitín, for instance, a woman of Spanish descent, lived in one of the nunneries for thirteen years as a "secular," supporting herself by odd jobs and with the charitable help of some nuns of the black veil. In 1683, the pious sodality of La O, directed by the Jesuits in their College of San Pablo, granted Catalina a dowry of 800 pesos to take the white veil. With that money Catalina Maitín was able to enter the novitiate, take the vows after one year, and become a nun of the white veil. Tiburcia de Chaberre and Jusepa Verdugo were also accepted into the same rank in that year. The document of admission clearly specified that they are accepted as nuns of the white veil "in view of the fact that at the present moment they do not have sufficient dowry to be nuns of black veil." Their modest financial status seems to have been in this case the only reason to relegate them to the more humble rank.[12]

Within the colonial convent, the *donadas* formed a buffer between nuns and the hundreds of servants and slaves who inhabited the cloisters. Their name derives from the Latin word *donata*, which menas "given," "offered," "consecrated." Although they wore the habit of a nun and led a community life, they were not nuns in the canonical and juridical sense. The *donadas* never took public vows recognized by the church, had no juridical obligation to remain for life in the nunnery, and were not subject by any vow to observe the rules and constitutions of the nunnery. They were, in fact, nothing but exalted maids who were allowed to live as "imitators of nuns."

Although they formed the lowest rank among those who wore the monastic robes, the *donadas* were segregated from maids and slaves and placed socially a notch above them in the complex hierarchical structure of the nunnery. Their roles within the convent were always subordinate ones, and their task was usually to help and assist the nuns of the white veil. The *donada* was seldom, if ever, given any independent position of authority even at the lowest level. The typical *donada* was poor, illiterate, almost without exception from the mixed-blood classes of the viceroyalty, and had been formerly a servant of the convent. Because of their humble status, the *donadas* tended to fade into the shadows of the cloisters, and their presence is difficult to detect within the walls of some of the convents.

We know that La Encarnación had forty-seven *donadas* in 1700, but we do not know who they were. We do know the names of some of the *donadas* of La Trinidad, thanks to a letter written in 1667 by Abbess Doña Gerónima Meléndez. In that year, María de Carbajal y Galindo, Petronila de San José, Nicolasa de Aguilar, Luísa Jusepa, and Josefa Narcisa were accepted as *donadas* of La Trinidad. All of them were mulattas, with the exception of Josefa Narcisa, who was a *cuarterona*, daughter of a mestizo father and a mulatto mother. All of them had been raised in the convent since early childhood and seem to have been daughters of maids of the nunnery. Their ages ranged from seventeen years old in the case of Petronila to thirty years old, the age of María de Carbajal. None of them had any means of support, but Doña Gerónima Meléndez accepted them as *donadas* because of their piety and virtue "to help the nuns in charge of different workshops." The rather bleak future of the *donada* was clearly described in a letter written in 1642 by the abbess of La Encarnación, Doña Violante de Guevara. The typical *donada*, she explained, is very poor, and "instead of a dowry they have a commitment to serve in the kitchen and other workshops of the convent for life."[13]

The candidates for any of the three categories—black veil, white veil, and *donada*—spent a year as novices. They were segregated from the rest of the community under the exclusive direction and guidance of a mistress of novices. The novices led an austere life of silence and prayer and were seldom allowed to leave the novitiate and mix freely with the hundreds of other women living in the nunnery. At the end of the year of novitiate, a delegate of the bishop came to the convent to administer a canonical exam to determine the competence of the candidates. Once the novices had been pronounced competent for the religious life, a step that usually was a pure formality, their candidacy was then submitted to the secret vote of the entire community of nuns of the black veil. In the closed meeting, the candidacy of each one of the novices was discussed. The results of the ballot were officially reported to the bishop, who gave the final and canonical license for the novice in question to take the vows.

In hundreds of these official reports, kept today in the archives of the bishopric of Lima, not a single case has been found of a rejected candidate. In fact, the vote of the community seems, suspiciously, to have always been unanimous for acceptance of the candidate. The criterion of selectivity was probably very lax, and anybody with the required dowry and the proper social background must have been acceptable.

A description of the different groups of women living in the colonial nunneries would be incomplete without mention of the large population of servants and slaves kept by the nuns within the walls of the convent. At their peak in the seventeenth century, each of the *conventos grandes* had several hundred women classified either as maids or slaves. Even toward the end of the eighteenth century, the twilight of female monasticism in colonial Peru, one still finds servants and slaves within the colonial cloisters. In 1790, when the nuns of the black veil had dwindled to only 59 in the nunnery of La Concepción, there were still 51 black slaves and 90 mestiza and mulatta servants. At that time, Santa Catalina had 61 professed nuns, 33 black slaves, and 91 maids. Santa Clara, with only 38 nuns, had 34 black slaves and 110 maids, and even the austere Barefoot Carmelites, who in 1790 had 41 nuns, kept in their convent one black slave and 36 maids. The total count of slaves and maids in the nunneries of Lima alone reached 932, while the nuns numbered 518 counting nuns of the black veil, nuns of the white veil, and novices.[14]

The presence of so many slaves and servants within the colonial nunneries can be understood only if one considers the historical origins of the Peruvian nunneries and the social and economic structures of the viceroyalty. Almost all the Peruvian convents were founded, as mentioned, by prominent and wealthy women of the colonial aristocracy. Rich households, served for years by maids and slaves, were converted into convents, and all their capital and property were transferred to the juridical ownership of the new religious institution. In this transformation process, many simple and illiterate maids and slaves passed unknowingly from the secular world into the realm of monastic life.

As the years went by, many candidates for the black veil, mostly daughters of wealthy families, came into the convent with their trusted maids and slaves, who might have found it attractive to move from the narrow confines of a single-family residence to the large cloisters, courtyards, and gardens of the colonial nunnery. Like nuns of the black veil, schoolgirls and retired women were usually allowed to bring their servants into the convent. As the nunneries grew, the need for servants also grew. The officers of the nunnery did not hesitate to buy slaves and hire more maids to fulfill their needs.

Indeed, the convent presented an attractive alternative to hundreds of unskilled and illiterate women, whose survival in the secular world was a constant, painful struggle. It was not easy for a women of the lower class to make a modest and respectable living in colonial Peru without a husband or male relatives. The nunnery offered her security and saved her from becoming "lost" or detained among the "protegées of the Conception." It is no wonder then that hundreds of women came to the nunneries seeking food and shelter in exchange for their services as maids.

A typical case, often repeated, is that of Antonia de los Rios in 1609. Antonia was an almost destitute widow with three daughters. She had failed to find even a modest dowry so that the girls could marry decent husbands, and finally made the decision to place them as maids in a convent. Antonia de los Rios went to the abbess of La Concepción and begged her to accept the three girls "to serve the nuns of the convent and, if the girls are willing and God would be served, to profess one day as *donadas*." What better solution to the worries of a devout mother than to know that her daughters had a secure future, free from abject poverty and the moral perils of a secular society. The three girls were accepted in La Concepción, where two of them became *donadas*.

At times, maids and slaves came into the nunneries either as "gifts" to the convent or lured by the sweet talk of some of the nuns. In the 1640s, Doña María Morán gave the convent of La Encarnación a very young slave girl named Ana to serve the community at the pleasure of the abbess. Doña María placed only one condition on her donation of the slave. Young Ana should be manumitted upon reaching her twentieth birthday and be allowed to determine freely her future life.

Barbola de Vargas was a ten-year-old maid in the convent of La Concepción in 1629, and the story of her arrival in the convent does not speak very highly of the ethical values of some of the nuns. A nun of the black veil, Doña Feliciana de Estrada, needed a maid, and through some outside persons had Barbola brought to the *locutorio* or parlor of the convent. There Doña Feliciana talked the young girl into entering the cloister to live with her in her large cell. Barbola de Vargas remained in the convent serving Doña Feliciana de Estrada until her mother appealed to the ecclesiastical tribunal. Barbola's mother was the *zamba* Pascuala del Espiritu Santo, who accused Doña Feliciana of "stealing my daughter . . . against justice and against my will." The nun was ordered immediately to return young Barbola de Vargas to her mother Pascuala.

A similar case occurred around 1644 with a slave named Lorenza owned by Doña Mencia de Guzmán. Doña Mencia had a sister, who was a nun of the black veil in La Encarnación, and the slave Lorenza, who was pregnant at the time, was a regular messenger between the two sisters. The nun befriended the slave and persuaded her that she and her baby could have a better life in the convent than in the outside world. Three months after her baby was born, the slave Lorenza ran away with her baby from the house of Doña Mencia de Guzmán and took refuge with her sister in the cloister of La Encarnación. Such unorthodox methods of acquiring maids and slaves, although not the rule, did occur with some regularity, if we are to believe the frequent appeals made by the injured parties to the ecclesiastical tribunal.[15]

This world of hundreds of nameless servants and slaves did not form within the cloister a uniform social group. Like the nuns themselves, the servants of the nunnery could be classified in different subgroups. The most obvious differentiation among those women was the one created by their juridical condition: some of them were slaves and some were free. The slaves were sold and bought, either among the nuns themselves or in commercial transaction with outside persons, and they had to work at the pleasure of the masters. The free maids, on the other hand, could earn a modest salary, and theoretically always retained the right to leave the cloister and return to the world. The free maid could also, as we have already seen, free herself of the purely servile world by one day becoming a *donada*, a higher rank in the hierarchy of the nunnery to which the slave had practically no access at all.

As thousands of documents attest, these women were divided by their juridical condition and also classified by their racial characteristics. Colonial Peru was an extremely color-conscious society, and the Peruvian nuns were an integral part of that society. A wide spectrum of social acceptability existed even within the cloisters between the two extremes of whiteness and blackness. Juridically, a conventual slave may have always been a slave, but the color of her skin was dutifully noted in the records as if it were a fact that made a difference. The slaves of the nunneries were either *bozales* or *criollas*. The *bozales* were deep black, African-born women, whose ignorance of the Spanish language and Peruvian customs seems to have been a justification to call them in many documents "wild" or "uncivilized." The criolla slave, Peruvian born and Spanish speaking, was much more acceptable, especially when she was *parda,* light dark, or *mulatta,* a mixture of Spanish and black, or even *morisca,* a slave woman of Moslem descent. Besides the *bozal,* the *parda,* the mulatta, and morisca slave—all classifications that made a social difference—in the convent of La Encarnación in 1630, there was at least one "yellow" or Oriental slave whose Christian name was Beatriz. She is described in the documents of the period as *"esclava Japona"* (Japanese slave), *"muchacha Japona"* (Japanese girl), and *"esclava . . . de casta caraga de la China"* (slave of *caraga* cast from China).[16] The maids of the nunnery were also differentiated in the documents by their racial backgrounds, and one can find among them Spanish, orphan girls, mulattas, mestizas, *cuarteronas, zambas,* and an occasional Indian.

Despite the juridical and racial differentiations in the servile population of the nunneries, the lives of the free maids and slaves could change depending on the social status of their mistresses and on their own skills and productivity. Some female servants belonged to the community as a whole, while others worked for, and belonged to, particular nuns of the black veil. The community servants lived in common dormitories under the constant watchful eye of a nun of the white veil or a *donada* supervisor. They were subject to a rigid and intense schedule of work and usually had to perform the most menial and unskilled tasks of the nunnery.

The maids and slaves of individual nuns, on the other hand, formed a class apart, more prestigious and socially superior to the common servants. They lived in the comfortable cells of their mistresses, serving them alone, were not subject to the supervisors

of servants, and did not engage in the most menial and heavy
work of the community: sweeping endless cloisters, scrubbing floors,
sweating in the laundry rooms, and the daily washing of hundreds
of pots and pans in the large kitchens. The servants of individual
nuns undoubtedly constituted an elite group within the servile
population of the nunnery. When their mistresses came from prestigious and wealthy families, the servants of those nuns lived much
better and worked much less than the average servant. Because
they were named after their mistresses, they shared the prestige
of socially prominent names.

The skills, productivity, and type of work exercised by the servants could also affect the social and economic status they enjoyed
within the nunnery. A skillful seamstress, a baker, a *curandera* or
folk healer, a good head cook, or an able gardener were several
notches above the unskilled servant in conditions of labor and in
social acceptability. Among these professional servants, one group
merits special mention because of the prestige of their office and
their impact on the community—the *recaderas* or messengers of
the convent, a small elite of about half a dozen women carefully
chosen by the abbess from among the most senior, best-educated,
and most trusted servants of the convent. The *recaderas* were the
ears and the eyes to the outside world, and they formed a sort of
movable drawbridge between the nunneries and the secular city.

Every morning the *recaderas* left the cloisters to deliver messages
and correspondence, to summon doctors, confessors, and other
officials, to place different orders of supplies with the city merchants, to buy medicines and articles urgently needed in the convent, and to bring gifts of conventual delicacies to the benefactors
of the nunnery. Being well known in the small colonial towns, the
recaderas were frequently stopped on their rounds and asked to
deliver all sorts of messages to the convent. Their arrival back into
the cloister was often like a stone thrown into a pond. The nuns
rushed to pick up their messages, to hear the latest news of the
outside city, and to share some gossip gathered in the markets
and shops of the town. Being in the good grace of the *recadera*
meant that many a cloistered nun could break the walls of isolation
and become aware of life in the outside world. No wonder, then,
that the *recaderas* were courted and pampered by many nuns, and

that the ecclesiastical authorities insisted that only trusted and respectable women should be allowed to become *recaderas* of the colonial convents.[17]

Family Clusters

In the convents, there were, surprisingly, large and frequent family clusters formed by blood relatives. These relatives lived together in adjacent cells and maintained a cohesive family. Mothers and daughters, sisters and cousins, aunts and nieces, distant relatives and close family friends were present in almost all the colonial convents of Peru. They formed small communities within the larger communities of the nunneries. Many of these family groups refused to be absorbed into the common life of the convent and were protected by maids and slaves, who, in some cases, were also related by blood. In their spacious cells, which sometimes had small private gardens, these nuns led an existence that was a delightful mixture of monastic and family life. It was not rare to encounter three generations of the same family, from nuns in their seventies to baby girls who could not yet walk.

In their furnishings and in the number of maids and slaves, the family cells reflected the economic and social status of the family origin. During conventual elections, these family groups could form solid voting blocks which, led by the group matriarch, engaged in all kinds of political maneuverings. At other times, the family cluster could be rent asunder by bitter feuds over the ownership of cells, the control of slaves and maids, the disposition of common inheritances, or the responsibility for the nieces raised within the cloister. Sometimes these feuds spilled over the cloister walls, and brothers, uncles, and male cousins flocked to the *locutorios* to give moral support to one or another of the family nuns. But most of the time these blood relatives led a peaceful life very similar to that of secular families, with the exception that the nuns did not have to contend with the presence of dominant men.

In some of the colonial convents, the family cluster was present from its founding. The convent of Santa Catalina, as we have already seen, was founded in 1604 by two sisters, Doña Lucía and Doña Clara de la Daga, who, surrounded by their family maids, were for years the undisputed mistresses of the convent. At the end of the sixteenth century, the wealthy Doña Luisa Diaz de Oré founded the convent of Santa Clara in the provincial town of Huamanga, and her five daughters became nuns of the black veil there. For a generation, the five sisters Diaz de Oré were the unchallenged, aristocratic elite of the convent.

As the years went by, these family clusters began appearing in almost all the colonial nunneries, and they increased in numbers and in size. In 1622, Doña Angela de Zambrano was a nun of the black veil in the convent of La Encarnación, where she held the important office of secretary of the nunnery. She owned her own cell, and lived with two nieces, Doña Angela de Villoslada and Doña Beatriz de Zárate, also of the black veil. The three nuns lived a comfortable life, served by a young black slave and a mulatta maid, Catalina. In 1622, when Catalina's health began to fail, Doña Angela de Zambrano dismissed her and hired in her place a mestiza maid, María de los Angeles. Four years later, in 1626, we find another family cluster in the convent of La Trinidad formed by three sisters, daughters of the already mentioned Don Francisco Ramos Galbán. They also had their own cell, a gift of their father, in which the three sisters lived together like a family.[18]

One of the most remarkable family clusters of the early seventeenth century existed in La Encarnación. It consisted of seven nuns of the black veil, all members of the prestigious colonial family of the Garabito-Illescas. The head of the family was Doctor Francisco de León Garabito, who was married to Doña Isabel de Illescas, a prominent society lady of colonial Lima. Doña Isabel's four sisters, Doña Isidora, Doña Casilda, Doña Beatriz, and Doña Angela de Illescas had taken the black veil in La Encarnación early in the seventeenth century. They were followed into the convent by three daughters of Doña Isabel: Doña Eufrasia, Doña Casilda, and Doña Isabel de Illescas. The seven Illescas nuns—aunts and nieces—were the most powerful group in La Encarnación, where they also had cousins and distant relatives. They lived within the nunnery at the economic and social level worthy of such a family. They enjoyed the full ownership of their adjacent cells, and they had their own maids and slaves, including the Japanese slave Beatriz, mentioned above.

In addition to the property of their cells, the ownership of their slaves, and the free use of their dowries, the Illescas nuns enjoyed a yearly income of 150 pesos assigned to them by the head of the family Don Francisco de León Garabito, and which they were supposed to receive "during all the days of their lives." When Don Francisco's wife, Doña Isabel de Illescas died, she left 200 pesos in her testament to her professed sisters and daughters to renew their monastic wardrobe and to buy "other things they may need." There is no question that the seven Illescas were wealthy nuns, who also carried one of the most prestigious names of colonial Lima. The prestige and power of the seven Illescas within the nunnery of La Encarnación became even more apparent when they succeeded in having one of them, the young Doña Casilda de Illescas, elected abbess of the convent. Ruling over a small female kingdom of almost five hundred women, Doña Casilda de Illescas became one of the most powerful women of Peru in the second decade of the seventeenth century.[19]

The Illescas were not the only family cluster in La Encarnación at that time. The Izaguirres and the Pastranas also formed their own, smaller groups. Doña Francisca de Pastrana and Doña Teresa de Pastrana were sisters and nuns of the black veil, who had with them in the convent two young nieces, who were still students in the conventual school. The nieces were nine-year-old Doña Isabel de Pastrana and eight-year-old Doña Leonor de Pastrana whose parents, absent from the city, had entrusted them to the nuns of the family to be educated in the nunnery. The core of the Izaguirre clan was formed by the two sisters Doña Justina and Doña Eufrasia de Izaguirre, whose brother Don Bernardo was the powerful secretary of the Holy Office of the Inquisition.

In 1627, in the convent of La Concepción lived a widow Doña Beatriz de Estrada, who had taken the black veil after the death of her husband. Doña Beatriz's three daughters also became nuns of the black veil in La Concepción, and they lived together with their mother in the family cell. In the 1640s, the convent of Santa Clara also had a large family cluster formed by five sisters of the Tello Meneses family. Four of the sisters, whose first names we do not know, had taken the black veil in Santa Clara, while a fifth sister, Doña Ana Tello Meneses, was a professed nun in La Trinidad.

In 1644, Doña Ana wrote a letter to the bishop of Lima requesting permission to leave La Trinidad and join her four sisters in Santa Clara. She explained that her sisters "had their own cell,

where they lived in comfort, and I have no cell . . . I live with
great depression deprived of the communication and support of
my sisters." Obviously a bit homesick for the company of her
sisters, Doña Ana also knew that the other four girls were enjoying
a better life-style than hers in La Trinidad. When the license was
finally granted, Doña Ana moved to Santa Clara, where the five
sisters lived together in the comfort and privacy of their own cell.[20]

In the second half of the seventeenth century, the convent of
Augustinian nuns of Santiago de Chile housed another powerful
family group, whose family name was written in blood across all
the pages of the early history of Chile. The group included six
sisters, nieces of the notorious Doña Catalina de los Rios y Lisperguer, "La Quintrala," who, as we saw in Chapter 2, was one of
the most depraved women of colonial Peru. The six sisters, Doña
Agueda, Doña María Clara, Doña María, Doña Juana, Doña Mariana, and Doña Nicolasa, were all daughters of Don Juan Rudolfo
Lisperguer, a first cousin of the infamous La Quintrala. Like the
Illescas nuns in Lima, the Lisperguer sisters lived in comfort in
the nunnery of Santiago, served by faithful family maids, and
surrounded by the dubious prestige of the family name. Each one
of them brought to the convent a dowry of 2,300 pesos, and from
their private, personal cells they exercised a clear influence in the
nunnery, where they controlled several important offices.[21]

In the eighteenth century, we still find family clusters in the
nunneries of colonial Peru. The four daughters of the general of
the royal militia, Don Juan de la Fuente y Rojas—Doña Petronila,
Doña Leonor, Doña Feliciana, and Doña Juana María de la Fuente
y Rojas—lived together in Santa Catalina with their aunt Doña
Leonor, who was also a nun of the black veil. They took care of
a third generation of young nieces, who were still in the conventual
school and would one day become nuns of Santa Catalina. The
five de la Fuente sisters, like the Illescas and the Lisperguers, were
wealthy women, whose lives in the nunnergy were not much different from their relatives' in the outside world. They owned one
of the best cells in the convent and had it furnished with all the
items required for the comfort of five persons. They were served
by four slaves, who also formed a family. The slave Juana Cazalla
and her three daughters, Petronila, Rafaela del Carmen, and Ana
María Cazalla, attended the needs of the de la Fuente sisters. It
is quite clear from the testaments of two of the sisters that these

nuns enjoyed a large income, which, in spite of the monastic vows, they could use at will. Doña Petronila de la Fuente opened her last will and testament with the following words:

It is my will and my desire to reserve, and by the present document I do reserve, all my properties, dowries, and all future inheritances, in whatever manner they may come to me, to enjoy them myself during the days of my life, and dispose of them according to my will either during my life or at the moment of my death.[22]

Doña Petronila went on to will part of her estate for the foundation of several chaplaincies to be served by clerics of the de la Fuente family. She also established an endowment of 3,000 pesos, and gave orders that from its interests her most trusted maid, María Esperanza, should be supported in the convent as a *donada*. Doña Petronila left a yearly income of 50 pesos to each one of her sisters, to whom she also transferred the ownership of all her slaves. The condition was added that the slaves should be manumitted after the death of the last surviving sister. Her cell and all the silver objects in it were bequeathed to her sisters, and after their deaths to her nieces, also nuns of the black veil of the convent of Santa Catalina.

The testament of Doña Leonor was similar; she named as her executrix her aunt and namesake Doña Leonor, who was the senior nun of the family. She assigned her aunt 50 pesos of yearly income. Two thousand pesos were left to celebrate masses for the repose of her soul, and 3,805 pesos were to be distributed among her sisters and nieces in the convent. Doña Leonor also established several chaplaincies and left a few monetary gifts to chapels and saints of her devotion.[23] Besides the five nuns of the family whose names are known to us, there were several nieces and half a dozen slaves and maids in their group. Such a large group of nuns, all related to a prestigious general, was bound to leave a noticeable mark on the life of the nunnery.

The cohesiveness of these family groups was enhanced a great deal by their living together in spacious cells. These cells were the property of the family, where private lives could be hidden from the rest of the community. In fact, the ownership of the cells was always considered a family right, and it was jealously defended with appeals to the bishop and with legal action in the ecclesiastical and secular tribunals. In 1618, a small family cluster formed in La Encarnación by Doña Justina de Guevara, her sister Doña Leonor de Guevara, and their niece Doña Justina de la Cerda, three nuns of the black veil, informed the bishop of Lima that they were being harassed by the abbess and other powerful nuns about the lawful possession of their cells and their slaves. Obviously, some serious doubts had been raised about the validity of the titles held by the Guevara sisters, and the dispute could not be solved within the nunnery itself. The Guevara sisters ended the appeal to the bishop with the following words:

> We humbly request that Your Most Illustrious Lordship order the Mother Abbess, under ecclesiastical penalties and censures, that we should not be disturbed and harassed in the possession we enjoyed of the mentioned cells and slaves. She should not permit that other nuns of the convent disturb and harass us . . . as long as we live, and after our death the same should hold during the lives of our nieces.[24]

Doña Justina and Doña Leonor de Guevara were not only defending their titles to the cells and the slaves, but also the right to maintain that property in the hands of the family as long as Guevara nuns resided in the nunnery. The bishops' usual format in cases of this nature was first to inform themselves by calling third parties to testify and by having the titles in question examined by experts in the law. Then, they tried to reach a friendly compromise between the nuns and thus avoid a formal court action, which was open only as a last resort.

Several other cases, also in the nunnery of La Encarnación, illustrate these procedures. The first involved a nun of the black veil, Doña Cecilia Pizarro. The abbess of the nunnery recognized Doña Cecilia's right to live in a cell that had been for some years in the Pizarro family. After her profession when Doña Cecilia tried to move from the novitiate into her cell, her aunt, the nun Doña Juliana de Valenzuela, would not allow her to do so. Doña Juliana had taken possession of the Pizarro cell with a group of her friends and refused to let her niece, Doña Cecilia, move in. Doña Juliana and her friends ignored the orders of the abbess, and Doña Cecilia had no other recourse but to appeal to the bishop. After the testimony of several witnesses and the examination of the ownership titles, the bishop backed the orders of the abbess and recognized Doña Cecilia as the rightful owner of the cell. Doña Juliana de Valenzuela finally yielded to her niece when the bishop threatened her with the severe penalty of excommunication.

At times, not even the intervention of the bishop could bring an agreement, and the dispute over the ownership of the cells had to be taken to court. In 1630, Don Luís Fernández de Córdoba, a well-known gentleman of Lima, brought a suit before the ecclesiastical tribunal in the name of his sister, Doña Francisca de Córdoba, a nun of the black veil in La Encarnación. Their story shows again how cells could stay in the same family for several generations, and how certain families sent some of their women into the nunneries generation after generation. At the turn of the century, a great-grandmother of Don Luís and Doña Francisca had bought a plot in La Encarnación and had built a cell for the nuns of the family. The cell, which had its own private courtyard, had been occupied in succession by great-grandaunts, grandaunts, and aunts of Doña Francisca, who lived in it in 1630. Then Doña María de Vergara, who probably owned an adjacent cell, clashed with Doña Francisca over the ownership of the small courtyard or *patiecillo*.

According to Doña María, she had bought the *patiecillo* many years before from an aunt of Doña Francisca and had paid ninety pesos for it. Fernández de Córdoba tried first to deny the fact. When Doña María produced the documentation of the sale, they claimed that the sale had been illegal and invalid, since no individual nun could alienate a property that belonged to the entire family. The case was first brought to the attention of the abbess and, when she failed to resolve the dispute, it was sent to the bishop. The bishop made efforts to mediate between Doña Francisca and Doña María, but he also failed to resolve the issue through extrajudicial channels. At that point, Don Luís Fernández de Córdoba brought a formal legal action before the ecclesiastical tribunal in the name of his sister and the other nuns of the family. The final resolution of the case is unknown to us, but the judges questioned witnesses and examined hundreds of documents, going all the way back to the original purchase by the great-grandaunt of Doña Francisca at the turn of the century.

A similar case occurred decades later in 1683 in the convent of La Concepción. A group of nuns of the Sanz Dávila family had been challenged about the possession of their cell by other nuns of the nunnery. Once again, the extrajudicial mediation of the abbess and bishop failed to resolve the dispute, and the case ended up in court. Sergeant Major Don Manuel Sanz Dávila represented the nuns of the family in their legal battle for the possession of their cell.[25]

As we turn our attention in the next chapter to the way of life led within these convents, it should be kept in mind that the large Peruvian nunneries were not just religious institutions in the modern sense of those words. The *conventos grandes* were *pueblos formados,* miniature, self-contained cities of women, islands in the midst of the secular city of men. The cloisters, the gardens, the hamlet formed by the cells, the common rooms, and the workshops of the nunneries were filled with hundreds of women of all social and economic classes. From the rich white heiress to the black African slave, the nunneries reflected the full spectrum of the racial and social differentiations of the outside world. The strong and prevalent cultural current of marianism, with its ideals of virginity and consecration to God, shaped many women of Iberian societies. Yet, even a fanatic marianism can hardly explain the large numbers of nunneries in colonial Peru and the constant exodus of thousands of women who took refuge there.

The hundreds of slaves lived in the cloisters not because of marian ideals, but because they were held there in bondage by the wealthy nuns who owned them. Most of the maids entered the nunneries, not in search of Christian perfection, but to obtain shelter, food, and security. For many of them, the nunnery was an escape from poverty and from a society in which sexual harassment and abuse of poor women was common. A great number of the nuns were the product of the conventual schools, where they had lived since a young age. The nunnery was the only world they had ever known. The consecrated women could find an independence and freedom in the nunnery which they could never have enjoyed in the outside world. They were free from the burdens and responsibilities of the common large families of those days. They had time to read, play musical instruments, and socialize with their friends. They enjoyed a political life unknown to the women of the secular city. They could vote by secret ballot on almost all issues that affected their lives, and they could aspire to and even campaign for conventual offices which carried a great deal of power.

The many babies and young girls in the convent could fulfill the nuns' maternal instincts. Religious and secular fiestas were celebrated in the nunnery with a luxury and zest not always paralleled in the outside world. Finally, the professed nuns enjoyed an economic independence known to very few women outside the cloisters. They owned their own cells and controlled their dowries and properties, which they could use at will without the approval or consent of a husband, a father, or an elder brother.

8

❦

Life in the
Colonial Nunneries

COLONIAL NUNNERIES OF PERU, following a tradition as old as monasticism itself, carved out of the crowded and noisy cities a space thought to be sacred, where religious and contemplative life was supposed to flourish. Silence and stillness hung over the court-yards and gardens, the long, ornate cloisters, and the shrines and chapels of the convent. The monastic way of life made the nunneries into something much more than a space segregated from the city of men. It transformed them into a world where humans seemed to touch the boundaries of the supernatural city of God. Even today, a visitor to any of the ancient abbeys still seems to cross the threshold into another world.

This unique quality was not merely the result of a religious architecture of vaulted cloisters with gardens and fountains but was created, in part, by the way in which time passed within the walls of a monastic institution: little ever changed within them. Whereas time in the secular city is linear and stretches inexorably toward an unknown and unpredictable future, time in the cloisters coils around itself in a slightly ascending spiral, making each day a repetition of the previous one. The contemplative nun spent long hours in meditation and adhered daily to a rigid schedule which seemed to freeze time. She denied her bodily senses to achieve an inner awareness of things unworldly.

201

Las Nazarenas

The sacred character of the monastery was utterly shattered in the *conventos grandes* of colonial Peru. By the early seventeenth century, large nunneries, with populations exceeding 1,000, had become chaotic republics of women who made a mockery of monastic discipline with their worldly life-style. As we shall see, in trying to reestablish a semblance of monastic discipline, bishops and viceroys failed repeatedly to reform the nuns of the *conventos grandes*. Yet colonial Peru had many small, observant nunneries, where monasticism at its best blossomed for more than two centuries. Las Nazarenas was such a nunnery. Life within that cloister had a character of religiosity and austerity totally unknown in the *conventos grandes*.

The founder of Las Nazarenas was a woman of very modest origin named Antonia Lucía del Espíritu Santo. Born in Guayaquil on June 12, 1646, she lost her father when she was eleven or twelve years old. Her mother took her to El Callao, the port of Lima, where both women struggled to make a living as *cigarreras*, or cigar makers. Worried about the future of her daughter, the mother arranged the marriage of Antonia Lucía to a "virtuous and poor" gentleman of El Callao named Alonso Quintanilla. After the death of her husband, Antonia Lucía, with the economic support of a Captain Francisco Serrano, founded a retreat for pious and poor women. The new foundation was called Beaterio de Las Nazarenas, but it never became the austere monastic institution envisioned by Antonia Lucía.

Captain Serrano, who had donated the money for the foundation, insisted that his seven-year-old daughter be appointed the first mother superior of that convent. Las Nazarenas of El Callao soon became the kind of place one would expect under the leadership of a seven-year-old child. In 1681, Antonia Lucía, on the advice of her confessor, left El Callao. Heartbroken, she traveled to Lima in search of her ideal monastic institution. For about a year, she lived as a guest in the Beaterio of Santa Rosa de Viterbo in Lima, still dreaming of her own foundation and eliciting the admiration of the other inmates by the austerity of her life.[1]

In Lima, the saintly life of Antonia Lucía attracted the attention of two wealthy gentlemen, Captain Roque Falcoa and Don Sebastián de Antuñano. With their generous donations, the foundation of Las Nazarenas of Lima became a reality. Antonia Lucía's new retreat house for pious women began as a beaterio, but as such, it lacked canonical recognition of the church to be a juridically approved nunnery. Canonical recognition was not bestowed upon Las Nazarenas until after the death of Antonia Lucía. On March 18, 1738, the viceroy marqués of Castelfuerte presided over solemn ceremonies, which transformed the *beaterio* of Las Nazarenas into a full-fledged nunnery, recognized by the church. On that day the elite of Lima's society gathered at the gates of the nunnery of the Barefoot Carmelites to accompany three of its professed nuns to Las Nazarenas. There these nuns would instruct the spiritual daughters of Antonia Lucía in the canonical and juridical obligations of true nuns.

The three professed Carmelites, Barbara Josefa de la Santísima Trinidad, Grimanesa Josefa de Santo Toribio, and Ana de San Joaquín were each accompanied by two prominent society ladies. They took their places in three ornate carriages drawn by six mules, and were carried through the streets of Lima to the cathedral, which was filled with common people and civil and ecclesiastical authorities. In a brief ceremony, the Carmelites received the official documents of Madrid and Rome, which established Las Nazarenas as a formal nunnery. Afterwards, the carriage of the viceroy, surrounded by the palace guard, and followed by the carriages of the nuns, led a procession of hundreds of people to the church of Las Nazarenas. There, a concert of sacred music and a choral presentation were offered for the entertainment of the illustrious guests.

When the concert was over, the viceroy marqués of Castelfuerte and the marchioness of Casaconcha took the nun Barbara Josefa by the hand and introduced her into the cloisters of Las Nazarenas. The other two professed nuns followed, led by ladies and gentlemen of Lima society. The group, headed by the viceroy, strolled through the cloister and gardens, while the three professed nuns took possession of the institution with a symbolic opening and closing of doors. Finally, Barbara Josefa de la Santísima Trinidad was installed as the first abbess of the nunnery of Las Nazarenas, and the viceroy with his lay entourage left the cloisters to return to their waiting carriages. With Las Nazarenas now a juridically recognized nunnery, the daughters of Antonia Lucía began their novitiate under the direction of the three Carmelite nuns.[2]

The canonical recognition of 1738 changed very little the austere way of life established by Antonia Lucía in the 1680s. Since the days of the foundress, the inmates of Las Nazarenas dressed in coarse, purple robes, went barefoot, and tied a rope around their necks. Under their veils, they wore a crown of thorns similar to that depicted in Christian iconography for Jesus. To underscore that resemblance even more, the nuns carried on their shoulders wooden crosses as they marched in procession at the appointed hours to some of the community functions. Their meals were very simple, and fasting and other corporal penances were encouraged.

The nuns of Las Nazarenas observed strict silence and followed a rigid schedule which seldom, if ever, was broken. They arose before dawn, at 4:00 A.M., from the wooden boards they called beds, and marched in procession to the convent's church. Wrapped in silence and shadows, the nuns meditated in the choir loft for almost two hours while the rest of Lima slept. By 7:00 A.M. the morning singing of the psalms was completed, and the nuns started preparations for the solemn celebration of the conventual mass. Before the start of the mass, the nuns were allowed to proceed to the confessionals, where they talked in private through the grill with their confessors and spiritual counselors. The celebration of the mass was usually finished by 8:00 or 8:30 A.M., and was followed by a light breakfast. From 9:00 until 11:00 A.M., the nuns, still observing strict silence, engaged in manual labor, such as sweeping the cloister, cleaning cells, and tending gardens; then they retreated to their pirvate cells for a short period of meditation, which was followed by the community's main meal.

The nuns ate in silence while listening to the reading of a pious book. After the meal was over, the nuns could return to their cells for a period of rest, reading, and tending to personal affairs until 2:00 P.M., when the community schedule was resumed with the singing of vespers. By 2:30, the nuns gathered in the common *sala de labor* or sewing room to do needlework until 4:00 P.M., when the schedule called for spiritual reading and the recitation of the rosary. By 6:00, the nuns were gathered again in the choir loft for an hour of meditation and prayer, which was followed by the communal singing of matins. After a light supper, the nuns formed a procession and, carrying their wooden crosses, they went through the cloisters in a symbolic recreation of the *via sacra*, or way of the cross. By ten o'clock, they had already retired to their cells for the rest of the night.[3]

This life-style was a world apart from the easy, secularized life in the *conventos grandes.* No wonder that the community of Las Nazarenas always remained very small, never exceeding 33 nuns. In fact, in the 1680s, Antonia Lucía had a difficult time persuading other women to commit themselves to such an austere way of life. The daughters of the best and most prominent families of Peru spurned Las Nazarenas. Most of them flocked to the *conventos grandes,* where they could lead lives of comfort and leisure. In 1790, the nun Josefa de la Providencia could truthfully write that "in the beginning the Lord brought Las Nazarenas neither countesses nor marchionesses, only poor and humble women." The very first companion to join Antonia Lucía in the community was an impoverished woman of very low social class, who in her youth "had been morally loose, and who had three children of tender age in spite of the fact that she had never been married."

The nuns' total lack of "proper" social background, coupled with the stern monastic rule imposed by Antonia Lucía, easily explains why Las Nazarenas always remained a small community. For a society girl imbued with the aristocratic mentality of the period, it must have been almost impossible, even if she felt called to a life of monastic austerity, to join a community whose foundress was a humble *cigarrera,* and whose first member was an unwed mother of dubious social background. Yet, there were enough women in Lima of modest social origin and deep religious faith to preserve Las Nazarenas as a viable institution. It eventually earned the admiration and respect not only of the common people, but of the civil and ecclesiastical authorities as well.

That admiration and respect were still shared in 1774 by the archbishop of Lima, Don Diego Antonio de Paredes. However, he was also concerned that the prolonged fasts and penances were ruining the health of many of the nuns. Without attempting to change the essential monastic character of the institution, he tried to mitigate somehow the austere asceticism observed by Las Nazarenas. The convent of Las Nazarenas survived the upheavals of the Independence period, and remains to this day a fine example of female monasticism in the heart of old Lima.

The cloister of Las Nazarenas was by no means the only observant convent of colonial Peru. There were others—Las Trinitarias, the Barefoot Carmelites, and Santa Clara of Tunja—where self-denial and monastic discipline flourished for more than two centuries. The documentation of the period calls these observant convents *conventos recoletos,* and in the religious landscape of the viceroyalty of Peru, they constituted strong centers of Christian monasticism. Yet because of their observance, practiced hidden and in silence, they hardly caused a ripple in the daily life of the colonial cities. The nuns of these observant convents, in the manner of elongated figures painted by El Greco, lived in a distant, metaphysical world of permanence rather than in the historical world of change. Constant observance of silence and long hours of repeated meditations created around them a historical vacuum.

Doña Francisca Josefa del Castillo, the mystical nun of the convent of Santa Clara de Tunja, lived from 1689 to 1742 in the northern region of the Peruvian viceroyalty. Yet, she could have lived one hundred years before in any other region of the Hispanic world. Her autobiography, written in superb Castilian, unfolds the inner life of a soul locked in a constant struggle with the ultimate issues of human existence. As a young child, Francisca Josefa was exposed to the writings of the great Saint Theresa of Avila which later drew her to the convent, where Francisca Josefa lived for more than fifty years. Nuns like Francisca Josefa del Castillo lived in many small, unknown convents scattered throughout colonial Peru, but their soft steps hardly left a footprint in the history of the viceroyalty.[4]

Life in the Conventos Grandes

Life in the *conventos grandes* stood in sharp contrast to the peacefulness and discipline of the *conventos recoletos.* The extended physical layout of the *conventos grandes,* their complex social structure, the clusters of relatives, and the hundreds of maids and slaves infused life in those convents with a faster tempo and greater drama than that experienced by women in the outside world. As their frequent reports to the crown show, viceroys and bishops were dazzled by the lively pace in the *conventos grandes.* They often declared themselves impotent to impose discipline and order upon those chaotic domains. Many nuns shunned their religious habits, and dressed in the best secular fineries; they acted with an independence and freedom that shocked civil and ecclesiastical authorities. Some of them, surrounded by faithful maids and slaves, refused to adopt the community's schedule and lived very much to themselves. At times, the community dining room stood half empty because the wealthiest nuns had special meals prepared by their maids, who served them in the privacy of their cells. Hundreds of religious and civil festivities observed in the viceroyalty gave the nuns a golden opportunity to organize boisterous evenings of music, fireworks, parades, and plays. During some of these occasions, it was not unusual for the abbess to suspend the law of the cloister and to admit secular persons of both sexes into the courtyards and gardens of the nunnery. The *locutorios* or parlors were always filled with all kinds of visitors: from the pious woman, who came to visit a daughter, to the young, perfumed dandy, who brought flowers or candy to a favorite nun.

Thousands of formal law suits originated in the cloisters of the *conventos grandes,* and nuns often clashed with each other. The frequency and legal complexity of these cases taxed the ingenuity of judges and lawyers, clogged the regular channels of colonial justice and, at times, forced some bishops to appoint special courts to clear the dockets of the regular tribunals. Disputes among nuns did not always remain within socially acceptable legal action; sometimes they erupted into physical violence. Cloisters, intended for silence and prayer, witnessed assaults, beatings, stabbings, and at least one well-documented murder. In a letter to the king, one eighteenth-century viceroy confessed his total inability to impose order on the *conventos grandes.* If husbands cannot control their own wives, he wrote with a touch of bitter humor, how was he supposed to control thousands of women living behind cloister walls in their semiautonomous kingdoms?

A typical outburst of violence occurred in the nunnery of La Encarnación in July 1707. Two sisters, professed nuns of the black veil, Doña Francisca de Merino and Doña Teresa de Merino, had developed some unclear, but serious disagreement with Catalina Negrón, the *campanera* or bellringer of the convent. The dispute had persisted for several months when the two Merino sisters sent a message to the *campanera.* They bid her to their cell for a friendly chat in order to settle their differences peacefully. The unsuspecting Catalina Negrón answered the call, unaware that four maids of the Merino sisters, armed with heavy clubs, were waiting for her. As Catalina crossed the threshold of the cell, she was assaulted by the maids Sabina Dorado, María de la Encarnación, and Juana de Llanos while the black slave, Juana de Peralta, stood guard at the door of the cell.

The three maids gave Catalina Negrón a savage beating and, throwing her on the floor of the cell, cut her hair and shaved her head. Catalina's screams of pain attracted the attention of several nuns who rushed toward the cell of the Merino sisters. Among them was the vicar of the choir, a woman and one of the most important officers of the nunnery. The nuns found access to the cell blocked by the menancing presence of Juana de Peralta. In trying to enter the cell, the vicar was assaulted and pushed aside by the black slave. She slapped the face of Juana de Peralta who, in turn, responded by drawing rivulets of blood on her arms and face. A pot of *locro,* the typical Peruvian stew of meat, potatoes and corn, stood simmering nearby. The slave grabbed the steaming pot, emptying its contents over the vicar's head.

When peace was restored at last, both the vicar and Catalina Negrón required medical attention in the convent's infirmary. Eventually, the two victims filed suit with the ecclesiastical tribunal against the Merino sisters and their maids. Three of the maids were expelled from the nunnery. Juana de Peralta, after receiving fifty lashes, also was expelled from the convent. No sentence was passed on the two Merino nuns. The tribunal merely instructed the abbess to punish the sisters commensurate with their guilt in the attack against Catalina Negrón.[5]

Scuffles of this nature were not uncommon in the *conventos grandes,* but none of them seem to have matched the tragic violence that wrecked the life of Doña Ana de Frías. Doña Ana, born early in the sixteenth century, entered at a very young age La Encarnación as a nun of the black veil. By the 1620s, she was already well known and feared throughout the convent for her violent character and erratic behavior. The most experienced women in the nunnery knew better than to cross her. She disdained wearing the monastic habit and veil, and at times would stroll half naked through the cloisters and gardens of the nunnery.

On one occasion, when a group of black laborers had entered the convent to do some heavy work, Doña Ana appeared "naked, without the habit, covered only with half a dirty sheet . . . and in that fashion she showed herself in front of the black men. . . ." Some members of the community realized that Doña Ana de Frías was crazy; however, others thought her possessed by an evil spirit, which should be driven away by charity, penitence, and prayers. At last, this difference of opinion came to be resolved. Henceforth only the most naive members of the community entertained any doubts about the mental balance of Doña Ana de Frías.

On the evening of November 24, 1624, the slaves and maids of the convent gathered in one of the torch-lit courtyards to celebrate one of the frequent fiestas of the nunnery with music, song, and dances. Special lyrics, alluding to life within the nunnery and certain of its inmates, had been written for the occasion, and each new song was greeted by a boisterous outburst of laughter. Mulattas and black slaves danced in a frenzy in the center of the courtyard, while torches threw their shadows against the walls of the cloister.

At about nine o'clock, Doña Ana de Frías appeared in the courtyard and made her way through the crowd of dancing servants to confront the slave Pascuala, owned by the nun Doña Isabel de Portugal. Doña Isabel, another troublemaker, had clashed with Doña Ana in the past, and eventually ended up in the jail of the convent. On this night, Doña Ana began to insult Pascuala. Before the bystanders realized what was going on, nun and slave were locked in a fight. Doña Ana tore Pascuala's dress to shreds, scratched her face and, with a loose stone from the floor of the courtyard, she opened a gash on Pascuala's head. Once she saw the blood gushing from the wound, Doña Ana, chased by a group of angry slaves, escaped through the cloisters toward the *locutorios*. In spite of the late hour, the *locutorios* were still filled with outside visitors, who spread news of the fight throughout the streets and plazas of Lima. While Doña Ana de Frías screamed insults and threats in the *locutorios*, the nun Doña Juana de Saavedra ran toward the backdoor of the nunnery to summon a *cirujano* or surgeon to stop the profuse bleeding of the wounded Pascuala.

Meanwhile the abbess of the nunnery, with other senior nuns, assembled a group of young and strong *donadas* to restrain the half-crazy Doña Ana. The task was not easy. Doña Ana ran again, throwing stones and broken bricks at them. It took four strong *donadas* to subdue Doña Ana de Frías. They dragged her screaming to the jail of the convent. By that time, many nuns and maids had gathered at the door of the jail to witness the incarceration of Doña Ana, and some of them were shocked again by the foulness of Doña Ana's language. As her legs and arms were clamped in the stocks and irons of the jail, Doña Ana shouted insults protesting that a wounded slave was not enough reason to imprison a professed nun. Doña Ana threatened that one of these days she was going to send Pascuala "to have supper with Christ." She also shouted, for all to hear, that other nuns had not been punished, even though they had thrown rope ladders over the walls of the convent to introduce their male friends. She, therefore, saw no reason why she should be punished with a jail sentence for merely wounding a black slave.

The troubles of Doña Ana de Frías had barely begun in 1624. For the next twenty years she was like the eye of a storm, leaving behind destruction and dissention at La Encarnación. During that time, Doña Ana de Frías was constantly in and out of jail for a variety of crimes. By the time she had completed her first sentence for the crime of 1624 and was released back into the community, she had become almost paranoid. She lived in fear that her life was threatened by other nuns and their maids and went around the nunnery concealing a sharp kitchen knife in the folds of her habit. She did not hesitate to brandish it during her frequent clashes with other members of the community.

Early in 1635, a double tragedy occurred within the walls of La Encarnación. One night, when most of the convent was already asleep, Doña Ana de Frías burst into the common dormitory that housed maids and slaves, shouting insults against the *priora,* a nun in charge of supervising the servants of the convent. When several maids tried to restrain her, Doña Ana took out her knife and threatened to stab anybody daring to approach her. A mulatta maid did, and Doña Ana stabbed her several times, nearly killing her. The nun Doña Juliana de Jesús was less fortunate. In another scuffle with Doña Ana de Frías, she received a mortal stab wound. Doña Ana was immediately thrown into the jail of the nunnery, but her case was sent to the Holy See for final disposition.

The pope discussed the case with the college of cardinals, whereupon he sent a special message to the bishop of Lima, instructing him on how to handle the dangerous nun. Apparently convinced that Doña Ana suffered from a serious mental illness, the pope imposed a rather mild sentence—six years in the jail of the nunnery. In addition, Doña Ana was to be deprived of the black veil for the same period. Furthermore, her right to vote in conventual elections was revoked for the remainder of her life. Finally, she could never again receive visitors from outside the nunnery, and was required to fast every Saturday during the six years she would spend in jail. Her sentence began on December 5, 1635.

Five years later, in December 1640, Doña Ana petitioned for an early parole from the ecclesiastical tribunal of Lima. The fear of the nuns had been such that in April 1640, they had a special jail built just to isolate Doña Ana from other imprisoned nuns. Upon learning of Doña Ana's petition to the ecclesiastical tribunal, the entire community of La Encarnación objected on the grounds that "they would all be dead at the hands of Doña Ana because she was incorrigible." However, since the process against Doña Ana ended abruptly in the closing weeks of 1640, one can assume that she died while still in the jail of the nunnery.[6]

Doña Ana de Frías's case may have been extreme, but it illustrates how profoundly monastic discipline could deteriorate within the *conventos grandes*. The outstanding feature of that case, however, is not so much the violence that was involved, but the length of time during which the violent behavior of Doña Ana was tolerated. Other episodes in Doña Ana's life were so commonplace as not to raise eyebrows within the nunneries. For instance, her penchant for not wearing the prescribed monastic habit was a widespread custom even before she entered the nunnery.

The archbishop of Lima, Don Melchor de Liñán y Cisneros, complained as early as 1681 that his repeated warnings about the modesty of conventual dress had either been ignored or "interpreted too freely" by the nuns. On October 1, Don Melchor issued new orders requiring the use of monastic robes and forbidding the application of white lace to undergarments and veils. Similar orders were repeated throughout the seventeenth century, and other bishops spoke of brightly colored ribbons, expensive lace, and secular garb displayed by some nuns even while receiving outside visitors in the *locutorios*. Clearly, many nuns ignored the prescribed dress code and wore whatever appealed to them.[7]

One aspect of conventual life which made it so pleasant and attractive to many women was the fun and entertainment enjoyed by nuns in the *conventos grandes*. In 1840, Fanny Calderón de la Barca wrote a letter to the American historian William H. Prescott which contained some very perceptive comments on Mexican women of her day. In that letter, Lady Calderón said that "I do not wonder that so many become nuns, as I think they amuse themselves quite as well in a convent as at home." These same words could have been written about the Peruvian nuns of the seventeenth and eighteenth centuries, who seem to have amused themselves more in a convent than they did at home.

Musical entertainment available in Peruvian nunneries became almost legendary, and its fame reached all the way to Madrid and Rome. Nunneries would vie with one another to attract talented musicians and singers in order to offer the most elaborate musical programs to the public. As mentioned before, a good singing voice, or the ability to play a musical instrument well was usually considered an acceptable substitute for a full dowry. The public was exposed to much of this musical talent during the liturgical services celebrated with great pomp in the conventual churches. Thousands of persons frequented churches and chapels of the nunneries. As a colonial observer noted, they did this not so much to worship God, but to enjoy some of the finest music available. Ecclesiastical authorities expressed their concern, now and then, about what they considered excesses in the liturgical celebrations, especially the widespread custom of hiring professional lay singers and musicians to enhance the musical quality of services. Their main complaint was that music in the *conventos grandes* greatly exceeded the accepted boundaries of liturgical celebrations, and was constantly used as a tool for purely secular entertainment.

Evenings of music and songs in the gardens of the nunneries became very popular. Frequently, musical events were organized in the *locutorios* for the entertainment of lay friends and relatives of the nuns. During these occasions, singers and musicians of the nunnery joined with hired secular musicians to produce excellent programs. Talented nuns stood always ready to write special lyrics to suit an occasion, and to weave the songs into a plot to produce a *juguete musical,* the Spanish equivalent to the French "opera bouffe."

The content of the nuns' musical productions did not always remain within the boundaries of good taste, as defined by bishops and civil authorities. To give but one exammple: Don Alvaro de Ybarra, a close advisor to the viceroy, wrote to the crown on December 20, 1669, complaining about the shocking behavior of the nuns of Lima. According to Don Alvaro, the nuns of the *conventos grandes* had been allowed to write and sing satirical and slanderous songs against the government of the count of Lemos in public. Had that type of criticism of the established authority emanated from lay and secular sources, it would have been punished severely by Don Alvaro. Yet, even the all-powerful Don Alvaro de Ybarra was impotent to take action within the walls of the nunnery. His letter to Madrid vented his frustration at not being able to control the nuns of Lima.

Other complaints accumulated against the nunneries' musical activities. The Diocesan Synod of 1668, attended by prominent representatives of the clergy of Peru, heard serious complaints on the matter: increasing attendance of the nunneries' musical performances by lay persons was accompanied by more raucous behavior. Nuns and lay persons mixed freely during those occasions, ignoring the laws of the cloister. The young pupils of the nunneries performed not only as singers, but also as dancers for the entertainment of lay visitors. At times, some of those musical events were attended by such crowds that the performance had to be moved from the spacious *locutorios* to the main body of the conventual church.

Canciones de negro, songs and rhythms of the black African slaves, constituted another element introduced by the nuns into their musical programs. Of the hundreds of slaves, some were *bozales,* or African-born, retaining many cultural traits of their native lands. It was only natural that eventually some of those songs and rhythms would find their way into the elaborate musical performances organized by the nuns of colonial Peru. The Diocesan Synod of 1668 took a very dim view of all these musical developments, and issued some stern orders in an effort to correct the most blatant abuses against religious discipline.[8]

The dramatic arts constituted another great source of entertainment in the *conventos grandes.* As mentioned in a previous chapter, drama was widely used in colonial Peru in humanistic education. Jesuits had popularized school dramas shortly after their arrival in Lima in 1568. Their schools of humanities produced hundreds of plays to which the Jesuits invited friends and relatives of their students. Some of those plays were adaptations of Spanish classical dramas, while others were written by the Jesuits themselves in either Spanish, Latin, or Quechua, the language of the Indians of Peru. Religious dramas, the traditional Spanish *autos sacramentales,* were also produced in the Indian missions, vividly instructing the natives in the theological and moral complexities of Christianity.

It was only natural, then, for the nunneries, where young ladies of the best families were educated, to open their doors to the dramatic arts. This in itself would not have met with opposition by ecclesiastical authorities; their objections arose early in the seventeenth century, when drama in the nunneries had already gone beyond the purpose of education and instruction of the faithful and become a boisterous, secular affair. The bishops of Peru often had to intervene to restrain the dramatic fervor of the nuns. They had to remind them that convents could not be allowed, even occasionally, to become public playhouses for the amusement and entertainment of lay people. For the most part, the nuns ignored the bishops' fatherly remonstrances and in the mid-eighteenth century, drama still flourished in the nunneries. One or two examples may help us to understand the nature of the problem as perceived by the bishops.

In the winter of 1631, an unknown informant brought some very disturbing news to the archbishop of Lima, Don Fernando Arias de Ugarte. The nuns of La Encarnación were in the midst of feverish preparations for the feast of Saint Ann, which was going to be celebrated with fireworks, a grand parade through the cloisters and gardens, and the production of a play prepared by the mulatto playwright Luís Sánchez. At the end of June 1631, the nuns of La Encarnación had time for nothing else than the thousands of details to be resolved before the feast day of Saint Ann. The nuns neglected singing the canonical hours in the choir, and they constantly broke the rules of silence. Luís Sánchez and several professional actors entered and left the convent on a daily basis, helping the nuns with rehearsals, theatrical equipment to set up the stage, and with costumes and make-up required for the play. Since the play had several male roles, the nuns had to borrow the proper costumes for those roles from male relatives and friends. Also, an agreement had been reached between the convent and several professional mule drivers of the city to furnish the "many mules and donkeys" that the nuns were planning to ride in the parade preceding the play.

Lay friends and benefactors had been invited to attend the

festivities, and everyone was buzzing with expectation and excitement about the upcoming gala production. However, the archbishop, Don Fernando Arias Ugarte, had another idea. On July 3, 1631, he issued a stern edict ordering the nuns to desist immediately from all their preparations under penalty of automatic excommunication from the church. The effects of that edict on the nunnery reveal once more the independent and rebellious nature of many nuns, who firmly believed that not even the bishop had any right to interfere in their personal lives.

On the morning of July 3, a cleric commissioned by the bishop and accompanied by a notary public arrived at the convent. The convent's bells gave the customary signal for all nuns of the black veil to assemble in the choir of the church. About two hundred women rushed from cells, *locutorios,* and gardens toward the choir, where they were met by the bishop's deputy. With all the nuns seated in their choir stalls, the cleric signaled the notary public, who proceeded to read the bishop's edict. As soon as they grasped the significance of that edict, and before the notary was through with his reading, "almost all the nuns jumped from their stalls, shouting and saying a lot of disrespectful things. . . . They ran toward the door to abandon the choir, shouting that they did not want to hear the edict." When the abbess of the convent tried to lock the doors of the choir and to restore order, she was pushed aside and ignored. Nuns scattered in all directions.

Some headed straight for the *locutorios,* where they contacted their lay relatives in an effort to enlist their help against the bishop's orders. Others accused the abbess of not standing up for the rights of the nunnery. They screamed that by having shown deference and obedience to the bishop on previous occasions, the abbess had caused the nuns' present predicament. Still other nuns claimed that their objections were intended not so much against the bishop's orders, but against the harsh ecclesiastical penalties attached to those directives. The cleric Julio de Villoslada, who happened to be visiting the nunnery on that day, witnessed the events. He later spoke of "a tumult of the younger nuns." The noisy commotion lasted the entire day, and monastic silence and discipline of the cloister were shattered. With their violent behavior, the nuns of La Encarnación transformed the religious cloister into a city taken over by an unruly mob.

Events developing on the following day show that the younger nuns of La Encarnación had chosen to confront openly the highest ecclesiastical authority of the viceroyalty. Ignoring the bishop's order and disregarding the dreaded penalty of excommunication, the nuns again admitted the playwright Luís Sánchez and one of the professional lay actors to the convent. Excommunication or not, the younger nuns were determined to proceed with the production of their play.

The archbishop, Don Fernando Arias de Ugarte, was beside himself. This time, he delegated his authority to one of the best-known and most prestigious clerics of Peru, Don Feliciano de Vega, vicar-general of the diocese of Lima. Don Feliciano arrived at La Encarnación armed with all the authority of the archbishop, ready to appeal to the state to reduce the rebellious nuns. Don Feliciano had no luck learning the names of the leaders of the conventual riot. In the great Castilian tradition of resistance to authority, so well described by Lope de Vega in his play *Fuenteovejuna,* the nuns refused to identify any particular sister as responsible for the blatant act of disobedience. As far as they were concerned, the entire community of La Encarnación answered for the events of July 3.

To confront an entire community as powerful as La Encarnación was not a viable and diplomatic alternative. Therefore, Don Feliciano de Vega continued his search for a few suspect individuals to be punished as an example for the rest of the nuns. Finally, with the help and testimony of the cleric Julio de Villoslada, the vicar-general was able to identify four nuns as the principal leaders of the tumult. They were Doña Dorotea Leones, Doña Mencia de las Casas, Doña Jacoba de La Reinaga, and the already mentioned Doña Isabel de Portugal. After they refused to submit and to recant, Don Feliciano declared them excommunicated from the church and had them thrown into the jail of the convent.

This action upset the convent. The grand parade on mules and donkeys, together with the gala production of the play, were never offered to the public in the way envisioned by the nuns. In a sense, the ecclesiastical bureaucrats had won the confrontation, but not before the nuns had flaunted their rebellious nature in open opposition to episcopal encroachment upon their private kingdom.[9]

The confrontation of 1631 was due not so much to the nuns' desire to produce a play, but to the fact that in their dramatic zeal they had exceeded the limits considered proper by the bishop.

Many other plays were produced in the nunneries which were not advertised among the general public, and which did not require close cooperation of professional actors and playwrights. On these occasions, the ecclesiastical authorities raised few objections, especially if the play could be disguised as some sort of academic and scholastic exercise for the benefit of the female students of the convent. Yet, dramatic fever in the *conventos grandes* was difficult to control, and gala productions did not disappear with the excommunication of 1631. The archbishop Don Melchor de Liñán y Cisneros found that out very clearly in 1705.

Early in September 1705, Don Melchor, like his predecessor in 1631, was informed that the nuns of La Concepción were rehearsing a secular play involving male roles. It was to be presented not only to the community, but to lay friends and benefactors as well. Don Melchor, like Don Fernando Arias de Ugarte, issued orders calling for the immediate suspension of preparations for the play. The eighteenth-century nuns, perhaps with a bit more finesse and sophistication than their sisters of 1631, avoided overreaction. They kept a low profile and, ignoring Don Melchor's orders, went on with their rehearsals.

Opening night was September 12, and curtain time had been set for 8:00 P.M. An hour or so before the start of the play, the street in front of La Concepción resembled a colonial Hollywood Academy Awards night. A crowd of curious onlookers had gathered on the sidewalks to watch for the arrival of the distinguished guests. Some of them rolled up in calesas, luxurious colonial carriages, drawn by mules or horses, which were parked in front of the convent to await the end of the play. The gates of La Concepción were illuminated by torches. A group of nuns stationed there greeted the arriving guests and led them to their seats in the improvised theater within the cloister. The play went on as scheduled, and lasted for two hours. After the play, the acting nuns, some of them still in their male costumes, mingled freely with the lay guests, receiving congratulations and exchanging social pleasantries. Still in their costumes and make-up, the nuns accompanied their guests to the open gates of the nunnery. There, in full view of the remaining onlookers, they waited as the calesas pulled to the gates of the convent to return the lay playgoers to their homes.

On the next day, the rage of the archbishop Don Melchor de

Liñán y Cisneros knew no limits. The nuns of La Concepción had made a mockery of his episcopal authority, and in full view of the entire city of Lima. The women of La Concepción had refused to recognize his authority as the highest ranking prelate of the Peruvian church. They had acted as if they were totally free and independent of any canonical and episcopal constraints. Don Melchor could not possibly ignore that blatant act of defiance. Not only did he issue numerous excommunications and jail sentences, he proceeded personally to excommunicate and dismiss from her office the abbess of the convent, Doña María Dávalos. He also excommunicated and dismissed from their offices the vicar of the abbess and the *porteras*, senior nuns who kept the keys to the nunnery and controlled the access of outsiders to the convent. The nuns, of course, must have known all along that they could not possibly get away with their disobedience and, obviously, they had accepted beforehand all the consequences of their actions. It is doubtful that all the penalties imposed by Don Melchor changed their minds as to the life-style they wanted to pursue within their own community.[10]

This event was certainly not the first time that the nuns of La Concepción had rebelled against episcopal authority. Like their sisters in other *conventos grandes,* they had a long history of flaunting their independence and ignoring episcopal orders. On two occasions in the seventeenth century the nuns of La Concepción not only angered the archbishop but also shocked the pious citizens of Lima with their behavior. In 1663, several vaqueros or cowboys led two young bulls through the backstreets and alleys toward La Concepción. The nuns were waiting for them at the backgate of the convent, which swung open to admit the vaqueros and their bulls into the cloister.

Generally, large deliveries were brought to the backgate, and the meat of slaughtered cattle and sheep, destined for the conventual table, came through those doors weekly. However, live bulls had never before passed through those doors. The swift and harsh reaction of the archbishop, coupled with the scandalized response of the people of Lima, clearly indicated that the nuns might have been planning some sort of bullfight within the walls of La Concepción. The archbishop Don Pedro de Villagómez excommunicated the vaqueros and all the nuns directly implicated in the unusual affair. However, his penalties did not produce a very lasting impact on the convent.

A few months later, the community of La Concepción was once again in trouble with the archbishop. On that day, the Holy Tribunal of the Inquisition celebrated one of its frequent *autos-da-fé* with great solemnity and pomp. A somber procession led the *penitenciados* or condemned persons through the streets of the city, exposing them to the curious gaze of the masses. The procession ended in the main plaza, where the best of Lima's society had gathered to hear the reading of the sentences and to witness the imposition of penalties. An auto-da-fé always attracted great crowds and gave the city an air of gay festivity. For many women confined to convents by the laws of the cloister, it must have been hard to be excluded from participation in these events.

On January 23, 1664, forty-eight inmates of La Concepción decided to sneak out of the cloister and join the crowds in watching the colorful parade led by the inquisitors of Lima. All of the escapees of 1664 were maids and lay women who, living in the nunnery, were subject to the laws of the cloister. Friends and relatives must have recognized them in the city streets, and news of their escapade soon circulated from one end of the city to the other. When the archbishop Don Pedro de Villagómez found out, he was angry and appalled. He excommunicated the culprits and ordered the abbess of La Concepción to expel them from the nunnery. The aborted bullfight and the escapade of the auto-da-fé represent two more occasions during which the inmates of the nunneries ignored the laws of the cloister, challenged the authority of the archbishop, and decided "to amuse themselves" regardless of the consequences.[11]

Social Visits

The well-established and almost ritualized custom of social visitations constituted another source of entertainment and amusement among women of Iberian societies. Prolonged and elaborate social visits, usually paid during the early evening hours, were extremely popular among secular women of the colonial cities. They presented the ladies a frequent opportunity to dress in their finest garments. Wearing their best jewelry, they displayed their silver and crystal, serving light refreshments. They also dazzled their friends with the luxurious furnishings of their houses and the excellent services rendered by their maids and slaves.

The founders of the *conventos grandes* came from the upper classes of colonial society, and the transformation of their ancestral homes into nunneries did not interrupt the flow of social visits. In fact, almost from the beginning, the large nunneries became popular centers of social gatherings. As the number of cloistered women increased throughout the seventeenth century, so did the number of relatives and friends who came to pay social calls to the nuns. The *locutorios* or parlors became a focal point of life within the nunnery. Hundreds of documents attest that what took place, at times, in the *locutorios* was frowned upon by ecclesiastical authorities. One of the authorities' greatest concerns was that the constant flow of visitors was not always contained within the restricted area of the parlors. Some of the colonial abbesses considered it within their rights occasionally to ignore the laws of the cloister, and to let secular visitors stroll through the gardens or gather in designated areas within the convent.

The extended physical layout of the nunneries made it almost impossible to monitor all contacts between nuns and their outside friends. A low or broken fence, street-level balconies or windows, a terrace overlooking a deserted alley, and the back delivery gates presented willing nuns with many opportunities to maintain contacts with the outside world. What troubled the bishops the most was not the occasional serious infraction of the convents' rules or vows, but the incredible amount of time the nuns wasted on the social ritual of entertaining secular visitors and the expenses incurred in serving abundant and elaborate refreshments.

By the beginning of the seventeenth century, the ecclesiastical authorities of the viceroyalty had already begun to clash with the Peruvian nuns in the effort to restrict and control the numbers of secular visitors to the *conventos grandes*. Yet the nuns and their secular friends either ignored the episcopal guidelines or appealed to a higher authority to continue with their visits. Some powerful and wealthy families did not hesitate to appeal all the way to the Holy See. On May 28, 1628, Pope Urban VIII issued an apostolic brief addressed to *"Dilectae in Christo filiae Sebastianae de Muris mulieri nobili Civitatis Regum in Indis,"* to the beloved daughter of

Christ, Sebastiana de Paredes, noble woman of the City of the Kings in the Indies, entitling Doña Sebastiana to enter the cloisters of the nunnery where her three daughters were professed nuns of the black veil. In addition, she was allowed the company of two other noble matrons. Dressed modestly, they could stroll through the convent, eat with the nuns, and be entertained by her daughters.

The Paredes family, aware of the royal patronage of the crown over the church, presented the apostolic brief to the Royal Council of the Indies and obtained the king's approval of its content. In view of such papal and royal approval, no local Peruvian authority, whether ecclesiastical or secular, could prevent Doña Sebastiana de Paredes and her friends from entering the nunnery and spending long hours socializing with the nuns. Of course, in most instances, this kind of appeal to the pope and the king was not necessary. Most abbesses displayed real ingenuity in finding loopholes in the law, and by their own authority granted innumerable exceptions to the rules prohibiting the entrance of secular persons into the cloisters. Nevertheless, a number of powerful families followed the example of Doña Sebastiana de Paredes.

In a society permeated by religious beliefs and dominated by the institutional presence of the church, a personal apostolic brief from the pope must have been a source of great social prestige. One can imagine the pride and conceit of those matrons who could flaunt such a document in front of their friends, and who saw viceroys and bishops yield to the rights they had obtained from the Holy See. Such was the case of Doña Petronila de Guzmán y Tobar.

In 1640, Doña Petronila, wife of General Don Rodrigo de Mendoza, obtained an apostolic brief, which allowed her to enter the cloisters of La Encarnación, La Concepción, and Santa Clara. She could exercise this privilege three times a year in each convent, and she could take her mother, Doña Brianda de Luna y Zuñiga, and her daughter, Doña Jordana de Mendoza y Guzmán, with her. The three women were allowed not only to stroll through the cloisters and to visit with their friends, but also to "partake of some corporal refreshments" with the nuns.[12]

Although social visits within the cloistered areas of the nunneries were not infrequent, nuns entertained the majority of secular visitors in the large and well-furnished *locutorios* or parlors of the convent. The *locutorios* were not affected by the laws of canonical closure, and common law of the church permitted access to both men and women. In most convents, the rule demanded that secular visitors be segregated according to sex, with separate parlors for each. All visitors had to identify themselves to the *portera,* or doorkeeper, and request the presence of the nun or nuns they wished to visit. The *portera* was supposed to inform the abbess or her vicar of the arrival of the visitors and to summon the nuns only after having obtained the abbess's permission. In addition, visits were to take place only in the presence of an independent chaperone. Documents of the period refer to them as *escuchas* or listeners. Their duty consisted in reporting to the abbess any suspicious conversations or unbecoming behavior on the part of the nuns or their visitors.

Each convent was also required to post visiting hours and never to allow visitations outside of those hours, so that community life would not be constantly interrupted. Finally, nuns were urged not to receive visitors other than their parents, brothers and sisters, and close relatives. All of these rules were obviously designed to protect the religious character of the nunneries, and to prevent the secular contamination of the cloisters. Yet, all those guidelines were universally ignored by the nuns of the *conventos grandes,* and all the efforts of viceroys and bishops could not change that fact.

A constant stream of visitors passed through the *locutorios* of the *conventos grandes.* They were seldom segregated by sex or limited to close relatives of the nuns. Posted visiting hours were mostly ignored, and one could find visitors in the parlors from the early morning hours until well into the evening. To the dismay of bishops and viceroys, these visits were not subdued affairs, filled with "edifying" and spiritual conversations, but noisy social gatherings, little different from receptions in the outside world. Many nuns took advantage of these visits to display their culinary talents and their artistic skills before friends and relatives. Black slaves brought delicacies from the conventual kitchens to the parlors frequently filled with the pleasant singing voices of the nuns and the sounds of guitars, violins, and harps. The official chaperones, often friends of the nuns and their secular visitors, seldom remained the detached, objective observers required by the rules. Most of the time they ended up actively participating in the festivities. Thus ecclesiastical authorities were caught wondering how to chaperone the chaperones.

At times, the *locutorios* of the *conventos grandes* were much more than a stage where the nuns engaged in boisterous, but innocent, fun and entertainment. Occasionally, events occurred that hardly fit into the legal and ethical framework of a monastic institution. Through the years a multitude of clerics served as chaplains and confessors of the nunnery and made a living from the income derived from their chaplaincies. Many of these clerics visited the parlors of the convents almost daily, cultivating the friendship of important nuns and securing a loyal following in the community. Their acceptance by the most powerful nuns obviously affected not only their economic status, but also their potential influence on the internal affairs of the nunnery.

Clashes between some of these clerics and one or another faction of the community were not unheard of. In 1680, the chaplains of the convent of Santa Clara, Don Antonio Arias de Ugarte, Don Juan de la Guardia, Don José Ternero, and Don Antonio Pérez de Vargas, caused a small crisis in the nunnery when they refused to attend in their ecclesiastical robes the ever-increasing religious festivities and liturgical services organized by the nuns. Long discussions and drawn-out negotiations between the four chaplains and groups of nuns took place in the *locutorios*. However, these efforts ended in a stalemate. When the nuns attempted to hire other clerics to attend their liturgical functions, the four official chaplains objected and physically prevented the new clerics from entering the convent. At this point, the nuns decided to seek legal counsel. In a meeting between the abbess, her advisors, and some experts in canon and civil law, the decision was reached to present the case to the ecclesiastical tribunal. Representatives of the tribunal came to Santa Clara to take depositions and to examine witnesses. Finally, the ecclesiastical tribunal dispatched the notary public, Alonso de los Carneros, to the convent, ordering the chaplains either to serve in the liturgical festivities at the pleasure of the nuns, or to allow other clerics to take their place.[13]

Every *convento grande* had its own cluster of clerics. As chaplains and confessors, they were essential to the religious life of the nunnery since only they could celebrate mass, conduct liturgical services, and hear the nuns' confessions. Quite often, the nuns would pamper many of these clerics and, at times, they would exercise great influence on the life of the community from their confessionals and the *locutorios*. However, few clerics of the colonial era became as powerful as the two brothers Don Juan and Don Gerónimo Sarmiento in the 1670s.

Their sister, Doña Catalina de Sarmiento, abbess of La Concepción, was for years one of the most influential nuns in the viceroyalty of Peru. Don Juan and Don Gerónimo, acting as advisors and agents of their sister, represented the nunnery in many of its outside business affairs. In addition, Don Gerónimo Sarmiento had secured the powerful position of mayordomo or business manager of the nunnery of La Encarnación. In this capacity, Don Gerónimo acted as buyer and seller on behalf of the convent, managed its investments and properties, and officially represented the nunnery in all its dealings with ecclesiastical and civil bureaucrats.

Using their power in the nunneries of La Concepción and La Encarnación, the Sarmiento brothers extended their influence over other convents, where they had relatives and friends among the professed nuns. Don Juan and Don Gerónimo were constantly seen in the *locutorios* of the nunneries, being entertained by their cloistered friends, or receiving different commissions from the community or from individual nuns. By 1674, many nuns regarded the Sarmiento brothers as their hired agents to protect their assets and personal rights against possible encroachment by the outside world. In 1674, the archbishop of Lima took some unusual action, clearly indicating that the ecclesiastical authorities understood and feared the unique position of the Sarmiento brothers. The archbishop had decided to conduct a canonical visitation of all the nunneries of Lima in order to reaffirm monastic discipline and to audit financial records. He was advised that his canonical visitation would end in failure as long as the Sarmiento brothers were in Lima, acting as agents for the nuns.

On December 17, 1674, the archbishop issued an order, exiling the two brothers from Lima under the penalty of excommunication. Don Juan and Don Gerónimo were given six days to abandon the city. One was directed to proceed south, toward the valley of Ica, while the other was supposed to go north, to the town of Barranco. Evidently, the ecclesiastical authorities considered such a harsh measure essential to ensure the success of the canonical visitation. The Sarmiento brothers and their cloistered friends were shocked by the order and tried to buy time. Assuming a humble and submissive tone, Don Juan wrote a letter to the archbishop, asking for more time to borrow money for the trip and to buy some mules to carry his belongings. Don Gerónimo also wrote, explaining that he was well advanced in years and infirm, adding that he could hardly face the trouble of being exiled from the city alone. The archbishop, nevertheless, reiterated his order, although softening it a bit. He granted the Sarmiento brothers a few more days in Lima and allowed them to go into exile together.[14]

As indicated above, the *locutorios* of the nunneries, at times, provided the stage for small dramas that broke the routine of monastic life, while engaging many nuns in the excitement of unexpected events. One such event occurred on May 16, 1689, in the convent of Saint Joseph in Lima. At around seven o'clock in the evening, the chief chaplain of the convent, Don Roque Valcázar, arrived to supervise the ritual closing of the convent's main gate. In spite of the hour, the nuns Isabel de San José, Juana de San Bernardo, and Francisca de San Javier were still engaged in an animated conversation with a lay friend, Don Santiago de Albarisqueta. Another chaplain, the priest Don Esteban Flores, was standing at the door of the nunnery, awaiting a physician who had been summoned to examine a sick nun. A group of slaves, led by the mestiza Bernarda de León, were tidying the parlors for the night. Outside, a calesa, its curtains drawn, stood parked near the entrance of the convent, as if waiting to return a visitor home. Two men sat resting on a stone bench to one side of the convent's main gate. One of the men appeared to be giving some kind of instructions to the other. He was known to many of the nuns, and his name was Domingo González Argandoña.

Don Roque Valcázar, the chief chaplain, had already closed the heavy front door but had not yet locked it with the three keys. He kept waiting for Don Santiago de Albarisqueta to finish his conversation with the nuns and to leave. While the chaplain waited, another nun appeared in the hall and joined the group talking to Don Santiago. She was the novice María de San Juan, whose wordly name had been Doña María Prieto. That night she appeared in the parlor without the veil that was supposed to cover a novice's head and shoulders at all times. The arrival of a novice at that late hour at the entrance hall was highly irregular and had obviously been prearranged. As María de San Juan joined in the conversation of the other three nuns and Don Santiago de Albarisqueta, the doorbell rang. A deliveryman requested permission to enter the nunnery to deliver several jars of honey, which had been ordered by the nuns.

As soon as the door opened, the two men who had been sitting on the stone bench by the gate rushed into the hall of the convent and, aided by Don Santiago de Albarisqueta, grabbed María de San Juan, dragging her toward the front door. The chief chaplain, Don Roque Valcázar, shouting for help, tried in vain to prevent what he deemed a kidnapping. The priest Don Esteban Flores, the physician Don Pedro de Utrilla, nuns, maids, and even some of the neighbors, all came rushing in confusion to answer Don Roque's shouts for help. However, all of them arrived too late. The abductors had thrown Doña María into the waiting calesa, which had already sped away into the night.

The convent of Saint Joseph was stunned by the novice's abduction, and by the fact that two of the abductors were well-known merchants of Lima. Both Santiago de Albarisqueta and Domingo González de Argandoña owned clothing stores in the *calle de los mercaderes* (merchants' street), and were well known to the nuns of Saint Joseph. It took several weeks and an official inquiry by the archbishop Don Melchor de Liñán y Cisneros to untangle the bizarre abduction. When the facts became clear, it turned out that there never had been an abduction at all. Doña María Prieto had arranged her own kidnapping with her friends and relatives in order to marry secretly Captain Alonso de Tenas Cabeza.

The case of the ex-novice Doña María Prieto, as clarified by the inquiry ordered by the archbishop, reveals a great deal about female society in colonial Peru, the power of the church, the way of life within the nunneries, and the character of Doña María herself. The ecclesiastical prosecutor, supported by the state, jailed the three male accomplices, Don Santiago de Albarisqueta, Don Domingo González de Argandoña, and Captain Alonso de Tenas Cabeza. All their properties and funds were seized and confiscated by the church. Their future would have been bleak indeed but for the frank testimony of Doña María Prieto. The ex-novice appeared before the ecclesiastical tribunal and completely exonerated the three men, who were then freed on bond.

According to Doña María, she had entered the convent of Saint Joseph with no real desire of becoming a nun; she merely obeyed the wishes of her devout father. As soon as she had taken the veil of a novice, Doña María realized that she had made a serious mistake. Therefore, she resolved to abandon the cloister. Fearful that the professed nuns would pressure her into remaining and into taking the final vows, Doña María took advantage of the loose discipline reigning in the nunnery. She secretly contacted her married sister and brother-in-law. At times in the *locutorios* or parlors, at times in the conventual church, and at times through the mediation of a faithful maid, the two sisters plotted Doña María's flight from the convent. Although they could have gone through proper canonical channels to obtain an official release from the novitiate, the two sisters chose to ignore the ecclesiastical bureaucracy and to act on their own, regardless of the consequences.[15]

Another curious and revealing affair occurred in the parlor of La Concepción on December 1, 1691. As usual, groups of the nuns' friends and relatives filled the *locutorios;* busy maids and slaves moved in and out of the parlors, serving refreshments to nuns and lay visitors. The hour was getting late, but the large entrance hall of the convent still resounded with loud voices, music, and laughter. However, this carefree gaiety came to an abrupt ending when a terrific fight erupted in the entrance hall. A few minutes before the outbreak of violence, the baker Domingo de Herrera, while delivering a basket of bread, had been admitted to the nunnery. The nun Doña Juana Molina had been summoned to the entrance hall to inspect the bread and to pay Domingo for his delivery. Doña Juana found the bread not only cold, but a bit stale. She refused to accept the delivery and to pay for the bread. Domingo de Herrera became indignant and, losing his temper, threw the basket of bread at the head of the nun. He also punched her with his fists, screaming insults at her.

When other nuns and maids tried to restrain him, Domingo de Herrera, blind with rage, attacked them, hitting and poking them with an umbrella. The women finally subdued the enraged baker and had him delivered to the city jail. After consulting with their friends and some of the lay witnesses to the events in the *locutorios* on the following day, the nuns decided to prosecute the baker Domingo de Herrera before the ecclesiastical tribunal. Domingo never had a chance against the powerful nuns of La Concepción. He was found guilty and sentenced to a jail term, during which his bakery was confiscated by the tribunal. To make his punishment even more severe, he was excommunicated "for having placed his hands sacrilegiously on a spouse of Jesus Christ." For weeks, Domingo's sad story and the nuns' revenge remained one of the favorite topics of conversation and gossip at La Concepción.[16]

As indicated above, contacts between the nunneries and the secular world were by no means limited to social gatherings in the parlors or to informal and, at times, violent meetings in entrance halls of the convents. Indirect evidence suggests that many unlawful meetings and conversations took place between nuns and secular friends through broken fences, or over low balconies and terraces overlooking deserted streets and alleys. As mentioned before, Doña Ana de Frías accused some of her sisters of throwing rope ladders over the walls of the nunnery to introduce lay friends into the convent. Doña Ana could not prove her accusations in ecclesiastical court, and the modern historian is hard put to find any specific and solid proof for those illegal meetings. Like clever smugglers of the period, the nuns of colonial Peru were very resourceful when it came to covering up incriminating evidence. Nevertheless, repeated warnings issued by the ecclesiastical authorities and records of the nunneries themselves contain enough allusions to substantiate the occurrence of such illicit meetings.

There was one event that, although rather innocent, was well documented because the principal eyewitness was the priest Don Juan Martín de Castro, prosecutor of the ecclesiastical court of Lima. On the evening of April 7, 1676, Don Juan Martín de Castro was walking toward his home when he passed the backstreet of the nunnery of La Concepción. As he made his way along the rear wall of the convent, he spotted a nun of the black veil. This nun, Doña Mariana de Molino, leaned out of an embrasure in the fence of the nunnery and talked to a man who, wrapped in a long cape, was armed with a sword. Don Juan must have suspected the worst, and in his later deposition, he testified as follows: ". . . committed to preventing such scandalous behavior, I approached the man and told him that such visit and conversation [with the nun] were out of order in that place and that late hour."

Don Juan should have known about the *pundonor* or pride of a Spaniard, who becomes truly dangerous when that pride is wounded; his friendly admonition unleashed a storm of rage. The stranger drew his sword and, not recognizing the ecclesiastical prosecutor because of the lateness of the hour, began to insult him in language that passersby did not dare repeat before the ecclesiastical tribunal. Doña Mariana de Molino, who according to an eyewitness was by now "hanging out" of the embrasure in the wall, also heaped all kinds of insults upon poor Don Juan Martín de Castro. His life was saved only by a few passersby who managed to restrain the nun's night visitor.

The nun and her friend eventually came before the ecclesiastical tribunal of Lima, where the affair was clarified and settled. It was revealed that on April 7, 1676, Doña Mariana had been visited by her own father, the priest Don Francisco de Molino. Don Francisco had been ordained into the priesthood only after the death of his lawful wife. Earlier that evening, a messenger had notified Don Francisco that one of his daughter's slaves had fallen from an upper corridor of the nunnery and was seriously injured. Don Francisco, moved by fatherly concern, rushed to the nunnery only to find the front gate already locked for the night. Eager to talk to his daughter, Don Francisco summoned her to the back fence "by giving a prearranged signal." The judges of the ecclesiastical court, aware of the mitigating circumstances, incarcerated Don Francisco for a brief period and fined him 300 pesos. Doña Mariana de Molino was ordered to spend some time segregated from the nuns of the black veil, secluded among the young novices of the convent.[17]

Although Don Francisco de Molino's motivations on that night were honest and reasonable, his irregular visit with his daughter at the fence of the nunnery seems to indicate that such meetings could easily be arranged. Don Francisco's admission that he summoned his daughter "by giving the prearranged signal" implies, of course, that there was prior agreement between father and daughter, and that lookouts or accomplices within the nunnery knew this signal and stood ready to convey the summons to Doña Mariana. The repeated warnings of the ecclesiastical authorities and their efforts to repair fences and to wall up low windows and balconies are strong indications that Don Francisco de Molino was not the only night visitor to the nunneries of Lima.

On July 17, 1683, for instance, the ecclesiastical prosecutor, Don Juan Martín de Castro, informed the bishop in an official report that five of the nunneries were not in compliance with the strict rules of the cloister. The convents of La Concepción, Santa Clara, Santa Catalina, Santisima Trinidad, and San José had low and broken fences through which the nuns were communicating with outsiders. At San José, Don Juan Martín de Castro noted that the cells of Doña Inés de los Reyes and Doña Isabel de Jesús had terraces and balconies over which anybody could easily climb in and out of the convent. No specific accusations were brought by the ecclesiastical prosecutor at that time, but the bishop issued a stern order to the abbesses of those convents, commanding them immediately to repair the fences and to wall up the low balconies. By the mid-eighteenth century, the problem still persisted. In 1755, the archbishop, Don Antonio de Barroeta y Angel, noticed extremely low fences in the convent of Santa Clara, and found the cells of Doña Petronila de Castro and Doña María Mancilla at the back wall of the convent built in such a way that they had very easy access to the street.[18]

Reform Efforts

Since the opening years of the seventeenth century, ecclesiastical authorities of the viceroyalty of Peru had been deeply concerned, and rightly so, about the lack of religious and monastic discipline within the *conventos grandes*. Peruvian bishops tried, mostly in vain, to influence their rebellious, spiritual daughters through chaplains and confessors. In addition, they availed themselves of their rights under canon law of the church to conduct a yearly official and canonical visitation of each nunnery. These canonical visitations were solemn and colorful affairs, lasting for several days and creating in the nunneries the atmosphere of a religious festival.

Early in the morning of the appointed day, the bishop, wearing his most awe-inspiring pontifical robes and surrounded by an entourage of high-ranking clerics, would be received at the main door of the conventual church by the abbess and the officers of the nunnery. With the nuns' choir, accompanied by organ, violins, lutes, and harps, singing flawlessly the hymn "Ecce Sacerdos et Pontifex" (Behold the High Priest), the bishop, wrapped in clouds of burning incense, would proceed toward the main altar. There, under the canopy, His Excellency celebrated the stirring pontifical mass of the Holy Spirit, while the church resounded with splendid music. Once the celebration of the mass was over, the bishop found himself honored with an exquisite breakfast prepared by the best cooks of the convent, after which he would stroll through the nunnery, inspecting the entire physical layout of the convent.

He scrutinized chapels, *locutorios*, cloisters, a few private cells, workshops, and common facilities, and paid special attention to the fence separating the nunnery from the secular city. Occasionally, the bishop would pause in his tour of inspection to dictate a few hurried notes to his secretary, who always followed a few steps behind. Given the extended physical layout of *conventos grandes*, such a tour of inspection would last most of the day.

For the next few days the bishop returned to the nunnery to begin an intensive inquiry into the spiritual and financial status of the convent. Usually, he held long conferences with the abbess, her advisors, other officers of the nunnery, and some of the chaplains. Then, at random, he would interview a dozen or so members of the community, ranging from prominent and proud nuns of the black veil to young novices and an occasional *donada*. At the end of these meetings, conferences, and interviews, the canonical visitation was completed and the nuns began a patient vigil, awaiting the bishop's official report. After a week or so had passed, the report was delivered to the nunnery by an ecclesiastical notary. The entire community would gather either in the chapel or in the chapter room. Before handing a notarized copy of the lengthy report to the mother abbess, the ecclesiastical notary would read it to the nuns. The document usually contained a long list of orders and guidelines and threatened harsh ecclesiastical penalties should these be ignored. Such documents clearly reveal the dichotomy that existed between ideals and realities in the daily life of the colonial nunneries.

These reports and episcopal orders affected the convents of colonial Peru like a firecracker thrown into the middle of a sleepy chicken coop. Having endured the episcopal visit, nunneries erupted into a flurry of protests, appeals, legal maneuverings, and consultations with canonical experts. However, after a while, everything returned to normal. The nuns, once more, returned to doing the same things they did before the bishop's visitation.

Although the bishop could issue orders, other than imposing ecclesiastical penalties, he never had any means to enforce his directives. Nuns either ignored these penalties or "interpreted" them to suit their own advantage. Factions of followers in the cities formed to cheer and support one or the other party, and hundreds of hours were spent in heated discussions of legal precedents or of fine points of obscure ecclesiastical laws. Year after year these canonical visitations served to underscore the stubbornness of the nuns, who were determined to persevere in their established ways. They also reveal the frustration of the bishops, who vainly attempted to reform the convents. Official reports of the ecclesiastical authorities list the same issues over and over again: lack of monastic discipline; chaos in *locutorios;* multitudes of unruly maids and slaves; excessive luxury in private cells; negligent *escuchas,* doorkeepers, and other officials; unlawful types of entertainment; widespread substitution of fashions of the day for religious veils and robes; excessive expenditures to finance religious and secular fiestas; and suspicious and secret contacts with all kinds of outsiders.

From a purely religious and theological point of view, these episcopal warnings, repeated yearly, are depressing, and they easily explain the frustration of colonial bishops. On the other hand, they also furnish clear proof that large groups of colonial women had taken hold of their own lives, and neither historical tradition nor theological and canonical arguments could prevent them from living in the manner they desired.[19]

Of the many clashes that occurred between nuns and bishops in the course of the seventeenth century, one illustrates especially well some of the above generalizations. It happened in December 1630 in La Encarnación which, housing several hundred women, and extending over two and one-half city blocks, had been a beehive of secular activities for many years. Several times it had been shaken by the erratic behavior exhibited by Doña Ana de Frías, as mentioned above.

In the late 1620s, the archbishop of Lima undertook a canonical visitation to the convent. He brought with him a thick book containing summaries of all reports made during previous visitations, as well as a list of all the orders issued during those occasions and the ecclesiastical penalties they carried. Forty of those episcopal precepts called for excommunication from the church. The compilation of these ordinances was inscribed with the title "Libro de Ordenanzas y Faltas de Religiosas." Periodically, this book was supposed to be read aloud during the community meal to ensure that none of the nuns could claim forgetfulness or ignorance of the bishop's orders and censures.

During the course of the visitation, the bishop of Lima discovered, to his dismay, that not only had the book not been read in years, but also it could not be found anywhere in the convent. Deeply disturbed, he began immediately to inquire as to the whereabouts of the missing book, which to him represented the bishop's juridical authority over the nuns. Early evidence, based on testimony by several nuns, implied that the cleric Luciano Guillén was responsible for the disappearance of the book.

Guillén, a frequent visitor of La Encarnación and a friend to many of the nuns, was accused of stealing the book to please his cloistered friends since they had been upset at the length of so many episcopal precepts. Subsequently, he was imprisoned in the ecclesiastical jail in spite of his repeated claims of innocence. Several days later, the bishop began having second thoughts about the trustworthiness of Guillén's accusers and returned to La Encarnación to pursue his inquiries in more depth. On December 5, he threatened all nuns with the penalty of excommunication if they were to mislead him and hide the truth. Then, a representative of the bishop summoned the oldest and most important nuns of the cloister before him in order to listen to their testimony one by one.

One of the first nuns to testify was Doña Luisa Altamirano who, in 1625, had been abbess of La Encarnación. In 1630, she was still one of the most powerful and influential nuns of the convent. Her testimony exonerated the imprisoned Luciano Guillén and shifted blame for the disappearance of the book to another well-known cleric. According to Doña Luisa, the canon and *maestrescuela* of the cathedral, Don Fernando de Guzmán, had written an official letter in 1625 to the nunnery, in which he requested all the books and papers related to the canonical visitations of the convent. Doña Luisa testified that she sent the books to Don Fernando, and, to her knowledge, he had never returned them. At first Doña Luisa's story sounded plausible, but further testimony revealed that she had been bluffing in an attempt to cover her own tracks in the unfolding saga of the missing book.

Testimony given by the nun Dorotea Leones, the next witness, not only unveiled Doña Luisa's bluff, but broke the case wide open.

Doña Dorotea exonerated the clerics Guillén and Guzmán, revealing that "she had heard many times a great number of nuns
of the convent saying . . . that they wished the book would be
burned because, according to them, it contained certain things
against their own reputation. Some time later, when the abbess
Doña Lorenza Serrato began looking for the book, . . . it could
not be found." She also heard many nuns saying that "it was useless
to look for the book because it had already been burned and
rightly so. . . ." Two other witnesses, Doña Ana de Guzmán, one
of the oldest members of the community, and Doña María San-
tillán who, as prioress of La Encarnación, held the second highest
rank in the nunnery, confirmed Doña Dorotea's testimony almost
word by word. A long stream of witnesses followed, confirming
the story of the burning of the book. Amazingly, however, not one
of the nuns could remember the name of a specific sister involved
in the plot of burning the book.

Once again the bishop met with silence, and the case finally got
lost in the labyrinth of ecclesiastical bureaucracy. The burning of
the book of visitations was, of course, a blatant act of defiance on
the part of the women living at La Encarnación. Their refusal to
identify the guilty parties served notice to the ecclesiastical authorities that no outside interference would be tolerated in the
internal affairs of the nunnery. The nuns of La Encarnación, like
their sisters in other *conventos grandes,* were determined to live
independent lives, and the opinions of viceroys and bishops mat-
tered little to them.[20]

Occasionally *conventos grandes* housed some individual nuns who
were saintly and devout women. However, by the seventeenth
century, these institutions ceased to be truly religious and monastic
communities. By the middle of the eighteenth century, discipline
in the Peruvian *conventos grandes* had deteriorated to such an extent that the situation required royal intervention. At least four
times in the second half of the eighteenth century, the crown
addressed stern orders to the nuns of the viceroyalty, commanding
them to obey bishops and viceroys and to conform to the rules of
monastic life. The crown even urged viceroys to use the power of
the state to force the rebellious nuns to obey the bishops. Extant
documentation clearly reveals that the crown was as unsuccessful
in its efforts to reform the nuns in the eighteenth century as
viceroys and bishops had been in the seventeenth. Neither eccle-

siastical nor civil authority were ever able to restore a semblance of monasticism to the *conventos grandes* of Peru. Behind their walls, the Peruvian nuns resisted all efforts by civil and ecclesiastical authorities to curtail their independence and freedom.

The lengthy visits of precepts and censures, contained in the eighteenth-century reports point to the same life-style already observed in the early decades of the previous century. Many nuns had practically abandoned the religious monastic robes and dressed in silks and jewels. In addition, they offended Christian modesty by displaying parts of their breasts and arms. The nunneries were still centers of public entertainment, and lay musicians and actors were admitted to the convents to help in the production of plays. If the plot of a play required it, nuns would appear on stage dressed as men, carrying pistols and swords. In 1755, Don Antonio de Barroeta y Angel had to remind the nuns that under no circumstances was it permissible to introduce bulls and calves into the cloisters to organize their own bullfights.

The presence of too many slaves and maids was still destroying the monastic character of the convents. Some of those servants, ignoring the rules of the cloister, paraded freely through the streets of the city. At times, they were spotted in the public bullring of Lima. The nunneries were filled, as usual, with many lay visitors, not only in the approved *locutorios,* but also in the cloisters and gardens. Frequently, lay persons were observed conversing with nuns over the outer walls of the nunneries, even though the main gates had been closed for the night. Community kitchens and dining rooms stood unused because the nuns preferred to have their meals prepared and served in the privacy of their cells. Babies were still being cared for by nuns, who obviously enjoyed being surrogate mothers. Too much time and money were spent on noisy parties to honor the birthdays or saint days of abbesses, officers of the convents, chaplains, and even lay friends. Some of the bishops were shocked to see the number of pets kept by the nuns and gave orders to rid the convents of all animals. In a couple of convents, bishops even found several small donkeys, which the nuns enjoyed riding through the extensive property of the nunneries.[21]

Deterioration within nunneries had reached such a point by the mid-eighteenth century that a concerted effort by bishops, viceroys, and the crown itself was required to curb the rebelliousness of the colonial nuns. With the encouragement and support of the viceroy, the archbishop of Lima, Don Antonio de Parada, prepared an *Auto General de Reforma* (General Charter of Reform) containing forty-two articles which, the bishop and viceroy hoped, would arrest the deterioration of female monasticism in the *conventos grandes* of Peru. The king approved the charter of reform on May 14, 1785, and the approval arrived in Lima, accompanied by royal orders to use all powers of the state to force the nuns to comply.

In 1786, the bishop of Arequipa, Don Miguel de Pamplona, proclaimed the charter of reform as approved by the king within his own diocese. Bishops of other provincial cities soon followed his example. The forty-two articles were primarily a repetition of all warnings, orders, and censures issued by bishops since Don Bartolomé Lobo Guerrero in the early years of the seventeenth century. The only noticeable differences were a harsher, more specific language, more severe ecclesiastical penalties, and the threat of criminal prosecution by royal authorities. In spite of these measures and close cooperation of altar and throne, the effects of the general charter of reform were disappointing. The nuns refused to yield, even in the face of explicit royal commands.

By 1782, they had already assembled a battery of lax confessors and canon lawyers, who rendered them an advantageous interpretation of the juridical language contained in the articles and who informed the nuns that "they are not morally obliged to obey a good number of the forty-two articles, because those articles are against the rules and principles under which the nuns took their vows. . . ." Once again, the legal and canonical battle resumed to last another two decades, into the early years of the nineteenth century.[22]

The Abbess and the Archbishop

The most dramatic of these reformation battles occurred in the 1790s in the nunnery of Santa Catalina. A woman of boundless ego, magnetic power, and Machiavellian mind, Doña Augustina Palacios, confronted the archbishop of Lima, successfully resisted the reform of her convent, and repeatedly defeated and humiliated the highest-ranking prelate of the Peruvian church. Not only the archbishop, but two viceroys, Don Francisco Gil de Lemos y Taboada and the marqués de Osorno, also felt Doña Augustina's scorn. In 1800, she still battled to prevent the reform of Santa Catalina, and to preserve a life-style which, to the archbishop, was anathema.

The confrontation between the abbess and the archbishop began in 1789. On March 21, the archbishop had written to the king to inform him of the slow progress in the reform of the *conventos grandes,* expressing his anguish and sorrow over the never-ending task of trying to reform the nuns of Lima. According to the archbishop, some progress had been made in the convents of La Encarnación, Santísima Trinidad, and La Concepción, but the situation at Santa Catalina was deteriorating. Headed by the abbess Doña Augustina Palacios, Santa Catalina displayed "scandalous and criminal disorder."

Doña Augustina, ignoring repeated warnings by the bishop and viceroy, had allowed the doors of her nunnery to remain wide open until very late at night. Male visitors had permission to enter the cloister at all hours, and some of them spent the whole day inside the nunnery, having their meals served by the nuns. According to the archbishop, inmates of Santa Catalina "went out into the city streets with total freedom, even attending public bullfights, and returning to the cloister at whatever hour they pleased. Not even novices of the rank of donadas were exempt from this abuse. . . ." The outer walls of the convent were "crowded with people" at all hours, and had become a popular place for the nuns to meet with their secular friends. This type of behavior, the archbishop informed the king, not only tore to shreds the moral fabric of Santa Catalina, but also made it more difficult to proceed with the reforms of the other convents of the city.

On August 8, 1790, the king responded to these charges with a royal cedula. He urged the viceroy and bishop to reduce the rebellious nuns to obedience by whatever means necessary, including the removal of the recalcitrant abbess. Despite mounting pressure applied by the viceroy and archbishop, three more years went by without any visible change in the behavior of the nuns. Short of taking extreme and drastic measures, which would have shaken the city of Lima, the two top-ranking officers of the viceroyalty were impotent to control Doña Augustina Palacios. At last, however, in March 1794, a final drastic step was taken.

At the end of February 1794, Doña Augustina Palacios, ignoring explicit and clear legal principles of canon law, allowed the funeral of a lay female friend to take place in the nunnery. In addition, she permitted the burial of her friend within the walls of the cloister, in ground reserved by law for consecrated virgins. Funeral services and burial were attended by many outsiders, thus making the affair a "public scandal" which required public punishment. The archbishop confronted Doña Augustina to inform her that her latest transgression could not be overlooked. Although aware of Doña Augustina's disrespectful and indomitable personality, the archbishop did not expect the answer she gave him: "Your Excellency, take care and rule your house and I will take care and rule mine."

That same day, the shaken archbishop went to see the viceroy, Don Francisco Gil de Lemos. The two men decided to remove the rebellious abbess from office, even if it would take military force to do it. They also decided to appoint a *presidenta* or acting abbess, who would govern the nunnery of Santa Catalina under their direction. Their problem, however, was to locate a nun who would show respect for monastic discipline and who would not be controlled by Doña Augustina. The task was not easy. Finally, they settled on Doña Josefa Próspera Gómez. On March 6, an ecclesiastical judge arrived at Santa Catalina to depose Doña Augustina and to install Doña Josefa in her place.

The two nuns, accompanied by other officers of the nunnery, met the ecclesiastical judge at the front gate. They led him toward the choir loft, where the installation of Doña Josefa was supposed to take place in front of the assembled community. By the time the ecclesiastical judge arrived at the choir loft and was ready to begin the ceremony, both Doña Augustina and Doña Josefa had disappeared. Without the presence of Doña Josefa to receive her appointment from the judge, the ceremony of installation could not take place. After waiting for a considerable period of time, the archbishop was finally informed that Doña Josefa had suddenly been taken ill. She was in no condition to accept the heavy responsibility of governing the nunnery. Viceroy and archbishop knew this unexpected excuse was really a new new ploy on the part of Doña Augustina. Both men determined not to let the imperious nun get away with it this time.

For two weeks, from March 6 to March 21, concerted efforts of civil and ecclesiastical authorities failed to restore order in the nunnery of Santa Catalina. On March 21, the ecclesiastical judge arrived once more at Santa Catalina, armed with orders to install Doña Josefa as *presidenta* of the convent, whether she was sick in bed or not. If Doña Josefa was truly ill, then members of the community were to assemble in her cell to acknowledge her as new acting abbess, and to pledge their obedience to her. This time Doña Augustina Palacios chose to retreat, but not to accept defeat. Doña Josefa Próspera Gómez was finally installed as *presidenta* for a term of three years, although Doña Augustina remained in the shadows, the true leader in the affairs of the nunnery.

Very much aware that within three years the community would have to elect a new abbess, and being thoroughly familiar with politics within the nunnery, Doña Augustina began to plot her canonical reelection in 1797. To his dismay, the archbishop discovered in March 1796 that through bribes, promises, and threats, Doña Augustina had already won over a majority of the nuns. She had also assembled a strong group of lay supporters from among the most powerful royal officials and professionals of Lima. Many of the nuns were obviously looking forward to a return of the good old days of Doña Augustina's rule, when they had been able to mock the authority of the archbishop and lead lives of unrestrained freedom. Many of Doña Augustina's outside supporters also remembered when the nunnery was their playground, and they could visit their nun friends at will. For two months, the archbishop of Lima tried desperately to persuade the nuns not to vote for Doña Augustina Palacios in the upcoming election.

By May 1796, however, the archbishop knew that his efforts had failed. Seven months ahead of the actual election, its outcome had already been decided in favor of Doña Augustina. Therefore, he took the only road open to him within the framework of canon law. He accused Doña Augustina before the ecclesiastical tribunal of trying to buy her election with unethical and illegal means. The ecclesiastical tribunal accepted his accusation and decided to try her case. Doña Augustina was found guilty and sentenced to lose her *voz pasiva* in the upcoming election. In canonical terms, to lose one's passive vote meant that the person in question could cast a ballot to elect somebody, but she could not be elected to office by the votes of others. In other words, the sentence of the ecclesiastical tribunal prevented Doña Augustina from being elected abbess. Any votes cast in her favor would be declared null and void.

The archbishop, pleased with the sentence, was convinced that the case was closed and finally resolved in his favor. Once again he underestimated the almost satanic pride and ego of Doña Augustina, who would not recognize any authority or accept any laws contrary to her imperious will. With the help of her powerful lay friends, Doña Augustina found a lawyer who was not afraid to challenge the authority of the archbishop, and through him appealed her case to the royal audiencia of Lima, the highest court of law in the viceroyalty of Peru.

This procedure was highly irregular, for Doña Augustina's case was clearly religious and ecclesiastical in nature, and should have remained under the jurisdiction of the ecclesiastical tribunal. However, the lay judges of the audiencia, pressured undoubtedly by the nuns of Santa Catalina and their influential friends, accepted the appeal. They lost no time in getting the trial under way. Once again, the citizens of Lima witnessed a dramatic clash between civil and ecclesiastical authorities, and the successful efforts of a rebellious nun to ignore the orders and wishes of the highest-ranking prelate of the Peruvian church. Much to the delight of the nuns and to the shock of the archbishop, the audiencia decided in favor of Doña Augustina, reversing the ruling of the ecclesiastical tribunal. It held her removal from office back in 1794 contrary to the law, calling it null and void. The legal implication of this decision was that Doña Augustina Palacios had been and still was the only lawful abbess of the nunnery of Santa Catalina.

In the days following the verdict of the audiencia, the archbishop was ridiculed in songs and poems in the cloisters of Santa Catalina, and Doña Augustina's friends humiliated him in public. In a letter to the king, he complained that the supporters of the nuns had even tried to attack him personally. Heartbroken, the archbishop turned to the new viceroy of Peru, the marqués de Osorno. On September 22, 1797, he dispatched a lengthy report to the marqués, recounting the efforts by the ecclesiastical authorities to reform the nunneries during the last two decades of the eighteenth century. He pointed to Doña Augustina as the single most important stumbling block toward reform of female monasticism in Peru. His report went on to summarize the events of 1796 and 1797, and ended with an urgent plea to reverse the verdict of the royal audiencia.

The new viceroy, caught uncomfortably between conflicting jurisdictions, tried to reach a friendly compromise. By September 1797, however, the case of Doña Augustina had passed well beyond that point. In trying to buy time and to avoid an open break with the judges of the audiencia, the viceroy followed his bureaucratic instincts, and at the end of 1797, he sent the entire case to the Royal Council of the Indies in Madrid. Three years elapsed without a final decision from Madrid. Doña Augustina used this period wisely to continue her hold on the nunnery of Santa Catalina.

A long letter written in 1800 by the archbishop to the king turned out to be the last salvo in the long war between the abbess and the archbishop. The letter, a pathetic confession on the part of the archbishop, confirmed his impotence to impose his authority on the nuns of Lima and, specifically, on Doña Augustina. At the same time, the letter contained a humble request for direct and prompt royal intervention in the case of the rebellious nun. Although the Spanish empire in America had already begun to crumble at the beginning of the nineteenth century, the colonial nuns, symbolized by Doña Augustina Palacios, still stood erect and unshakeable in their determination to preserve their freedom and autonomy.[23]

Even a cursory examination of records reveals that, ever since the early seventeenth century, life in the *conventos grandes* had ceased to reflect the true ideals of Christian monasticism. This pattern would endure throughout the colonial period, until the beginning of the nineteenth century. The hundreds of women who flocked to those convents did not look for Christian perfection or for a life of ascetic denial, silence, and prayer. They may have rationalized their motives with symbols and language of monastic rule, but, in fact, they found the nunneries an ideal setting to retain control of their properties; to live in comfortable "cells," surrounded by maids and slaves; and to amuse themselves with all sorts of pleasant social entertainments.

In the city within a city represented by the *convento grande,* nuns of the black veil enjoyed the right to vote on most matters that affected their personal lives. The typical nun of the black veil seems not to have been a humble and subdued "spouse of the Lord," but a strong, independent woman, very capable of manipulating things to suit her convenience.

Orderly discipline and prayerful silence practiced in small *conventos recoletos* were completely ignored in the *conventos grandes,* where a highly secularized life rushed on with a fast and dramatic tempo. With uncanny ability, inhabitants of the convents resisted, decade after decade, all the efforts of ecclesiastical and civil authorities to restore discipline and to impose monastic reforms. Like the breastless amazons of classical tradition, colonial nuns seem to have truncated their femininity by renouncing motherhood and marriage. In reality, however, they gained a personal independence and freedom seldom enjoyed by their sisters in the secular city.

9

❦

Monastic Riots
and
Partisan Politics

FOR THREE CENTURIES, NUNS of colonial Peru were the most "liberated" women in the viceroyalty. Their broader general education and higher human development placed them above their sisters in the secular city, and they fought with incredible stubbornness to preserve their independence and autonomy in the face of the challenge posed by the authority of viceroys and bishops. As was said unfairly of the great Saint Theresa of Avila, they were *"féminas inquietas y andariegas,"* restless and wandering women.

Although the autonomy they enjoyed was unheard of in the secular world, the nuns of Peru tried time and again to shake the light juridical bonds that tied them to the authority of the local bishop. Yet, these well-educated women knew that the rigid canonical structures of the Catholic church hierarchy dominated by males permitted no such thing as total juridical autonomy for female monastic institutions. Therefore, in spite of their constant clashes with the bishops, Peruvian nuns preferred episcopal jurisdiction as the lesser of two evils. The alternative, canonical jurisdiction, was dreaded by most nuns; it meant a much more constrained way of life because it placed a nunnery under the direct jurisdiction of a male religious order.

Some of these orders, such as the Augustinians, Franciscans, and Dominicans, had attracted clusters of pious and devout women since the beginning of the colonial period. These women regularly attended services in those orders' churches, and chose their confessors and spiritual counselors from among the friars of these communities. Eventually, some women organized themselves into religious communities, adopting the constitutions and habits of their favorite male order, and taking vows as Franciscan, Augustinian, or Dominican nuns. The practice and legislation of the church recognized them as female branches of the original male orders. They were granted exemption from episcopal jurisdiction, and juridically placed under the superiors of their corresponding male order. Many of the male orders treated their female branches as a "women's auxiliary," whose sole reason for existence was for the benefit of the friars. When such a juridical relationship existed between a nunnery and a male order, the friars frequently considered the convent as "their nunnery," and felt free to interfere constantly in its internal affairs.

The friars' provincial superior, aware of his canonical jurisdiction over the nuns, forced his own friars as confessors and counselors upon the nuns, appointed their chaplains and administrators and, finally, did not hesitate to manipulate monastic elections in favor of the nuns of his choice. The friars also kept a very close eye on the finances of a nunnery and, at times, they diverted some of the nuns' financial resources for their own benefit. Allowed to enter the nunnery as counselors and confessors, the friars could exercise daily control over the lives of the nuns. No wonder, then, that the nuns preferred the more distant and less stringent episcopal jurisdiction of the bishop, whose orders and directives they had learned to ignore with impunity.

The nunneries' efforts to break away from the jurisdiction of the friars became evident in the 1570s. On September 24, 1572, Don Francisco de Toledo, the great viceroy and lawgiver of Peru, wrote to His Majesty Philip II about the Augustinian nuns of Lima. According to the viceroy, these nuns had received the habit and the rule from the friars of Saint Augustin, and their nunnery had begun to develop in Lima as a female branch of the already well-established male Augustinian order. Some conflict had developed between friars and nuns before the latter took their final vows, and the juridical relationship between the nunnery and the convent of Augustinian friars had been broken by both parties. Nevertheless, the nuns had proceeded to take their final vows, claiming that they were now under episcopal jurisdiction.

Don Francisco de Toledo viewed this step as highly irregular, since the transfer of jurisdiction had taken place without royal or papal approval. In his letter of September 24, the viceroy asked the king to petition the pope for an apostolic brief to establish the nunnery canonically under the jurisdiction of the bishop of Lima. The canonical approval of the nunnery was needed, Don Francisco went on to write, "so that many daughters of conquistadores and servants of Your Majesty (some forced by necessity and others taking the habit of their own free will), may find a place to lead a secluded life."[1]

Monastic Riots

Although juridical separation of the Augustinian nuns from the friars of the same order seems to have been accomplished peacefully in the 1570s, there were other instances when the efforts of the nuns to break away from the jurisdiction of the friars erupted into violent riots. To the modern observer, these monastic riots reveal not only the violence latent in colonial society, but also the overlapping complexities of civil and ecclesiastical jurisdiction, the unyielding stubbornness of many nuns, and the power of monastic politics to break the walls of the cloister and to involve hundreds of lay persons. Two of those riots occurred at opposite ends of the viceroyalty of Peru: one in the city of Santiago de Chile in 1656, and the other in the Andean city of Quito in 1679. The first riot involved the nuns of Santa Clara and the Franciscan friars of Santiago, while the riot of Quito was ignited by a clash between the nuns of Santa Catalina and the powerful Dominican order.

The nuns of Santa Clara had lived in their convent of Santiago under the jurisdiction of the Franciscan friars since 1603, but by mid-century, juridical dependence on the Franciscan order had become an unbearable burden to the nuns. Sometime around 1650, the nuns undertook the first legal step to sever their juridical relationship with the Franciscans, and they petitioned to be placed under the jurisdiction of the local bishop. The ecclesiastical authorities did not want to offend the powerful Franciscans, and for almost six years they delayed resolution of the case. During that time, tension mounted in the convent of Santa Clara, where the nuns became the target of the wrath and vengeance of the Franciscans. By 1656, with their petition still lost in the tangle of the ecclesiastical bureaucracy, the nuns of Santa Clara decided to act on their own. They refused to obey the provincial superior of the Franciscans, Fray Alonso Cordero, and began to block the entrance of their nunnery to any Franciscan friar.

Since the Franciscan convent stood practically next door to the nunnery of Santa Clara, the Franciscan community could not suffer the rebelliousness of their female neighbors in silence. Because the bishop had taken no action and appeared to be sympathetic toward the nuns, the provincial, Fray Alonso Cordero, appealed to one of the judges of the audiencia, Oidor Don Pedro de Azaña Solís. On December 19, 1656, Don Pedro and Fray Alonso led two companies of soldiers and the entire Franciscan community toward the nunnery of Santa Clara, ready to force open the gates of the nunnery and to subdue the nuns. The soldiers carried loaded firearms, while the Franciscans concealed swords and clubs under their monastic robes. Violence, always close to the surface of colonial life, was now unavoidable.

News of the impending clash spread rapidly through the streets of Santiago, and groups of concerned relatives and curious onlookers began to gather in the vicinity of the nunnery of Santa Clara. The nuns realized that they could not resist a long siege of their nunnery and, as soldiers and friars began to surround the convent, the decision was made to flee the buildings. In the resulting panic and confusion, some nuns jumped from low balconies and windows, a few pulled up their long robes and tried to climb the fence of the cloister, while still others fled through the back gate of the nunnery into the surrounding alleys. Waiting soldiers and friars caught most of the nuns, who were then physically abused by the armed men. They were beaten with clubs, kicked, poked with swords and pikes, and some of them dragged by their hair over the rough cobblestones of the street back into the nunnery.

Relatives and friends of the nuns who had gathered did not remain uninvolved. Many of them drew their swords and clashed with friars and soldiers in an effort to rescue the nuns. However, their efforts, as well as those of the city fathers and other officials, were in vain. When the latter arrived with the intention of restoring peace, four or five shots rang out over their heads, sending them rushing for cover. The day ended with the Franciscans in total control of the nunnery, and the nuns imprisoned in their own cells under the custody of armed soldiers.

After the shocking events of that day, the clash could no longer be contained within the city limits of Santiago. Both the viceroy in Lima and the king in Spain were informed of the violent actions of the Franciscans, and they decided to hear the appeal of the nuns of Santa Clara. The royal bureaucracy took six years to resolve the case but, finally, in 1662, a royal decree exempted the nuns from juridical control of the Franciscan order. That same decree placed the nunnery under the jurisdiction of the local bishop. After twelve years of struggle, the nuns of Santa Clara had finally succeeded in shaking the yoke of the Franciscans and in winning a degree of autonomy denied them by the daily interference of the friars.[2]

Another, more violent and more dramatic, clash between a nunnery and a male religious order occurred in the city of Quito in 1679. The nunnery of Santa Catalina of Quito had been founded by Dominican friars who, for several decades, maintained strict juridical control over the nuns. Around 1663, the nuns of Santa Catalina, seeking greater freedom and autonomy, had initiated legal steps to dissociate themselves from the Dominican order. Their struggle for liberation lasted almost twenty years. During that period, the nuns not only challenged the authority of the Dominicans, but also confronted civil and ecclesiastical judges and divided the entire city into two factions: those supporting the nuns and those defending the juridical rights of the Dominicans. Before the struggle was over, the monastic passions unleashed by the nuns of Santa Catalina had drawn into the fight the bishop of Quito, the archbishop of Lima, hundreds of secular and regular clerics, the viceroy of Peru, and audiencia of Quito, the audiencia of Lima, the Council of the Indies in Spain, King Charles II, and the pope in Rome. With cunning persistence, the nuns of Santa Catalina cleared canonical hurdles placed in their way by royal and ecclesiastical bureaucracies.

The long-simmering dispute between the nuns and the Dominicans finally erupted into a violent monastic riot in April 1679. The sudden death of the mother abbess, Doña Lorenza de San Basilio, precipitated the crisis. According to established rule, the nuns began immediate preparations for the election by secret

ballot of a new abbess. By mid-April, it became quite clear that
Doña Leonor de San Martín had an overwhelming majority of
the votes already pledged to her. The Dominican friars, who had
constantly interfered in the internal affairs of the nunnery, strongly
objected to the election of Doña Leonor. Through the provincial
superior of the Dominican order, Fray Gerónimo de Cevallos,
they issued orders to the nuns to elect Doña Catalina de San
Dionisio instead. The Dominican friars not only used the secrecy
of the confessional to pressure the nuns to elect Doña Catalina,
but also threatened them with all kinds of ecclesiastical penalties,
including excommunication, should they elect Doña Leonor.

Fifty-three nuns of the black veil among the eighty-two inmates
of Santa Catalina refused to yield to the Dominican pressures.
Instead, they appealed to the bishop of Quito, Don Manuel Alonso
de la Peña y Montenegro, a gentle priest whose most fervent desire was to preserve peace within the restless nunneries, to take
them under his episcopal jurisdiction, thus preserving the freedom of their upcoming election. The bishop of Quito, tired of
long years of quarrels between Dominican friars and nuns, accepted their petition and severed the juridical bond between the
nunnery and the Dominican order.

On the morning of April 24, unusual activities took place around
the cathedral and the episcopal palace. A number of secular clerics,
armed with swords and clubs and accompanied by armed lay persons, awaited the appearance of the official representative of the
bishop, the cleric Don Manuel Morejón, in front of the episcopal
palace. His task was to announce to friars and nuns that the Dominican convent and the nunnery of Santa Catalina were now two
separate juridical entities. He must have felt some comfort when
he spotted the crowd of clerics and lay persons milling around
the cathedral, swords and clubs held ready. They were waiting
there, he knew, to accompany him on his dangerous errand, and
to support the decision of the bishop with their weapons. Should
the Dominicans try to resist the episcopal order by force, the
armed secular clerics and their friends stood ready to break the
Dominicans' hold on the nunnery of Santa Catalina.

Shortly after 8:00 A.M., Don Manuel Morejón, followed by his
small army, entered the nunnery and gathered all the nuns to
hear the bishop's edict. Doña Leonor de San Martín and her fifty-
three followers were delighted. They were free, at last, from the

jurisdiction of the Dominican order, and free to hold their election without any outside interference. By temporarily appointing Doña Leonor de San Martín mother superior of the convent, the bishop had also given strong indication of his intention to respect the will of the majority. That same day the Dominican friars also received notification of the episcopal order, and to everybody's surprise, their reaction was rather subdued and calm. They chose not to contest their rights with swords and clubs in the streets and alleys surrounding the nunnery, but to use legal and canonical arguments in the civil tribunal of the audiencia of Quito.

The following day, April 25, the entire community of Dominican friars, led by Provincial Fray Gerónimo de Cevallos, and followed by lay friends and supporters, marched to the audiencia in the center of town. The white-robed Dominicans filled halls and corridors of the courthouse, waiting for the arrival of the judges. When the tribunal finally opened its morning session, Fray Gerónimo de Cevallos presented an appeal to the bishop's orders. He asked the judges to declare that the Dominican order still retained jurisdiction over the nunnery of Santa Catalina. To reinforce his petition, Fray Gerónimo also introduced a letter signed by Doña Catalina de San Dionisio and twenty-eight other nuns of the black veil, who wanted to remain under Dominican jurisdiction and live as Dominican nuns. Later that day, however, the judges received another letter signed by Doña Leonor de San Martín and her followers. This document listed all grievances by the nuns against the friars and clearly indicated that the undersigned would never go back to live under Dominican jurisdiction. The enumeration of grievances, later confirmed by the bishop himself, brought the majority of the nuns to a point where compromise with the friars had become impossible.

The nuns began their letter by informing the judges that the nunnery had obtained a papal bull, which allowed them to break their juridical relationship with the Dominican friars. Yet, that solemn document, signed by the pope himself, had been stolen from the archives of the convent, either by the Dominicans themselves or by some misguided nuns manipulated by the friars. The friars had shown no respect for the rules and constitution of the nunnery and had constantly tried to impose their whims on the community. Each new Dominican provincial superior had changed things around, issuing new policies and rules. The Dominicans had also refused to send qualified confessors to the nunnery, and the nuns had no other choice than to confess to secular priests. The friars "treat[ed] the nuns worse than slaves bought with money, without any respect for their religious habit, social class, and virtues." Instead of appointing a venerable and learned friar as chaplain of the nunnery, the Dominicans assigned to this important office an ignorant priest, who spent the whole day in the cloister "checking what the nuns eat and how they dress." The letter of the nuns ended with a strong protest against the policies of the current Dominican provincial, Fray Gerónimo de Cevallos, who interfered with the free election of a new abbess and who was trying to impose his own candidate, Doña Catalina de San Dionisio upon the community. They also warned that compromise was very unlikely. If the Dominicans were not prevented from interfering in the life of the nunnery, the nuns stood ready to abandon their cloistered lives "to save their freedom of conscience."

The nuns' letter presented an excellent case for dissolving the legal bond between the nunnery and the Dominicans, reinforcing the decree already acknowledged by Don Manuel Alonso de la Peña y Montenegro, bishop of Quito. Yet, the judges of the audiencia, pressured by the powerful Dominicans and moved to act against the bishop by bureaucratic jealousies, decided to uphold the authority of the Dominican order over the nunnery of Santa Catalina and chose April 28, 1679 as the day when they would notify the nuns of their decision.

Both the notary of the audiencia, Don Alonso Sánchez Maldonado, and Fray Gerónimo de Cevallos, the Dominican provincial, were ordered to inform the nuns in private that, in accordance with the decision handed down by the highest tribunal in the province of Quito, they were still under the jurisdiction of the Dominicans. Had the Dominican provincial observed the guidelines of the audiencia, perhaps one of the most shocking events in the history of the city would have been avoided. But Fray Gerónimo de Cevallos was more eager to humiliate the rebellious nuns than to execute the orders of the audiencia. He took with him not only the entire Dominican community, but also the chief constable, Don Antonio Laso de la Vega, and his officers, and the captain of the militia, Don Juan de Medrano, with a full company of armed soldiers. In the early afternoon of April 28, more than one hundred friars, soldiers, and constables began to move toward the nunnery of Santa Catalina as if they were marching into battle. In a small colonial city with narrow, twisting streets, such a procession did not go unnoticed, and a crowd of lay persons and secular clerics soon began following the soldiers and friars. Fray Gerónimo de Cevallos was pleased. In his great hour of victory over the nuns, the whole city of Quito was watching.

The strange army arrived at the nunnery shortly before 2:00 P.M. A cordon of soldiers and constables was stationed around the convent, while Fray Gerónimo de Cevallos and his friars went into the conventual church to inform the nuns that the Dominicans were still in charge. The nuns were summoned to the church, where the notary, Don Alonso Sánchez Maldonado, read the decision of the audiencia. The reaction of the nuns was swift and unmistakable. Doña Leonor de San Martín jumped from her seat, and facing the notary and the assembled Dominicans shouted: "I shall not obey [the decision of the audiencia] because I have already a superior to whom I have given my obedience." With that, she turned to the sacristan of the nunnery, ordering her to bring out the processional cross so as to lead the nuns out of the convent and into the streets of Quito.

Almost sixty nuns of the black veil, determined to abandon the cloister altogether rather than to submit to the Dominican friars, followed the processional cross through the center aisle of the church and toward the street. At the main door of the church, the nuns encountered a wall of Dominican friars armed with clubs and swords, bent on blocking their exit. The procession of nuns never made it to the street. The two groups clashed in what eyewitnesses described as a barroom brawl. The Dominicans insulted the nuns with words so gross and obscene "that the pen and tongue refuse to repeat them." The friars shoved, kicked, and punched the nuns, beating them back into the church. Unable to exit through the door of the church, the nuns ran back into the cloisters, trying either to escape through the back gate or to jump over the fence of the gardens. The friars, blinded by rage, pursued them into the cloisters, and for the next two hours the nunnery turned into a battleground. Doors were broken, cells searched and ransacked, and furniture destroyed. At least one nun was wounded by a sword, while others were beaten with clubs.

Doña Leonor de San Martín, acting as abbess and symbol of the rebellion, was cornered by a group of Dominicans and beaten by

Fray Juan de Ribadeneira. She sustained a torn habit and a swollen face. A few nuns made it to the streets only to be caught in another violent confrontation. Friends and relatives of the nuns, aided by secular clerics carrying swords and shields, had clashed with the soldiers and constables, who were surrounding the nunnery. An especially tense moment occurred when a nun, who had fled to the belfrey of the church, threatened to throw herself from the tower into the horrified crowd below if she was not freed from the control and harassment of the Dominicans. Only the arrival of the president of the audiencia, Don Lope Antonio de Munibe, accompanied by the judge Don Carlos de Cohorcos, prevented the suicide. Don Lope Antonio shouted from the street to the nun that her grievances would be heard, thus giving the rescuers time to pull her back into the tower.

With the arrival of the chief justice of the audiencia, a semblance of order returned to the nunnery and the surrounding streets. A group of nuns were still held by the Dominicans within the nunnery, while others had fled either to the episcopal palace, to neighboring convents, or to the houses of friends and relatives. The president of the audiencia was shocked and outraged as he surveyed the aftermath of the monastic riot and heard the eyewitnesses' accounts. He blamed the Dominican provincial, Fray Gerónimo de Cevallos, for all the tragic events of that day. Fray Gerónimo had ignored the orders of the audiencia and, by taking with him the entire Dominican community, plus a small army of soldiers and constables, he had ignited a volatile situation into a violent riot. Don Lope Antonio de Munibe began to realize that, given the uncompromising attitude of the nuns and the abuses of the friars, the nunnery of Santa Catalina could not possibly survive as a monastic institution if it remained under the jurisdiction of the Dominican order.

The chief justice of the audiencia conferred with the bishop of Quito, Don Manuel Alonso de La Peña y Montenegro, and with the provincial superior of the Franciscan order, Fray Marcos Terán; they reached an agreement to resolve the monastic crisis. The audiencia would announce a reversal of its decision, and the Dominicans would be ordered out of the nunnery, while the nuns, for the time being, would be placed under the episcopal jurisdiction of the bishop. The evening was spent gathering together the scattered nuns, and clearing the nunnery and its surrounding streets of Dominicans and soldiers. Shortly after 6:00 P.M., the reassembled nuns, accompanied by a large crowd of lay persons, secular clergy, and led by the bishop, the president of the audiencia, and the Franciscan provincial, marched in procession from the episcopal palace to the nunnery of Santa Catalina. There, in a short ceremony, the president of the audiencia commended the nuns to the protection and jurisdiction of the bishop. The nuns accepted their new juridical status with great joy. After five long and dramatic hours, the violent confrontation of April 28 had finally ended, but legal and canonical battles between nuns and friars were far from resolved. In the nearby Dominican convent, the friars plotted new legal appeals. Within the nunnery itself, Doña Catalina de San Dionisio, the Dominican candidate for abbess, and a handful of her friends determined not to recognize Doña Leonor de San Martín as the lawful abbess of the convent.

Two days later, on April 30, the Dominican provincial, Fray Gerónimo de Cevallos, presented a new appeal to the audiencia of Quito, requesting that the Dominican order regain jurisdiction over the nunnery. He explained to the judges that he had taken the Dominican community and the soldiers to the nunnery on April 28 in order to avoid a greater evil. According to the provincial, a number of secular clerics and lay persons had armed themselves in order to free the nuns of Dominican control by taking them away from the cloister. Fray Gerónimo believed his actions of April 28 to be justified in the face of the threat presented by secular clerics and their friends. The judges of the audiencia, still smarting from the events of April 28, rejected the Dominican appeal, and urged the bishop, Don Manuel Alonso de la Peña y Montenegro, to proceed with the pacification of the nunnery of Santa Catalina. Aware that the interference of the friars in the election of the new abbess had been the spark that ignited the crisis, the bishop ordered the nuns to prepare for a new election on May 18. He assured the nuns that their new election would be totally free of any pressures or interference on his part or on the part of any other outsiders.

On May 12, Doña Catalina de San Dionisio, still clinging to the hope of becoming abbess under a Dominican regime, wrote to the audiencia and tried to stop the election of May 18. However, the judges had learned their lesson and refused to be drawn into the quicksand of monastic politics. Instead, they informed the

bishop of the potential disruption threatened by Doña Catalina
and her friends and supporters. Don Manuel Alonso acted quickly.
He identified six leaders of the group who wanted to return to
the Dominican jurisdiction and who supported the appointment
of Doña Catalina de San Dionisio as abbess of the nunnery. On
May 15, those six nuns were taken from the nunnery and sent to
two other convents of Quito. With the potential troublemakers
out of the way, the election took place as scheduled on May 18.
Sixty votes were cast, and Doña Leonor de San Martín, the fearless
fighter against the Dominican friars, obtained fifty-eight of them.
The remaining two votes were cast in a symbolic act of defiance
"in favor of Santa Catalina of Siena," the Dominican nun who had
lived in Siena, Italy during the fourteenth century.

The Dominicans of Quito were determined to recover their lost
authority over the rebellious nuns of Santa Catalina at all costs.
Aware that they had exhausted all the avenues of appeal available
in Quito, they requested an official review of their case by the
audiencia of Lima and by the viceroy of Peru. In 1679, by a rare
coincidence, Don Melchor de Liñán y Cisneros was both archbishop of Lima (the highest-ranking prelate in Peru), and also
viceroy and captain-general of Peru. The Dominican friars of
Lima placed the case of their Quito brethren before the judges
of the audiencia and the archbishop-viceroy. They also enlisted
the support of their many friends in the viceregal capital.

Their shrewd political know-how turned the case lost twice before into a legal victory for the Dominican order. On June 19,
1679, the archbishop-viceroy, in his capacity as president of the
audiencia of Lima, chaired a special meeting of the justices. Their
unanimous decision was to overturn the opinion of the audiencia
of Quito, and to restore the jurisdiction of the Dominicans over
the nunnery of Santa Catalina in Quito. This unexpected turn of
events reached Quito about a month later. On August 19, 1679,
civil authorities of the northern city officially recognized and accepted the decision of Lima, and urged Bishop Don Manuel Alonso
de la Peña y Montenegro to comply immediately with the orders
of the archbishop-viceroy.

On August 20 and 23, the prelate visited the nunnery of Santa
Catalina, gently breaking the news to the nuns, and begging them
to obey the Dominicans while new appeals to the Council of the
Indies and the king were prepared. A few days later, he wrote to

the crown, saying that what he had witnessed in those two days at the nunnery had so moved him that he committed himself to fight against the orders of Lima, which to him were "against the service of God . . . and the public peace and tranquility" of the city.

What the bishop witnessed in the nunnery of Santa Catalina closely resembled mass hysteria. Upon hearing the news from Lima, the nuns broke into sobs, and even the most mature among them fell into despair. Talk of mass suicide circulated, and many nuns assured the bishop that they would rather hang themselves or become loose women in the world than obey the Dominicans again. Quite a few nuns began moving all of their belongings out of the nunnery, ready to flee the cloister as soon as the Dominicans were allowed to return. Lay friends and relatives filled the parlors, and all kinds of wild scenarios were prepared to resist encroachment of the Dominican friars. Secular priests, whose dislike and resentment of the Dominicans was almost obsessive, also frequented the nunnery, offering their support by patrolling the cloisters and surrounding streets with swords and clubs. Not only was the nunnery in an uproar, but "public peace and tranquility" had disappeared once more from the streets of Quito.

His Excellency, Don Manuel Alonso de la Peña y Montenegro, was convinced that, regardless of the decision of the archbishop-viceroy and of the audiencia of Lima, the nunnery of Santa Catalina could never again be placed under the jurisdiction of the Dominican order. Therefore, on August 26, he took the only lawful step possible to suspend the implementation of the viceroy's orders. He issued a formal appeal to the king and to the Holy See.

In his appeal Don Manuel Alonso wrote with a candor and passion that he had not used before. The nuns may not have been blameless and humble "spouses of the Lord," but they were right in saying that no human being should be required to suffer what they had to endure under Dominican jurisdiction. Even natural law concedes them the right to defend their autonomy and freedom from Dominican control. The bishop's appeal to king and pope listed all grievances already mentioned, but added some new and damaging information concerning the unethical and criminal behavior of some of the Dominicans of Quito. According to the bishop, some monks of this order entered the cloister of the nunnery at all hours, without reasonable cause, and only for their own personal convenience and pleasure. Once inside the cloister, they would spend time in some nun's private cell, entertained by their female friends and served delicate meals. This atmosphere of personal, unsupervised contacts between friars and women living in the cloister fostered the development of certain friendships and emotional attachments which went well beyond the ethical tenets of the church.

The bishop knew of at least four young women who led devout and religious lives within the convent, only to have been seduced by the friars. The women were removed from the convent by their Dominican friends, and "today are kept in this city at the disposal [of the friars]." The most shocking example of this kind of immoral behavior occurred one night when four Dominicans had entered the cloister to keep watch at the bedside of a dying nun. One of the friars, taking advantage of the stillness and darkness of the cloister, found his way to the bedroom of one of his female lay penitents and "raped her, robbing her of her virginity." The bishop was, of course, outraged at this type of crime, but the thought of leaving the Dominicans in control of the nunnery upset him even more. Certain that the Dominicans "commit public and scandalous crimes against God and the Republic, which are tolerated and covered up," he was determined that no one tolerate and cover up those crimes any longer.

The immediate effect of this appeal was the suspension of the decision reached by the audiencia of Lima, with the nunnery remaining under episcopal jurisdiction and waiting for Madrid and Rome to take action. The Dominicans, scared perhaps that the shortcomings of their order could become public knowledge in royal and papal courts, chose to keep a low profile and not to force the issue of jurisdiction over the nunnery. Within the nunnery itself, things were not entirely peaceful. The twenty nuns who had supported the candidacy of Doña Catalina de San Dionisio for the office of abbess under Dominican sponsorship refused to obey abbess Doña Leonor de San Martín, who was recognized by the bishop and by sixty nuns of the black veil. In fact, the Dominican sympathizers fell victim to the hatred that the majority of the nuns felt toward the Dominican order. They were not allowed to participate in the choir and other community events; they were forbidden to have visitors; they were forced to perform the most servile offices of the nunnery; they lost their maids and slaves; they were deprived of the right to vote in community matters; they were constantly threatened with ecclesiastical penalties; and they were thrown into the conventual jail for a variety of flimsy reasons.

Tension between the two factions within the nunnery exploded, at times, into violent fights. Some members of the Dominican minority were hurt and beaten, and at least one of them, Doña Josefa de Santa Casilda, was stabbed with a knife by Doña Ana de Santa Margarita. Since the bishop would not or could not stop these abuses, Doña Catalina de San Dionisio, representing the minority, appealed to the audiencia of Quito. She informed the justices that her group lived in constant fear of the supporters of Doña Leonor. In an effort not to polarize the inmates of the nunnery even more, the audiencia did not proceed officially in the case. Instead, the justices unofficially contacted the bishop and the Dominican provincial to enlist their cooperation in the pacification of the nunnery. Both officers, aware that a new legal battle would not benefit anybody, cooperated with the audiencia.

Things began to improve in the nunnery of Santa Catalina. Internal tensions were never fully resolved in the convent, but the main issue concerning the question of Dominican jurisdiction was finally confronted in 1680. In May, a royal decree arrived in Quito declaring the nunnery of Santa Catalina juridically independent from the Dominican order and recognizing the bishop of Quito as juridical superior of the nuns. After seventeen years, the struggle for autonomy that had begun in 1663 was finally over, and the nuns of Santa Catalina emerged as the winners of the monastic war. Recognizing their loss, in a last official letter to the Dominican faction within the nunnery, the provincial, Fray Gerónimo de Cevallos, exhorted and urged Doña Catalina de San Dionisio to obey the abbess Doña Leonor de San Martín and to recognize Don Manuel Alonso de la Peña y Montenegro as the new canonical superior of the nunnery.[3]

Monastic Politics

One of the most striking features in the life of the nunneries was the way in which political power was obtained, shared, and used by the inmates of the convents. Politics of a colonial nunnery, although exercised mainly by the oligarchical elite made up of nuns of the black veil, were amazingly democratic in nature. As stated before, all nuns of the black veil, because of their rank, had the right to vote in most matters affecting the life of the community. Some of the most complex issues concerning the governance of a nunnery were resolved through a majority vote. Any nun of the black veil had the right to speak up in the conventual chapter, where those issues were discussed, and her vote counted as much as the vote of any other nun. Acceptance of candidates into the novitiate of the nunnery was decided in this democratic fashion by all the nuns of the black veil. The candidate's life, family background, and financial resources were scrutinized by professional nuns, who then voted by secret ballot to accept or to reject her. At the end of the novitiate, and before she was granted permission to take the vows, the candidate underwent the same process once again. By casting secret ballots, the community as a whole made the decision on whether or not the novice in question should be allowed to take the vows and thus become a full-fledged member of the community.

Most *conventos grandes* employed this same democratic procedure to accept candidates to either white veil or the rank of *donadas* or to approve the admission of young girls to the conventual school, and of women who wished to retire in the cloister. In addition, the community was consulted on the admisison, retention, and possible expulsion of the hundreds of lay servants and slaves who were either hired or bought to perform services for the community as a whole. The very nature and composition of the population at any given time was thus controlled and determined by the vote of the majority.

In colonial nunneries, the vote, totally unknown in the world of secular women, was by no means limited to acceptance or rejection of new members. The purchase or sale of communal properties, the establishment of internal policies, and any legal actions taken in the name of the community required, if not a formal vote of the community, then at least its advice and consent. For triennial elections of officers heading the nunnery, the right to vote was most jealously guarded and most passionately exercised by the nuns. In accordance with monastic rule and tradition, power to govern the nunnery would be obtained only by the majority vote of the community. Any effort by bishops or viceroys either to appoint directly or to influence the election of these officers was resisted by the nuns as an intolerable interference in the internal matters of the nunnery.

In theory, and in accordance with monastic rule, triennial elections were supposed to take place *secundum Spiritum,* under the inspiration of the Holy Spirit. The great colonial theologian Diego de Avendaño dedicated quite a few pages of his massive *Thesaurus Indicus* to explain how these elections should be conducted. First of all, the nuns were to proceed in an atmosphere of peace and mutual trust, to avoid, by all means, the formation of factions, and to reject any earthly motivation in reaching their decision. The solicitation of votes through promises, bribes, or pressure constituted sufficient grounds to invalidate an election.

In conventual elections nobody could vote for herself, and secrecy and confidentiality had to be maintained or risk having the election declared null and void. A simple plurality vote did not suffice to have someone elected to conventual office. The successful candidate needed *plura medietate,* more than one-half of all votes cast in any given election. If nobody obtained more than one-half of the vote on the first ballot, the election was inconclusive and had to be repeated. Finally, reelection to a second consecutive term of office ran counter to monastic tradition and ecclesiastical legislation. Diego de Avendaño supported all these rules with the best theological and canonical arguments, and exhorted the Peruvian nuns and their confessors to adhere faithfully to these moral and canonical principles.[4]

However, canonical guidelines, so thoroughly explained by Avendaño, were universally ignored by Peruvian nuns in the *conventos grandes.* For one thing, they had no faith in the benign and divine guidance of the Holy Spirit to determine the outcome of triennial elections. During the months preceding an election, the nunnery was a beehive of political activity. Inmates of the nunneries employed pressure groups, propaganda campaigns, trading of votes, secret deals, promises and bribes, articulation of "platforms," and patronage with zest and efficiency. That such methods had been outlawed by ecclesiastical legislation, and some of them were clearly unethical, did not seem to have disturbed them. Since a successful candidate needed more than one-half of the vote, supporters of minor candidates tended to be absorbed

by larger and more powerful groups until a "two-party system"
emerged. Documents of the time describe these two factions or
parties as *Las Encarnadas* and *Las Verdes,* the Pinks and the Greens.

As the day of the election approached, members of the two
groups wore either pink or green ribbons to identify themselves
as supporters of one or the other candidate. Although nuns of
the white veil, maids, and slaves had no vote in conventual elections, they also wore pink or green ribbons to symbolize support
for the candidate of their choice. Proudly displaying their party
identifications, nuns visited with relatives and lay friends in the
conventual parlors. Many of these people also ended up by wearing the ribbon of their favorite nun. One can imagine the pressure
put on those nuns wearing neither a pink nor a green ribbon.
They constituted the uncommitted faction whose vote could, at
times, swing an election. Committed nuns, or even the candidates
themselves, visited them in their private cells to make promises
or to offer outright bribes in exchange for their votes. Many of
those meetings took place late at night after the nunnery bell had
given the signal to put out all the lights and to retire for the night.

Family clusters took a very active part in these secret political
meetings in preparation for upcoming elections. Any senior nun
who was the matriarch of a large family cluster of sisters, cousins,
and nieces (all of them of the black veil), had a natural constituency
to form the core of a political machine. Many of the women who
became powerful abbesses in the *conventos grandes* achieved that
rank because they were supported by twenty or thirty blood relatives.[5]

Few men of colonial Peru, aside from a select group at the top
of the civil and ecclesiastical bureaucracies, ever held the power
and prestige of a colonial abbess. During her three-year term of
office, a colonial abbess enjoyed social, political, economic, and
religious power that few people inside or outside the nunnery
could ignore. For instance, she represented the nunnery in all
negotiations with viceroys and bishops, and handled all official
correspondence with the crown, the Holy See, and ecclesiastical
and civil tribunals. She usually left a visible imprint on the life of
the nunnery by imposing certain rules and guidelines, or by choos-
ing to ignore others. An abbess also controlled and administered
all common assets and properties of the nunnery. This power
made her, as we shall see later, one of the most influential persons

in the financial circles of the city. An abbess also had an extended right of patronage, and thus she could appoint her friends and supporters to a myriad of offices within the nunnery.

In the daily life of the community, she was always surrounded by the symbols of authority. She lived in a stately cell, attended by advisors and servants. She kept the keys and the official seal of the nunnery, presided over community functions from an elevated throne not unlike the throne of a bishop, and even senior nuns knelt before her, kissing her right hand. A shrewd abbess could manipulate affairs during her term of office to secure for herself an excellent future once her term expired. Many ambitious women used all the political means at their disposal to secure that office for themselves or for the candidate of their choice.

After several months of intense political activities, the day of the election itself was somehow anticlimactic. Pledged votes were counted and recounted by the political operatives of the candidates; political deals had been finalized, and only the most naive among the nuns of the black veil did not know the name of the future abbess on the eve of the election. The day of the election itself was filled with ceremony and pageantry, but no one showed any expectation or curiousity about the result of the election. Election day ceremonies remained nearly unchanged throughout the colonial period. One example from 1630 epitomizes the common characteristics of all election days in Peruvian nunneries.

This particular election took place on August 6, 1630 in the convent of Las Descalzas of Lima. Early in the morning of election day, the archbishop of Lima, Don Fernando Arias de Ugarte, accompanied by two high-ranking clerics, the *maestrescuela,* Don Fernando de Guzmán, and the vicar, Don Feliciano de Vega, arrived at the nunnery to preside over the election of a new abbess. The officers of the nunnery led the archbishop and his companions into the conventual church, which had been adorned by the nuns for the solemnities of the day. Prayers and hymns offered to the Holy Spirit ensured that the election would be carried out in accordance with the will of God. After the liturgical ceremony was completed, Don Fernando Arias de Ugarte took his seat on the episcopal throne erected in the sanctuary of the church and called for the retiring abbess to approach him. Abbess Doña Beatriz de Jesús knelt in front of him and, for all to hear, acknowledged that her term of office had come to an end. She further declared herself legally disqualified for reelection to a second consecutive term. After the archbishop had accepted and confirmed her declaration, Doña Beatriz handed him the official seal and keys of the nunnery thereby relinquishing her authority as abbess of the covent. At this point, the archbishop delivered a short sermon exhorting the nuns to reject any earthly and worldly motivation and to vote for a new abbess under the guidance of the Holy Spirit.

The nuns then knelt and recited the act of contrition as a symbol of sorrow for their sins and transgressions. Then, to ensure a valid election, the archbishop stood up and absolved the entire community and each nun individually from all censures and ecclesiastical penalties that she might have incurred unknowingly. At the completion of this act, all nuns of the black veil proceeded through the center aisle of the church to the sanctuary. There they knelt in front of Don Fernando Arias de Ugarte and one by one deposited their written ballots in a silver tray held out by one of the two clerics in attendance.

On that morning, fifty-three nuns of the black veil approached the throne of Don Fernando. Only one did not carry her written ballot because she did not know how to write. This nun was allowed to whisper the name of her candidate into the ear of the vicar, Don Feliciano de Vega. The attending clerics counted the votes in the presence of the archbishop. Of the fifty-three cast, Doña Ana María de Dios obtained forty votes. She was called to the throne of the archbishop, who asked if she would accept the office of her own free will. When Doña Ana María agreed, Don Fernando Arias de Ugarte declared her the new abbess of the nunnery, handing her the official seal and the keys of the convent as symbols of her new authority. Then, while the monastic choir sang hymns of thanksgiving, the new abbess was led to the abbatial throne to receive the pledge of obedience from her community. The entire population of the cloister, nuns of black and white veil, novices, and *donadas,* came to kneel in front of her, pledging their obedience, kissing her right hand, and receiving her blessing.[6]

Once the election proper had been completed, the remainder of the day was dedicated to gay celebrations. The new abbess, surrounded by relatives and friends, took possession of the large abbatial cell, and then would visit the extended property of the nunnery to be congratulated by the different subcommunities of the convent. Nuns, novices, *donadas,* schoolgirls, maids, and slaves all vied with one another to entertain their new abbess with songs, poems, and skits related to her personal life. The nunnery's community dining room was filled to capacity, and the cooks of the cloister served one of the best and most elaborate meals of the year. Daytime festivities carried over into the evening and were moved to the *locutorios* or parlors of the nunnery.

Lay friends and relatives, who had come to offer the new abbess their congratulations and gifts, turned the parlors into a sort of county fair. Slaves and maids served abundant refreshments; nuns and lay friends milled around entrance halls and parlors; musical instruments were played, and everybody tried to be noticed by the new abbess and speak a few personal words to her. Quite frequently judges of the audiencia, members of the powerful merchants' guild, canons of the cathedral, and important secular and regular clerics of the city mingled with the crowd of visitors. If the nunnery was a *convento grande* and if the new abbess belonged to an important family, the viceroy himself might have paid a surprise visit. The evening usually ended with a play or concert.

After all the excitement of election day had died down, the new abbess would plunge into the government of her nunnery. One of her first official actions, which created a great deal of expectation in the community, was the announcement of new assistant officers. The names of new officers, chosen by the abbess and confirmed by the bishop, were usually read to the nuns in the choir or in the dining room during a community function. To nobody's surprise, they usually included names of friends and supporters of the new abbess. Some nuns worked for her candidacy and voted for her with the understanding that their names would appear on that list of officers.

In the closed world of these nunneries, officers carried power and prestige that placed them above the common nun in the hierarchical structure of the convent. One of the most important offices was that of *definidora* which, depending on the size of the nunnery, was held by four to six nuns of the black veil. *Definidoras* formed a sort of personal cabinet of the abbess. They met regularly with her to discuss and decide important issues in the life of the community. Some of the nunneries required their advice and consent before a policy or decision by the abbess became binding on the community. Appointment to *definidora* meant access to formulation of policies and active participation in the decision-making process. Of paramount importance to the success of an abbess was, of course, that the *definidoras* were at all times loyal to her and supported her personal style of government.

The office of *priora* ranked as the single most important post in the nunnery, right after that of the abbess. A *priora* was an executive officer who ran the day-by-day affairs of the nunnery under the direction of the abbess. If the abbess became ill or otherwise incapacitated, the *priora* would act as her deputy. In many instances, this office was an important stepping stone toward the office of abbess.

The offices described in some of the sources by the generic term of *pedagogas* probably ranked next in importance and influence on the daily life of the convent. As the word clearly implies, *pedagogas* were nuns in charge of teaching and training other members of the community, while maintaining discipline within their assigned groups. The mistress of novices undoubtedly held the most crucial position among the *pedagogas*. As already mentioned, young novices lived segregated from the rest of the community; they were forbidden to talk to professed nuns and were placed under the sole guidance of the mistress of novices. In the eyes of many young novices, the nun in charge of this post became an idealized woman, loved more and esteemed higher than any other person in the convent. Mistresses of novices turned the love and respect of their former pupils into support for their candidacies as *priora* or abbess.

Next to the mistress of novices ranked the headmistress and teachers in the *seglarado* or convent school. They were the only nuns in daily contact with lay society girls whose parents had placed them in the convent to receive an education. Since these students led a cloistered life and, like the novices, were segregated from the rest of the community, their teachers became the primary influence of their young lives. In some of the *conventos grandes*, the list of *pedagogas* also contained a mistress for nuns of the white veil, a mistress for servants, and a mistress for slaves.

The right of patronage and appointment enjoyed by the abbess was not limited to the above-mentioned offices. She could also appoint *porteras* or doorkeepers, whose task was one of the most important and sensitive assignments in colonial nunneries. *Porteras* controlled access to the outside world—the entrance halls and *locutorios* of the convent. Bishops never failed to underscore the importance of this office, constantly urging abbesses to appoint only the most experienced and trusted nuns of the black veil to this position. In the *conventos grandes,* teams of fifteen to twenty performed as *porteras* at any given time, and no door could be opened without the presence of at least three of them. The entire community depended on the cooperation and good will of the *porteras* so as to communicate freely with the outside world.

Escuchas, mentioned in a previous chapter, were nuns appointed by the abbess to chaperone the hundreds of visitors in the parlors. In most of the *conventos grandes,* the abbess would appoint two different teams of *escuchas,* each composed of eight to ten nuns of the black veil. One group served as *escuchas de hombres,* chaperons for male visitors, and the other as *escuchas de mujeres,* chaperons for female visitors. Cooperation of nuns appointed to the office of *escuchas* was also essential to assure the community's free and confidential communication with lay friends and relatives.

Many of the nunneries had special endowments to support pious sodalities and chaplaincies founded by lay benefactors. Therefore, *patronas de cofradias y capellanias,* or sponsors and patrons of sodalities and chaplaincies was another important office. Nuns appointed to this rank administered the assets of the foundation, assigned duties to chaplains and officers of the sodality, and saw to it that the founder's will was observed in all matters.

Overall discipline in the nunnery was the responsibility of the *celadoras,* a group of monastic constables who, under the direction of the abbess, were supposed to maintain law and order within the walls of the cloister. *Celadoras* were called upon to suppress fights and to restrain those inmates of the convent whose violent behavior became a threat to the rest of the community. When less extreme means failed, *celadoras* would lead guilty nuns or servants to the jail of the convent, where they placed them in the custody of the *carcelera* or jail warden. The abbess of the nunnery further appointed a *boticaria* or pharmacist, an *enfermera* or nurse of the convent, supervisors of chapels, kitchens, and gardens, *provisoras* or buyers, and *acompañadoras.*

Acompañadoras were nuns assigned to accompany any man who, by reason of his office, was allowed to enter the cloistered part of the nunnery. At times, medical doctors, chaplains, and lay workers were needed inside the convent; however, they could not proceed beyond the parlors without the presence of official *acompañadoras*.[7]

Although the right to appoint the officers of the nunnery bestowed upon the abbess a great deal of power over the community, her control of the convent's finances made her a person to be reckoned with not only by the nuns, but also by lay merchants and royal officials. Most nuns of the black veil by custom, if not by rule, were allowed to dispose freely of their personal property. Yet, at times, approval by the abbess was required to give legal status to many of the financial operations agreed upon by the nuns themselves. The buying and selling of private cells and of slaves, the transfer of properties held by individual nuns outside the convent, the authority to issue last wills and testaments, and the borrowing and lending of monies—all of which occurred frequently—had to be approved by the abbess so that these transactions would stand up in any court of law.

Control and administration of the common assets of the nunnery provided the chief source of economic power held by the abbess. In this capacity, her role in the economic life of the city could not be ignored. For example, the abbess of a *convento grande* could hire or fire hundreds of women of modest means to work as servants of the nunnery. She also could buy or sell, almost at will, the many female slaves held as common property by the community. There is some evidence that certain nunneries were granted or inherited encomiendas of Indians; thus some of the colonial abbesses could count themselves among the powerful encomenderas mentioned in a previous chapter.

The nunnery of La Concepción, for instance, obtained from the king the encomienda of Anauhuancas in the Andean valley of Jauja. When Doña Ines Muñoz de Rivera was abbess of La Concepción from 1584 to 1594, she also was encomendera of Anauhuancas, with all the prestige and economic power inherent in that office. A similar case occurred in the 1570s in the Augustinian nunnery of Lima, when Don Francisco de Toledo served as viceroy of Peru. The nunnery claimed the right to control a small encomienda in the province of Huamanga, which had been part of the dowry of the nun Doña Isabel de Estete. Viceroy Toledo frowned upon such an arrangement, and attempted to relieve the nuns of the Huamanga encomienda by offering them a yearly pension to compensate the convent for the loss of Indian tributes. However, the viceroy did not always oppose ownership of encomiendas by Peruvian nunneries. On July 29, 1571, he granted the encomienda of Juliaca in the province of Lapa to the nunnery of Santa Clara of Cuzco. Abbesses of Santa Clara controlled that encomienda for nearly two hundred years. Finally, in 1743, royal officials took the encomienda away from the nuns, offering them, instead, a yearly pension, which was paid by the royal treasurer in Cuzco.

In 1786, the powerful abbess of Santa Clara, Doña Josefa de Ibarrena, protested to the crown, claiming the annual pension had not been paid regularly and that 6,821 pesos were in arrears. The king, taking into consideration that the nuns of Santa Clara "were daughters of conquistadores," agreed on August 7, 1787 to restore the annual payments to the nuns of Cuzco.[8]

At times, colonial abbesses, while carrying out their financial duties, had contact with the most powerful treasury officials of the crown and the merchant guild or *consulado*. Those men who held real power in the monopolistic economic system of the viceroyalty often had to humbly resort to the financial means controlled by the abbesses in order to solve moments of monetary crises. During such instances, colonial abbesses bailed out royal administrators and merchants from the constraints of an impossible financial situation. In 1664, for example, the *prior del consulado,* or president of the merchant guild, had to obtain a loan from the abbesses of La Concepción and of Santa Catalina *para engrosar el envío.* The annual fleet stood ready to sail for Panamá and Seville, but the merchant guild of Lima found itself without sufficient funds to send as investments to Spain. Ready cash had to be obtained in a hurry, and the merchants turned to the nunneries of Lima. The abbesses of La Concepción and Santa Catalina offered a portion of the needed cash, but not before making sure that the president and officers of the merchant guild were legally accountable for prompt repayment of the loan.

In addition, on December 6, 1664, eight of the most powerful abbesses of the viceroyalty informed the king of a financial arrangement between the nunneries of Lima and royal officials of the viceroyalty. Their strong letter, which requested royal intervention in order to hold the royal officials to the terms of their financial agreement, was signed by Doña Augustina Osores de

Ulloa, abbess of La Encarnación; Doña Juana de Amaya, abbess of La Concepción; Doña Luísa del Espíritu Santo, abbess of the convent of San José; Doña María Antonia de la Cruz, abbess of the Augustinian nunnery; Doña María de Bustamante, abbess of La Santísima Trinidad; Doña Catalina de Gamoa, abbess of Santa Clara; Doña Clara de la Asunción, foundress and abbess of the convent of Our Lady of the Rosary; and Doña María Teresa del Espíritu Santo, prioress of the Barefoot Carmelites. The eight nuns informed the king that royal officials approached the nunneries of Lima to borrow "a very considerable" amount of silver to meet financial emergencies in the administration of the viceroyalty.

Their letter reveals that the abbesses had invested the dowries of their nuns in order to keep the viceregal bureaucracy solvent and to increase the amount of silver destined for Spain. The abbesses had granted the loan based on the premise that royal officials would repay it with interest on a regular schedule. By 1664, however, the crown owed the nunneries *"crescidas cantidades,"* a great deal of money. The abbesses did not hesitate to remind the king of the repayment of their loan, explaining that without regularly scheduled repayments the nuns could not possibly support themselves.[9]

Loans did not constitute the only form of financial aid offered by colonial abbesses to officials of the viceroyalty. Royal officials approached the powerful abbesses of the *conventos grandes* on countless other occasions, requesting all kinds of monetary donations. In a society lacking a banking system, nunneries were one of the few places where cash could be obtained readily in cases of emergency. Colonial nunneries, through their abbesses, donated monies to pay for the reception of new viceroys or bishops, shared in the expenses to celebrate royal birthdays or funerals, and met emergencies, such as attacks by pirates or devastation caused by earthquakes and floods. Without generous cash gifts by monastic institutions, royal officials would have been hard pressed to confront such emergencies.

An example typifying such hardships occurred in 1780 when the Andean regions of Peru were rocked by the bloody revolution of Tupac Amaru. In the course of the Indian rebellion, many towns and villages came under attack and Cuzco itself was sieged and threatened with destruction. In the opening weeks of the revolt, royal officials found themselves without sufficient resources to contain the fury of Tupac Amaru. As they had done many times before, they asked the nunneries for money to supply the royal militia and to organize the defense of Cuzco. In her letter to the king in 1786, the abbess of Santa Clara of Cuzco reminded him that her cloister had contributed 2,000 pesos to help the royal cause at a time when the royal treasury of Cuzco was almost empty. Her words seem to imply that without the help of the nuns of Santa Clara, the imperial city of Cuzco would have fallen into the hands of the rebels.[10]

Although loans and donations made abbesses important persons in the financial circles of the viceroyalty, their daily administration of the nunneries' common assets probably had a greater impact upon the economic life of colonial cities. Colonial abbesses ranked among the largest employers in the viceroyalty, and hundreds of persons were able to make a living thanks to the opportunities provided by the nunneries. In addition to maids and other servants, there were many men whose livelihood depended on the good graces of the women who ruled the nunneries. The convents' account books list a variety of jobs performed by men with regular salaries paid from the common assets of the nunneries. There were chaplains, confessors, medical doctors, surgeons, carpenters, masons, lawyers, legal executors, gardeners, sextons, master musicians and, finally, artists who worked on the beautification of churches, chapels, and cloisters and who received either a regular monthly or annual salary from the nuns.

The most important post held by a man in a colonial nunnery was the office of mayordomo or business manager of the convent. A mayordomo was the abbess's right hand in the myriad of economic and legal transactions, which she had to handle outside of the cloister. He also bought the hundreds of supplies needed every month to maintain the large population of the nunnery. Always under the direction of the abbess, he administered the properties owned by the convent in the city and in rural areas and saw to it that the convent's debtors paid on time. In addition, he represented the abbess in many of her dealings with royal and ecclesiastical bureaucracies. The importance of his office is underscored by the fact that he was the highest-paid secular employee of the nunnery. For example, early in the eighteenth century, a convent mayordomo could make close to 1,500 pesos a year plus free housing, while a doctor or a lawyer received an annual salary of only about 300 pesos from the nuns.

The case of Doña Bernarda Merino best exemplifies the economic power of a colonial abbess. Doña Bernarda became abbess of La Encarnación on December 24, 1714. While providing work within the cloister to many female servants and maids, she also employed almost fifty men in the nunnery, paying them regular salaries. Her account books reveal that she paid twenty-six chaplains and several confessors, four lawyers and legal agents, a couple of sextons, a barber, a medical doctor, a surgeon, a collector of rents, some gardeners and, of course, the all-powerful mayordomo. Those account books also show that under Doña Bernarda Merino's administration, the nunnery of La Encarnación either owned or had an interest in 103 urban or rural properties. During her term of office, Doña Bernarda was landlady of more than forty residential houses in Lima. The value of those properties can be inferred from the social and economic status of the tenants who paid rent to La Encarnación. The count of Portillo, General Don Martín de Zamudio, the royal accountant Don Nicolás de Mancilla, the marqués de Villar de Tajo, the royal treasurer Don Lorenzo Fernando de Córdoba, General Don Nuño de Espiñola Villavicencio, the canon of the cathedral, Don Bernardo de Zamudio, Don Diego Hurtado de Mendoza, and General Don Juan Bautista de Raigada were among those who paid monthly rents to the abbess of La Encarnación.

Doña Bernarda Merino also administered interests of her nunnery in thirteen stores, two barbershops rented by the barbers Juan Mexía and Pedro Collantes, two *pulperias,* a warehouse, an *obraje* or cloth factory named Santa Petronila de Cisco, several *chacras* or vegetable gardens and orchards, and at least one large rural property or hacienda, which was burdened with a mortgage by the marchioness of San Miguel, payable to the nuns of La Encarnación.[11]

The Temptation of Power

There is little doubt that colonial abbesses of the *conventos grandes* were among the most powerful individuals in the viceroyalty of Peru. They enjoyed social prestige and economic power that very few persons outside the nunneries could match. Both the institution of monasticism and their status as consecrated virgins in pursuit of the marian ideal helped them gain positions of honor, respect, and economic influence. Therefore, it is not surprising that many ambitious women sought the rank and office of abbess with all the legal and illegal means at their disposal. Neither is it shocking that some of those women who had become abbesses did not find it easy to relinquish their power after the expiration of their legal term in office. At times, they fought to be reelected to a second and even a third term, ignoring the law of the church and the customs of the nunnery. When their efforts for their own reelection failed, some of the abbesses worked for the candidacy of a close friend, and some had themselves appointed to other prestigious offices within the nunnery. Power and prestige, once tasted and enjoyed, were not easily discarded, even by supposedly "humble spouses of the Lord."

Before the end of the sixteenth century, this problem was already a serious one in colonial Peru. Some of the founders of the early nunneries, women like Doña Inés Muñoz de Rivera in La Concepción, and Doña Mencia de Sosa in La Encarnación, enjoyed papal dispensation and were privileged to remain abbesses of their convents for life. Those dispensations, however, established a dangerous precedent. If founders could remain in office for life, why not allow some other important and gifted individuals to have a second and even perhaps a third term? In 1599, Pope Clement VII answered that question with a papal bull addressed to the archbishop of Lima and to the nuns of the Peruvian viceroyalty. He insisted that, regardless of an occasional papal dispensation, no abbess could remain in office beyond the three years prescribed by canonical legislation. The king of Spain, acting in his capacity as patron of the church, restated the same directive in 1626, and fifteen years later Pope Urban VIII had to repeat those orders once more since, obviously, they were being ignored by the Peruvian nuns.

In spite of such clear directives by the crown and the Holy See, there were nuns in almost all the convents of Peru who clung to their power and managed to retain it far beyond the term allowed by law. Among them was Doña Marcela de Aguilar, abbess of La Trinidad at the end of the seventeenth century. She headed a powerful family cluster of twenty nuns of the black veil, who provided the base of her political power within the nunnery. With the help of her blood relatives, Doña Marcela ran for reelection to the office of abbess and enlisted some influential lay friends to persuade the viceroy and the archbishop that an exception to the law should be granted in her case.

Doña Mariana de Contreras, several times abbess of La Concepción, was one of the great master politicians in the monastic political battles of seventeenth-century Peru. With the help of friends and relatives, Doña Mariana built an efficient and smooth political machine, one which repeatedly returned her to office. For years she avoided any canonical confrontation with the ecclesiastical authorities by observing the letter of the law, although her political manipulations and her repeated election made a mockery of the spirit of that law. During her first term in office as abbess of La Concepción, Doña Mariana developed a system that worked to her advantage for years to come. She would choose a close friend to succeed her as abbess, but with the understanding that she would retain power behind the throne. After her friend's three-year term expired, Doña Mariana de Contreras was re-elected to a second term and, then, continued to strike the same bargain with yet another friend at the end of her own triennium. By playing musical chairs with the abbatial throne, the shrewd Doña Mariana retained unchallenged power in the nunnery of La Encarnación for two decades. Her political manipulations finally came to an end when the new archbishop, Don Pedro de Villagómez, ruled her method a "pernicious corruption" of the spirit of monasticism and appealed to the pope to forbid future reelections of Doña Mariana de Contreras.

At La Encarnación, one of Peru's most powerful monastic institutions, Doña María de Tudela also fell victim to the temptation and corruption of power. Heading a strong party of supporters, Doña María de Tudela captured the abbatial throne of La Encarnación in 1704. During her three years in office, she managed to keep the loyalty of that party by dispensing patronage and by granting economic favors to some of the most influential nuns. By 1707, Doña María knew that she had more than enough votes to be reelected to a second term, provided that civil and ecclesiastical authorities did not openly oppose her reelection.

By means that are not entirely clear, she won the support of the viceroy and through powerful clerical friends began to work on the archbishop of Lima. In August 1707, only four months before the election, a handful of nuns appealed to the archbishop, asking him to forbid the election of Doña María to a second term. Their action came too late, for the archbishop had alrady been pressured by the viceroy not to interfere in the upcoming election, but to let the monastic politics of La Encarnación take their own course. On election day, the viceroy dispatched a company of soldiers to surround the nunnery in order to prevent any outside interference. In addition, he made it quite clear to the community that he desired to have Doña María de Tudela reelected to a second term. Naturally, such powerful backing swept Doña María into office for a second term as abbess of La Encarnación.

Since this kind of political deal was not always possible, an abbess could also manipulate the system to secure election to a lesser office once she had completed her three-year as abbess. Doña Tomasina de Mesa, abbess of La Encarnación in 1670, is a good example of this alternative. While still in office and with little hope of being reelected to a second term as abbess, Doña Tomasina obtained an episcopal decree appointing her headmistress of the convent school for life. That appointment meant that Doña Tomasina could live in the splendid isolation of the convent school, in a large and well-decorated cell, surrounded by maids and servants, and with little, if any, accountability to conventual authorities. For more than thirty years Doña Tomasina de Mesa was headmistress of the convent school, clinging to her independent life-style at the fringes of the monastic community.[12]

Although many nuns clung to positions of prestige and authority in the colonial nunneries, none seem to have wielded power with more zest and ruthlessness than Doña María de las Nieves Fernández Maldonado in the nunnery of La Encarnación from 1723 to 1735. Doña María de las Nieves not only controlled the majority of the votes within the nunnery, but had also become a master at manipulating civil and ecclesiastical bureaucracies of the viceroyalty to her advantage.

Like other *conventos grandes*, La Encarnación was divided into political factions of Las Encarnadas and Las Verdes, the Pinks and the Greens. By the early 1720s, Doña María de las Nieves had become the undisputed leader of the Pink party which swept her into office during the abbatial election of 1723. During her first term in office, Doña María consolidated and expanded the membership of the Pinks and, when the time arrived for a new election in 1726, La Encarnación was an ocean of pink ribbons. There were so many pink ribbons in the cloisters, gardens, chapels, and parlors of the convent that everybody realized that only outside interference, either by the viceroy or the archbishop, could prevent Doña María's reelection to a second consecutive term.

However, the shrewd abbess had made sure that no outside intervention could take place, and in 1726 she was reelected to a second term. By then, Doña María was one of the most powerful individuals in Lima. Making judicious use of her rights to dispense patronage, she controlled the large financial holdings of the nunnery, and was very close to the viceroy, the marqués of Castelfuerte, and to the archbishop, Fray Diego Morcillo. As her second term neared its end, with unchallenged control over the Pinks, Doña María made the fateful decision to run for an unprecedented third term. Obviously, she knew that since the founding of the nunnery more than a century before, not a single abbess had ever been elected to three consecutive terms, but she also realized that she had the votes and that she could persuade Fray Diego Morcillo to ignore her blatant disregard for the tenets of canon law.

Late in 1729, tension and political clashes mounted within La Encarnación. Doña Rosa de la Cueva, the Greens' chosen candidate, opposed the incumbent abbess. With Doña María still in charge as abbess, it was not prudent to wear a green ribbon, and the leaders of the Green party had to work cautiously and in secret. Among the 142 nuns of the black veil, at least 72 votes were needed to elect Doña Rosa de la Cueva. By November 1729, a month before the election, the Greens sadly realized that they lacked eight or ten votes needed to elect Doña Rosa de la Cueva. Their only remedy to prevent reelection of Doña María de las Nieves was to request the archbishop to nullify the votes cast in her favor.

On November 17, 1729, the leaders of the Green party, among them two ex-abbesses, Doña Bernarda Merino de Heredia and Doña María de Rojas, wrote to Fray Diego Morcillo asking the prelate to reaffirm the tenets of canon law and to declare Doña María de las Nieves legally incapable of being reelected to a third term. The archbishop of Lima was caught in a very uncomfortable position. As head of the Peruvian church, he had no choice but to reaffirm the law and to prevent the election of Doña María. As an admirer and supporter of the incumbent abbess, however, he wanted a third term for his favorite nun. His ultimate course of action was dishonest and threw the nunnery of La Encarnación into one of the most confusing and chaotic political crises in its history. Officially and in public, Fray Diego Morcillo acquiesced to the petition of the Greens and upheld the principle of no reelection. In private and secretly, he assured Doña María de las Nieves that if she had the votes, he would not prevent her reelection. On December 18, only five days before the election, after having publicly denounced her reelection several times, Fray Diego wrote a hurried note to Doña María:

> *Lady Abbess: I have already answered by word of mouth to the petitions and letters of that holy convent. At this juncture, I only ask you to have patience and I will take the steps to assure that you will be abbess once again, notwithstanding the legislation. To fully accomplish this the only thing needed is to have the votes and to keep quiet. At the Palace, December of 1729. Yours, Fray Diego Archbishop.*

The election was scheduled for the morning of December 23. Fray Diego Morcillo chose the cleric Don Andrés de Paredes to represent him and to preside over the election. Don Andrés, perpetuating the dubious policies of the archbishop, gave a clear signal to Doña María's supporters when he pronounced that he would make no efforts to restrict or to condition in any form "the entire freedom" of those who were about to cast their votes for a new abbess. The election ceremony took place as previously described, and 142 votes were cast. Don Andrés de Paredes counted the ballots, but waited to announce the results officially to the community until the archbishop could be informed. The election turnout was close, but, nevertheless, a stunning victory for Doña María de las Nieves, and a clear indication that after almost a decade, the Pink party could still deliver the vote. Doña María obtained seventy-six votes, or four more than required for canonical election. The Green party could only muster sixty-four votes for Doña Rosa de la Cueva, or eight votes short of the minimum required. Doña Gerónima Meléndez and Doña María de Rojas obtained one vote each. These two votes, however, would not have made a difference, even if they had been switched to Doña Rosa.

In postponing official announcement of the election result, the archbishop, Fray Diego Morcillo, wanted to buy time to see if Doña María de las Nieves could slide into her third consecutive term as abbess without causing a political riot in the nunnery of La Encarnación. He should have known better. The election had been much too close to silence the losers. In addition, the unofficial number of votes obtained by each candidate was well known to all political operatives of the convent. The Greens, headed by Doña Rosa de la Cueva, publicly and officially protested the results of the election. They drew up a legal petition to have the votes for Doña María declared null and void. Even though this action pinned the archbishop against a canonical wall, Fray Diego Morcillo still wanted to stall for time in an effort to save the office of abbess for his favorite nun. Instead of nullifying the votes, he appointed Doña Bernarda Merino interim president of the nunnery, conferring upon her all rights and privileges of an abbess, but withholding that title. The archbishop's diversionary tactics did not bring about the expected result. The Greens refused to compromise, and continued to press their demands through all available legal channels. They wanted Doña Rosa de la Cueva the declared abbess of La Encarnación.

By December 28, 1729, only five days after the election, Fray Diego Morcillo realized belatedly not only that the battle to save the abbatial throne for Doña María de las Nieves was lost, but that he could no longer skirt the tenets of canon law. Within the nunnery, neither the Pinks nor the Greens paid the slightest attention to their interim president, Doña Bernarda Merino. The two monastic parties clashed violently with each other. Also, outside the nunnery, the citizens of Lima had begun taking sides in the monastic dispute, and civil and ecclesiastical tribunals stood ready to intervene. Left with no choice, Fray Diego Morcillo had to nullify Doña María's votes on December 28 and declare Doña Rosa canonical abbess of La Encarnación.

When representatives of the archbishop arrived at the nunnery the following day to install Doña Rosa as the new abbess, they found the entrance of the convent barred by followers of Doña María bent on preventing their rival's installation. On December 30, forces of the state had to be used in order to gain access to the nunnery. The viceroy sent two detachments of infantry and cavalry with orders to surround the nunnery and to open the doors of the convent by force. The colonial militia did as they were ordered, and representatives of the archbishop entered the cloisters to notify the nuns officially that Doña Rosa de la Cueva was their new abbess.

During January 1730, utter confusion reigned in the nunnery of La Encarnación. Doña María de las Nieves, trying to avoid confrontations with civil and ecclesiastical authorities, disappeared from her cell and went into hiding somewhere on the property of the convent. Her followers, the Pinks, refused not only to obey Doña Rosa, but also to surrender to her the keys and official seal of the nunnery. For nearly a week Doña Rosa was a virtual prisoner of the Pinks, who had cornered the new abbess in her cell and had posted loyal maids and slaves to guard the entrance. Clashes between the Greens and the Pinks occurred almost daily and, once again, soldiers had to be sent to the nunnery to patrol the cloisters and to keep the two factions apart. The royal audiencia of Lima intervened in the case, upholding the rights of Doña Rosa de la Cueva and urging members of the Pink party to submit. On January 14, 1730, Fray Diego Morcillo excommunicated all nuns who did not immediately recognize and obey Doña Rosa as the lawful abbess. However, the Pinks did not yield, and instead, on January 30, 1730, they appealed their case to the Holy See and to the king of Spain.

The political upheavals of the nunnery of La Encarnación lasted for two more years. On April 18, 1730, archbishop Fray Diego Morcillo died in Lima, and the cathedral chapter took over the governance of the diocese for the duration of the episcopal vacancy. Such collective leadership was not suited to handle the volatile situation at La Encarnación efficiently, and the nuns took advantage of the situation. The Pink party once more took the offensive, and by February 1731, they controlled the convent and had again imprisoned Doña Rosa de la Cueva in her own cell. Doña María de las Nieves, still in hiding, manipulated events through four of her most trusted lieutenants, Doña Juana de Ampuero, Doña Paula de Alzamora, Doña Francisca Montejo, and Doña Francisca Torrejón.

Pressured by the viceroy and the judges of the audiencia, the cathedral chapter tried to break the impasse. Don Francisco de Velasco y Reina was sent to La Encarnación to confront the four lieutenants of Doña María de las Nieves, to order them, under penalty of excommunication, to free the imprisoned Doña Rosa, and obey her as lawful abbess. Don Francisco was probably psychologically unprepared for the rebellious nuns' shocking reaction. With unbending stubbornness, they assured Don Francisco that they would rather "relinquish the veils" than obey Doña Rosa de la Cueva. To "relinguish the veils" meant, of course, they would give up their lives of consecrated virgins. Many of the Pinks came rushing in from all parts of the convent, stripping themselves of their veils in front of Don Francisco and angrily throwing them at his feet. They also threatened that if they ever saw Doña Rosa holding the abbatial crosier, symbol of supreme authority within the nunnery, they would take it away from her and would break it into pieces.

After this violent confrontation, the cathedral chapter became even more impotent in dealing with the crisis of La Encarnación. The year 1731 ended with the nunnery still involved in suits, countersuits, appeals and counterappeals, all of which turned life in La Encarnación into a nightmare of vicious passions.

The political struggles of La Encarnación finally ceased in 1732 when the vacant episcopal See of Lima was filled by a new archbishop, the able Don Francisco Antonio Escadón. Within a few weeks of his installation, he managed to restore peace in La Encarnación. His approach to the political clashes within the nunnery was so simple and reflected such obvious common sense that the nuns readily accepted the compromise suggested by the new archbishop. Don Francisco Antonio went to La Encarnación as a pastor and father, bent on persuading the nuns with love instead of confronting them with juridical commands and canonical penalties. He gathered the community, lifted all censures imposed by his predecessor, and reminded the nuns of an obvious fact: namely that by 1732 the results of the 1729 election had become meaningless and purely theoretical. Whoever had held the office of abbess, whether Doña María or Doña Rosa—and archbishop Escadón refused to pass judgment on this point—her term of office had already expired. Don Francisco Antonio suggested that the obvious way to proceed was to elect a new abbess in a spirit of reconciliation.

Doña Gerónima Meléndez, who in the election of 1729 had not identified herself with either of the two monastic factions, and who had obtained one of the two votes that did not go to either

Doña María or Doña Rosa, emerged as the compromise candidate. Heeding the advice of the archbishop, Doña Gerónima promised that she would distribute the offices of the nunnery equally between the Pinks and the Greens. Furthermore, she pledged that nobody would be excluded from office on the basis of previous party affiliation. When the election of 1732 took place at last, 140 votes were cast and Doña Gerónima emerged as the unanimous winner. A few months after the election, on June 1, 1733, the nuns of La Encarnación wrote an official letter to the king informing him that peace and union had returned to the nunnery. This letter was signed by the new abbess, the prioress, the deputy prioress, and the *definidoras* or cabinet of the abbess. Their signatures reveal that Doña Gerónima had kept her promise of a fair distribution of conventual offices. The prioress was Doña Francisca Torrejón, an activist in the Pink party; the deputy prioress was Doña Petronila de Céspedes, a member of the Greens; and among the *definidoras* were Doña María de las Nieves and her rival, Doña Rosa de la Cueva.[13]

In the cloisters of Spanish Peru lived some of the strongest, most liberated, and best-educated women of the viceroyalty. One is tempted to accept that colonial nunneries were the best institutional setting for a woman in the Spanish Empire in South America. She owned her own cell, controlled her properties, servants, and younger relatives, was constantly entertained by excellent music and drama, and was free to vote in all kinds of elections. The Peruvian nun of the black veil had much more autonomy and freedom than her average sister in the secular city.

IO

❀

Beatas
and *Tapadas*

FOR MOST WOMEN, LIFE outside the cloisters lacked the autonomy, freedom, and drama that made the life of a consecrated virgin so attractive to thousands of colonial women. Many women of Spanish Peru led hidden, uneventful lives within the home, constantly watched by jealous husbands or demanding fathers. Their virtue, that is, their virginity or marital fidelity, was a matter of family honor, and had to be protected beyond the slightest shadow of suspicion. The burden of responsibility for the family honor, and society's demand that their personal behavior reflect the ideals of a Christianity obsessed with marianism restricted the lives of many women, obscured their visibility, and stifled their own personal and independent growth.

Yet, in the secular city two types of women emerged who were so visible and ubiquitous that they became, in the popular imagination, symbols and prototypes of women's life in the colonial cities of Spanish Peru. They were regarded with curiosity by European travelers, were frequently mentioned in the diaries and letters written by colonial observers, became at times the subject of pastoral letters issued by the bishops of the viceroyalty and of the sermons delivered by colonial preachers, and even occasionally caught the watchful eyes of the members of the Holy Tribunal of the Inquisition. Those two types of women were the beatas and the *tapadas*. The former was a living symbol of the doctrines of marianism, while the latter exhibited in her daily living all of the characteristics of a restless and stubborn female Don Juan.

The beata was usually a single woman who, without ever attaching herself to a juridically recognized religious community, wore the habit of a consecrated virgin, practiced daily hundreds of religious devotions and acts of charity, never missed the myriad of liturgical celebrations performed in the colonial temples, and spent much of her day in chapels and churches. To the common people the beata was a person endowed with special gifts and power to whom one could turn for religious and supernatural help. In a deeply religious society, the beata enjoyed a high degree of social respectability and prestige and could make a good, modest living by the alms and monetary gifts from her many devotees. Bishops and priests, although always ready to recognize and encourage the saintly lives of many of those women, were also concerned with the existence of false beatas who, devoid of any true Christian virtues, exploited the credulity of the simple people and used religion to improve their social and economic status. The false beatas, frequently found among the ignorant and illiterate women of the lower classes, were condemned by the bishops, attacked from the pulpits of the viceroyalty, and occasionally ended in the clutches of the Holy Inquisition.

The *tapada* was a worldly woman; in the eyes of many she was the prototype of the temptress and the sex symbol of colonial Peru. She was always dressed in the latest fashions, and her clothing was made of the most expensive, imported materials. She favored lace from the Low Countries, exquisite silks from China, and exotic perfumes and jewelry from the Orient. The length of her gown was shortened several inches to reveal the lace trim of her undergarments and to draw attention to her small feet covered with embroidered velvet slippers. The distinctive mark of the *tapada* was the long veil or shawl, which covered the upper part of her body. Although the shawl was a very common garment and used daily by most women of the viceroyalty, the *tapada* wore it with such flirtatious style that it had a devastating effect in arousing the erotic interest of males. With the shawl over her head leaving only one eye partially uncovered, she wrapped it tightly below her shoulders to enhance her bust and to accentuate the curvaceous lines of her hips and waist. The Peruvian *tapada* knew how to

handle her shawl with the same artful and teasing skills the bull-
fighter used to entice the bull with his cape. She could reveal her
sensuous mouth by lifting the edges of her shawl, or she could
let a shoulder slip free from the shawl to show the rising curve
of her breasts and the plunging neckline of her gown.

Many foreign visitors were amazed at the looseness and freedom
of the *tapada,* who behaved in public in a way unseen even in the
most progressive cities of Europe. The preachers of the viceroyalty
castigated and condemned her from the pulpit, but the *tapada*
never disappeared from the streets and plazas of the colonial cities.
She was constantly seen walking with other *tapadas* in the prom-
enades and parks, mixing with the crowds to watch the frequent
parades and processions, hurrying into churches to offer a prayer
or to light a candle to her favored saint, crossing the city on her
way to markets and shops, visiting friends and acquaintances, and
faithfully attending bullfights, plays, and musical events.

One of the most disturbing characteristics of the *tapada,* from
the point of view of the moral watchdogs of the viceroyalty, was
that she used the shawl both as a tool of enticement, and to conceal
her identity. In the popular language of the period, *"tapada"* meant
"a woman who covers herself with the shawl or veil in order not
to be recognized." Protected by this anonymity, the *tapada* dared
to do things that she never would have done with her face uncovered. Any young wife or daughter of a respectable family could
leave the house with her face uncovered and the shawl loosely
hanging from her shoulders in a modest fashion, and a few blocks
from the house rearrange her shawl and transform herself into
a *tapada* to do as she pleased without being recognized by anybody.
Once transformed, many young Peruvian women went through
the streets of their cities doing more damage to the souls of men,
to use the delightful hyperbole of a colonial observer, than the
damage done by the royal galleon in attacking a fleet of small and
flimsy rowboats.

The Rose of Lima

Among the thousands of beatas who crowded the temples and
streets of the Peruvian cities during colonial days, none had a
stronger impact on her society or exhibited the characteristics of

marianism better than Isabel Flores de Oliva. More than three centuries after her death, her memory is still alive among the popular classes of Peru, who know her not by her real name but by the traditional and affectionate appellation "Holy Rose of Lima." Soon after her death, her fame and the story of her saintly life spread across the oceans into Spain and other Catholic countries of Europe. Clerics, playwrights, poets, painters, and sculptors perpetuated in their works the name of the Rose of Lima. The superb painting of Isabel Flores de Oliva by Claudio Coello, kept today at the Prado Museum in Madrid, is but one example of the fascination she aroused in the artistic imagination of Spain. The names of many royal officials, rich merchants, and influential clerics are all but forgotten, while the name of the Rose of Lima remains a household word in Peru today. Since 1671, the year Isabel Flores de Oliva was canonized by the Catholic church, thousands of Peruvian women have been baptized with the name of Rose in honor and in memory of the great Peruvian beata.[1]

Isabel was born in Lima on the last day of April 1586, to a modest and poor Spanish family of eight children. Her father, Gaspar Flores, was an impoverished Spaniard, whom Viceroy Don Andrés Hurtado de Mendoza had appointed to a minor position in the royal militia of Lima. Her mother, María de Oliva, was also of pure Spanish ancestry and worked at home all her life as a seamstress to supplement the meager earnings of her husband. Nothing distinguished the Flores Oliva family from hundreds of other modest Spanish families that in the last decades of the sixteenth century struggled to make a living in the capital of the viceroyalty of Peru. The birth of Isabel rescued them from anonymity, and their modest house, not far from the Rimac River, became, with time, one of the most popular shrines of Peru. In an age permeated by pious legends and religious beliefs, an alleged miracle set Isabel apart from all other children of her age; relatives, neighbors, and friends perceived it as a divine sign that Isabel was chosen of God and was destined to become a living example of all of the virtues of marianism. The so-called miracle was such an undramatic and normal occurrence that in a different time and place, only a loving mother or a doting grandmother would have thought it extraordinary.

An Indian maid who helped Isabel's mother with the household chores checked the crib of Isabelita one day and "saw" that two

beautifully formed roses were clearly visible in the healthy pink
cheeks of the baby. The excited maid called relatives and neighbors and most of them also saw that two fresh roses had blossomed
on the face of the baby girl. The attribute of Venus, the goddess
of love, in pagan antiquity, the rose had been introduced into
Christian iconography as the symbol of divine love, purity, and
sacrifice. The Virgin Mary was known as "the rose without thorns,"
and her statues and paintings were frequently decked with roses
to symbolize her immacualte conception, her love of God, and
her perpetual virginity. The thought that the roses on Isabel's
cheeks had marked the little girl as a new Mary and an embodi-
ment of all the marian virtues must have crossed the mind of
many. From then on, the original baptismal name, Isabel, was all
but forgotten, and the little girl was called by family and neighbors
"the Little Rose." Only Isabel de Herrera, the grandmother after
whom the girl had been named, objected to the change of name
and punished her granddaughter when years later she refused to
answer to the name of Isabel. The name change was made official
in 1597. That year, Isabel received the sacrament of confirmation
at the hands of the archbishop of Lima, Toribio Alfonso de Mogrovejo, who confirmed her with the name Rosa de Santa María.

Rose was eleven years old in 1597 when she was confirmed.
Until her death in 1617, Rose of Saint Mary was, without ever
abandoning secular life or the paternal house, one of the most
visible and most influential women in the city of Lima. As a well-
recognized and respected beata and under the spiritual guidance
of several prominent priests, the young woman of modest family
had access to the upper strata of colonial society, gained social
status and prestige, obtained generous economic aid from wealthy
donors, and influenced a great number of women of different
social classes. Even some prominent gentlemen of Lima gravitated
toward Rose, whose words and saintly deeds became for them a
respected norm of life. Of the thousands of consecrated virgins
in the cloisters of the colonial cities, none had the emotional impact
on her contemporaries that Rose had.

Still a very young woman, Rose spurned the common female
dress of her time and hid her recognized creole beauty under the
coarse brown robe of a Franciscan monk. For several years, she
always appeared in the street and churches of Lima wearing the

Franciscan habit, until 1606 when she adopted and wore until her death the white robes of the Dominican order. The monastic robes made Rose stand out among the throngs of worshippers that filled the temples and followed through the streets of Lima the frequent religious parades. One of her early established religious practices identified Rose in the popular imagination with Mary, the Mother of Christ.

There were many statues and paintings of Mary in the churches of Lima. By 1600, the doctrine of the Immaculate Conception had become in the Spanish world not only a theological but also a social and political issue as well. Many sodalities and religious corporations of secular membership had begun to require from all of their members an oath to defend that doctrine. Schools, colleges, universities, and merchants and artisans guilds had followed suit. Even viceroys and royal governors issued guidelines from time to time instructing the masses how to celebrate properly the many festivities dedicated to Mary, the Mother of God. The viceroy himself presided over the congregation in the great marian solemnities and marched close to the float when the statue of Mary was paraded through the streets of Lima. In this atmosphere, Rose had taken upon herself to visit almost daily three of the most popular madonnas of Lima: Our Lady of the Rosary, kept in the Dominican church of Lima; and Our Lady of Loreto and Our Lady of Los Remedios, both venerated in the church of the Jesuit College of San Pablo.

Rose was soon recognized by the priests of those churches and by the faithful as the *camarera* or maid-in-waiting of the three popular madonnas. The office of *camarera* was, and has remained to this day, a great status symbol in many cities and towns of the Spanish world. The *camarera* was the only person who had free and daily access to the *camarin* of the madonna, the ornate and hidden enclosure behind the altar where the statue of the Virgin was dressed and adorned for the many marian festivities. The *camarera* alone was in charge of changing the robes, the crown, and the jewels of the madonna, and was the person sought after by the common faithfuls to place candles and ex-votos or religious offerings close to the statue of the Virgin. In a society deeply influenced and shaped by religious symbols, a *camarera* was frequently perceived by the popular masses as a close aid or adviser to a president is perceived today: a person not only close to the source of power, but sharing in and distributing that power. For her constant and close attendance to three of the great madonnas of Lima and for her daily wearing of the monastic robes, Rose of Saint Mary was seen by her contemporaries as a living extension of Mary Herself and as a mystic presence of the Virgin Mother in the midst of the secular city.

This reputation, already well established early in the seventeenth century, was enhanced by the life-style she adopted within the home of her parents. She lived secluded from the family living quarters in a small and humid cell built in a corner of the garden, where she led a life of intensive work and prayer. Like her mother, Rose was very skilled at sewing and embroidering. Those skills, highly regarded in colonial days and coupled with Rose's reputation as a living saint, brought to her cubicle in the garden some of the most aristocratic ladies of Lima. They paid Rose generously for her work, and many of them lingered for hours in the small cell, lost in conversation with the beata. Other lay persons came by the garden just to visit Rose and to bring her donations of money, food, and clothing to help the poor. Rose also received from her lay friends enough money to have masses celebrated or other religious services performed. Rose's Dominican and Jesuit counselors often celebrated those masses without charge, and let Rose keep the donations to support herself, her family, and the poor. Occasionally, the most ornate carriages of Lima stopped at the door of the Flores Oliva family to pick up Rose. The aristocracy brought Rose with them to pay social visits, to attend religious services in a favored church, or to visit the sick. It was indeed a mark of honor and prestige to be seen in public with Rose and to be able to call her companion and friend.

Rose's cubicle in the garden was also a place where women gathered to pass the time and amuse themselves "in an honest fashion." Rose was gifted with a very pleasant singing voice and could play the guitar with skill and feeling. She also composed excellent poetry and, like Saint Theresa of Avila, had the uncanny talent of changing popular, secular love songs into beautiful *coplas a lo divino,* songs of divine love. One of her most charming poems, probably inspired by a popular love song of the times, is a delightful play on words with the family surnames and her own name:

Oh Jesus of my soul
How handsome you look
Among roses and flowers
And green olive branches.

It is already midnight
My Jesus has not arrived
Who could be the lucky one
Who is keeping Him?[2]

Her music and poetry, her charm and wit, and her personal beauty attracted many lay persons to Rose's little cubicle in the garden. The popularity of the small cell in the garden was enhanced by the constant rumors of miracles Rose performed there with the charm and simplicity of a Saint Francis of Assisi. Her miracles, it was whispered in the streets and homes of Lima, were undramatic, playful, and even humorous things, whose sole purpose seems to have been to show that she was a beloved, almost spoiled child of God. It was said that Rose could grow the most beautiful plants and flowers in the city almost overnight and entirely out of season. Her music and songs attracted to the garden all kinds of birds, which joined Rose in perfect melody to praise the Lord. She could throw into the air the petals of her miraculous flowers and form with them garlands, crosses, and religious symbols, which were carried away by the winds without breaking the patterns. Because of the high humidity of Lima and its proximity to the riverbed, the garden of the Flores Oliva family was always infested by thick clouds of mosquitoes. Rose, many of her visitors testified later, could command the mosquitoes not to come near her and her lay friends while they visited and engaged in conversation. Clouds of mosquitoes hovered over the garden, but one was never bitten by them as long as Rose was around.

These "miracles" may have been nothing more than charming, but empty, legends, but Rose's contemporaries did not dismiss them. The pious and the curious flocked daily to that little garden in the hopes of catching a glimpse of one of those miracles and of being close to Rose, whom they perceived as a source of supernatural power. With the passing of years, a group of well-known and influential ladies clustered around the Rose of Saint Mary, who became their spiritual mentor and the dominant figure of the group. Among the ladies were Doña María de Uzategui, wife of the royal accountant Don Gonzalo de la Maza; Doña María de Pimentel, the powerful niece of the archbishop of Lima, Don Toribio Alfonso de Mogrovejo; Doña Jusepa de Guzmán, wife of the royal secretary Don Juan de Tineo; Doña María Eufemia de Pareja, niece of the bishop of Huamanga and wife of Don Juan de la Raya; Doña Luisa de Melgarejo, married to Doctor Juan de Soto who served in the royal audencia; Doña Teresa de Grijano; Doña Isabel Mejía; and Doña Luisa de Mendoza.

These women vied with each other for the friendship and company of Rose, and many of them placed their daughters and female servants under her guidance. A second cluster of young women was thus formed around Rose, who taught them sewing, embroidering, some music and singing, and how to become worthy Christian women within the contemporary value system. The young disciples of Rose of Saint Mary included Doña Micaela and Doña Andrea de la Maza, daughters of Doña María de Uzategui; Doña Francisca and Doña Isabel de Tineo, daughters of Doña Jusepa de Guzmán; the female servants Barbara López and Ana de los Reyes; and the four sisters, Catalina, Lucía, Felipa, and Francisca de Montoya, daughters of Andrés López, the oldest and most trusted servant in the household of the royal accountant Don Gonzalo de la Maza. These women formed the core of a larger group of Rose's followers, and some of them wore religious robes and became beatas in their own right.

The influence of Rose was not limited to the pious womenfolk of Lima. Through her female friends she had access to the men in their families, and in the early seventeenth century, many clerics and laymen fell under the spell of the beata. As already mentioned, Don Gonzalo de la Maza, Don Juan de Soto, and Don Juan de Tineo were among the most ardent admirers of Rose of Saint Mary. They were men who enjoyed a prominent social and political status in Lima, and as their friend, Rose acquired a social acceptance and respectability that were not hers by virtue of her birth. Don Gonzalo treated her as a daughter, and Rose spent long periods living in the rich mansion of Don Gonzalo in the heart of old Lima. She died in Don Gonzalo's house, surrounded by his family, servants, and friends. Don Juan de Tineo, a royal secretary of the audiencia, considered himself Rose's spiritual brother because of a pact between them to share the merits of the prayers and acts of charity they each performed.

With her charismatic religious appeal, Rose also had significant influence on two of the most powerful male religious orders of Peru, the Jesuits and the Dominicans. Men who were leading theologians and spiritual directors of these elites became strong supporters of the beata and vouched before ecclesiastical authorities for Rose's saintly life. Among Rose's friends and advisors were the Dominicans Fray Pedro de Loaysa, Fray Francisco Nieto, Fray Juan de Lorenzana, and Fray Alonso Velásquez, and the Jesuits Antonio de Vega, Diego Martínez, Juan de Villalobos, and Diego de Peñalosa. With the support of such clerical and secular friends, Rose became the most respected beata of the viceroyalty and one of the best-known and influential women of Lima.

An extraordinary event attributed to her saintly life took place in Lima a few months before Rose's death. The new "miracle" had a deep effect on the popular masses, increasing even more the reputation of the beata, and causing, in part, the explosion of religious hysteria which gripped Lima a few months later at her death. On the evening of April 15, 1617, following a well-established custom, Doña María de Uzategui, accompanied by her two daughters, Doña Micaela and Doña Andrea, and by Rose, entered the private chapel of her house to start preparations for the family evening prayers. Her husband, Don Gonzalo de la Maza, had left the house a few minutes before to go next door to visit his friend Don Juan de Tineo, who had just returned from a business trip to Callao. While Rose and her daughters settled in the chapel, Doña María unveiled a painting of Christ, which was hanging over the small altar, set some candles in front of the painting, and left the chapel to gather other members of the household for the evening prayers. Doña María was in the living room talking with her black maid Gerónima, when her daughter Doña Micaela came rushing excitedly from the chapel.

While Rose was praying to Christ, the girl told her mother, the painting of the Lord had begun to perspire and the hair, face, and beard of Christ were covered with sweat. Doña María went back into the chapel and saw that the girl was right, the painted face of Christ appeared to be perspiring. The slave Gerónima ran with the news to the servants quarters and came back with Juan

Costilla and Pedro Leandro, who, upon entering the chapel, also saw the sweating face of Christ. Almost ten persons were by now in the chapel, all of them overcome by excitement and religious emotion. Only Rose remained calm and silent, her eyes fixed on the painting, totally oblivious to the noise and commotion around her.

Then, not knowing what else to do, Doña María sent a servant next door to tell her husband to return home immediately. Don Gonzalo arrived, accompanied by his neighbor Don Juan de Tineo, and both of them tried to calm the mounting excitement of those in the chapel. Don Gonzalo proceeded to examine the painting carefully. While he was trying to establish the source and cause of the perspiration of Christ, other friends and neighbors began to arrive. Word of the "miracle" taking place in the presence of Rosa had obviously spread through the neighborhood. Andrés López arrived with two of her daughters, followed shortly by the lawyer of the audiencia, Don Juan de Soto, and his wife, Doña Luisa Melgarejo. Doña Barbara Fajardo with her son Don Diego and several maids also rushed to Don Gonzalo's house and found a placed in the already overcrowded little chapel.

Don Gonzalo de la Maza, a level-headed gentleman, realized the need to control the emotions of his neighbors and friends whose eyes, filled with tears, shifted with mounting religious emotion from the perspiring face of Christ to the luminous transfixed face of Rose of Saint Mary. Don Gonzalo spoke calmly to those in the chapel and suggested that perhaps the perspiration on the face of Christ was not a miraculous but a simple, natural phenomenon. After all, the lit candles had been placed too close to the painting, and the heat emanating from them could have melted some of the paint, creating the illusion that the face of Christ was perspiring. Don Gonzalo's efforts to gave a rational explanation of the event had little impact on those gathered in the chapel. By then, they were so overcome by religious emotion and so moved by the proximity of Rose that they were convinced a true miracle was taking place before their eyes. Don Gonzalo de la Maza knew that he alone could not handle the strange event. He called aside the manservant Pedro Leandro and sent him in haste to summon a priest and the artist Angelino Medoro, who had painted the canvas of Christ a few months before.

Angelino Medoro was a well-known Italian painter, born in

Rome, who had been attracted to Peru by the boom in religious art created by the construction of new churches, chapels, and convents. Don Gonzalo de la Maza had commissioned him to paint an *Ecce Homo,* a portrait of the suffering Christ at the moment of being sentenced to death. Medoro had finished the painting by December 1616, and brought it to Don Gonzalo's house to be placed over the altar of the family chapel. He was called now, in April 1617, to examine his painting and to see if there was a natural explanation for the perspiration phenomenon. When Angelino Medoro arrived with his wife at Don Gonzalo's house, the first thing he noticed was that the perspiration covered only the hair, face, and beard of Christ, while the rest of the canvas was completely dry. Medoro touched the oozing liquid with the tips of his fingers to feel its thickness and texture and to smell it for any odors of varnish, oils, or paints. He concluded that the layers of colors he had used on the canvas were not melting, that the strokes of his brushes were still visible, and that the mysterious liquid had no traces of the oils and paints he had used in his work. Then he turned to those in the chapel and told them that "on the basis of his experience and skill in the art of painting, [the phenomenon of perspiration] was a supernatural and miraculous thing . . . and that he considered the greatest of fortunes to have happened in a painting made by him with so much care."

Meanwhile, two Jesuits from the nearby College of San Pablo, Fr. Diego de Peñalosa and Br. Francisco López, had answered Don Gonzalo's summons and were now waiting at the entrance of the chapel. After Medoro spoke declaring the phenomenon miraculous and supernatural, all eyes turned to the Jesuit priest. Fr. Peñalosa approached the painting and, still a bit skeptical, began drying the perspiration with small cotton balls. The face and hair of Christ appeared dried and normal for a little while, but then the perspiration began again. Once more the priest dried the face with cotton balls, only to see the unusual phenomenon repeated a third time. The painting had perspired three times in about three hours. Fr. Diego de Peñalosa decided to cover the painting with a veil, to dismiss those in the chapel, and to report the strange events of the evening to the archbishop of Lima, Don Bartolomé Lobo Guerrero.

The archbishop delegated the vicar general, Don Feliciano de Vega, assisted by the notary public of the royal audiencia, Dr. Juan de la Roca, to conduct an official inquiry into the alleged miracle. Twelve eyewitnesses were called to testify under oath, and all of them, without exception, confirmed the events of April 15. The Peruvian church never made an official pronouncement on the matter, but the faithful believed that a true miracle had taken place, owing to the prayers and presence of the beata Rose of Saint Mary. Rose had only four more months to live, and in those last months of her life she was venerated more than ever as a living saint by the people of Lima.[3]

Rose died in the house of Don Gonzalo de la Maza shortly after midnight on August 24, 1617, in a room close to the chapel, where the miraculous Christ of Angelino Medoro was still displayed. At her passing, the emotional explosion of the city of Lima indicated what a beata meant to the people of seventeenth-century Peru. In spite of the late hour, word of Rose's death spread through the city and very soon the street in front of the house was filled with people pleading to view and touch the body of the beata. Long lines formed all through the night, and clerics, gentlemen and ladies of Lima society, common people, servants, and even slaves passed in front of the body. They came in a continuous stream through the front door of the house, and were ushered out through a back door to avoid overcrowding the main street in front of the house.

The following morning found Lima in an atmosphere of uncontrolled religious excitement. The crowds waiting in front of Don Gonzalo's house grew larger. Later in the afternoon when the body was transferred to the Dominican church, the streets and plazas in the center of Lima were a solid mass of humanity. The clerics of the Cathedral Chapter, the most prestigious secular clerics in Lima, bore Rose's body on their shoulders through the streets of the city toward the Dominican convent. Every time they stopped to rest or change the pallbearers, the crowds surged forward trying to touch the body and had to be restrained by the royal militia. The viceroy himself, with his wife and the entire viceregal court, waited for the funeral procession in the main plaza of Lima in front of the viceroyal palace. The procession came to a halt in front of the palace, and the highest authority in the land fell to his knees to pay his respects to the young laywoman who had captured the heart and the imagination of Lima. The Dominican community of Lima, presided over by the archbishop

Don Bartolomé Lobo Guerrero, received the body of Rose at the main door of the church, which for several hours had been filled with a large and restless crowd of Rose's devotees.

The arrival of the body turned the faithful inside the church into an uncontrollable hysterical mob. The soldiers sent by the viceroy could not contain the crowds, and Rose's funeral robe was almost torn to pieces by the devotees eager to keep a relic of the saint. The Jesuit Antonio Vega told later of the barbaric action of one of his lay friends who, in a frenzy of religious hysteria, broke through the crowd and bit off one of Rose's fingers with his bare teeth. The bishop of Guatemala Don Pedro de Valencia, who was visiting Lima and had been asked to conduct the funeral service, was unable to calm the crowds or to approach the altar to begin the service. With a new reinforcement of additional troops, the viceroy began slowly restoring order and gave the Dominicans the opportunity to take the body to the safety of the cloister, which was then hastily buried in the chapter room inside the Dominican convent, where lay persons could not easily enter. The funeral service was postponed until the following day, and the crowds were finally persuaded to return home. That night, the empty Dominican church looked more like a battlefield than a temple. The floors were strewn with torn veils, unstrung rosaries, over-turned pews, broken chairs, prayerbooks, and candles. The Dominican lay brothers and a few servants had to work all night to get the church ready for Rose's funeral the following day.

The fame of the great Peruvian beata grew in the months and years after her death. In 1618, seventy-five witnesses were called by the archbishop to testify under oath about the life of Rose of Saint Mary. While ecclesiastical authorities in Lima, Madrid, and Rome took their time in lengthy deliberations about Rose's virtues, the people of Peru hastened to turn in their popular verdict: Rose was to them the most beloved woman in the city of Lima, and her virtues represented an ideal of Christian womanhood. Rose's little cell in the garden of the Flores Oliva family became a popular shrine, and prayers and candles were offered daily in the Dominican church to honor her memory. This popular and unofficial cult worried the judges of the Holy Tribunal of the Inquisition, and in 1624, they issued orders to stop the veneration of the young Peruvian woman. Her portrait was removed from the Dominican church, and all of her relics were gathered in an effort to restrain the growing popular devotion to Rose. These efforts did not succeed, and in 1630, a new judicial inquiry was ordered by the archbishop, Don Fernando Arias de Ugarte. Once again the ecclesiastical bureaucracy moved slowly, but Isabel Flores Oliva, the Rose of Lima, was finally canonized by the Catholic church on April 12, 1671.[4]

Beaterios and False Beatas

The influence of the beatas in Peruvian society, at times, went beyond the cluster of their friends and devotees to blossom into an institutional presence in the city. Some beatas displayed a great talent in pooling their spiritual and economic resources and, by using the prestige and power of their lay friends, organized themselves into informal communities known by the common people as beaterios or houses of beatas. The beaterios, as suggested in a previous chapter, were retreat houses, where the beatas lived a communal life and where, as a cohesive group of laywomen, they could control better their spiritual and economic assets. From the beaterios, united into one body, the beatas could and did exercise a greater influence on their friends and followers than the influence exercised by individual pious women. Although the beaterios may appear almost identical to the canonical nunneries, in reality they were substantially different.

The beaterios were not officially recognized by the canonical legislation of the church, and the beatas living in them were not allowed to take official vows; therefore, they remained always laywomen from a canonical point of view. In the case of the beaterios, ecclesiastical authorities lacked the legal powers so clearly granted them by canon law to rule and control the official nunneries. Nearly every major city of colonial Peru had one or two beaterios. The Beaterio de Amparadas, Beaterio de Viterbo, Beaterio de Copacabana, Beaterio de Nazarenas de Lima, Beaterio del Patrocinio, and Beaterio de Nazarenas del Cuzco, among others, established the existence of these unofficial, female communities in the Peruvian cities. Some of the beaterios acquired a noticeable amount of wealth and prestige and tried to transform themselves eventually into canonically recognized communities of professed nuns.

The Beaterio de Nazarenas of Cuzco, for instance, was founded in the 1690s and by 1752 had rural and urban properties that yielded a yearly income of more than 100,000 pesos. Considering that only about twenty-five beatas lived in the Nazarenas of Cuzco in 1752, that yearly income represents an extraordinary amount, indicating the business acumen of those women. A better example of how piety and religiosity became, at times, the foundation of an affluent economic status for some women is the one afforded by the Beaterio of Copacabana.

Copacabana, the only Peruvian beaterio that received Indian and mestizo women exclusively, owned in the 1730s several houses in the San Lázaro section of Lima, which yielded an average income of 4,400 pesos every year. In 1738, the beatas of Copacabana invested some of their money to buy a few small houses and several city lots from the *licenciado* Don Juan del Cerro. The beaterio also owned the estancia or ranch of Casacoto in the municipality of Ocoros, which produced several loads of *cecina* (dried, salted meat) and cheese every year. One of the beatas of Copacabana, the Indian Catalina Guaman Capac, spent several months every year traveling through rural Peru to collect money and donations for the beaterio. She must have been a shrewd business woman because in 1756, the wealthy landowner of the Valley of Chincha, Don Felipe Cogentes, made her his business agent in Lima. Catalina transported the grain produced in the farms of Don Felipe to Lima, stored it in the beaterio, and then sold it for a commission in the markets of the viceroyal capital.[5]

The institutionalization of the life-style of the beata would have not been possible without the help and constant support of wealthy and socially prominent ladies. Every true beata, as seen in the case of Rose of Saint Mary, attracted some powerful women, who became her benefactors and supporters. In the world that formed around the beatas and the beaterios, no woman had a higher stature than the illustrious Doña María Fernández de Córdoba. Doña María not only carried one of the most illustrious names of the viceroyalty, which tied her to some of the noble houses of Spain, but she was also one of the wealthiest women of Peru in the eighteenth century. She had been married for years to General Don Alonso Calderón de la Barca y Bolta, but by 1720, she was a widow without children and the sole owner of several large estates or *mayorazgos*. She used her wealth generously in works of charity and to help other pious women of the viceroyalty. By 1715, she was already recognized as the most important lay benefactor of the beaterio of the Nazarenas, to which she assigned in perpetuity the interests of an endowment of sixty thousand pesos. When the devastating earthquake of 1746 almost destroyed the dwellings of the beatas, Doña María spent twenty thousand pesos of her own money to rebuild the house. Four years later, in 1750, she began planning one of her most ambitious projects, a retreat house under the care of the Jesuits for the society ladies of Lima.

The Jesuits had introduced in Peru the *Spiritual Exercises* of Saint Ignatius, one of the most influential books of the Spanish Counter-Reformation, and thousands of their students and lay, male friends had made the spiritual exercises in the secluded environment of the Jesuit colleges of Peru. In 1750, Doña María Fernández de Córdoba decided to offer the same opportunity to the women of her own social class, so they could experience the silence and peacefulness of the monastic life by withdrawing from the world into the cloister of a Jesuit retreat house. For this purpose, she donated her ancestral mansion, located two blocks from the vice-royal palace and half a block from the Jesuit College of San Pablo. Doña María also bought some adjacent houses, which she began remodelling to serve as a temporary monastic enclosure for the society ladies of Lima.

The new retreat house for women opened in 1752 to a group eager to spend a week of monastic silence and prayer under the guidance of a Jesuit retreat master. In that first group were, among others, Doña María de Perales, widow of General Eugenio de Alvarado; Doña Mariana de Córdoba, countess of Polentinos; Doña María Josefa de Colmenares, wife of Don Juan José de Alliaga; Doña Josefa de Urdanequi, granddaughter of the marqués of Villafuerte; Doña Francisca Ortiz de Foronda, countess of Valle-hermoso; and the wives of royal officials and judges of the audiencia. By the end of 1753, 314 women had spent a week in the house built by Doña María Fernández de Córdoba.[6]

Not all Peruvian beatas were women of such high moral character. The false beatas, who made a mockery of religion and exploited the credulity of the simple people, were ubiquitous in the colonial cities. Most of them were poor, ignorant women, whose alleged supernatural powers brought them money and social prestige among the people of their class. They spent their days practicing sorcery and witchcraft, preparing love potions, reading palms, and telling fortunes. These false but rather harmless beatas usually fell into the hands of the Holy Inquisition, which condemned them to short jail sentences, made them serve in the city hospitals, or exiled them from their neighborhoods and communities.

These humble women, although harassed by the Inquisition and the Peruvian clergy, were never taken very seriously or punished too severely. Inquisitors and bishops were more concerned with other types of false beatas, who belonged to a better social class, were more educated, and pretended to live in Christian mysticism. They claimed to have revelations and the gift of prophecy, and pretended to be inspired interpreters of the mysteries of Christian dogma. Because of their social class and better education, they sometimes won fanatic followers from among the common faithful and even from the ranks of the clergy. They were undoubtedly a serious threat to the unity of doctrine and to the pastoral monopoly of bishops and priests, and were therefore persecuted with a vengence and punished with great severity. Two prominent and well-known women, Doña María Pizarro and Angela Carranza, exemplify this second type of false beata.

Doña María belonged to a prominent Peruvian family and was the sister of a well-known Jesuit, and a distant relative of the Pizarro brothers, conquerors of Peru. By 1560, still a very young woman, Doña María enjoyed the reputation of a beata, who had direct revelations from God and was in daily contact with saints and angels. A devout and fanatical group of followers clustered around Doña María, whose words they accepted as a new oracle of God. By the end of the decade, Doña María was the emotional and religious center of a group formed by Doña Elvira de Avalos and her daughters Doña Beatriz, Doña Isabel, and Doña María; Doña Leonor de Valenzuela; Doña Ana Pizarro; Isabel de Contreras; the servant María "La Morisca," the Dominican friars Pedro de Toro, Alonso Gasco, and Francisco de la Cruz; and the Jesuit priests Jerónimo Ruiz de Portillo and Luís López. By 1568 or 1569, all these people were leading confused lives overshadowed by the phantasmagorical visions of María Pizarro. They perceived themselves as a specially chosen group placed beyond the normal tenets of doctrine and morality. Some of the priests had fallen into the pitfall of erotic mysticism and sacred, religious sexuality, and were persuading some of the women that sexual intercourse with the priest was the best way to reach the divine. The Dominican fray Francisco de la Cruz, a victim of *dementia theologica,* impregnated Doña Leonor de Valenzuela and persuaded himself and Doña Leonor that their son was sent by God to build a "new Jerusalem" in the pagan wilderness of Peru. Doña María Pizarro claimed to have had sexual relations with the Jesuit Luís López, and she declared years later that the first time they slept together was "the night of the feast of the eleven thousand virgins."

This twisted world came tumbling down in 1572. The Holy Inquisition, which for months had had the group under surveillance, imprisoned Fray Alonso Gasco on May 8. On July 5, Fray Pedro de Toro was brought to the dungeons of the Inquisition, followed shortly by the madman Fray Francisco de la Cruz, his lover Doña Leonor de Valenzuela, Doña Beatriz de Avalos, the Jesuit Luís López, and Doña María Pizarro herself. The sordid story of revelations, exorcisms, spiritual compacts, and erotic mysticism was revealed under the refined tortures of the Inquisition. Some of the priests were suspended from the ministry and exiled from Peru. Fray Francisco de la Cruz, convinced to the last that he was the father of a new Peruvian savior sent by God, was burned at the stake. The Jesuit Luís López was sent to prison in Spain. Doña María Pizarro, weakened by months of harsh treatment in the inquisitorial jails, died in prison on December 11, 1573, before the inquisitors had reached a verdict on her case. Her properties were confiscated by the Holy Tribunal, and her body was buried in an unmarked grave in a chapel within the cloister of the Mercedarian convent.[7]

Angela de Carranza, who called herself Angela de Dios, was born in Córdoba of Tucumán in 1641 and arrived in Lima around 1665, already with the reputation of a powerful beata. Clad in the robes of an Augustinian friar, Angela Carranza dominated for twenty years the imagination of the viceroyalty with her alleged visions, raptures, prophecies, and miracles. She was known in Mexico, Panamá, Madrid, and Rome, and letters arrived in Lima from those places requesting the prayers and the relics of "the saint." She was an avid reader of all kinds of theological works and wrote more than seven thousand pages of her own theological interpretations. In a period dominated by theological disputes about the Immaculate Conception of Mary, Angela Carranza believed that she had been chosen by God as *doctora de la Inmaculada Concepción*. The simple people, in awe of the holiness of the young woman, called her "the saint of the century," "the marvel of the planet," and "the doctor of mystical theology." Angela used this reputation to develop one of the most prosperous businesses of religious articles known in colonial Peru. From 1665 to 1668, she sold thousands of rosaries, religious statues, medals, relics, and holy candles, supposedly imbued with her supernatural power. Her output of religious articles was unmatched even by large religious communities, and the income derived from her business kept Angela in a comfortable economic position for twenty years.

The Holy Inquisition put an end to the economic and spiritual prosperity of Angela Carranza. Some of her writings, copied perhaps by devout followers, came to the attention of the inquisitors, who found them full of theological errors and immoral doctrines. In 1688, Angela de Dios was locked in jail while the judges examined her writings and took the deposition of witnesses. The process lasted six years, until finally the Inquisition declared Angela Carranza an impostor and a false beata and gave orders to collect all the religious articles she had sold during two decades. Loads of rosaries, medals, candles, and relics were brought to the Holy Tribunal, which burned all of them, together with Angela's writings. On December 20, 1694, Angela Carranza was brought from the jails of the Inquisition to the Dominican church to hear her sentence. She was forbidden to write or teach, to sell religious articles and to wear monastic robes, and was condemned to five more years in prison.[8]

The Tapadas

If the beata was a woman shaped by the pervasive currents of marianism, the *tapada* was the symbol of Don Juanism. As a wife or a daughter, she had to conform to the tenets of her society and to lead a life subservient to the males of the family. Covered and hidden by her shawl, the *tapada* could do as she pleased, go where she wanted, and break social conventions without fear of family retribution. In the eyes of the civil and ecclesiastical authorities, the *tapada* was a menace to society not simply because she often used the shawl to hide occasional sexual escapades, but also because the shawl had become a tool and symbol of a powerful social, religious, and political protest. The *tapada* may not have been fully aware of it, but with her shawl she was making a loud and public statement against the established and widely accepted code of female behavior.

Dress codes are a social language that reveal values, status, roles, and the relationships between individuals and certain times and places. One who breaks the dress code is either an eccentric or a rebel, and sooner or later will be attacked by the social majority. He or she may be expelled from a school or a club, denied access to a restaurant or a social gathering, or even be excommunicated from the church or ostracized by civil authorities from normal civic and political activities. The famous "mutiny of the capes and the hats" is a good example of the political and social language potentially contained in the way people dress. In 1767, the people of Madrid revolted against the crown by wearing the hats and capes that had been forbidden by the king. The mutiny rocked the capital of the Spanish empire, briefly halted the reforms of Charles III, brought about the fall of a powerful minister, and was indirectly linked with the expulsion of the Jesuit order from the Spanish dominions.

The Peruvian *tapada* was not merely a mischievous and flirtatious woman. Her shawl was not a fad, but a flag of her revolt against the stereotyped image of women as religious madonnas. She resisted for three centuries, with the selfish independence of a true Don Juan, the constant pressures of husbands, priests, bishops, and viceroys to abandon the shawl and to dress with modesty and simplicity. That impudence and independence of spirit, more than the sensuous contours of her body enhanced by the shawl, captured the heart and imagination of many and made the *tapada* a folk heroine of colonial Peru.

In his book *Velos Antiguos y Modernos en los Rostros de las Mujeres: Sus Conveniencias y Daños,* published in Madrid with royal approval in 1641, Don Antonio de León Pinelo explains the historical origin of the Iberian and Peruvian *tapadas* and why they became such an obsession to the civil and ecclesiastical authorities. After the fall of the Moslem kingdom of Granada in 1492, the Spanish crown forbade the Arab women of Andalusia to wear the Islamic veils, which covered their faces and hid their identities. It was not easy to uproot such an ancestral and secular custom, and the prohibition was repeated by Emperor Charles and his son King Philip II. When finally the moriscas were forced to abandon their veils and to adopt the Castilian shawl, they began using the new garment to cover their faces, leaving only one eye uncovered. This new fashion in the use of the traditional shawl, León Pinelo assures us, was exceedingly graceful, sensuous and appealing because of the exotic beauty of the eyes of the moriscas.

Christian women of Granada, Córdoba, and Seville were soon imitating the new fashion of wearing the shawl, and the Iberian *tapada* was born. From Seville the fashion went to the overseas colonies, and became especially entrenched in Peru. León Pinelo explains that the fashion of the *tapada* had become so popular and widespread that "great offenses against God and a notable damage to the republic have resulted from such a fashion. . . ." The Council of the Indies and the Spanish cortes saw three causes for this notable damage to the commonweal of the empire: the *tapadas,* cannot be recognized by anybody and therefore "they have the freedom, the opportunity, and the places to act as they please"; men take indecent liberties with the *tapadas* that they would not take with recognized, respectable ladies; and finally, men are adopting the female dress of the *tapada* to commit "great sins and sacrileges" because they cannot be recognized as males.[9]

The Peruvian *tapada* had been under pressure to uncover her face since the rule of the stern viceroy Don Francisco de Toledo in the 1570s. Toledo issued several ordinances to regulate the behavior of women and to curtail what he thought were excessive and dangerous fashions. Don Francisco de Toledo, committed to a life of celibacy as a Knight of Alcántara, was a bit of a misogynist and had an exceedingly narrow view of the proper role in society of respectable Christian women. Toledo's efforts to persuade women to dress modestly were taken up by his successors and by the preachers and bishops of the viceroyalty. The continuous and escalating warnings against immodest fashions, which emanated almost yearly from the city councils, the audiencia, the palace of the viceroy, and the pulpits of the viceroyalty, indicate that women were paying little attention, and went on dressing as they pleased and using the shawl in the fashion of the *tapada*.

In 1583, when all the bishops of Peru gathered in Lima for the opening of the Third Council of the Peruvian church, the assembled fathers had to admit that the immodesty of the female fashions was even worse than in the times of Viceroy Toledo. The bishops were shocked at the liberties taken by the Peruvian *tapadas* and issued a stern order against them, which found its way into the official decrees of the Third Council of Lima. The words of the council fathers are clear: ". . . No women should walk the street or be seen at their windows with their faces covered. This decree should be kept and observed by all women in such a way that their frivolity will not distract the people from the cult of God. Women should rather show their inner faith and piety with modest countenance and religious dress."[10] In their private directives to preachers and confessors, the bishops insisted that women be urged to conform to the ideals of Christian womanhood, meaning, of course, the ideals of marianism. They were distressed at seeing that many women of Peru, regardless of their acceptance of the marian virtues, had rejected them in their daily lives and were living "as they pleased."

The decree of the council and the directives of the bishops had the same effect as the efforts of Toledo a few years earlier. Most women paid very little attention to them, and the number of *tapadas* in Lima and other cities of the viceroyalty had increased by the opening years of the seventeenth century. In 1609, a group of royal officials, among them the *licenciado* Blas de Torres Altamirano, urged the new viceroy, the marquis of Montesclaros, to put an end to the abuses of the *tapadas* which, they thought, "were causing great sins . . . , scandals, and damage to the republic." The marquis, a wise man who was convinced that values and customs could not be changed just by legislating against them, hesitated to commit his prestige and authority to a losing battle against the *tapadas*. He agreed to consult the Council of the Indies and the king, but refused in the meantime to issue a new order against the *tapadas*.

The viceroy understood that the *tapada* did not conform to the expectations of a culture permeated by marianism, and that, in a sense, she was a rebel against the cultural status quo. Yet, he felt that to curtail the liberties taken by the *tapadas* was a task better left to fathers, husbands, confessors, and preachers. This cavalier attitude did not please the conservative faction of Blas de Torres Altamirano, who wrote to the king on May 15, 1613, accusing Montesclaros of neglecting his duty in this important issue. Altamirano informed His Majesty of the growing boldness of the *tapadas,* whom he accused of liberties and dishonesties taken not only in the streets and plazas, but even in the temples. The preachers have lost their voices, wrote Altamirano, shouting from the pulpits against the *tapadas,* but to no avail. The Lima gentleman pleaded with the king to force the Peruvian viceroy to use the power of the government to exile from Peru the pernicious customs of the *tapadas.*

The marquis of Montesclaros tried to defend himself and justify his course of action on the issue of women's fashions. In one of the last documents he wrote in Lima shortly before leaving office, he explained that all the efforts of his predecessors in office had failed in abolishing the shawl of the *tapadas,* and that there was no reason to expect that he would succeed. In the face of the impossible, inaction was obviously better than to expose royal authority to the ridicule and scorn of the women of the viceroyalty. He added a wise and amusing comment: ". . . since I have seen that each husband cannot control his own wife, I have no confidence whatsoever that I will be able to control all of them together."[11]

The watchdogs of morality, who wanted to keep women "in their place," had to wait for another decade to see any serious official action taken against the *tapadas* of Peru. On July 25, 1622, a new viceroy, Don Diego Fernández de Córdoba, marquis of Guadalcazar, arrived in Lima. Many pressing issues of royal finances, administration, and trade occupied his early years in Peru, but eventually he turned his attention to what many thought was a serious social problem of Peru—the *tapadas.* The marquis of Guadalcazar understood that the unique fashion of the *tapada* was much more than a problem of individual morality or a convenience to indulge in dangerous, sexual flirtations. He saw the *tapada* as the Spanish cortes had seen her in 1586, a person who was inflicting "a notable damage to the republic" by taking liberties that destroyed the traditional position of women in society. A problem of individual morality could be left to preachers and confessors. An issue that threatened the established social order had to be met by the viceroy himself. With this conviction, the marquis of Guadalcazar prepared a lengthy royal ordinance against the *tapadas,* which was signed on December 4, 1624, and consequently proclaimed by towncriers "in all the cities, towns, and villages of this kingdom [of Peru]."

The royal pragmatica of 1624 began with a brief history of the problem: there were many orders of the king and of the Spanish cortes forbidding women to cover their faces to hide their identities. In Peru, almost all the viceroys had issued similar orders, which unfortunately "had either been forgotten little by little or scorned" by the women of the viceroyalty. The problems had not yet been solved, and, in fact, the "excesses" of the *tapadas* had increased in the last few years. After this brief introduction, the marquis of Guadalcazar explained that many private citizens, preachers, confessors, the members of the city council, and the canons of the ecclesiastical council had repeatedly approached him to put an end to the "liberties of the *tapadas*." Finally, with the advice and consent of the judges of the royal audiencia, the viceroy issued his orders in the name of His Majesty the King: Within the term of five days, namely beginning on December 10, 1624, no woman of the viceroyalty, regardless of social class, should be seen wearing the shawl in the fashion of the *tapadas*. This order should be obeyed by all women in the streets, in the parks, in the churches, in the outskirts of the city, and even when they are riding in a carriage or standing on the balconies or in the windows of their own houses. In all those places, "their faces must be uncovered so that they may be seen and recognized at all times."

The marquis of Guadalcazar knew that the prohibition would have no effect by itself, and he added to the royal ordinance the most severe penalties yet decreed against the *tapadas* in the viceroyalty of Peru. Law enforcement officers were ordered to detain immediately any woman, regardless of social class, whom they saw wearing the shawl in the forbidden way. The shawl should be confiscated, and the woman sentenced to ten days in prison and fined sixty pesos. If the *tapada* was riding in a carriage, the carriage and the horses would also be confiscated. If the woman in question was a mestiza or a mulatta, the fine was the same, but she would serve thirty days in prison. In cases of ladies of "good families," the judges were given the authority to allow them to serve their sentences in private homes approved by the judges themselves. If a woman were caught for a second time, she would automatically be exiled from her city or town for a whole year.[12]

It is obvious by the severity of these penalties that the viceroy was convinced that the *tapadas* were a true menace to traditional society, and that he was committed to eradicate their abuses from the viceroyalty. Yet, the zeal of the marquis of Guadalcazar could have been tempered by the wisdom of the marquis of Montesclaros. The royal ordinance of 1624 did not scare the women of Peru into adopting a more modest fashion of dress. As explained, any woman could transform herself into a *tapada* in a matter of seconds as she went around a street corner or crossed the threshold of a house. Likewise, any *tapada* could become in an instant a "normal" woman by letting her shawl hang loose and thus uncovering her face. As the marquis of Montesclaros had foreseen, there was no way in such a situation that a handful of law enforcement officers could possibly control all the *tapadas* of any given city. After the ordinance of 1624, the *tapadas* exercised perhaps a bit more caution; a few of them may have been fined and sentenced to prison, but the majority of them were still very much in evidence in the streets and plazas in the 1650s and in the opening decades of the next century. Juan del Valle y Caviedes, the great satirical Peruvian poet, described them in the 1680s:

> *While walking you must see*
> *flirtatious steps and suggestive moves*
> *since it is a skill of self-respecting ladies*
> *to imitate the positions of the fencing arts.*[13]

Amadée François Frézier, the French naval engineer mentioned in a previous chapter, saw the *tapadas* of Lima on his visit to Peru in 1712 and described *"le visage voilé de maniere qu'on ne leur voit le plus souvent qu'un oeil"* (the face covered in such a way that you can only see one eye). Although he was a sophisticated man of the world and was very familiar with the social life of the French women, Frézier was amazed and even a bit shocked when observing the freedom of the Peruvian *tapadas*. He saw them going out in the late evening and walking the streets of the city unchaperoned. They moved around the city, he thought, with the same unrestrained freedom that men have in France. He was amazed at the luxury in dress and adornments exhibited in the streets by the worldly Peruvian women.

They were clad in the most expensive, imported materials from the Far East and from Europe, and their dresses and gowns were fashioned not to hide but to reveal their physical attributes. Bare arms, bare shoulders, and plunging necklines to expose the breasts were common. The shawl covered those parts of the body most of the time, but Frézier observed that the *tapadas* were quite generous in lifting their shawls to reveal their physical charms. He felt that this flirtatious behavior would be considered in France not freedom and independence but licentiousness. These worldly women led a social life as free and independent as one could see in the cities of France. They entertained male and female friends in their houses with music and dances, which Frézier found exceedingly sensuous. They went freely, and at times unchaperoned, to plays, bullfights, and popular fiestas. They could be seen almost every day, between five and seven in the evening, in the Alameda Park of Lima for the traditional evening promenade. There, among the orange trees, flowers, and fountains of the Alameda, the *tapadas* were queens of the promenade. Frézier was again amazed at the free interaction between the sexes, the flirtatious games, and the risqué conversations. Many *tapadas* accepted with gaiety and laughter propositions, "which no lover would dare to make in France without meriting the indignation of honest women."[14]

The testimony of Frézier, confirmed by the observations of other eighteenth-century travelers, seems to indicate that all the efforts of the viceroys and bishops to force women to live by the tenets of marianism had utterly failed. Like the sharp and sporadic jolts of an Andean earthquake, the *tapadas* had shaken the rigid structures of Peruvian society and had opened the way for a secular and worldly woman, who was no longer a creature of the church and a male-dominated society. The Peruvian *tapada* flaunting her shawl in Alameda Park and the modern, radical feminist burning her bra in New York's Central Park have a few things in common. They were both jolting society out of its complacency with a high degree of drama. They were both shouting their protest symbolically against the constraining and stereotyped positions of women in society. And they were both opening the way for their less daring and radical sisters to enter into positions and to play roles that would have been unthinkable a few years before. The *tapada* and the modern radical feminist may be seen by many as aberrant cases of extreme social behavior, but without them most women would have continued to be prisoners of images and symbols, which distorted the full potential of their human femininity. Once the old images and symbols were shattered, it became possible for women to start the search for new and more fulfilling images of themselves.

In the eighteenth century, a new type of more secular and more liberated woman appeared in Peruvian society. There were clusters of women in Lima, Cuzco, and other large cities of the viceroyalty who pursued with enthusiasm all kinds of secular knowledge, presided over some of the best literary and artistic salons of Peru, and wrote letters and essays in the early periodicals of the viceroyalty, voicing their views on the social and cultural issues of the day. Doña Manuela de Orrantia was fluent in French and Italian, read with avidity French and Italian authors, and attracted to her literary salon some of the most progressive men and women of Lima. Doña Juana, marchioness of Casa-Calderón, was an outstanding intellectual by the standards of any period. Besides French and Italian, she had command of Greek and Latin and produced a remarkable translation in Castilian verse of the *Song of Songs,* an Old Testament book which the church had always considered unsuitable reading for lay persons. The marchioness, who also presided over her own literary salon, could stand her ground in any discussion with clerics, university professors, and other educated men. Her fields of expertise included philosophy, mathematics, and ancient history. Doña Rita Unamunsaga and Doña Isabel de Orbea were friends and collaborators of the founders of the prestigious *Mercurio Peruano,* the best Peruvian periodical of the eighteenth century. Doña Isabel was known in the literary circles of Peru as one of the most avid readers of the French encyclopedists, authors considered dangerous by ecclesiastical authorities. Doña Josefa Cruzat y Munive had the reputation of being an accomplished humanist with an unsurpassed knowledge of the Greek and Roman classics. Doña Josefa de Silva, wife of a rector of the University of San Marcos, and Doña Mariana de Querejazu were also active members of the intellectual elite of Peru during the *siglo de las luces,* the century of enlightenment. None of these women obtained official degrees, but they learned disciplines and read authors not yet taught in the colonial universities. They did not enter the professions, but through their literary salons, they exercised a new kind of intellectual leadership in the late years of the empire.[15]

The founders of the *Mercurio Peruano* were fully aware of the

many educated women among the readers of the periodical, and
in one of the early issues invited "the many enlightened female
philosophers so abundant in this city" to submit letters and essays
to the editors defending the female point of view on the social
and cultural problems of the day. That invitation was answered
with eagerness by women from Lima and Cuzco. Doña Lucinda
del Cuzco wrote a lucid essay—a model of logic and literary skill—
defending the right of every woman to be called señora and be
treated as one. One did not need to be a member of the nobility
or the wife or daughter of a royal official to be called a señora
nor to be treated with the dignity and respect due a lady. Doña
Lucinda reveals in her essay not only literary and polemic skills,
but a good knowledge of theology, history, literature, and a fa-
miliarity with modern French ideas.

This essay defending the dignity of every woman raised a storm
of discussions in the literary salons of Lima and Cuzco. In the old
imperial city of the Incas, more conservative and more backward
than Lima, the discussions became verbal clashes, and women
rallied to support Doña Lucinda's views. The reaction of a young
wife of Cuzco, moved by the ideas of Doña Lucinda, is a good
example of the mentality. Presented by her attorney with a document which began "Doña ——, legitimate wife of Don ——," the
young lady refused to sign the document, tore it to pieces, and
demanded that it be rewritten. She instructed her attorney to
begin the document with the following words: "Doña ——, lawful
lady and conjoint person with Don ——." When the story was
reported in the *Mercurio Peruano,* the young wife of Cuzco became
the heroine of all the women who wanted freedom and equality,
while most males were shocked by her "incredible" behavior.[16]

Another essay published in the *Semanario Crítico* attacked the
blatant double standard prevalent in traditional Peruvian society.
The anonymous author claimed that it was unjust and illogical to
condemn women for one single marital infidelity, while husbands
could break their marriage vows publicly and habitually as a normal and accepted social custom. The essay demanded equality for
both sexes and asked for a marriage partnership in which, to use
the words of the young wife from Cuzco, both partners were equal
and conjoint persons. Quite a few other women took advantage
of the pages of the *Semanario* to air their views and to exercise
their freedom of expression. Perhaps the most outstanding con-

tribution by a female on the subject of women's rights appeared
in the *Mercurio.* An anonymous wife of Lima published a lengthy
and passionate letter, which attacked the crippling chauvinism of
many husbands for whom wives were nothing but charming toys.
The letter is filled with rage against husbands and against the
editors of the *Mercurio* for allowing publication of articles injurious
to the reputation and dignity of women. A brief quotation from
that letter should be sufficient to show that a new climate of wom-
en's freedom and equality had begun to spread throughout the
length of the viceroyalty:

> *I warn you [the editors] not to manhandle the ladies in your articles.*
> *I will avenge any insults against women with my tongue, if I am not*
> *allowed to do so with my pen. In any case, you better follow a different*
> *policy and let us, women, live our lives in peace.*[17]

By the end of the Spanish empire in the early nineteenth century, the women of Peru had not yet won a full social and legal
equality with men. But the beata filled with the ideals of marianism
had practically disappeared from the cities and towns of the viceroyalty, and the *tapada* had succeeded in shattering the traditional
beliefs about what a woman could do. In addition to the two
equestrian statues to honor the memory of two liberators, Bolivar
and San Martín, in Lima, the city needs to erect a new statue to
the Peruvian *tapada.* She should be shown as she walked the streets
of the city in real life, her face covered and her true identity
hidden from all viewers. With one eye uncovered, the statue of
the *tapada* would thus honor the colonial women who refused to
submit to standards of behavior that curtailed their freedom. Bolivar and San Martín gave Peru political freedom. The *tapada*
fought for an inner and deeper freedom of the mind and of the
spirit, without which political freedom is ultimately meaningless.

II

❦

Conclusion

WALTER PRESCOTT WEBB, IN HIS BOOK *The Great Frontier,* developed a theory to explain modern history and the expansion of Europe which has challenged historians since its publication in 1952. Webb's "boom hypothesis of modern history" implies that the unexpected windfall of land and wealth discovered by the Europeans in the great frontier changed dramatically the course of human history. The New World, the "great frontier" in Webb's theory, nurtured a new way of life unknown in Europe before the journeys of Columbus. Many ancestral customs and institutions of Europe, Webb contends, were challenged and, at times, discarded in the new environment of the Americas, where a freer and more prosperous society was born. The great frontier of the new world gave rise to new ideas, values, and institutions which could never have flourished in the close and rigidly institutionalized societies of Europe. Modern capitalism, social equality, and economic and political democracy are, in Webb's views, the ideological and institutional offspring of the great frontier.

Webb's theory can hardly be applied without qualifications to the total, historical experience of colonial Peru. It does not sufficiently account for the strong Iberian continuity in the new Spanish viceroyalty, although it provides an excellent working hypothesis to explain some of the profound changes that took place in Spanish Peru. If we reflect on the historical data contained in this book, we would need to accept both continuity and change in the lives of Peruvian women. As we reassert Iberian continuity in women's lives, we need to account also for the changes that made the daughters of the conquistadores so different from their Castilian sisters. Perhaps the nature of a boom society may help us to understand better the changes experienced by women in the new environment of Peru.

The women of Spanish Peru lived in, and were shaped by, a society that was highly institutionalized and had a strong and predominantly urban character. Even at the earliest stages of the conquest of Peru, representatives of the royal bureaucracy and of the church were already present in the lands of the Incas. By the mid-sixteenth century, the Spanish church and the Spanish state had a strong hold on the new Peruvian society, and both institutions had a profound influence on women's lives. The church upheld traditional Iberian values related to the behavior of women, influenced deeply their education, and tried constantly to exercise its authority over the young maiden, the married woman, and the consecrated virgin. Throughout the colonial period, the state issued hundreds of guidelines and regulations to define and to uphold the traditional status and role of women within the newly founded Spanish cities of Peru.

The daughers of conquistadores lived, for the most part, in urban centers. Santa Fé de Bogotá, Quito, Piura, Trujillo, Lima, Santiago, Cuzco, La Paz, Asunción, Córdoba, and Buenos Aires held together the extended territories of the viceroyalty of Peru and provided an urban frame to the lives of countless women. The cityscape of those centers was dominated by the cathedral, the government palace, the city hall, the courthouse, and the numerous convents of the religious orders. These powerful institutions, Iberian in origin and character, gave men's and women's lives a distinctive Spanish profile. Many Iberian customs, legal practices, and religious beliefs took root in the new Spanish lands as firmly as olive trees, grapevines, and wheat.

Marianism was as paramount in Lima and Arequipa as it was in Madrid and Seville. Marian shrines dotted the landscape of Peru from New Granada (Colombia) to Chile, and from the Pacific coast to the cities of Paraguay and Argentina. For three hundred years, Mary was proclaimed by preachers, confessors, and even some royal officials as the ideal of womanhood. Nevertheless, romantic love repeatedly shattered the rigid, ethical standards of

Catholic morality to produce the concubine, the mistress, and the woman of love in numbers unknown in the more austere cities of Castile. The proud and arrogant personality of Don Juan was shared by the encomendera, the *tapada,* and the campfollower, as well as by the nuns of the *conventos grandes.*

Although essentially Iberian, the daughters of the conquistadores were by no means exactly like their Spanish sisters across the ocean. An emerging Peruvian and American character was already discernible among those women in the sixteenth century, and became more distinct in the seventeenth and eighteenth centuries. The tempo and drama of their lives, the sharpness of their personalities, and the independence and freedom of their behavior, shocking to many European visitors, could hardly be found among Spanish women in the Iberian peninsula. This book has attempted to illuminate the complex and, at times, contradictory nature of women's lives in colonial Peru. The schoolgirl and the child bride, the housewife and the encomendera, the concubine and the divorcee, the woman of love and the consecrated virgin, the beata and the *tapada,* all crowded in the cities of Peru, present a picture that appears much more American and Peruvian than Spanish. How does one begin to explain these contradictory female types and the unique, dynamic tension that held them together in the colonial cities? Why, in spite of their essential Iberian character, did royal officials, preachers, and traveling dignitaries find them so shockingly different from Spanish women living in Castile?

Perhaps there are as many answers to these questions as there are Latin American historians. If he could have dealt with the specifics of Peruvian history, Walter Prescott Webb would have undoubtedly advanced his boom theory of modern history as an explanation of the profound changes that took place among the women of Spanish Peru.

The wealth of Peru was well beyond anything the average Spaniard had known before the 1530s. The mines of Potosí and Huancavelica; the booming trade on new kinds of goods and commodities; the fortunes paid in labor, goods, and monies by the Indians of the encomienda; the availability of land and the creation of the haciendas; and the biological explosion that revolutionized the sheep and cattle industries created in Peru a climate of luxury and prosperity that deeply changed the life-style of the Peruvian woman.

She flaunted a luxury and freedom in her dress and behavior that shocked not only pious monks, but even worldly males newly arrived from Europe. The wealth of her apparel, we are told by almost every visitor to Peru, could not be matched by anything seen in Seville, Madrid, Paris, or Rome. That wealth, and the presence in Peru of a large population of poor Indian, black, and mixed-blood women, gave the daughters of the conquistadores an aristocratic mentality that they would have not developed in Castile. They appropriated to themselves the titles of Doña and Señora, which would not have been theirs in the less prosperous and rigidly structured society of Spain. Even wives of Spanish craftsmen and clerks were served in Peru by Indian maids and black slaves. Thus the average Spanish woman of Peru behaved in public and within the house in a way possible in Castile only to a handful of noble, wealthy ladies.

The economic boom of Peru did not destroy, but changed deeply, the traditional, Iberian institutions of female monasticism and marriage. The colonial nunneries, cities of women within the secular cities of men, could not have existed without the wealth of Peru. The great numbers of women with wealthy dowries who took refuge in the colonial nunneries were a constant worry to the administrators of the viceroyalty. Too much wealth was concentrated in the hands of the Peruvian nuns, and that wealth gave the consecrated virgins an independence and power hardly compatible with traditional Iberian monasticism. The luxury of their cells, the hundreds of servants and slaves, the ample gardens and orchards, the richness of cloisters and chapels revealed an affluence hardly to be found in the convents of Castile. That affluence made the Peruvian nun into a lady of independence and leisure, a world apart from the nuns described by Saint Theresa of Avila. Without their wealth, the Peruvian nuns could not have challenged with impunity the authority of bishops and viceroys.

The institution of marriage also was affected in Peru by the unique conditions of a boom society. A constant flow of males, royal officials, merchants, and fortune seekers arrived in Peru determined to marry colonial wealth. Their pure Spanish ancestry, regardless of their economic and social status in Spain, made them ideal husbands in the eyes of wealthy criollo families. Many parents perceived the newcomers as a source of social status and prestige for their daughters and for the entire family. Those criollos families were eager to commit parts of their fortunes to marriages of social convenience to avoid the progressive miscegenation of colonial Peru and to identify themselves more closely with the mother country. Many women became, therefore, pawns manipulated by parents and male relatives in the financial and social plays of Spanish Peru.

It is no wonder that many of those marriages of convenience lacked the traditional stability envisioned within an ideal Christian marriage. The thousands of annulments and separations granted by the church in Spanish Peru support the contention of colonial observers that many Spanish Peruvians divorced and separated almost as easily and frequently as they married.

Two other conditions, created in part by the Peruvian boom, further eroded the stability of marriages in the viceroyalty. The lure of prosperous mining towns, the imperatives of an expanding trade, and the need to supervise encomiendas, ranches, and haciendas tore many husbands away from the cities and from their families. This male mobility, unknown in the more static society of Castile, created thousands of abandoned wives and made marital infidelity more frequent, and eventually more acceptable, than in Spain.

This mobility, coupled with the large numbers of females of lower social class, created a fertile ground for the growth of a well-established concubinage. The mistress and the concubine appear so frequently in the colonial records that one cannot doubt that they presented a serious and widespread challenge to the lawful wife. Many of those concubines were not "loose women" that engaged lightly in extramarital affairs. Most of them were, for years and even for life, faithful to their lovers, and they raised their children as well as or better than the legitimate wives. Regardless of the condemnation of the church, the Peruvian concubine could be, and many times was, a respectable and respected woman.

The late Spanish scholar Salvador de Madariaga points out in his work *The Rise of the Spanish American Empire* that liberty and freedom, born of the wealth of the Indies, were the most dominant characteristics in the life-style of the Spanish colonies. Madariaga, obviously, is not talking of institutionalized political and religious freedoms as we understand them today. Echoing the testimony of countless colonial observers, Madariaga refers to a social and cultural liberty, which made the inhabitants of the Spanish vice-royalties abandon many Iberian traditions and values to flaunt a freedom of behavior shocking those newly arrived from Spain.

It would be hard to find any social group in which social freedom was as visible as it was among the Spanish women who lived in the colonial cities. The early campfollowers, the women politically active at the time of the Civil War, the female entrepreneurs, the encomenderas, the concubines, the divorcees, the nuns of the *conventos grandes,* and the *tapadas* seem to have enjoyed an inner freedom that flourished, in spite of the efforts of the church and state to control their lives. For more than two centuries, the *tapada* was a fighter for personal independence and freedom, and clergy and royal officials were impotent in subduing her. The colonial nun managed to institutionalize her freedom, whether she was aware of it or not, by creating the Peruvian *conventos grandes.* The women of Spanish Peru challenged the preconceived patterns of life of the traditional Iberian women, and when they succeeded, it was due in great part to their economic independence made possible by the wealth of Peru.

The women of Spanish Peru were undoubtedly rooted in the Iberian cultural tradition. They lived in a society that politically and religiously was highly institutionalized. Yet, the untold riches of Peru created a social climate of liberty and freedom that enabled many women to assert themselves with the courage and intensity unknown in Spain. Already by the opening decades of the seventeenth century, the women of Spanish Peru were more Peruvian and American than Spanish.

Notes

Abbreviations

AAL   Archivo Arzobispal de Lima
AGI   Archivo General de Indias, Sevilla
ANP   Archivo Nacional del Perú
BNP   Biblioteca Nacional del Perú
CV   Colección Vargas Ugarte

2
The First Spanish Women of Peru

1. Bartolomé de las Casas, *Historia de las Indias* (Madrid: Ediciones Atlas, 1957), 328. Francisco Morales Padrón, *Historia de America* (Madrid: Espasa Calpe, S.A., 1962), 5: 294–95.

2. Las Casas, *Historia de las Indias*, 120–22, 241, 354.

3. Gonzalo Fernández de Oviedo, *Historia General y Natural de las Indias* (Madrid: Ediciones Atlas, 1959), 88–89.

4. Carl Ortwin Sauer, *The Early Spanish Main* (Berkeley and Los Angeles: University of California Press, 1966), 199–200.

5. Quoted by Juan Friede, "The Catálogo de Pasajeros and the Spanish Emigration to America," *HAHR,* 31 (1955): 341.

6. For a summary of this chaotic period of Peruvian history, see Luís Martín, *The Kingdom of the Sun: A Brief History of Peru* (New York: Charles Scribner's Sons, 1974), 21–44.

7. Juan Bromley Seminano, *Virreyes, Cabildantes y Oidores* (Lima: P. Barrantes Castro, 1944), 44. James Lockhart, *Spanish Peru 1532–1560: A Colonial Society* (Madison: University of Wisconsin Press, 1968), 151.

8. Bernabé Cobo, *Historia del Nuevo Mundo* (Madrid: Ediciones Atlas, 1956), 1: 406–7.

9. Inca Garcilaso de la Vega, *Historia General del Perú* (Lima: Librería Internacional del Perú, S.A., 1959), 1: 115.

10. Ibid., 117.

11. Lockhart, *Spanish Peru*, 151–52. Nancy O'Sullivan-Beare, *Las Mujeres de los Conquistadores: La Mujer Española en los comienzos de la Colonización Americana* (Madrid: Compañia Bibliográfica, S.A., 1956), 139.

12. For a brief and clear definition of encomienda, see Lockhart, *Spanish Peru*, 11.

13. Raul Porras Barrenechea, *Cronistas del Perú* (Lima; Sanmartí y Cía., 1962), 91. O'Sullivan-Beare, *Las Mujeres de los Conquistadores*, 140.

14. Ibid., 141–42.

15. Garcilaso de la Vega, *Historia General*, 2: 595.

16. José Antonio de Lavalle y Arias de Saavedra, *Estudios Históricos* (Lima: Librería e Imprenta Gil, S.A., 1935), 43–52.

17. Garcilaso de la Vega, *Historia General*, 1: 448–49. O'Sullivan-Beare, *Las Mujeres de los Conquistadores*, 144–47.

18. C. R. Boxer, *Mary and Misogyny: Women in Iberian Expansion Overseas, 1415–1815* (New York: Oxford University Press, 1975), 48–49.

19. Ibid., 51.

20. Diego Fernández, El Palentino, *Primera Parte de la Historia del Perú* (Madrid: Colección Hispano Americana, 1913), 2: 27, 40, 66–67.

21. Garcilaso de la Vega, *Historia General*, 2: 594.

22. O'Sullivan-Beare, *Las Mujeres de los Conquistadores*, 222–24, 226–27, 229–32.

23. Ibid., 233.

24. William Bollaert, *The Expedition of Pedro de Ursua and Lope de Aguirre in Search of El Dorado and Omagua in 1560–61* (London: Hakluyt Society, 1861). This is an excellent English edition of the work written by the colonial historian Fray Pedro Simón.

25. Walker Chapman, *The Golden Dream: Seekers of El Dorado* (Indianopolis, Kansas City, New York: Bobbs-Merrill Co., 1967), 207.

26. Bollaert, *The Expedition of Pedro de Ursua*, 12–13, 36.

27. Ibid., 87.

28. Quoted by O'Sullivan-Beare, *Las Mujeres de los Conquistadores*, 183.

29. Guillermo Furlong, S. J., *La Cultura Femenina en la Epoca Colonial* (Buenos Aires: Editorial Kapeluz, 1951), 95–96. The letter of Doña Isabel to Queen Juana has been published in the original Spanish in *Revista de*

la Real Academia Hispano Americana de Ciencias y Artes de Cadiz, 2 (1913–), 74–76.

30. Justo Zaragoza, *Historia del Descubrimiento de las Regiones Australes Hecho por el General Fernández de Quirós* (Madrid: Imprenta de Manuel Hernández, 1876–80) contains the contemporary and original account of the expedition, in which Doña Isabel de Barreto took part. For a modern biography of Doña Isabel, see M. Bosch Barret, *Doña Isabel de Barreto, Adelantada de las Islas Salomón* (Barcelona: Editorial Juventud, S.A., 1943).

31. Bosch Barret, 1–23. Zaragoza, *Historia del Descubrimiento,* 1: 1–22.

32. Zaragoza, 1: 23–51. Bosch Barret, *Doña Isabel,* 23–46.

33. Bosch Barret, 48–77. Zaragoza, *Historia del Descubrimiento,* 1: 53, 55–57, 82–83, 85–100, 108–14.

34. Bosch Barret, 100–114. Zaragoza, *Historia del Descubrimiento,* 2: 170–82.

3
Homemakers and Encomenderas

1. *Monografías Históricas sobre la Ciudad de Lima* (Lima: Librería e Imprenta Gil. S.A., 1935), 1: 408–9.

2. Lockhart, *Spanish Peru,* 164–70.

3. Ibid., 159–60.

4. Ibid., 160–61. ANP: Cabildo-Gremios, 1577–1704, Legajo L, Cuaderno 2.

5. *Harkness Collection in the Library of Congress. Documents from Early Peru: The Pizarros and the Almagros, 1531–1578* (Washington, D.C.: U.S. Government Printing Office, 1936), 171–77, 274. Manuel de Mendiburu, *Diccionario Histórico-Biográfico del Perú* (Lima: Imprenta Enrique Palacios, 1932), 3: 50–51.

6. Cobo, *Historia del Nuevo Mundo,* 1: 407.

7. Ibid., 1: 407–8.

8. O'Sullivan-Beare, *Las Mujeres de los Conquistadores,* 139. Garcilaso de la Vega, *Historia General del Perú,* 1: 115.

9. Cobo, *Historia del Nuevo Mundo,* 1: 309–95, 406–7.

10. Ibid., 1: 386–87; 2: 431. Fernando Silva Santisteban, *Los Obrajes en el Virreinato del Perú* (Lima: Museo Nacional de Historia, 1964), 14–23.

11. *Harkness Collection,* 170–76, 233.

12. Ibid., 162–68, 233–34.

13. Lockhart, *Spanish Peru,* 18.

14. Roberto Levillier, *Gobernantes del Perú: Cartas y Papeles* (Madrid: Sucesores de Ribadeneyra, S.A., 1921–26), 1: 515.

15. Ibid., 1: 454–55.

16. Ibid., 5: 231–32.

17. Ibid., 9: 134–209.

18. Mendiburu, *Diccionario*, 7: 183–84.

19. Benjamín Vicuña McKenna, *Los Lisperguer y La Quintrala (Doña Catalina de los Ríos)* (Santiago de Chile: Empresa Editora Zig-Zag, 1950), 254–58.

20. AGI: Audiencia de Lima, Legajo 1626. Mendiburu, *Diccionario*, 1: 197.

21. Vicuña McKenna, *Los Lisperguer*, 75–78.

22. Ibid., 67–72.

23. Ibid., 306–9.

24. Ibid., 96–100, 116–17.

25. Ibid., 271–78.

4
Women's Education

1. *Constituciones Synodales del Obispado de Arequipa* (Lima: Joseph de Contreras, 1688), folio 7, numero 30.

2. Luís Martín and Joann G. Pettus, *Scholars and Schools in Colonial Peru* (Dallas: Southern Methodist University School of Continuing Education, 1973), 118.

3. Cobo, *Historia del Nuevo Mundo*, 2: 302, 428, 434.

4. Rubén Vargas Ugarte, S. J., *Concilios Limenses* (Lima: Talleres Gráficos de la Tipografía Peruana, 1952), 2: 106–7. AAL: Monasterio de La Encarnación, Expedientes 1630–32, Legajo 3.

5. AAL: Monasterio de La Encarnación, Expedientes 1630–32, Legajo 3.

6. Ibid.

7. Ibid.; AAL: Monasterio de La Concepción, Expedientes 1628–30, Legajo 4.

8. Ibid.; Vargas Ugarte, S. J., *El Monasterio de La Concepción de la Ciudad de Los Reyes* (Lima: Editorial Lumen, 1942), 16–17.

9. ANP: Joseph del Corro (1649), folio 344. Furlong, *La Educación Femenina*, passim.

10. AAL: Monasterio de La Concepción, Expedientes 1603–14, Legajo 1; Expedientes 1683–84, Legajo 23.

11. AAL: Monasterio de La Trinidad, Expedientes 1662–74, Legajo 6.

12. AAL: Monasterio de La Concepción, Expedientes 1683–84, Legajo 23.

13. AAL: Monasterio de La Trinidad, Expedientes 1662–74, Legajo 6.

14. AAL: Papeles Importantes 1630–39, Legajo 7.

15. AAL: Papeles Importantes 1660–90, Legajo 8.

16. CV: Papeles Varios MS 36, Documento 1. Cobo, *Historia del Nuevo Mundo,* 2: 406–8.

17. Ibid., 447–50. *Mercurio Peruano* (Lima: Biblioteca Nacional del Peru, 1964), 1: 11–12, 97–98.

18. Cobo, *Historia del Nuevo Mundo,* 2: 434–36.

19. Furlong, *La Educación Femenina,* 104–8.

20. Ibid., 124–25.

21. Cobo, *Historia del Nuevo Mundo,* 2: 452–53.

22. *Mercurio Peruano,* 1: 169–73.

23. *Constituciones del Colegio de Santa Cruz* (Lima: Imprenta de la Plazuela de San Christoval, 1756).

24. ANP: Tribunal de la Inquisición. Fundaciones: Colegio de Santa Cruz, 1667–1745, Legajo 1.

25. *Constituciones de Colegio de Santa Cruz,* Artículo 26.

27. ANP: Tribunal de la Inquisición. Fundaciones: Colegio de Santa Cruz, 1667–1745, Legajo 1 and 1746–87, Legajo 2.

5
Marriages, Dowries, and Annulments

1. *Sacrosanti et Oecumenici Concilii Tridentini . . . Canones et Decreta* (Antverpiae: Apud Hieronymum Verdussen, 1677), 195–205. Vargas Ugarte, *Concilios Limenses,* 1: 108–12.

2. Ibid.; Jean Descola, *Daily Life in Colonial Peru, 1710–1820* (New York: Macmillan Company, 1968), 113–14.

3. Vargas Ugarte, *Concilios Limenses,* 2: 75, 109, 111–12.

4. Josephe de Mugaburu and Francisco de Mugaburu, *Diario de Lima, 1640–1694* (Lima: Imprenta C. Vásquez L., 1935), 2: 63, 75, 133, 255. Vargas Ugarte, *Concilios Limenses,* 1: 278–79.

5. Diego de Avendaño, *Thesaurus Indicus* (Antverpiae: Apud Jacobum Meursium, 1668–78, and apud Hieronymum Berdussen, 1686), 1: 142–43.

6. Mugaburu, *Diario de Lima,* 2: 113.

7. AAL: Papeles Importantes 1590–1662, Legajo 10.

8. AAL: Nulidad de Matrimonios, Expedientes 1600–1604, Legajo 1.

9. Descola, *Daily Life,* 117–18.

10. Ibid., 116–18. José Antonio de Lavalle y Arias de Saavedra, *Estudios Históricos* (Lima: Librería e Imprenta Gil, S.A., 1935), 315–29.

11. *Recopilación de las leyes destos reynos hecha por mandato de la magestad Catholica de Rey Don Philipe Segundo* . . . (Alcalá de Henares: Andrés de Angulo, 1569). *Las Partidas*, Partida IV, Titulo XI. *Leyes de Toro*, Nos. 29, 53, 82.

12. Avendaño, *Thesaurus Indicus*, 5: 318.

13. Vicuña McKenna, *Los Lisperguer y La Quintrala*, 309–10.

14. BNP: "Carta Dotal de Da. Lucía de Pastene, Los Reyes, Febrero 5, 1635," MS Z147.

15. Luís Martín, *The Intellectual Conquest of Peru: The Jesuit College of San Pablo, 1568–1767* (New York: Fordham University Press, 1968), 131–42.

16. ANP: Tribunal de La Inquisición. Fundaciones: Colegio de Santa Cruz, 1746–87, Legajo 2.

17. Mugaburu, *Diario de Lima*, 2: 3, 12, 104.

18. BNP: "Exclamación de mi Señora Da. Isabel de Menacho . . . ," MS Z149. AAL: Divorcios, Expedientes 1609–11, Legajo 4; Nulidad de Matrimonios, Expedientes 1631–33, Legajo 9.

19. Vargas Ugarte, *Concilios Limenses*, 2: 112.

20. Amadée François Frézier, *Rélation du Voyage de la mer du sud* . . . (Paris: Chez Jean-Geoffroy Nyon, 1716), 207.

21. AAL: Nulidad de Matrimonios, Expediente 1605, Legajo 2, and Expedientes 1606–1607, Legajo 3.

22. Avendaño, *Thesaurus Indicus*, 5: 311–13.

23. AAL: Nulidad de Matrimonios, Expedientes 1608, Legajo 4.

24. AAL: Nulidad de Matrimonios, Expedientes 1606–1607, Legajo 3, and Expedientes 1635–37, Legajo 12.

25. AAL: Nulidad de Matrimonios, Expedientes 1608, Legajo 4.

26. AAL: Nulidad de Matrimonios, Expedientes 1635–37, Legajo 12.

27. AAL: Nulidad de Matrimonios, Expedientes 1660–61, Legajo 21; Expedientes 1606–1607, Legajo 3; Expedientes 1631–33, Legajos 9 and 10.

6
Divorcees, Concubines, and Repentant Women

1. Furlong, *La Cultura Femenina*, 197–98. AAL: Nulidad de Matrimonios, Expedientes 1634, Legajo 11.

2. AAL: Nulidad de Matrimonios, Expedientes 1634, Legajo 11.

3. AAL: Causas de Divorcios, Expedientes 1612, Legajo 5.

4. AAL: Causas de Divorcios, Expedientes 1701–1702, Legajo 71.

5. AAL: Causas de Divorcios, Expedientes 1607–1608, Legajo 3; Expedientes 1609–11, Legajo 4; Expedientes 1650–52, Legajo 29.

6. AAL: Causas de Divorcios, Expedientes 1703–1707, Legajo 62.

7. Vargas Ugarte, *Concilios Limenses*, 2: 111–12.

8. *Memorias de los Virreyes que han governado el Perú durante el coloniaje español* (Lima: Librería Central de Felipe Bailly, 1859), 1: 36, 166, and passim.

9. Frézier, *Rélation du Voyage*, 230–31.

10. *Mercurio Peruano*, 1: 52–54. AGI: Audiencia de Cuzco, Legajo 17.

11. AAL: Causas de Divorcios, Expedientes 1703–1707, Legajo 62.

12. AAL: Causas de Divorcios, Expedientes 1612, Legajo 5; Expedientes 1635–37, Legajo 12; Expedientes 1703–1707, Legajo 62.

13. AAL: Causas Criminales Reservadas de Clérigos, Legajo Siglo XVIII. This material is not in the open section of the archives, but it is kept under key in the private office of the archivist.

14. Ibid.

15. Ibid.

16. Ibid.

17. *Colección de Memorias o Relaciones que escribieron los Virreyes del Perú . . .* (Madrid: Imprenta del Asilo de Huérfanos, 1921), 1: 173.

18. Mendiburu, *Diccionario Histórico*, 2: 97; 4: 92–93, 291. *Mercurio Peruano*, 4: 231–66.

19. AAL: Causas Criminales Reservadas de Clérigos, Legajo Siglo 17.

20. Carlos Alberto Romero, *Memoria del Virrey del Perú Marqués de Avilés* (Lima: Imprenta del Estado, 1901), 14–18.

21. AAL: Nulidad de Matrimonios, Expedientes 1634, Legajo 11.

7
Islands of Women

1. Cobo, *Historia del Nuevo Mundo*, 2: 302, 431–34. *Mercurio Peruano*, 1: 97–98; 4: 143. Manuel A. Fuentes, *Lima: Apuntes Históricos, Descriptivos, Estadísticos, de Costumbres* (Paris: Librería de F. Didot Hermanos, Hijos y Cía., 1867), 30–35.

2. AGI: Audiencia de Lima, Legajo 333.

3. Benjamín Vicuña McKenna, *Historia de la calle de las Monjitas* (Santiago de Chile: G. E. Miranda, 1904), 5–15. Darío Achury Valenzuela, *Obras Completas de la Madre Francisca Josefa de la Concepción de Castillo* (Bogotá: Talleres Gráficos del Banco de la República, 1968), xxxix–lx.

4. The description of the nunneries is drawn from hundreds of indirect references kept in AAL and in AGI. See as examples AGI: Audiencia de Lima, Legajo 2 and Legajo 554; AAL: Monasterio de La Concepción,

Expedientes 1628–30, Legajo 4; Expedientes 1700–1720, Legajos 20 and 21.

5. Rubén Vargas Ugarte, S. J., *El Monasterio de La Concepción de la Ciudad de los Reyes* (Lima: Editorial Lumen, 1942), 16–17.

6. AGI: Audiencia de Lima, Legajo 102.

7. *Mercurio Peruano,* 1: 97–98.

8. María Josefa de la Santísima Trinidad, *Historia de la Fundación del Monasterio de Trinitarias Descalzas de Lima* (Lima: Editorial San Antonio, 1957), 98. Vargas Ugarte, *El Monasterio de La Concepción,* 16–17. AAL: Monasterio de La Concepción, Expedientes 1615–22, Legajo 2.

9. BNP: *"Escritura de venta otorgada por la Abadesa y Monjas del Monasterio de la Santísima Trinidad . . . ," MS Z215.* AAL: *Monasterio de Santa Catalina, Expedientes 1624–31, Legajo 1; Monasterio de Las Nazarenas, Expedientes 1722–96, Legajo 1.*

10. AAL: *Monasterio de La Encarnación, Expedientes 1700–1709, Legajo 20.*

11. AAL: *Monasterio de La Concepción, Expedientes 1603–14, Legajo 1 for the case of Tomasa Polanco, and Monasterio de La Encarnación, Expedientes 1605–25, Legajo 1 for the case of the young mulatta.*

12. AAL: *Monasterio de La Trinidad, Expedientes 1622–74, Legajo 6.*

13. AAL: *Monasterio de La Encarnación, Expedientes 1642–45, Legajo 6.*

14. *Mercurio Peruano,* 1: 97–98.

15. AAL: Monasterio de La Concepción, Expedientes 1603–14, Legajo 1, and Expedientes 1628, Legajo 4; Monasterio de La Encarnación, Expedientes 1642–45, Legajo 6.

16. AAL: Monasterio de La Encarnación, Expedientes 1630–32, Legajo 3. The presence of Oriental slaves in Lima as early as 1630 should not surprise us. The Peruvian historian Emilio Harth-Terré has clearly shown that already in 1602 a gang of Oriental laborers worked in the construction of the "new" stone bridge over the River Rimac.

17. AAL: Monasterio de La Concepción, Expedientes 1615–22, Legajo 2; Monasterio de La Encarnación, Expedientes 1605–25, Legajo 1; Expedientes 1630–32, Legajo 3, and Expedientes 1700–1709, Legajo 20.

18. BNP: "Escritura de venta . . . ," MS Z215. AAL: Monasterio de La Encarnación, Expedientes 1605–25, Legajo 1. Furlong, *La Cultura Femenina,* 69.

19. BNP: "Testamento de Doña Isabel de Illescas. Los Reyes, 16 de diciembre, 1622," MS Z1119. AAL: Monasterio de La Encarnación, Expedientes 1630–32, Legajo 3.

20. AAL: Monasterio de La Encarnación, Expedientes 1638–41, Legajo 5; Monasterio de La Trinidad, Expedientes 1622–74, Legajo 6. Doña Ana's petition is obviously misfiled in this Legajo 6.

21. Vicuña McKenna, *Los Lisperguer y La Quintrala,* 216–17.

22. BNP: "Renuncia de Doña Petronila de la Fuente y Rojas. Los Reyes, 3 de febrero, 1712," MS Z1219.

23. BNP: "Renuncia de Doña Leonor de la Fuente y Rojas. Los Reyes, 4 de enero, 1715," MS Z1393.

24. AAL: Monasterio de La Encarnación, Expedientes 1605–25, Legajo 1.

25. AAL: Monasterio de La Encarnación, Expedientes 1630–32, Legajo 3; Monasterio de La Concepción, Expedientes 1638–84, Legajo 23.

8
Life in the Colonial Nunneries

1. Josefa de la Providencia, *Relación del Origen y Fundación del Monasterio . . . de las Religiosas Nazarenas . . .* (Lima: Imprenta Real de los Ninos Expósitos, 1793), 1–14.

2. Ibid., 116–71.

3. Ibid., 32–40, 58–65. Andrés Paredes Armendariz, *Constituciones de las Religiosas Nazarenas . . .* (Lima: Imprenta de la Calle de la Encarnación, 1765), 16–19, 20–26.

4. Her autobiography is reproduced by Achury Valenzuela in his *Obras Completas de la Madre Francisca,* 1: 3–214.

5. AAL: Monasterio de La Encarnación, Expedientes 1700–1709, Legajo 20.

6. AAL: Monasterio de La Encarnación, Expedientes 1605–25, Legajo 1, "Autos contra Doña Ana de Frías . . . ;" Expedientes 1642–45, Legajo 6, which contains also the accounts of the nunnery from 1639 to 1642.

7. AAL: Papeles Importantes, Expedientes 1600–1610, Legajo 4.

8. AAL: Ibid. The letter of Don Alvaro de Ybarra can be found in AGI: Audiencia de Lima, Legajo 103.

9. The confrontation between the archbishop Don Fernando Arias Ugarte and the nuns is well documented with the deposition of eyewitnesses in AAL: Monasterio de La Encarnación, Expedientes 1630–32, Legajo 3.

10. Vargas Ugarte, *Un Monasterio Limeño,* 68–70.

11. Ibid.

12. AAL: Papeles Importantes, Expedientes 1630–39, Legajo 7 contains the Latin apostolic brief granted to Doña Sebastiana de Paredes. The privilege obtained by Doña Petronila de Guzmán can be found in AAL: Monasterio de La Encarnación, Expedientes 1638–41, Legajo 5.

13. AAL: Papeles Importantes, Expedientes 1660–90, Legajo 8.

14. Ibid.

15. AAL: Causas Criminales Reservadas de Clérigos, Legajo Siglo 17.

16. Ibid.

17. Ibid.

18. AAL: Papeles Importantes, Expedientes 1660–90, Legajo 80; Visitas Monasterio, Legajo Unico.

19. AAL: Papeles Importantes, Expedientes 1600–1610, Legajo 4; Expedientes 1630–39, Legajo 7; Expedientes 1660–89, Legajo 8. Monasterio de La Concepción, Expedientes 1638–84, Legajo 23.

20. AAL: Monasterio de La Encarnación, Expedientes 1630–32, Legajo 3.

21. AAL: Visitas Monasterios, Legajo Unico; Monasterio de La Encarnación, Expedientes 1709–14, Legajo 21. CV: "Ordenes del Arzobispo Juan Dgo. de la Reguera . . . 1793," Papeles Varios MS 38 Iglesia, Documento 42.

22. CV: Papeles Varios MS 32, Documento 82, and MS 38, Documento 38.

23. CV: Papeles Varios MS 32, Documento 84 and Documento 85.

9
Monastic Riots . . .

1. Levillier, *Gobernantes del Perú*, 4: 412.

2. Vicuña McKenna, *Historia de la Calle*, 16–26.

3. AGI: Audiencia de Quito, Legajo 95.

4. Avendaño, *Thesaurus Indicus*, 5: 226–33.

5. AAL: Visitas a Monasterios, Legajo Unico.

6. AAL: Papeles Importantes, Expedientes 1630–39, Legajo 7.

7. AAL: Monasterio de La Encarnación, Expedientes 1700–1709, Legajo 20; Monasterio de La Concepción, Expedientes 1683–84, Legajo 24; Monasterio de La Trinidad, Expedientes 1662–74, Legajo 6.

8. AGI: Audiencia de Cuzco, Legajo 15. Levillier, *Gobernantes del Perú*, 4: 412–13, 421; 5: 455–56.

9. AGI: Audiencia de Lima, Legajo 102 and Legajo 333.

10. AGI: Audiencia de Cuzco, Legajo 15.

11. AAL: Monasterio de La Encarnación, Expedientes 1714–19, Legajo 22, and Expedientes 1642–45, Legajo 6; Monasterio de La Concepción, Expedientes 1628–30, Legajo 4.

12. AAL: Monasterio de La Encarnación, Expedientes 1700–1709, Legajo 20, and Expedientes 1709–14, Legajo 21. AGI: Audiencia de Lima, Legajo 555.

13. AGI: Audiencia de Lima, Legajo 555.

10
Beatas and Tapadas

1. AGI: Audiencia de Lima, Legajo 333.

2. These poems and all the information summarized above on the life of the beata Rosa are taken directly from "Proceso original de la vida, santidad, muerte y milagros de la Beata Sor Rosa de Santa María . . . ," an original document preserved in the Lilly Library of Indiana University, Bloomington, Indiana.

3. Ibid.

4. Ibid.; AGI: Audiencia de Lima, Legajo 333.

5. AGI: Audiencia de Cuzco, Legajo 64; AAL: Beaterio de Ntra. Sra. de Copacabana, 1692–1818.

6. Balthasar de Moncada, *Descripción de la casa fabricada en Lima . . . para que las Señoras Ilustres . . .* (Sevilla: Joseph de Padrino, 1757).

7. José Toribio Medina, *Historia del Tribunal de la Inquisición de Lima, 1569–1820* (Santiago de Chile: Fondo Histórico y Bibliográfico José T. Medina, 1956), 1: 63–114.

8. Mendiburu, *Diccionario Histórico*, 3: 417–18.

9. Antonio de León Pinelo, *Velos Antigüos y Modernos en los rostros de las mujeres: Sus consecuencias y daños* (Madrid: Por Juan Sánchez, 1641), 2: 245–46.

10. Vargas Ugarte, *Concilios Limenses*, 1: 274.

11. AGI: Audiencia de Lima, Legajo 35 and Legajo 143. *Colección de las Memorias o Relaciones que escribieron los Virreyes del Perú*, 1: 172–73.

12. The entire document is reproduced in Mendiburu, *Diccionario*, 3: 242–44.

13. For the poems of Caviedes, see Vargas Ugarte, *Obras de Don Juan del Valle y Caviedes . . .* (Lima: Tipografia Peruana, 1947).

14. Frézier, *Rélation du Voyage*, 187, 196, 231–37.

15. Furlong, *La Cultura femenina*, 72–75.

16. *Mercurio Peruano*, 2: 44–46; 4: 62–67, 267, 278–82.

17. Ibid., 1: 161–64. Semanario Crítico, 10: 94–96; 11: 101–4; 13: 115–17.

Bibliography

Selected Manuscript Sources

Archivo Arzobispal de Lima
    Autos contra Doña Ana de Frías. Monasterio de la Encarnación. Expedientes, 1605–25.
    Causas criminales reservadas de clérigos, Siglo 17.
    Causas de Divorcios. Expedientes. (Siglos 16 y 18).
    Cuentas Tomadas . . . a la M. Doña María de Santillán, Abadesa que fue de la Encarnación. 1645. Monasterio de la Encarnación. Expedientes, 1642–45. Legajo 6.
    Nulidad de Matrimonios. Expedientes. (Siglos 17 y 18).
    Papeles Importantes, 1630–39. Legajo 7.
    Razón de las Rentas que tiene el Monasterio de Ntra. Sra. de la Encarnación. Año 1715.
    Monasterio de la Encarnación. Expedientes, 1714–19. Legajo 22.
    Visitas Monasterios. Legajo Unico.
Archivo General de Indias
    Autos contra la Abadesa Doña María de las Nieves Fernández Maldonado. Audiencia de Lima. Legajo 555.
    Autos de las Monjas de Santa Catalina de Quito. Audiencia de Quito. Legajo 99.
    Informe de Virrey Marqués de Castel-Dos-Rius al Rey sobre Doña Josefa de Portocarrero. 1708. Audiencia de Lima. Legajo 554.
Archivo Nacional del Perú
    Registros Notariales de Joseph del Corro, 1649.

Tribunal de la Inquisición. Fundaciones: Colegio de Santa Cruz, 1667–1747. Legajo 1; 1746–87, Legajo 2.

Biblioteca Nacional del Perú

Carta Dotal de Da. Lucía de Pastene. Ms. Z 147.

Escritura de Venta Otorgada por la Abadesa y Monjas del Monasterio de la Santísima Trinidad . . . Z 215.

Expediente sobre la Confirmación de las Constituciones que . . . Han Hecho para el recogimiento de Doncellas que se pretende Fundar. B 122.

Poder para testar a Doña María Casimira Vázquez de Velasco, viuda de José de la Fuente y Roxas . . . 1713. Z 1221.

Renunciación de Doña Petronila de la Fuente y Roxas . . . 1712. Z 1221.

Testamento de Doña Antonia Romaní . . . 1703. Z 1322.

Colección Vargas Ugarte

Auto de Don Pedro Bravo de Rivero, Obispo de Arequipa, sobre los trajes inhonestos de las mujeres. 1744. Papeles Varios, MS 14, Documento 37.

Auto del Obispo de Arequipa, Don Juan Cavero de Toledo reprimiendo el abuso de los Trajes femeninos . . . 1734. Papeles Varios, MS 14, Documento 35.

Auto del vicario General de Arequipa . . . sobre trajes inhonestos. 1747. Papeles Varios, MS 14, Documento 38.

Declaración . . . sobre el auto de Reforma . . . 1782. MS 38, Documento 38.

Descripción de los Conventos de Arequipa por el Obispo Miguel de Pamplona, 1786. MS 32, Documento 82.

Papeles Varios. MS 36, Documento 1.

Lilly Library, Indiana University, Bloomington

Proceso original de la vida, santidad, muerte y milagros de la bendita Sor Rosa de Santa Maria . . . Criolla de esta Ciudad de los Reyes. Hecho por orden del Arzobispo D. Bartolomé Lobo Guerrero.

Primary Printed Sources

Achury Valenzuela, Darío, ed. *Obras Completas de la madre Francisca Josefa de la Concepción de Castillo.* 2 vols. Bototá: Talleres Gráficos del Banco de la República: 1968.

Aguilar, José, S. J. *Sermones varios morales.* Madrid: Por Don Gabriel del Barrio, 1723.

Aguilar, José, S. J. *Sermones varios predicados en la Ciudad de Lima.* Bruselas: Por Francisco Tserstevens, 1704.

Amat y Junient, Manuel de. *Memoria de gobierno*. Edición y estudio pre-liminar de Vicente Rodríguez Casado y Florentino Pérez Embid. Sevilla: Escuela de Estudios Hispano-Americanos, 1947.

Ansalone, Pedro. *La Religiosa ilustrada*. 6a. edición; Lima: Casa de los Niños Huérfanos, 1788.

Arriaga, Pablo de. *The Extirpation of Idolatry of Peru*. Translated and edited by Clark Keating. Lexington: University of Kentucky Press, 1968.

Avendaño, Diego de. *Thesaurus Indicus seu generalis instructor pro regimine conscientia, in iis quae ad indias spectant*. Tomus Primus et Secundus. 6 vols. Antverpiae: Apud Jacobum Meursium, 1668.

———— *Auctarium indicum seu tomus tertius ad indici thesauri ornatius complementum*. Antverpiae: Apud Jacobum Meursium, 1675.

———— *Auctarii indici tomus secundus seu thesauri tomus quartus*. Antverpiae: Apud Jacobum Meursium, 1676.

———— *Auctarii indici tomus tertius seu thesauri tomus quintus*. Antverpiae: Apud Jacobum Meursium, 1678.

———— *Auctarii indici tomus quartus et thesauri tomus sextus*. Antverpiae: Apud Hieronymum Berdussen, 1686.

———— *Problemata theologica*. 2 vols. Antverpiae: Apud Engelbertum Gymnicum, 1668.

Barrasa, Jacinto, S. J., *Sermones varios predicados . . . en el reino del Perú*. Madrid: En la Imprenta Real, 1678.

Bollaert, William, ed. and trans., *The Expedition of Pedro de Ursua and Lope de Aguirre in Search of El Dorado and Omagua in 1560–61*. London: Hakluyt Society, 1861.

Carta del Arzobispo Melchor de Liñan a las religiosas, esposas de Jcto. de los monasterios de esta ciudad. S. L., S. R.

Cobo, Bernabé, *Historia del Nuevo Mundo*. Biblioteca de Autores Españoles, vols. 91, 92. Edited by Francisco Mateos, S.J. Madrid: Ediciones Atlas, 1956.

Coleción de memorias o relaciones que escribieron los virreyes del Perú. . . . Madrid: Imprenta del Asilo de Huérfanos, 1921.

Constituciones del Colegio de Santa Cruz de Las Niñas Expósitas en la casa de Nuestra Señora de Atocha de esta ciudad de Los Reyes . . . año de 1659. añadidas y en parte mudadas . . . año de 1756. Lima: s. d.

Constituciones generales para todas monjas y religiosas, sujetas a la obediencia de la orden de nuestro padre San Francisco. . . . Madrid: Imprenta de las Causa de la V. Madre María de Jesús de Agreda, 1748.

Constituciones synodales del obispado de Arequipa. Lima: Joseph de Contreras, 1688.

Dahlgren, B. E. *Travels of Ruiz, Pavón, and Dombey in Perú and Chile (1777–1788)*. Chicago: Field Museum of Natural History, 1940.

Documentos para la historia de la Beata Mariana de Jesús Azucena de Quito. Quito: Imprenta del Clero, 1902.

Documents from Early Peru: The Pizarros and the Almagros. Harkness Collection in the Library of Congress. Washington: U.S. Government Printing Office, 1936.

Fernández de Oviedo, Gonzalo, *Historia general y natural de las Indias.* Biblioteca de Autores Españoles, vol. 97. Edited by Juan Pérez de Tudela. Madrid: Ediciones Atlas, 1959.

Frézier, Amadée François. *Relation du voyage de la mer du sud aux côtes du Chile et du Peru . . .* Paris: Chez Jean-Geoffroy Nyon, 1716.

Garcilaso de la Vega, Inca. *Historia general del Perú.* 2 vols. Lima: Librería Internacional del Perú, 1959.

Gijón y León, Thomas de. *Compendio histórico de las prodigiosa vida, virtudes, y milagros de la venerable sierva de Dios, Mariana de Jesús Flores y Paredes, conocida con el justo nombre de la azucena de Quito.* Madrid: Imprenta del Mercurio, 1754.

Juan, Antonio Jorge y Ulloa. *Noticias secretas de América.* Londres: Imprenta de R. Taylor, 1826.

Las Casas, Bartolomé de. *Historia de las Indias.* Biblioteca Autores Españoles, vol. 95. Edited by Juan Pérez de Tudela and Emilio López Oto. Madrid: Ediciones Atlas, 1957.

León Pinelo, Antonio de. *Velos antiguos y modernos en los rostros de las mujeres: Sus conveniencias y daños: Ilustración de la real prematica de las tapadas.* Madrid: Por Juan Sánchez. Año de 1641.

Levillier, Roberto, *Gobernantes del Perú: Cartas y papeles.* 14 vols. Madrid: Sucesores de Rivadeneyra, 1921.

Lisson, Emilio, *La Iglesia en el Perú: Colección de documentos para la historia de la iglesia que se encuentran en varios archivos.* 5 vols. Sevilla: Editorial Católica Española, S. A., 1943–56.

Loayza, F. A., ed. *Mártires y heroinas (documentos inéditos del año de 1780 o 1782)* Lima: Librería e Imprenta D. Miranda, 1945.

Los Procesos de beatificación de la azucena de Quito. Quito: Tipografía Salesiana, 1896.

Memoria del Virrey del Perú marqués de Avilés. . . . Lima: Imprenta del Estado, 1901.

Memorias de los Vireyes que han gobernado el Perú durante el tiempo del coloniaje español. 6 vols. Impresas de Orden Suprema. Lima: Librería Central de Felipe Bailly, 1859.

Mercurio Peruano. 12 vols., edición facsimilar. Lima: Biblioteca Nacional del Perú, 1964.

Miguélez Domínguez, Lorenzo, ed. *Código de derecho canónico y legislación complementaria.* Madrid: La Editorial Católica, S. A., 1954.

El Monasterio de La Concepción de la Ciudad de Los Reyes. Lima: Editorial Lumen, 1942.

Moncada, Balthasar, S. J. *Descripción de la casa fabricada en Lima . . . para que las señoras ilustres de ella, y las demás mujeres devotas . . . puedan tener . . . los exercicios de San Ignacio.* Sevilla: J. Padrino, 1757.

Monografías Históricas sobre la Ciudad de Lima. 2 vols. Lima: Librería e Imprenta Gil, S. A., 1935.

Mugaburu, Josephe de, and Francisco de Mugaburu. *Diario de Lima (1640–1694). Crónica de la epoca colonial.* 2 vols. Lima: Imprenta C. Vásquez L., 1935.

Paredes Armendariz, Andrés. *Constituciones de las religiosas nazarenas.* . . . Lima: Imprenta de la Calle de la Encarnación, 1765.

Peralta Barnuevo Rocha y Benavides, Pedro de. *Lima fundada o conquista del Perú.* . . . Lima: Imprenta de Sobrino y Bados, 1732.

Polo, José Toribio, ed. *Memorias de los vireyes del Perú marqués de Mancera y conde de Salvatierra.* Lima: Imprenta del Estado, 1897.

"Pretension de Una Beca del Colegio de Sta. Cruz de Niñas Expósitas . . . de Juana de Atocha y Azcona, Niña Expósita. Se Casó con D. Rosendo Gao," *Revista del Archivo Nacional del Perú,* 20 (1961): 76–81.

Providencia, Josefa de la. *Relación del origen y fundación del monasterio . . . de religiosas nazarenas.* . . . Lima: Imprenta Real de los Niños Expósitos, 1793.

Ramos Gavilán, Fr. Alonso. *Historia de célebre santuario de nuestra señora de Copacabana y sus milagros.* . . . Lima: 1621.

Recopilación de las leyes destos reynos hecha por mandato de la magestad catholica del rey Don Philippe Segundo. . . . Alcalá de Henares: Andrés de Angulo, 1569.

Romero, Carlos Alberto, ed. *Memoria del Virrey del Perú Marqués de Avilés.* Lima: Imprenta del Estado, 1901.

Sacrosanti et oecumenici concilii tridentini . . . canones et decreta. Antverpiae: Apud Hieronymum Verdussen, 1677.

Santísima Trinidad, María Josefa de la. *Historia de la fundación del monasterio de trinitarias descalzas de Lima.* . . . Lima: Editorial San Antonio, 1957.

Suardo, Juan Antonio. *Diario de Lima: 1629–1634.* Edited by Rubén Vargas Ugarte, S. J. Lima: Imprenta C. Vázquez L., 1935.

Terralla y Landa, Esteban de, *Lima por dentro y fuera.* París: Librería Española, s. d.

Valdivia, Pedro de. *Cartas: Introdución por Jaime Eyzaguirre.* Santiago de Chile: Editorial del Pacífico (1955).

Vargas Ugarte, Rubén, ed. *Concilios Limenses.* 3 vols. Lima: Talleres Gráficos de la Tipografía Peruana, 1952.

—— *Nuestro Romancero. Clásicos Peruanos.* Vols. 4 and 6. Lima: Tipografía Peruana S.A., 1951, 1958.

—— *Relaciones de Viajes (Siglos XVI, XVII, y XVIII).* Lima: Instituto de Investigaciones Históricas, 1947.

—— *Rosas de Oquendo y otros. Clásicos peruanos.* vol. V. Lima: Tipografía Peruana S.A., 1955.

Virreinato Peruano. *Documentos para su historia.* 50 vols. Lima: Instituto Histórico del Perú, 1954–.

Zalduendo, Francisco Xavier, S. J., *Sermones varios.* 4 vols. Madrid: Viuda de Juan García Infançón, 1717; Don Gabriel del Barrio, 1723.

Zaragoza, Justo, ed., *Historia del descubrimiento de los regiones australes hecho por el General Fernández de Quirós.* 2 vols. Madrid: Imprenta de Manuel Hernández, 1867–80.

Secondary Sources

Archury Valenzuela, Dario. *Análisis crítico de los "afectos espirituales" de Sor Francisca Josefa de la Concepción de Castillo.* Bogotá: Ministerio Educación Nacional, 1962.

Acosta de Samper, Soledad. "La mujer española en Santafé de Bogotá." *España Moderna* 4 (1892): 161–68.

Angulo, P. Domingo, O.P. *Santa Rosa de Santa María.* Prologue by Carlos Alberto Romero. Lima: Sanmartí, 1917.

Anton, Ferdinand. *Woman in Pre-Columbian America.* Translated by M. Herzfeld, revised by G. A. Shepperson. New York: Abner Schram, 1973.

Arciniegas, Germán. "La fronda genealógica." In *América, Tierra Firme; Sociología.* Santiago: Eds. Ercilla, 1937.

Arias, Augusto. *Mariana de Jesús.* Quito: Talleres Gráficos del Ministerio de Educación, 1944.

Balbontín Moreno, Manuel G., and Gustavo Opazo Maturana. *Cinco Mujeres en la vida de O'Higgins.* Santiago: Arancibia Hnos, 1964.

Barden, James C. "Three Literary Ladies of Spain's American Colonies," *Bulletin of the Pan American Union* 75 (1945): 150–58.

Bayle, Constantino. "La Educación de la Mujer en América," *Razón y Fe* 124 (1941): 216–21.

Bermúdez, José Manuel. *Breve Noticia de la vida y virtudes de la Sra. Da. Catalina de Yturgoyen Amasa y Lisperguer, Condesa de la Vega Del Reu.* Lima: Imprenta Del Rio, 1821.

Bermúdez, José Manuel. *Vida de la Gloriosa Virgen Dominicana Santa Rosa.* Lima: Librería de Benito Gil, 1869.

Blomberg, Héctor Pedro. *Mujeres en la historia americana*. Buenos Aires: Librerías Anaconda, 1933.

Bonham, Milledge L., Jr. "A Trio of American Heroines," *Boletín de la Unión Panamericana* 68 (1934): 708–11.

Bosch Barret, Manuel. *Da. Isabel Barreto Adelantada de las Islas Salomón*. Barcelona: Editorial Juventud, S.A., 1943.

Bowser, Frederick. *The African Slave in Colonial Peru, 1524–1650*. Stanford: Stanford University Press, 1976.

Boxer, C. R. *Mary and Misogyny: Women in Iberian Expansion Overseas, 1415–1815: Some Facts, Fancies and Personalities*. New York: Oxford University Press, 1975.

Bromley Seminario, Juan. "El Capitán Martín de Estete y Doña María de Escobar la Romana, Fundadores de la Villa de Trujillo," *Revista Histórica* 22 (1955–56): 122–41.

Bromley Seminario, Juan. "Virreinas del Perú," *Revista Histórica* 23 (1957–58): 64–84.

Bromley Seminario, Juan. *Virreyes, Cabildantes y Oidores*. Lima: P. Barrates Castro, 1944.

Busto Duthurbura, José Antonio del. "Una huérfana mestiza: la hija de Juan Pizarro." *Revista Histórica* 28 (1965): 103–6.

Cabrera, Pablo. "Acción gubernamental y privada en pro de las hijas de familia durante la colonia." In *Cultura y Beneficencia Durante la Colonia*, vol. 2. Córdoba, Arg.: Est. Gráfico La Elzeviriana, 1925.

Campo, Santiago del. *Pedro de Valdivia, el capitán conquistado, ensayo de biografía interior*. Madrid: Instituto de Cultura Hispánica, 1961.

Carvajal, María de. "Una carta de la viuda de Jorge Robledo al Rey," *Boletín de Historia y Antigüedades, Bogotá* 19 (1932): 639–40.

Carvajal, Morayma Ofyr. *Galería del Espíritu: Mujeres de mi Patria*. Quito: Edit. "Fr. Jodoco Ricke," 1949.

Catá de Calella, José Antonio. *Vida Portentosa de la esclarecida Virgen Santa Rosa de Santa María, Vulgo Santa Rosa de Lima*. Barcelona: Librería y Tipografía Católica, 1896.

Centurión, Carlos R. *La Mujer paraguaya de la historia*. Asunción: Imprenta Ariel, 1939.

Chapman, Walker. *The Golden Dream: Seekers of El Dorado*. Indianapolis, Kansas City, New York: Bobbs-Merrill Co., 1967.

Cocca, Aldo Armando. "La mujer en las culturas americanas." In *Ginecocracia (El Gobierno de las Mujeres)*, B.A.: Bibliográfica Omeba, 1963.

Compendio Histórico de la Vida de Santa Rosa de Lima con un Apendice de la Gloria Póstuma de la Misma Santa. Based on the writings of P. Leonardo Hansen. Valladolid: Imprenta de Aparveo, 1828.

Cordero, Héctor Adolfo. *María de los Santos Sayas, Carretera y Correo del Viejo Buenos Aires*. Buenos Aires: Eds. Delta, 1963.

Cornejo Bouroncle, Jorge. *Sangre andina, diez mujeres cuzqueñas.* Cuzco: H. G. Rozas Sucesores, 1949.

Cortés Alonso, Vicenta. "Los esclavos domésticos en América." *Anuario de Estudios Americanos* 24 (1967): 955–83.

Cruz, Josefina. *Doña Mencia la Adelantada.* Buenos Aires: Edit. La Resa, 1960.

Deleito y Piñuela, José. *La Mujer, La Casa y la Moda.* 3rd ed. Madrid: Espasa-Calpe, S.A., 1966.

Descola, Jean. *Daily Life in Colonial Peru, 1710–1820.* Translated by M. Heron. New York: Macmillan, 1968.

Dias Meza, Aurelio. "La Quintrala y los Agustinos." *Revista Chilena de Historia y Geografía* 54 (1927): 324–30.

Duarta, María Amalia. "La mujer en la historia argentina." *Revista de la Universidad Nacional de Córdoba* 10 (1969): 127–51.

Duque Betancur, Francisco. "La mujer en la historia de Antioquia." In *Historia del Departamento de Antioquia; Epocas del Descubrimiento y Conquista, Colonia, Independencia y República.* Medellín: Asamblea Departamental de Antioquia, 1967.

Eyzaguirre, Jaime. "La Quintrala en la lucha con la inglesia." *Boletín de la Academia Chilena de la Historia* 12 (1945): 5–16.

Fernández Duró, Cesareo. *La Mujer española en Indias.* Madrid: Tipografía de la Viuda de M. Tello, 1902.

Fitzmaurice-Kelly, J. "Women in Sixteenth Century Spain." *Revue Hispanique* 70 (1927): 69–71, 557–631.

Friede, Juan. "The Catálogo de Pasajeros and the Spanish Emigration to America." *HAHR,* 31 (1955):341.

Fuentes, Manuel Anastasio. *Lima: Apuntes Históricos, Descriptivos, Estadísticos y de Costumbres.* París: Librería de F. Didot, 1867.

Furlong, Guillermo. *La Cultura femenina en la época colonial.* Buenos Aires: Editorial Kapeluz, 1951.

Gandía, Enrique de. "Una expedición de mujeres españolas al Rio de la Plata en el siglo XVI." *Boletín de la Junta de Historia Numismática Americana Buenos Aires* 8 (1936): 117–31.

García y García, Elvira. *La Mujer peruana a través de los siglos.* 2 vols. Lima: Imprenta Americana, 1924.

García Vargas, Lucy Etel. "Doña Mencia Calderón." *Norte Revista Hispano-Americana* 259 (1974): 25.

García y Sanz, Pedro. *El Pastor, la patrona y el Apóstol de Lima; Panegíricos de Santo Toribio de Mogrovejo, de Santa Rosa de Santa María y de San Francisco Solano.* Lima: Imprenta y Librería de San Pedro, 1893.

González Arrili, Bernardo. *Mujeres de nuestra tierra.* Buenos Aires: Eds. La Obra, 1950.

González Zuñiga, Alberto. *La Rosita Limeña.* Lima: Editorial P.T.C.M., 1948.

Grez, Vicente. *Las Mujeres de la Indepencia: Prólogo y Notas de Raul Silva Castro.* Santiago de Chile: Zig-Zag, 1966.

Hansen, Fray Leonardo. *Vida Admirable de Sta. Rosa de Lima.* Translated from the Latin by P. Fray Jacinto Parra. Vergara: El Santísimo Rosario, 1929.

Henderson, James D. *Ten Notable Women of Latin America.* Chicago: Nelson-Hall, 1978.

Hernández de Alba, Guillermo. "Mujeres en la colonia." In *Estampas Santafereñas.* Bogotá: Edit. ABC., 1938.

Jerves, Alfonso A., O.P. *Rosa de Jesús Nazareno Terciaria Dominica* (1678–1731). . . . Quito: Imprenta de Santa Domingo, 1928.

Keyes, Frances Parkinson. *The Rose and the Lily: The Lives and Times of Two South American Saints.* New York: Hawthorn Books, Inc., 1961.

Knaster, Meri. *Women in Spanish America: An Annotated Bibliography from Pre-conquest to Contemporary Times.* Boston: G. K. Hall and Co., 1977.

Konetze, Richard. "La Emigración de las Mujeres Españolas a America Durante la Epoca Colonial." *Revista Internacional de Sociología* 3 (1945): 123–50.

Labarca Hubertson, Amanda. *Historia de la Enseñanza en Chile.* Santiago: Imprenta Universitaria, 1939.

——— "La Educación Femenina en Chile." *Revista de Filosofía* (La Plata) 11 (1925): 37–73.

Langdon-Davies, John. *A Short History of Women.* New York: Viking Press, 1927.

Lassaga, Ramón J. *Una Santafecina Virreyna del Río de la Plata.* Buenos Aires: Talleres Gráficos de L. J. Rosso y cía, 1917.

Loaysa, Fr. Pedro de, O.P. *Vida de Santa Rosa de Lima.* Lima: Sanmartí y Cia., S.A., 1937.

Lockhart, James. *Spanish Peru, 1532–1560: A Colonial Society.* Madison: University of Wisconsin Press, 1968.

Loor, Wilfrido. *Santa Mariana de Jesús.* Quito: La Prensa Católica, 1954.

Machado de Arnao, Luz. "Doña Isabel Manrique: primera gobernadora de la provincia venezolana." *Boletín de la Academia Nacional de la Historia* 45 (1962): 567–71.

Martín, Luís. *The Intellectual Conquest of Peru: The Jesuit College of San Pablo, 1568–1767.* New York: Fordham University Press, 1968.

Martín, Luís. *The Kingdom of the Sun: A Brief History of Peru.* New York: Charles Scribner's Sons, 1974.

Martín, Luís, and JoAnn G. Pettus. *Scholars and Schools in Colonial Peru.* Dallas: Southern Methodist Univeristy School of Continuing Education, 1973.

May, Stella Burke. *The Conqueror's Lady, Inéz Suárez.* New York: Farrar and Rinehart, 1930.

Maynard, Sara. *Rose of America.* London: Sheed and Ward, 1944.

McKendrick, Melveena. *Woman and Society in the Spanish Drama of the Golden Century.* Cambridge: Cambridge University Press, 1974.

Medina, José Toribio. *Ensayo de Una Bibliografía . . . de Santos y Venerables Americanos.* Santiago de Chile: Imprenta Elze-Veriana, 1919.

——— "Las Mujeres de la Araucana de Ercilla. . . ." *Hispania* 11 (1928): 1–12.

Medina, José Toribio, ed. *Vida de Doña Ana Guerra de Jesús . . . [1681–1745].* Santiago de Chile: Imprenta Universitaria, 1925.

Mendiburu, Manuel de. *Apuntes Históricos.* Lima: Imprenta del Estado, 1902.

Mendiburu, Manuel de. *Diccionario Histórico-Biográfico del Peru.* 2d ed., 11 vols. Lima: Imprenta Enrique Palacios, 1932.

Menéndez Rua, Angel. *Reseña histórica del santuario de Santa Rosa de Lima.* Lima: Sanmartí y Cía, S.A., 1939.

Miranda, Marta Elba. *Mujeres Chilenas.* Santiago: Edit. Nascimento, 1940.

Miró, César. *Cielo y Tierra de Santa Rosa.* Buenos Aires: Editorial Schapire, 1945.

Monge, Germania Moncayo de. *Mariana de Jesús Señora de Indias.* Quito: La Prensa Católica, 1950.

Morán de Burtón, Jacinto, S.I. *Vida de Santa Mariana de Jesús.* Quito: Imprenta Municipal, 1955.

Noguera V., Armando. "Micaela Bastidas Puyucahua." *Revista del Centro de Estudios Histórico Militares del Peru* 19 (1971): 186–90.

Opazo Maturana, Gustavo. "Doña Inés Suárez." *Boletín de la Academia Chilena de la Historia* 7 (1941): 141–55.

Osende, P. Victorino, O.P. *Vida de Santa Rosa de Lima.* Lima: Tip. de El Smo. Rosario, 1927.

O'Sullivan-Beare, Nancy. *Las Mujeres de los conquistadores: La mujer española en los comienzos de la colonización americana.* Madrid: Compañía Bibliográfica Española, S.A., 1956.

Otero Muñoz, Gustavo. "Figuras Femeninas de la Colonia." In *Conferencias de la Academia Colombiana de la Historia.* Bogotá: Academia Colombiana de la Historia, 1936.

Papasogli, Giorgio. *Vita di S. Maria Anna de Gesu.* Rome: Tipografía Pontificia Università Gregoriana, 1950.

Peristiany, J., ed. *Honour and Shame: The Values of Mediteranean Society.* Chicago: University of Chicago Press, 1966.

Pescatello, Ann M. *Power and Pawn: The Female in Iberian Families, Societies, and Cultures.* Westport, Conn.: Greenwood Press, 1976.

Pescatello, Ann M., ed. *Female and Male in Latin America: Essays.* Pittsburgh: University of Pittsburgh Press, 1973.

Phelan, John Leddy. "The Sinners and the Saint." In *The Kingdom of Quito in the Seventeenth Century; Bureaucratic Politics in the Spanish Empire.* Madison: University of Wisconsin Press, 1967.

Pittaluga, Gustavo. "Las Mujeres, el trigo y la quina." *Revista de América. Bogotá.* 6 (1896): 77–80.

Pólit, Aurelio Espinosa, S.I. *Santa Mariana de Jesús Hija de la Compañía de Jesús.* Quito: La Prensa Católica, 1956.

Portugal, Ana María. "La Peruana ¿"Tapada" Sin Manto?" *Mundo Nuevo* 46 (1970): 20–27.

Prieto de Zegarra, Judith. *Así hicieron las mujeres el Perú.* Lima: Gráficos E.R.V., 1965.

Proaño, Juan Félix, trans. *Vida Auténtica de Santa Rosa de Lima.* Lima: Imp. de El Bien Social, 1897.

Puga, Mario A. "La Mujer en el Perú." *Cuadernos Americanos* 62 (1952): 152–79.

Quesada, Vicente Gregorio. *Escenas de la Vida Colonial en el Siglo XVIII. Crónicas de la Villa Imperial de Potosí.* Buenos Aires: Edit. Huarpes, 1945.

Rivas, Raimundo. "Amores de Solís." *Boletín de Historia y Antigüedades* 12 (1920): 660–84.

Roca y Boloña, José Antonio. *Sermón Panegírico en Honor de Santa Rosa de Santa María.* Preached in the Cathedral of Lima, August 30, 1864. Lima: Imprenta y Librería de Benito Gil, 1886.

Romero, Carlos A. "La virreina gobernadora." *Revista Histórica. Lima.* 1 (1906): 39–59.

Romero de Valle, Emilia, ed. *Mujeres de América.* Mexico, D.F.: Secretaría de Educación Pública, 1948.

Sabat Pebet, María Matilde G. de. "Presencia de la mujer española en la conquista chilena." *Revista Nacional. Montevideo.* 48 (1950): 376–94.

Salvatierra, Sofonías. "La Ccsta de los Mosquitos. Episodio de doña María Manuela Rodríguez." *Revista de la Academia de Geografía e Historia de Nicaragua* 2 (1937): 105–29.

Sánchez, Luís Alberto. *La Perricholi.* Lima: Universidad Nacional Mayor de San Marcos, 1963.

Sauer, Carl Ortwin. *The Early Spanish Main.* Berkeley and Los Angeles: University of California Press, 1966.

Silva Santisteban, Fernando. *Los Obrajes en el Virreinato del Perú.* Lima: Museo Nacional de Historia, 1964.

Soeiro, Susan A. "The Social and Economic Role of the Convent: Women and Nuns in Colonial Bahia, 1677–1800." *HAHR* 54 (May 1974): 209–32.

Sosa de Newton, Lily. *Las Argentinas de Ayer a Hoy.* Buenos Aires: Librería y Edit. L.V. Zanetti, 1967.

Stevenson, R. *The Music of Peru: Aboriginal and Viceroyal Epochs.* Washington, D.C.: Pan American Union, 1959.

Stineman, Esther. *Women's Studies: A Recommended Case Bibliography.* Littleton: Libraries Unlimited, Inc., 1979.

Turner Hart, B. *Conquistador, Inca Princess, and City Fathers: The Ampuero Family of Lima in the 16th Century.* Coral Cables, Florida: University of Miami Press, 1962.

Vargas Ugarte, Rubén, S.J. *Vida de Santa Rosa de Santa María.* Lima: Talleres Gráficos de la Tipografía Peruana, S.A., 1951.

——— "Un Archivo de música colonial en al ciudad del Cuzco." *Mar del Sur* 26 (1953): 1–10.

——— *El Monasterio de la Concepción de la ciudad de los Reyes.* Lima: Editorial Lumen, 1942.

Vargas Ugarte, Rubén, S.J., ed. *Obras de Don Juan del Valle y Caviedes.* Lima: Tipografía Peruana, S.A., 1947.

Vicuña McKenna, Benjamín. *Historia de la Calle de las Monjitas.* Santiago: G. E. Miranda, 1904.

——— *Los Lisperguer y la Quintrala (Doña Catalina de los Rios): Episodio Histórico Social con Numerosos Documentos Inéditos.* 2d ed. Edited by Jaime Eyzaguirre. Santiago de Chile: Empresa Editora Zig-Zag, 1950.

Villafaña Casal, María Teresa. "La Mujer española en la conquista y colonización de America." *Cuadernos Hispanoamericanos* 59 (1964): 125–42.

Villamizar Berti, Arturo. "La Fundadora de Cúcuta, 1649–1736: Esbozo Genealógico y Biográfico." *Gaceta Histórica* (Cúcuta, Colombia) 27 (1963): 15–19.

Villasís Terán, Enrique M. *Mariana de Jesús Azucena de Quito.* Quito: La Prensa Católica, 1946.

Index